MW01026840

The Pathfinder
and the President

John C. Frémont, Abraham Lincoln,
and the Battle for Emancipation

John Bicknell

STACKPOLE
BOOKS

Essex, Connecticut
Blue Ridge Summit, Pennsylvania

STACKPOLE BOOKS

An imprint of The Globe Pequot Publishing Group, Inc.
64 South Main St.
Essex, CT 06426
www.globepequot.com

Distributed by NATIONAL BOOK NETWORK

British Library Cataloguing in Publication Information Available

Library of Congress Cataloging-in-Publication Data available

ISBN 9780811776653 (cloth)
ISBN 9780811776660 (electronic)

∞™ The paper used in this publication meets the minimum requirements of American National Standard for Information Sciences—Permanence of Paper for Printed Library Materials, ANSI/NISO Z39.48-1992

To John C. Frémont

Thy error, Frémont, simply was to act
A brave man's part, without the statesman's tact,
And, taking counsel but of common sense,
To strike at cause as well as consequence.
Oh, never yet since Roland wound his horn
At Roncesvalles, has a blast been blown
Far-heard, wide-echoed, startling as thine own,
Heard from the van of freedom's hope forlorn
It had been safer, doubtless, for the time,
To flatter treason, and avoid offence
To that Dark Power whose underlying crime
Heaves upward its perpetual turbulence.
But if thine be the fate of all who break
The ground for truth's seed, or forerun their years
Till lost in distance, or with stout hearts make
A lane for freedom through the level spears,
Still take thou courage! God has spoken through thee,
Irrevocable, the mighty words, Be free!
The land shakes with them, and the slave's dull ear
Turns from the rice-swamp stealthily to hear.
Who would recall them now must first arrest
The winds that blow down from the free Northwest,
Ruffling the Gulf; or like a scroll roll back
The Mississippi to its upper springs.
Such words fulfil their prophecy, and lack
But the full time to harden into things.

—John Greenleaf Whittier

Contents

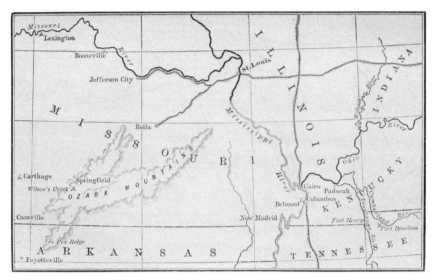

COURTESY OF WIKIMEDIA COMMONS

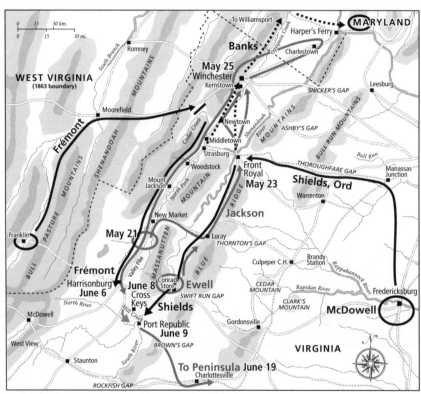

Jackson's Valley Campaign Actions May 21–June 9, 1862

ADAPTED FROM ENCYCLOPEDIA VIRGINIA

INTRODUCTION

HISTORY IS RARELY KIND TO LOSERS, AND THE CIVIL WAR WAS ESPECIALLY unkind to John C. Frémont.

From 1861 to 1865, Frémont lost two military commands, the only major battle in which he fought, a presidential campaign, a good chunk of his fortune, his home, and much of the renown he had accumulated over the previous twenty years that had made him one of the most famous men in the world.

But Frémont, born in Georgia and educated in South Carolina, was also the first official of the U.S. government to issue an emancipation proclamation, freeing the slaves of Missouri, where he was military commander. Abraham Lincoln quickly revoked Frémont's order but would follow in the general's footsteps less than a year later and use the same argument of military necessity to justify his own Emancipation Proclamation, declaring free all the slaves in rebel-held territory.

The conflict over when and how to free the slaves divided the two men. But Lincoln and Frémont might have been allies. Both were born in humble circumstances in the slaveholding South; through their own efforts, both became successful men of the West. Both had strong, politically ambitious wives. They were among the founders of the Republican Party and stood as its first two presidential candidates. The convention that nominated Frémont for president in 1856 strongly considered Lincoln for vice president, though Lincoln had supported Supreme Court Justice John McLean rather than Frémont for the nomination. When the time came for Lincoln to fill his cabinet and senior diplomatic posts, Frémont was a contender for each.

But their differences outweighed the similarities, with personalities defined by their professions. Lincoln approached problems in a methodical, lawyerly fashion. Frémont, the great "Pathfinder," had the improvisational survival skills of one who battled the elements beyond the pale of civilization. At heart, Lincoln was a conservative. He hated slavery but viewed the law and the Constitution as immutable foundations and abhorred mob rule. His considerable ambition was in service to this philosophy. Frémont was quick to ignore his superiors and set rules aside if he believed he was right. He, too, hated slavery but had no long record of activism or fixed political philosophy—thus, his ambition served only itself. "Lincoln," in Shelby Foote's perceptive phrase, "was his own psychiatrist." If Frémont had one, it was his wife, who was too partial to be effectively therapeutic. Lincoln was practical, Frémont a romantic. Lincoln was a talented politician. Frémont was not.[1]

The conflict between Lincoln and the Frémonts—and he interacted with both husband and wife at crucial moments during the war—creased a few extra lines into the president's careworn face. It finished Frémont as a political and military figure and embittered his wife for the rest of her life. If it did not make winning the Civil War more difficult, it certainly made the commander in chief's life more difficult. If it did not ruin Frémont outright, it set him on the road to ruin.

Lincoln misjudged Frémont, as he did many other generals. But he was not alone. Frémont's appointment as commanding general of the Western Department in summer 1861 was met with nearly universal acclaim, outside the West Point officer class. Lincoln's closest advisers enthusiastically endorsed the appointment. Underinformed journalists, abolitionist supporters, and ordinary citizens hailed Frémont as the next Andrew Jackson, George Washington, and even Joan of Arc.

He was obviously not the equal of Old Hickory or Washington. And he was certainly not saintly. But Frémont did accomplish things during the war that have been forgotten or dismissed, in large part because he ultimately failed as a commander, a soldier, and a candidate. Lincoln recognized this fact in 1863 when, responding to a suggestion from an abolitionist delegation that Frémont be made military governor of North Carolina, he compared the Pathfinder to Moses, who had led the Israelites to the Promised Land but would not enter the land of milk and honey himself: "It looks as if the first reformer of a thing has to meet such a hard opposition and gets so battered and bespattered that afterward, when people find they have to accept his reform, they will accept it more easily from another man."[2]

While it's worth remembering that Lincoln, the Joshua of this scenario, was the one who had done some of the bespattering, bringing Frémont out from under Lincoln's shadow would take a monumental work of revisionism. That is not the purpose of this book. But by shining a light on the relationship between Abraham Lincoln and John and Jessie Frémont, we can get a clearer picture of all three and a better understanding of the Civil War.

Prologue

"We all saw war ahead"

Jessie Benton Frémont spent her life around politics. When she was born in 1824, her senator father—one of Missouri's first two—had been in the post for three years. Thomas Hart Benton would go on to serve twenty-seven more, plus one term in the House of Representatives, with Jessie often serving as an unofficial aide-de-camp. As the wife of famed western explorer John C. Frémont, she played an unprecedented role as editor of his best-selling expedition reports and as de facto campaign manager of his unsuccessful run as the Republican Party's first presidential candidate in 1856. Her long exposure to government had inured her to grandiosity, but even she was impressed by the speaker she heard on the night of October 26, 1860, at San Francisco's American Theater.

"Four years ago this night, in front of this very house, I had the honor to attempt to lay a little deeper and broader the principles of Republicanism by trying to show why we should elect as President an eminent citizen, who I believe is here tonight," said the newly elected senator from Oregon, Edward D. Baker.[1]

At the mention of Frémont, Baker turned in acknowledgment toward a private box where he assumed the Pathfinder to be seated. A close friend of Abraham Lincoln's for thirty years, Baker had traveled the state on Frémont's behalf in 1856, enduring bad roads and hundreds of miles on horseback to deliver the message of "free speech, free press, free territory, and the Pacific Railroad." But Frémont was not in attendance on this night. The box was occupied instead by Jessie and one of her protégés, Unitarian minister Thomas Starr King. King had moved to California in April 1860 from Boston, where he had befriended Ralph Waldo Emerson. Even with the great Transcendentalist as a standard of comparison, King was still more impressed with Baker than was his new California mentor.[2]

They were not alone. Baker, who had struggled with a political career in California before decamping to Oregon, was welcomed back to San Francisco as a conquering hero by local Republicans. Stores and offices closed early so employees could get a seat for his speech. That night, in a theater designed to seat four thousand, estimates put the crowd inside and out at three times that number, jamming the adjacent streets and sidewalks. "So dense and tightly packed was the crowd in the aisles and standing places that persons who fainted were passed out over the heads of others," remembered a patron who had traveled twenty-four hours from the Sierra Nevada town of Marysville to attend the event. At one particularly rousing point in the speech, when Baker invoked the Italian freedom fighter Giuseppe Garibaldi, a man raced to the footlights at the front of the stage waving an American flag and shouting, "It is true! It is [t]rue! We are slaves, compared to the rest of the world."[3]

The distinguished Baker—balding on top with gray on the sides, flashing blue eyes, "indomitable energy, true English perseverance [he was born in London], fine natural parts, great elegance and popular manners"—pressed on after the interruption. He was already an hour and a half into the speech, extolling the antislavery virtues of Frémont and his party, as well as their support of a transcontinental railroad.[4]

"Pierce professed to recommend the road; Buchanan professed to recommend it," Baker asserted, citing the empty promises of the current Democratic president and his immediate predecessor. "If, four years ago, we had elected Frémont, in four months after, he would have recommended a railroad, and would have sent two regiments of dragoons in the meanwhile to tamp the track." This statement brought a rousing cheer, as nearly any mention of a railroad to the West Coast was bound to do in San Francisco. "He would have had no constitutional scruples himself, and would not have tolerated them in any one else. He would not, as this man [Buchanan] has done, have hesitated because somebody said that Mason, or Toombs, or somebody else, did not like it." This last point was a castigation of southern senators James Mason and Robert Toombs, who favored a southern route and blocked all efforts at a central or northern route for the railroad. "There is not a more incorruptible man in the world, I believe, than Frémont," Baker averred—then, possibly realizing that this might be a bit much, caught himself. "But if anybody had been corrupted, I assure you it would have been in favor of and not against the railroad," he added, sparking laughter and more applause.[5]

After two hours and fifteen minutes, Baker brought his oration to a close, assuring his audience that Lincoln would be just as incorruptible as Frémont— and toward the same policy ends: a railroad across the country and an end to the expansion of slavery. "There were loud cries for Frémont," and the chairman of the event quieted the crowd enough to tell them that the man was not in the building. "Well, hunt him up, then," someone yelled, inspiring another round of raucous laughter. But Baker would have to wait until Monday for his personal audience.[6]

Three days later, he joined the Frémonts and other members of their salon (which at various times included King, Baker, aspiring writer Bret Harte, fellow writers such as Herman Melville and Samuel Langhorne Clemens [who would soon take the pen name Mark Twain], artist Albert Bierstadt, photographer Carleton Watkins, and other luminaries) to discuss John C. Frémont's potential role in bringing the antislavery and pro-railroad policies to fruition. They met at the Frémont home at Black Point, a rocky promontory on the north edge of the city opposite the Golden Gate (the name Frémont had given the spot in 1848). King, who made use of a small cottage on the property to write, called it "our Lodge by the Golden Gate," and Jessie described it as "where the waters of the great bay washed the rocks of our headland and we looked down over roses and geraniums to the decks of passing ships making their way out to the Pacific." The "black" of Black Point came from the dark pine and scrub oak that covered the peninsula. Harte was a regular attendee at Sunday dinners. Navy man Edward F. Beale, who had known and defended Frémont during the Mexican War and served as superintendent of Indian affairs in the state, was a frequent guest. Frémont had paid $42,000 for the Black Point house and surrounding dozen acres earlier in the year to provide his wife with a more civilized situation than she tolerated in the mining-camp atmosphere of Las Mariposas (the butterflies), the couple's home in the wilderness of the Sierra Nevada foothills, near Yosemite Valley. Perched atop a hundred-foot bluff, Black Point had, as Frémont described it, "the three things we have always held as requirements for a home. The sound of the sea, a view, and a gentle climate."[7]

Baker was familiar with the Frémonts, the "first lady and gentleman" of California; Baker also knew the state's politics, and he came to Black Point that day as Lincoln's personal representative. He had first met Lincoln when both served in the Black Hawk War in 1832. Baker practiced law alongside Lincoln in Springfield, Illinois, and served with him in that state's legislature. His two terms as a congressman in Illinois in the 1840s bracketed Lincoln's one term. A mark of their closeness came in 1846, when Lincoln named his second son Edward Baker Lincoln after his friend.[8]

Baker also had things in common with Frémont. Both served in the Mexican War, although in different theaters. Baker had given up his Illinois political career to emigrate to California in 1852, where Frémont was already living.

Frémont won and lost a Senate seat. Baker had enjoyed legal and financial success in San Francisco but lost races for the state legislature and Congress. Both had gained fame and wealth, and both had a penchant for spending more than they earned. Baker had even gone through his own cabinet consideration in 1848–1849 before being rejected for a position by President Zachary Taylor. (At the same time, Lincoln had turned down an offer from Taylor to become governor of the Oregon Territory.)[9]

Now Baker was a senator from the new state of Oregon, to which he had retreated after losing the 1859 California congressional race. Local worthies had recruited him specifically to run for the Senate in 1860, and Baker was more than happy to oblige. The newcomer, benefiting from a split in the state Democratic Party that reflected the one that would boost Lincoln to his victory a month later, won the October 2 election and became the first Republican to represent the West Coast in Congress (Frémont had been elected as a Democrat in 1850). Lincoln had other connections to the state, but Baker was, as one historian called him, "the most influential nationally of Lincoln's personal connections in Oregon," and he had been deputed to feel out Frémont.[10]

At the Black Point meeting on October 29, Baker still had to speak unofficially on behalf of his old friend. Lincoln's prospects were bright, but Election Day remained eight days away. News of the positive results (for Republicans) of October state elections had not yet reached California. Baker "was authorized to offer a Cabinet position or a first class foreign appointment to Mr. Frémont," Jessie recalled. "The mission to France would have been tempting in time of peace, but we all saw war ahead and it was not a time to leave one's country."[11]

Frémont, a naturally reticent man, heard Baker out but committed to nothing. His reluctance was not simply a case of typical nineteenth-century faux humility. Though he had lost the 1856 election and largely left the political playing field in the wake of that defeat, he had kept a hand in. He and King, for example, were working together to raise money for drought-stricken farmers "of all shades of political belief" in Kansas—and he still had something of a following in the party, as the reception in absentia at Baker's speech indicated. Horace Greeley observed, "There are many thousands who cherish for Col. Frémont a personal regard and affection which render them profoundly solicitous with respect to his good or evil fortune." He had a claim on a top-level position if he wanted one, especially if California came in for Lincoln. The question was, did he want one? More to the point as far as Frémont was concerned, if secession came and war followed, would he be given a senior field command in any northern army?[12]

The truth was, although he was elated at the prospect of a Lincoln administration that would vindicate his unsuccessful 1856 crusade, Frémont's mind was on other things, and he told Baker as much. His claims of concentrating on business were legitimate and well documented. A decadelong battle to secure title to the forty-four thousand acres of land and mining operations at Las Mariposas had been successful, and the mines and stamping plants were producing tens of thousands of dollars a week in revenue. The land he had paid $3,000 for in 1847 included twenty-nine ore-bearing veins and was now valued at $10 million. However, the costs of running the operation, dealing with multiple creditors, and ferreting out squatters were overwhelming in terms of both time and money. State courts had held that any "unoccupied" claim could be jumped, and they offered a loose definition of that term. "A small miner working alone would go to his dinner, and immediately men watching for the chance would seize and hold against him his lawful property," Jessie Frémont wrote. It kept "every mine-owner in the position of sentinel." Newspapers in the weeks after the election were reporting on lawsuits that Frémont was filing in attempts to recover gold that had been taken from his land, along with regular reports on how much gold was being produced.[13]

A decade before, Frémont had turned down a $1 million offer from a purchaser Benton had recruited. An 1851 trip to Europe, during which John and Jessie were received by Queen Victoria, had yielded no takers. Now he needed new investors and more capital; for the moment, that would have to take precedence over any political appointment. Turning to Jessie, John asked, "And what do you wish?" He probably knew what she would say: "Above all, to stay here where I have taken root along with my rose bushes; otherwise, to do what you think best." What Frémont thought best was that business came first. But if war came, he assured Baker, he would serve his country in uniform as he had done before. Considering Frémont's long record of insubordination and defiance of authority, that promise might not have reassured the emissary of the soon-to-be president-elect in quite the way Frémont intended.[14]

"THE LATTER-DAY JACKSON"

That record stretched back to the very beginning of the Frémont-Benton relationship.

Frémont's early exploration work for the Army Corps of Topographical Engineers in the 1830s led to his meeting Thomas Hart Benton, who headed the Senate Military Affairs Committee. When the young lieutenant returned from an expedition to the Coteau des Prairies between the Mississippi and Missouri Rivers, Benton invited him to his Washington home. There, in 1840, the twenty-seven-year-old John met Benton's sixteen-year-old daughter, Jessie Ann.

It was, on both sides, love at first sight. Benton and his wife, however, were less than thrilled. Mrs. Benton had hoped to marry Jessie off to the widowed president, Martin Van Buren (who was more than four decades her senior, so it couldn't have been Frémont's age that stood in the way). The elder Bentons took steps to keep the couple separated, pointing out that Frémont had no family fit for society. His mother and roguish father had not been legally married when he was born in Savannah, Georgia, in 1813. A promising student, he had been admitted to the College of Charleston but was expelled for failing to attend class regularly. Even with the expulsion, Frémont's math and drawing skills had caught the attention of future secretary of war Joel Poinsett, a former South Carolina congressman and minister to Mexico. Poinsett both launched Frémont's career as an explorer by hiring him to do a railroad survey and was instrumental in getting him a commission with the Army Corps of Topographical Engineers. Still, with no money and the meager career prospects typical of an army officer, Frémont seemed like a bad bet to the Bentons. Jessie, accustomed to getting what she wanted, refused to listen. John was in a more difficult position as a military officer under indirect supervision by Benton. Eventually the couple agreed to Benton's demand that they wait a year to see whether their romance would survive the test of time. To add a biblical touch to the proceedings, Benton arranged for Frémont to be sent off on an expedition to the Des Moines River, in which he had nearly drowned two years earlier, in 1838.[15]

Time and distance did not deter them, and unlike Uriah in II Samuel, Frémont survived his exile. The lovers were both used to getting their way, and the romance would prove no exception. John headed west in June 1841, he was back in Washington in August, and the couple eloped in October, marrying in the home of Kentucky senator John J. Crittenden, whose wife, Maria, was a friend of Jessie's. They did not tell the Bentons for nearly a month. The couple's defiance of authority created a template they would follow for the next three decades of Frémont's life in politics and the military.

Benton soon forgave his protégé and welcomed Frémont into the family and into his official good graces. This connection laid the foundation for Frémont's enduring fame. An 1842 expedition partway up the Oregon Trail was followed by a second expedition all the way to Oregon (and then, in defiance of orders, to California) in 1843–1844. This journey yielded an official report written by John that was subsequently edited by Jessie into a romantic adventure story and became a best seller. Published at the opportune moment as immigration to Oregon and California began to boom, the page-turner made Frémont into a national celebrity.

Frémont's decision to turn southward and cross the Sierra Nevada in February 1844 was without official sanction. California belonged to Mexico, and he had no authorization from the Corps of Topographical Engineers to venture into Mexican territory. To top it off, he was toting a howitzer, which he had requisitioned from the armory in St. Louis before heading west. On discovery of this possession shortly after his group had begun its journey, orders were sent for John to return with the weapon, endangering the entire expedition. Jessie held up the orders until her husband was too far down the trail to reverse course and then sent a message his way to keep going and not look back. John J. Abert, head of the Corps, was outraged. Benton smoothed things over for his son-in-law, so the commanding general in St. Louis, Stephen Watts Kearny, suffered the greatest share of embarrassment and castigation from the War Department. Kearny would not forget the humiliation.

More troubling than making off with a single piece of artillery was Frémont's insubordinate behavior on his next journey west, to California on the eve of war with Mexico. It was there that Frémont sealed his reputation as a loose cannon, offending the West Point officer class that would still be holding a grudge against him when he returned to the military in 1861.

War with Mexico was declared in April 1846, by which time Frémont had been agitating in California for several months. In late 1845, he had promised settlers and recent immigrants at Sutter's Fort (present-day Sacramento) that if war came, his men would protect them. His belligerent actions in the field and unofficial discussions with U.S. Consul Thomas Larkin got the attention of Mexican officials, who soon grew suspicious of Frémont's activities and ordered him to leave California. He took his men out of Monterey, but not California, camping atop nearby Gabilon Peak (now Frémont Peak) and raising the Stars and Stripes at the summit. When Mexican troops arrived in response to this provocation, Frémont and his men retreated to Oregon. By May 1846, they were back in California, looking (as Lt. Frederick Walpole of the Royal Navy described Frémont's corps) like "true trappers, the class that produced the heroes of Fenimore Cooper's best works."[16]

Heroes were needed. Lt. Archibald Gillespie caught up with Frémont in the first week of May and handed him dispatches from Washington that anticipated, but predated, the war declaration. Frémont moved south, setting up camp along the Bear River about two days north of Sutter's Fort. He was joined by American immigrants hoping to rise up against the Mexican authorities. On June 14, a few dozen of those men captured Sonoma and the next day hoisted the Bear Flag up a makeshift pole and declared formation of the California Republic. Frémont disavowed any knowledge of or participation in the Bear Flag Revolt, but he sent those taken prisoner by the rebels under guard to Sutter's Fort, and the rebels considered him sympathetic to their cause. His actions were questionable, but there was nobody in authority in California willing to question them.

The navy got to California before the army. When news of the war declaration came, Frémont's men, bolstered by local recruits and now numbering more than four hundred, were enlisted into service by Comm. Robert Stockton. When Army brigadier general Stephen Watts Kearny arrived on the scene in December 1846, he ordered Frémont to come under his command. Frémont refused, arguing that he was answerable to Stockton.

Stockton backed up Frémont and appointed him military governor of California in January 1847. Kearny got the same appointment from commanding general Winfield Scott. Frémont at first refused Kearny's order to return to the east. When he finally acquiesced, Kearny had him arrested when their party reached Fort Leavenworth, Kansas, despite President James K. Polk's order that Frémont be given the option to return to his regiment fighting in Mexico. Frémont was charged with mutiny, disobeying a superior officer, and conduct prejudicial to the public services. When he returned to Washington, he endured a grueling three-month court-martial. Convicted on all charges in January 1848, he was sentenced to discharge from the service, although a majority of the court recommended executive clemency.[17]

Stepping in because her husband had gone to South Carolina to tend to his dying mother, Jessie met twice with Polk, who doubted the legitimacy of the mutiny conviction but provided no succor. Polk, as he related to his diary but not to Jessie, believed "Frémont was greatly in the wrong when he refused to obey the orders issued to him by General Kearny." Jessie then met with Kearny, who hurled the St. Louis howitzer back at her, and she felt the game was up. Benton provided a more effective intervention with Polk, who admitted to Benton that he "regretted the whole affair." After consulting with his cabinet, the president commuted the sentence and offered to reinstate Frémont into service. But Frémont's stubborn pride would not countenance a deal. He refused Polk's offer, believing he was innocent of all charges and that accepting a pardon would effectively be an admission of guilt. Instead, he resigned his commission in 1848 and left the army. It was a sordid affair, instigated by vague orders and Frémont's insubordination, but likely would have amounted to nothing if not for

Kearny's tenacious grudge. On his deathbed in St. Louis in October 1848, the general sent a message to Jessie via the army doctor who was treating them both (Jessie had recently lost a baby), asking her to visit him. She steadfastly refused, and Kearny died, unvisited and unforgiven, on October 31.[18]

The Frémonts settled in California on forty thousand acres of land that John had bought for $3,000 with help from Consul Larkin in 1847. Having left the Topographical Corps, Frémont led a privately funded expedition up the Arkansas River in 1848–1849, during which some of his men nearly starved and at least some participated in cannibalism to stay alive. But he remained enough of a hero to the now American residents of California that when statehood came in 1850, he was elected one of the new state's first two senators. His brief tenure— he had drawn the short straw and faced reelection in 1852—was unremarkable. He supported legislation that would have guaranteed Mexican land grants, like the one he had purchased from Larkin. Another measure would have barred foreigners from owning gold claims. He backed abolition of the slave trade in the District of Columbia but not the abolition of slavery itself in the nation's capital. He served only 134 days and, after a long and extended debate in the state legislature, was not reelected.[19]

A fifth expedition in 1853–1854—like the fourth, funded by St. Louis businessmen recruited by Benton—sought a railroad route along the 38th parallel. Also like the fourth expedition, this one ran into harsh winter weather and accomplished little. At the age of forty, Frémont decided it was time to get out of the exploration business. He became serious about developing Las Mariposas into a going concern.

Despite the court-martial, the undistinguished and brief Senate career, and the failed expeditions, the handsome and dashing Frémont retained a hold on the public imagination. Both political parties, hoping to attach themselves to his enduring fame, considered him a viable nominee for president in 1856. His antislavery instincts led him to the new Republican Party, largely because the Republicans promised to stop the spread of slavery into the western territories he had done so much to popularize.

A leading proponent of Frémont's candidacy was Francis Preston Blair, a longtime Washington fixture, a close friend of Andrew Jackson and Thomas Hart Benton, and a founding member of the Republican Party who decades earlier had dandled little Jessie on his knee. The Blair family sat at the nexus connecting Lincoln and Frémont. One Blair son, Montgomery, had represented Frémont in the Supreme Court in the case that secured his land grant. Another son, Francis Preston Blair Jr. (known as Frank), was running for Congress as a Republican in the Benton stronghold of St. Louis. Daughter Elizabeth was one of Jessie's closest friends. When the Frémonts' infant daughter Anne had fallen ill in 1853, it was to the Blairs' Silver Spring home outside Washington that Jessie had retreated. The baby died there, and the Blairs helped nurse Jessie back to health.

Benton, by contrast, was not a Frémont supporter. He believed a Republican victory would split the country, leading to secession and civil war, and endorsed Democrat James Buchanan. Forced to choose between her husband and her father, Jessie sided with John. In effect, she served as his campaign manager, handling correspondence and controlling access to him. It was a unique role for a woman and a wife, and her performance in many ways outshined her husband's. "Our Jessie" became at least as popular a figure as the Pathfinder. By October 1856, leading national politicians were writing not about what Frémont might do as president but about what "the Frémonts" might do and what "they"—not "he"—might be able to accomplish. Acquaintances noted that "Frémont would never transact business without his wife being present, who had a much clearer head than he."[20]

When the campaign ended in defeat, the dispirited Frémonts took different tacks. Jessie's role was widely acknowledged, and some believed it portended a brighter future for women in the public sphere. "The ballot has not yet been yielded," noted women's rights activist Lucy Stone, "but it cannot be far off when, as in the last Presidential contest, women were urged to attend political meetings, and a woman's name was made one of the rallying cries of the party of progress. The enthusiasm which everywhere greeted the name of Jessie was so far a recognition of woman's right to participate in politics."[21]

For Jessie herself, it was a time of discontentment. It's not certain that she knew of accusations by some close associates that her husband had been unfaithful or, if she did, that she believed them. But her behavior implied that a certain distance had grown between the couple that went beyond the letdown that is natural after the exhilaration of a campaign and the disappointment of a defeat. When John headed to California, she headed to Europe with their children: Lily, John Charles Jr. (called Charley), and Frank, who was named in honor of Francis Preston Blair. John's niece and ward, Nina, also traveled with them, leaving in June 1857.

The Frémonts would not be reunited until November, in New York. Apparently reconciled, they headed back to California in March 1858 by ship, via Panama. It was the third time Jessie had made the perilous journey. Arriving the following month, they began in earnest to set up a home at Las Mariposas.

New York newspaper editor Horace Greeley visited Las Mariposas in spring 1859 as part of his western tour. For Frémont, it would be a rehearsal for the meeting the following year with Baker. Greeley talked politics and the 1860 election, but Frémont waved away the subject emphatically enough that Greeley "soon realized why Mr. Frémont would not reenter political life in a way which would again entail the abandonment of his property," Jessie wrote. A dedicated foe of New York senator William Henry Seward, however, Greeley "wanted and obtained, all the influence and helping good feeling Mr. Frémont could bring to bear in aid of Mr. Lincoln."[22]

That was Jessie looking back. In fact, Frémont played no role in Lincoln's nomination or election. Some loyal supporters still wanted Frémont to try again in 1860, and his name continued to come up as the May convention approached, despite his having officially demurred the previous November in a letter to the *Daily Alta California*, insisting he "would not again encounter the vexation, mortification and annoyance" of a presidential campaign. Among Frémont's most devoted followers were the Germans of St. Louis, who hoped that a deadlocked convention might turn the Pathfinder's way. "Our First Choice! As Presidential Candidate of the Republican Party J. C. Frémont, Subject to the Decision of the Republican National Convention," declared a March 1860 headline in the *Anzeiger des Westens*, one of the city's German-language newspapers, whose editor was a friend of Lincoln's. Just a week before the Chicago convention, the paper referred to Frémont as "the latter-day Jackson" and insisted, "We will continue to hold his name up at the head of our ranks as the first and only chosen one until a final and irreversible decision, and we shall parade until then for Frémont alone." Frémont acted to keep his name out of the convention, authorizing a friendly delegate to withdraw his name in the event it was raised. His primary concern was that the party nominate a candidate who was solid on the transcontinental railroad.[23]

Despite all this, Frémont remained a heroic figure in the popular imagination. At the San Francisco celebration of a decade of statehood in September 1860, his carriage led the procession through the city's streets. Baker's visit on behalf of Lincoln confirmed that Frémont hadn't been forgotten outside the state either.[24]

Frémont's antebellum career was marked by great success and unmatched fame as an explorer despite frequent carelessness with the lives of the men under his charge, electoral defeat, defiance of authority coupled with outright insubordination as a military officer, and a grade of incomplete on his political, financial, and business acumen. Civil war would again test Frémont on each of these counts. If he was a "latter-day Jackson," as his friends in the German press proclaimed, he would have plenty of opportunity to demonstrate it in the coming conflict.

CHAPTER ONE

"Great confusion and indecision in affairs"

BY THE TIME THE LONG ELECTION NIGHT WAS OVER, ABRAHAM LINCOLN HAD a pretty good idea of whom he wanted as the core members of his cabinet. After spending the evening in the Springfield telegraph office, "I had substantially completed the framework of my Cabinet as it now exists," he explained later. That would not stop him from vacillating on individual choices—or others from offering their advice. Some of that advice involved pushing the candidacy of John C. Frémont for a spot in the cabinet or a senior diplomatic post.[1]

Charles Billinghurst, a former two-term member of Congress from Wisconsin, was quick out of the gate in favor of Frémont. "Frémont at the head of the War Department in the government, would be found equal to any emergency," Billinghurst wrote Lincoln. "I am for Frémont for Secty of War first and foremost. In a time of profound peace I do not believe he would accept, but as the times are, I believe he would glory in it."[2]

Lincoln and his vanquished rival for the presidential nomination, New York senator William Henry Seward, had different visions for the cabinet. Seward was the leading candidate to become secretary of state, and he sought allies who would bolster his self-anointed position of prime minister. He wanted loyal Whigs, which meant excluding his chief political rival, Salmon P. Chase. By contrast, Lincoln wanted, in historian Doris Kearns Goodwin's phrase, a team of rivals who would balance each other while binding the factions of the party together. Lincoln the politician understood this approach would come with a high degree of intrigue, but it would be better to have those rivals working inside the tent than hectoring from outside.[3]

Frémont's executive ability had never really been put to the test beyond leadership of a few dozen men in the wild and a few hundred in California during the Mexican War, at which times his performances were hit-or-miss. His record of working as one cog in an executive team was more miss than hit.

Under the guiding hands of such mentors as Thomas Hart Benton, former secretary of war Joel Poinsett (the South Carolinian who gave Frémont his first exploring job), and French polymath Joseph Nicollet (who led the 1838–1839 Great Plains expedition), Frémont had prospered as a protégé, as an instrument of policy. Now all his mentors were gone. Benton had died just a couple weeks after the Frémonts departed for California in 1858. Unshackled and left to his own devices, Frémont had floundered. Working as a department head would require a level of political sophistication he had not, as yet, demonstrated. His tendency to go off half-cocked, somewhat kept in check when under the influence of older and wiser men, was a liability when he became untethered from their restraints. His troubling tendency to defy authority had mattered less when under Benton's overarching protection or when separated from civilization by thousands of miles of wilderness. With all his protectors gone, and operating at the center of power, Frémont would find that defiance came at a hefty cost.

Pennsylvania, because of its size and crucial role in the Republican coalition, was entitled to be rewarded with a senior administration post. The leading candidate for that place was Senator Simon Cameron, a possibility for either the War Department or the Treasury. If he was in at War, Frémont was out. If Cameron was tapped for the Treasury or left out entirely, the War Department was still in play and thus still a possible landing place for Frémont.

Although Cameron was the top Pennsylvania choice, he was not the only possibility. And he came with considerable baggage, the loading of which had begun behind Lincoln's back at the Republican convention in May—amid all the other chicanery typical of a brokered convention, such as using the home-field advantage of Chicago to print extra tickets for supporters so they could flood the Wigwam (the name given to the temporary structure hosting the convention). Lincoln's team physically separated the New York and Pennsylvania delegations on the convention floor and placed pro-Lincoln delegations between them, thus making it more difficult for the two big states to work together to bring the Seward and Cameron factions together on a deal.

Behind the scenes, Lincoln operatives persuaded Cameron to bring his delegates to Lincoln on the second ballot in exchange for the promise of a top cabinet position, probably the Treasury Department. Leonard Swett, a longtime acquaintance who had ridden the Eighth Judicial Circuit of Illinois with Lincoln, confessed as much postelection, when he had to explain to the president-elect why Cameron's supporters were channeling their supplications through Swett and his convention colleague David Davis.

"I am annoyed, a little, that these applications of Cameron's friends are made so prominently through Judge Davis & myself. Yet, on the whole, from what occurred at Chicago I think they have a right to do it," he owned up as introduction. "The truth is, at Chicago we thought the Cameron influence was the controlling element & tried to procure that rather than the factions." But that did not mean he was backing away from the agreement, however unsavory it might have been. "My belief is that no man, other than C. can be selected there without considerable dissatisfaction." Cameron's partisans were also lobbying Vice President–elect Hannibal Hamlin, who was getting appeals "from very strong and unexpected quarters in Pennsylvania, urging the appointment of General Cameron to a place in the cabinet."[4]

That might well have been true. But selecting Cameron came with its own set of dissatisfied customers stretching far beyond just devotees of Frémont. Alexander McClure, a leader in the state's anti-Cameron faction, thought it better for Pennsylvania to go unrepresented in Lincoln's cabinet than to have Cameron as the representative. "It is not at all essential that you should select a Cabinet officer from this State," he told the president-elect. "Surely it is better to take none than to do us positive wrong."[5]

From Swett, McClure, and countless others, Lincoln was getting plenty of advice (solicited and otherwise) about Cameron and every other potential cabinet nominee. Over the first few weeks, a couple of themes began to emerge. On November 16, a visitor from Lincoln's home state of Kentucky urged him to build a cabinet of conservatives, including at least one southerner. Lincoln's reply that this approach would effectively deliver the government into the hands of the men he had just defeated in an election was a message he would return to repeatedly over the next three and a half months. "I am not at liberty to shift my ground," he wrote that same day to a Missouri newspaper editor. "That is out of the question."[6]

In part, that was because he thought it would not be necessary. By the third week of November, the *New York Herald* was reporting that Lincoln "still adheres to the opinion that actual secession will not be attempted." At the same time, he was ready to make a stand if it did. "The tug has to come," he wrote to Illinois ally Lyman Trumbull a few weeks later, "& better now, than any time hereafter."[7]

Rather than rush to Washington and perhaps make things even worse by his presence, he stayed in Illinois. Springfield became for a short time the "Mecca of

American politics," as Lincoln secretaries John Hay and John Nicolay described it. The political mountains would come to Mohammed.[8]

In mid-December, Missouri congressman and presumed Frémont ally Frank Blair met with Lincoln in Springfield. Blair was not there to lobby on Frémont's behalf, however. Instead, he was angling for his lawyer brother, Montgomery (often called "The Judge" or "Brother" by the family), to receive a place in the cabinet, possibly as war secretary or attorney general. Trumbull also put forward Montgomery Blair, a West Point graduate, for the War Department. Frank Blair briefed Lincoln on the need to defend the St. Louis Arsenal, the largest military depot in the slave states, housing sixty thousand rifles, one and a half million cartridges, and ninety thousand pounds of powder. Losing the arsenal to southern sympathizers, Blair stressed, would likely mean losing the state.

A Blair presence in Lincoln's inner circle would seem to be good news for Frémont. Frank Blair had been working with Lincoln since 1857. The Blairs and Bentons had a long political and personal history together. Both Frank Jr. and Montgomery had been law partners with Thomas Hart Benton in St. Louis, and Benton had sponsored Montgomery's admission to West Point. Montgomery handled some of Frémont's legal work. Francis Blair Sr. had been a leading early proponent of Frémont's nomination in 1856. Jessie and Elizabeth Blair Lee, the congressman's sister, had grown up together as best friends and remained warm and frequent correspondents. Lincoln was also considering another Frémont ally, Nathaniel Banks, as an option to represent New England in the cabinet, in part because he wanted his New Englander to be a former Democrat, which favored Banks and Gideon Welles, a Connecticut newspaper editor and politician, over Charles Francis Adams, a former Free Soiler. Like the senior Blair, Banks had been an early Frémont supporter in 1856 and a candidate for the vice presidential spot on the ticket for which Lincoln was also considered and that eventually went to former New Jersey senator William Dayton.[9]

It might have been true that, as Lincoln later told Welles, "before the sun went down [on the day after Election Day], I had made up my cabinet." But more than a month later he was still looking for advice on that and a host of other topics.[10]

On December 10, Swett, acting on Lincoln's behalf, invited Seward's fixer, Thurlow Weed, to Hay and Nicolay's Mecca, seeking advice about the cabinet generally and to gauge Seward's interest in particular.[11]

Weed had previously invited Lincoln to join him at Seward's home in Auburn, New York, a move designed to signal Seward's desire to be the driving force in the administration—making the president-elect come to him. Lincoln was having none of that. Application would be made to the chief executive; the chief, however deferential he might sound, did not make application. On the same day Swett invited Weed to Springfield, Vice President–elect Hamlin caught his senatorial colleague Seward on the streets of the capital and invited the New Yorker to his hotel room to pigeonhole him on the State Department.

"No, no," was Seward's reply to Hamlin's inquiry. "If that is what you have come to talk to me about, Hamlin, we might as well stop here. I don't want the place, and if I did, I have reason to know that I could not get it; therefore let us have no more talk about it." Then Hamlin pressed into Seward's hands two letters from Lincoln, assuring him that the offer of secretary of state was in good faith, and Hamlin believed Seward's eagerness gave away his enthusiasm. "This is remarkable, Mr. Hamlin; I will consider the matter, and, in accordance with Mr. Lincoln's request, give him my decision at the earliest practicable moment." Seward's on-again, off-again, on-again game of political chess with Lincoln over the State Department would have implications for Frémont right up until the night of the inauguration.[12]

Before Seward could talk to Lincoln directly or take the oath as secretary of state, though, he needed to continue playing the role he had played for the past half decade, that of a Republican leader in Congress. While Lincoln entertained guests and fended off office seekers in Springfield (all the while maintaining a studied public silence), Washington was a nest of intrigue.[13]

As lawmakers reconvened in the first week of December, President James Buchanan sent up his annual message. Newspapers reported that Lincoln "awaits the appearance of his predecessor's Message with the greatest anxiety." It allayed no fears and stoked quite a few new ones. Buchanan insisted secession was illegal while paradoxically arguing that the federal government could do nothing to stop it. He called for compromise to avert a crisis but offered nothing to the North that would qualify as a concession. In essence, Buchanan, like Lincoln's postelection visitor from Kentucky, called on Congress to repudiate the verdict of the 1860 election. A young Henry Adams (son of Charles Francis) feared that was exactly what would happen. "Our men hardly dare say they'll take the prize they've won," he wrote to his brother.[14]

Committees were formed in each chamber—a Committee of 33 in the House (named for the number of members) and a Committee of 13 in the Senate—to come up with proposals. Among the members were one from each chamber under consideration for high office in Lincoln's administration: Seward and Charles Francis Adams. Also included was Mississippi senator Jefferson Davis.

What the committees produced was unpromising from a Republican point of view. Kentucky representative John Crittenden devised a plan that called for six constitutional amendments that would extend the Missouri Compromise line to California; bar Congress from abolishing slavery in any state where it already existed or in the District of Columbia without consent or compensation; protect the domestic, interstate slave trade; provide for compensation of slave owners whose fugitive slaves were assisted to freedom by rescuers; and bar further amendments that might interfere with slavery. For all his "masterly inactivity," Lincoln's line in the sand was clear. To William Kellogg, a Committee of 33 member from Illinois, Lincoln stated plainly, "Entertain no proposition in regard to the extension of slavery." He made similar remarks to several other correspondents.[15]

Lincoln was treading a fine line. Conscious that three out of five voters had chosen someone other than him, he understood the tenuous nature of the Republican plurality, and he was proceeding cautiously with that knowledge in mind. Leading a new party that had never governed at the national level, confronted by crisis, rent by internal divisions about how to proceed, and facing hostile Democrats in Congress, Lincoln saw silence as the safest course, except to repeat to "discreet friends" his "well-formed convictions." While many foes and some friends urged him to do more, close ally Trumbull spoke for many when he said, "Inactivity and a kind spirit is, it seems to me, all that is left for us to do, till the 4th of March." Compounding Lincoln's reluctance to engage was a lack of any real power to affect events until that date, coupled with a fond hope that reason would prevail and the fire eaters would be brought to heel before violence could break out.[16]

In that desire, he had plenty of company. The North had been hearing threats of southern secession at least since the Missouri crisis of 1820. Always there had been much smoke but no fire; always in the past an accommodation had been reached, and there was no reason to believe this time would be any different. That, at least, was the thinking of Lincoln and some of his partisans. Journalist John Bigelow described the situation as "the extraordinary and unprecedented spectacle of an insurrection provoked entirely by prospective grievances."[17]

Edward Bates of Missouri, under consideration for either secretary of state or attorney general, was confident "that (except with a few demented fanatics) it is all brag and bluster, hoping to make a better compromise with the timid patriotism of their opponents. . . . The letters and telegrams from the South, bear plain evidence of exagiration, and make a false shewing of the unanimity of the people, in support of the traitorous design."[18]

At the other end of the ideological and geographical spectrum, Senator William Pitt Fessenden of Maine was of the same mind. "My opinion is that much of the noise is got up for effect in the hope that the North will be frightened and the Republicans induced to lose the confidence of the people in their firmness and capacity."[19]

Less than a week before South Carolina's secession convention, Richard Corwine, a Cincinnati lawyer and political figure who had lived in Mississippi for eight years and would serve on Frémont's staff in 1861, assured Lincoln, "The great heart of the South is loyal to the Union, and it will be manifested whenever a suitable opportunity occurs."[20]

The financial markets were less sanguine. As Frémont was preparing to travel to Europe in search of investors for his mining venture, stocks fell into a pair of postelection panics, and several banks ceased exchanging gold for bank notes after edgy customers rushed to get their money. In Springfield, Lincoln was kept abreast of developments as "telegraphic dispatches, conveying the troubles and anxieties of Eastern financial commercial centers, constantly flashed upon him," wrote journalist Henry Villard. Antislavery Republicans like *New York Post* editor William Cullen Bryant worried that market disruptions might sway Lincoln from bold action. Bryant was particularly concerned about Thurlow Weed's influence. "The rumor having got abroad that you have been visited by a well known politician of New York who has a good deal to do with the stock market and who took with him a plan of compromise manufactured in Wall Street, it has occurred to me that you might like to be assured of the manner in which those Republicans who have no connections with Wall Street regard a compromise on the slavery question," he wrote to Lincoln. "The restoration of the Missouri Compromise would disband the Republican party."[21]

The visit to which Bryant alluded began when Weed arrived in Springfield on December 20—the same day the South Carolina state convention voted to secede from the Union. Even before Weed arrived, Lincoln had laid out his response to compromise proposals: "inflexible on the territorial question," "no State can in any way lawfully get out of the Union without the consent of the others," and "it is the duty of the President and the other Government functionaries to run the machine as it is."[22]

Lincoln and Weed had met before, as far back as 1848 and as recently as May 24. A pair of ambitious, experienced politicians, the two "took to each other" and spent most of the day talking, with only a brief break for lunch. Weed opposed the nominations of Blair and Welles (both former Democrats) and of Chase, who had bounced from the Liberty Party to the Free Soil Party before joining the Republicans but had long endorsed Democratic Party policies outside the realm of slavery. Regarding Montgomery Blair, Weed warned Lincoln that he would "regret it" if the Judge were brought into the cabinet, saying that the "Blair blood was troublesome." Weed also steered Lincoln away from Cameron for Treasury. Weed had surely discussed Frémont with Seward, who would recommend him, but Weed's opinion was not high. Weed had called Frémont's 1856 nomination "an inexcusable blunder" and said he had "no qualification for the position of Chief Magistrate." That was a journalist soaked in the life of politics talking about a nonpolitician who disdained that world, but it called into question Weed's—and thus Seward's—endorsement of Frémont for any executive branch position.[23]

After that marathon session with Lincoln, Weed wrote a pessimistic note to Seward on Christmas Day about Lincoln's resolve on Chase, Blair, and Welles. That same day, Seward wrote to Lincoln suggesting Frémont for secretary of war. Lincoln responded on December 29, saying he had thought of Frémont as well, "but not very definitely."[24]

Edward Baker, who had traveled to Washington after his October visit with the Frémonts, returned west to arrive in Springfield from the nation's capital on Christmas Eve. Newspapers called it a private visit, though Baker gave a forty-five-minute speech in which he extolled the West Coast's devotion to the Union and the need for a transcontinental railroad. It seems inconceivable that he and Lincoln did not discuss the political intelligence from Washington and California, including news of Frémont's preference for a senior field command over a cabinet post.

More significantly for Frémont's prospects, Pennsylvanian David Wilmot also spent part of Christmas Eve cloistered with Lincoln, making the case for Cameron, who arrived December 30 at Lincoln's invitation via Swett. A day before his arrival, a well-placed New York journalist had offered his "unshaken conviction that Mr. Cameron will not occupy a seat in the Cabinet." That journalist's preference for Wilmot might have influenced his reporting. Cameron's partisans had been lobbying Lincoln at least since the days immediately following the election and would continue right into the new year.[25]

Cameron, angling for the Treasury, told Lincoln that perhaps Chase was the right man for the War Department. "We are going to have armed conflict over your election," he said, somewhat to Lincoln's alarm, "and the place for an ambitious man is in the War Department. There he will have lots of room to make a reputation." Later that Sunday night, another cabinet candidate, Edward Bates of Missouri, arrived in town at Lincoln's request. Lincoln, Cameron, and

Bates "had a sort of general conversation" for about two hours in the Pennsylvanian's room. When Lincoln left, Bates stayed, and they were joined by lawyer and editor John Sanderson, a close ally of Cameron. The senator spilled no beans to Bates, and before leaving Springfield, he had a written promise from Lincoln that he would have a place in the cabinet, though the final landing spot was yet to be determined.[26]

Where Cameron landed had major implications for Frémont's future. The *New York Herald's* Springfield correspondent reported on New Year's Day that one of the cabinet positions "positively disposed of" was Frémont for the War Department. The paper had to acknowledge that "Frémont has not been heard in reply to the tender of what is but justly due him; but he is expected to manifest no resistance to the pleasure of the President elect, and the current of popular opinion, that, to all appearances, flows very strong in his favor throughout the free States." *Frank Leslie's Weekly* on January 19 had "a strong expectation that Col. Frémont will be made War Minister," while admitting, "We are half afraid of the Colonel, he is too fond of land speculations," and suggesting his southern birth might be disqualifying.[27]

However certain the *Herald* was, and whatever was "justly due" to Frémont, Lincoln's commitment to Cameron would last only a few days. Hard on the Pennsylvania senator's heels came his home-state detractors: Alexander McClure, a state legislator, and Governor Andrew Curtin, leveled hair-raising accusations of corruption. They were not alone. A former congressional colleague of Lincoln's wrote, "Under no circumstance or contingency will it answer to even dream of putting Simon Cameron in the Cabinet. He is corrupt beyond belief. He is rich by plunder—and cannot be trusted anywhere." Thaddeus Stevens told Chase that Cameron would turn any department he led into a "den of thieves." Lincoln asked the Pennsylvania visitors for proof, and McClure claimed he provided it, although no written record of what he gave Lincoln exists. Whatever it was, it moved Lincoln to revoke the offer made just days earlier. It seemed the War Department was once again in play.[28]

Ignorant of all of Lincoln's deliberations, politicians' machinations, and newspaper reporters' faulty conclusions, Frémont boarded a ship in San Francisco Bay headed for Panama, and thence to New York and on to Europe, on the same day the *Herald* named him a lock for the cabinet.

At first, the new year seemed to clarify little in Springfield or Washington. Bates had confirmed to his friend, Indiana congressman Schuyler Colfax, on Christmas Eve that Lincoln had invited him into the cabinet, although the exact spot at that point was still uncertain.[29]

Meanwhile, Mississippi, Florida, and Alabama joined South Carolina in seceding from the Union, on January 9, 10, and 11, respectively. Jessie Frémont's close friend Elizabeth Blair Lee (Lizzie to her friends) despaired in a letter to her husband, navy officer Samuel Phillips Lee, a unionist Virginian and grandson of Richard Henry Lee, "Civil War seems inevitable." Lizzie was in the Senate gallery when Jefferson Davis gave his valedictory, a speech he delivered in a voice his wife, Varina—another good friend of Lizzie's—compared to "a silver trumpet." Lizzie took a slightly different view of Davis and his compatriots, saying, "I wished in my heart for Old Hickory to arrest them all."[30]

On January 14, Lizzie's father, Francis Preston Blair, weighed in with a long letter to Lincoln. Reminding the president-elect that he was about "to assume a position of greater responsibility than Washington ever occupied" (a phrase Lincoln would borrow a few weeks later in his farewell speech to Springfield), Blair urged the appointment of men of the same caliber as John Adams, Thomas Jefferson, Alexander Hamilton, and others who had attended Washington. Seward was not on that list, and neither was Cameron. Lincoln's greatest asset, Blair wrote, was his "acknowledged purity of character." Bringing in someone with Cameron's reputation for "greedy & unscrupulous ambition" would erode public trust in his administration before it had a chance to get off the ground. Better to provide "a first class mission" to Cameron and ship Seward off to France. "I am sure that both Seward & Cameron might do themselves & the country more essential service by defeating the plots of our conspirators abroad than they could do for either at home—They have many good points & are on the whole good men." Then, as Blair was wont to do, he invoked Andrew Jackson, citing how he was able to put even the pirate Jean Lafitte to good use in New Orleans.[31]

If the image of Seward and Cameron as latter-day pirates brought a smile to Lincoln's face, the moment is lost to history. Blair's letter did not dissuade Lincoln: three days after he read it, the president-elect publicly announced his intent to nominate Seward as secretary of state and Bates as attorney general; then he said he wouldn't be naming any more cabinet picks until he arrived in Washington. He also wrote a letter meant for Cameron, inviting the potential nominee back to Springfield for another session, and then chose not to send it.[32]

Lincoln's declaration that he was done announcing cabinet selections did not put an end to the lobbying. Two days later, a delegation of Californians showed up in Springfield "laying close siege to the President-elect." If they were there to lobby on Frémont's behalf, they kept it to themselves. News reports noted their appearance but offered no details on their mission. Lincoln might have changed his mind about inviting Cameron for another visit, but on January 24 a delegation of Pennsylvanians arrived in Springfield to lobby on his behalf. Lincoln told them he had "every reason to hope that your wishes will be gratified. I feel a strong desire to do something for your big State, and I am determined she shall be satisfied, if I can do it." However, he asked another Pennsylvania delegation what would happen to his reputation as "Honest Old Abe" if one of his first acts as president was to nominate someone with Cameron's notorious reputation, "whose very name stinks in the nostrils of the people for his corruption?"[33]

Perhaps sensing that Frémont's chances for a spot in the cabinet were slipping away, Horace Greeley in the first week of February publicly pushed the Pathfinder for minister to France. "I believe that John C. Frémont ought to be Minister to France, not so much for his own sake as because the Republicans of '56 will feel that they are slighted if he is not recognized by the new Administration," Greeley wrote Lincoln, perhaps forgetting that Lincoln was one of those "Republicans of '56." "I pray you to consider this. Col. F. never intimated to me that he desired or would take any office whatever; but whether he will or will not accept, it is due to the Frémonters of '56 that he be offered a position of dignity and honor." The Washington rumor mill was still racing. While Greeley was fretting on behalf of Frémont, Ohio senator-elect John Sherman told Elizabeth Blair Lee that Frémont would enlist Frank to lobby on his behalf for the War Department, and "he is likely to get the post." When Lincoln was in New York, however, he was paid a visit by Pennsylvania judge James Millikin, who informed him that much of the in-state opposition to Cameron had melted away. Lincoln expressed relief, but he was still not quite ready to commit to Cameron for the War Department and hinted that he might retain Kentuckian Joseph Holt in the post, at least for a short time.[34]

By the end of the month, with the president-elect safely in Washington, Lincoln had told Governor Curtin, "When I have friends who disagree with each other, I am very slow to take sides in their quarrel." Perhaps that reluctance had helped move the Pennsylvanians toward a peace of convenience. Realizing that the factional infighting in the state might mean Pennsylvania could be left out of the cabinet entirely likely helped smooth the way to a temporary unification. Cameron and Lincoln met on February 27 at the Willard Hotel in Washington, where Lincoln offered, and Cameron refused, the Interior Department. Interior would instead go to Indiana's Caleb Smith. Had Cameron accepted, the way might still have been clear for Frémont to head the War Department. Lincoln and Cameron met again two days later, and the president-elect finally reoffered the job he had first offered at the turn of the year, and Cameron accepted. "In accepting Lincoln's offer, Cameron embraced a job for which he was temperamentally unsuited," a friendly biographer wrote. It's by no means clear that the same would not have been true of Frémont.[35]

But just when things appeared settled, Seward threw another wrench into the works. Complaining about Lincoln's cabinet choices and that he had not been consulted about them to his satisfaction, he threatened on March 2 to withdraw his acceptance of the State Department. The maneuver annoyed Lincoln, who saw it for the power play it was and quickly set about coming up with a new slate that excluded both Seward and Chase, bringing Frémont back into play yet again.

Lincoln confided to George G. Fogg, a New Hampshire politician and newspaper publisher who would serve Lincoln as ambassador to Switzerland, that he had devised a Seward-less cabinet that would place New Jersey's Dayton at State and Frémont at the War Department, while sending Seward to London. In this scenario, Cameron was out altogether. Lincoln sent that list to Weed to show he meant business while at the same time asking Seward to withdraw his withdrawal in "the public interest." Seward, seeing that he was beaten, retreated. In an inauguration night meeting with the new president, he agreed once again to take the post Lincoln had offered. With that, Frémont's last chance to join the cabinet evaporated.[36]

Despite Frémont's insistence that he wanted a field command if war came, Lincoln was still hawking Frémont to Seward as ambassador to France a week after the March 4 inauguration, although as "suggestion merely, and not dictation." The *Daily Alta California* liked the idea, opining that Frémont "will command more respect and attention in Europe than any mere politician in the whole nation." Thomas Starr King suggested Jessie would be the better choice. Seward's purposes were better served by mere politicians, though, and he was unenthusiastic, with concerns on personal and political grounds. "As to Frémont and France—the prestige is good," Seward responded. "But I *think* that is all. If as I have heard, he is to be engaged in raising money there for his estates, it would be a serious complication. Beside this he is by birth and education a South Carolinian," which left Seward questioning "his being very decided in the defence of the Union." He preferred Dayton for Paris and eventually got his way.

Seward's objections based on Frémont's days in Charleston seem odd given that he had previously suggested him to lead the War Department—the last position in which the new administration would want someone with southern sympathies. Furthermore, Seward had endorsed others still living in the South—Randall Hunt, a New Orleans attorney; congressman John A. Gilmer; and state legislator Kenneth Raynor of North Carolina—for various positions. Hamlin had also suggested tapping a southerner without specifying any one in particular, though he sought "a man of pluck" for the War Department in a Christmas Eve letter to Lincoln. Lincoln himself had held out the possibility of adding a southerner and early on considered Kentuckian James Guthrie (Franklin Pierce's Treasury secretary) for the War Department. Gilmer was mentioned most often, although even the name of failed Constitutional Unionist presidential candidate John Bell of Tennessee came up. But finding a southerner who would adhere to Republican principles proved too high a mountain to scale. How, asked New York journalist Villard, could Lincoln put such men in his cabinet "when the same men may be made foreigners by the progress of disunion even before the inauguration of his Administration?" In the end, he could not. But considering what was to follow on the slavery question, Seward's concerns about any vestigial southern feeling held by Frémont—certainly a man of pluck—seem absurd.[37]

And so the stage was set. As Nicolay and Hay put it, Lincoln "wished to combine the experience of Seward, the integrity of Chase, the popularity of Cameron; to hold the West with Bates, attract New England with Welles; please the Whigs through Smith, and convince the Democrats through Blair," who got the patronage-rich job of postmaster general. It was a collection of men that perhaps only Lincoln could manage. Speaker of the House Galusha Grow later wrote that a President Seward could not "have kept such a cabinet as Lincoln selected in harness two weeks without broken traces, cracked whiffletrees, and a general smash-up." Frémont was not part of the cabinet equation. But he would still figure in Lincoln's plans for dealing with the west and placating the Blairs.[38]

"Not a little uneasy touching the transaction"

The newspapers reported on December 23 that Frémont would leave San Francisco for Washington on January 1. The reporters had the date right but not the destination. Having begged off a cabinet or diplomatic post during the meeting with Edward Baker, he had no plans to visit the capital during the secession winter.[39]

He sailed January 1. Jessie saw him off with a salute from a "cherished old flag" her husband had carried with him on a western expedition and that he had given to her as a gift on his return. Among the 215 passengers joining Frémont aboard the steamer *Golden Age* were San Francisco lawyer Frederick Billings, a native Vermonter and investor in Las Mariposas; Mariposa Land and Mining Company partner George W. Wright; and a portfolio of Carleton Watkins photos of the mining operations that Frémont hoped would induce European money men to invest in the enterprise. The prospectus, illustrated with Watkins's photos, promised a net gain of $16,000 to anyone willing to buy in. By this point, one of Frémont's creditors, San Franciscan (and another Vermonter) Trenor Park, had a $250,000 mortgage on the property and had been installed as manager of the estate, effectively running the operation in return for a 6.25 percent stake. Billings collected the same amount as his fee for accompanying Frémont to Europe.[40]

Also accompanying Frémont was a San Francisco woman named Margaret Corbett and a child who might or might not have been fathered by Frémont. He apparently paid for the separate cabin the mother and child occupied and made a halfhearted attempt at discretion by suggesting, to no avail, that Billings sail on a separate ship. Billings, who was fond of Jessie, claimed to be disgusted by the sordidness of it, but he was not so disgusted that he didn't later join Frémont and Corbett at a reading in London by Charles Dickens. Frémont was taken aback by Billings's reaction, telling the lawyer, "I thought more highly of you than I suppose that you could be shocked by any of the small rascalities." The affair went public, at least aboard ship. But there's nothing in the record to indicate Jessie knew about it, and Wright, under pressure from Francis P. Blair, would later deny that anything untoward happened on the journey, contradicting Billings's contemporaneous account in letters and the ship's own passenger list. As with many nineteenth-century sexual escapades, the evidence is scanty and circumstantial. The couple apparently spent time together in Philadelphia and New York, according to one Frémont biographer, although Corbett slept in a separate stateroom aboard ship. Jessie's lonely post-1856 sojourn to Europe was a strong indication that she had uncovered at least one previous liaison, even if she remained unaware of the latest dalliance.[41]

Having crossed the continent five times by land, Frémont took the sea route on this journey—to Panama, across the isthmus by train, and then north to New York. There he intersected at the Astor House with the president-elect, who was traveling by circuitous train route from Springfield to Washington. In what the newspapers called "a strictly private interview" on the afternoon of February 20, Lincoln and Frémont covered much of the same ground Frémont and Baker had during their October meeting at Black Point. Frémont explained his reasons for declining any cabinet or diplomatic post and expressed his preference for a field command. Lincoln confided his regret that he had been powerless to resist the tide of secession. Jessie would write later that "Colonel Frémont and the President were in full sympathy in their views of the situation." That didn't seem to be the case at the time, however. Although both expressed hope for a peaceful resolution, John wrote to Jessie of the meeting, "With the inflammatory press and inflammatory conversation on every hand, I am convinced that actual war is not far off," while Lincoln was "unwilling to believe in actual war," revealing a fundamental division in how Frémont and Lincoln viewed the rebels that would color their relationship for the next four years. On that note of discord, Frémont sailed for Liverpool aboard the steamer *Africa*.[42]

Frémont made an honest effort to raise money for his mining operations, and he checked in with the U.S. embassy shortly after his arrival. The legation's secretary, Benjamin Moran, recorded visits on March 12 and 21, describing Frémont as "slight" with "quick pleasant grey eyes." On the first visit, Moran noted Frémont was "en route to Paris with a Mrs. Corbett," whom Frémont had indiscreetly brought along with him to the embassy; on the second, he came with Billings. Outgoing U.S. ambassador George M. Dallas—described by Moran as "a weak, vain man, with a certain amount of lawyer-like talents," but less a statesman than a politician, "and a trimmer at that"—was of little help. Moran told Frémont he "hoped the rumor was true that he would be appointed minister to Paris," but Frémont "would not express an opinion."[43]

Even with Frémont's fame and his being in play for a senior administration or diplomatic position, the search for money proved quixotic. He and Billings invited multiple potential investors to meetings, and some even got invitations to travel to the mines in California. They reached out to the Rothschilds and received at least two offers of sizable loans. But Frémont wasn't interested in further indebtedness. He wanted investors, not more creditors. In the end, the unsettled situation in America as Lincoln prepared to take the reins of power was simply too precarious for European money men to risk their capital, even on behalf of the world-famous Pathfinder. The *Times of London* wrote nice things about Las Mariposas, but the effort had run its course. "If I had a million [friends in France] and the estate was all gold, I don't think I could work up anybody to the scratch," Billings moaned.[44]

On April 12, Confederate forces under P. G. T. Beauregard fired on Fort Sumter in Charleston Harbor. War had come, and Frémont's search for investors was effectively over. Contradicting Seward's concern that Frémont was fending for himself in Europe, he quickly put aside his Las Mariposas fund-raising the moment it became clear that war had put the kibosh on any hopes of securing funds and turned his attention to buying arms for the Union cause. Confirmation of the attack on Fort Sumter reached Britain, home to eight thousand American expatriates—about half of them living in London or Liverpool—on April 26. At a soirée at Cambridge House two days later, outgoing U.S. ambassador Dallas recorded, "Nothing else engaged the conversation of the whole company." Three days after that, on May 1, his replacement, Charles Francis Adams, left Boston Harbor bound for Britain.[45]

Adams, who was following in the footsteps of his father and grandfather as minister to the United Kingdom, arrived on May 13. On May 15, Frémont was at his door, one among the "great crowds" who pushed their way into the embassy that day. "I am called upon by a great variety of people on a multiplicity of errands. Some like Colonel Frémont desire to know what aid can be given towards the transmission of munitions of war to America, some are on visits of civility, some soliciting work." Adams's advice to Frémont about obtaining arms in France was to first check in with U.S. Ambassador William Dayton, who had won the post for which Lincoln had considered Frémont. Some had also said of the Frémont-Dayton ticket in 1856 that it "had the head where the tail ought to be." Legation secretary Moran, who had expressed hope that Frémont would get the Paris post, duplicitously described Dayton as "a tall manly gentleman of great dignity, & yet as polite and courtly as the most polished peer. . . . Intellectually he would make a dozen of Frémont." This time, Dayton had gotten the prize, and Frémont was obliged to appeal to his former number two.[46]

After sizing up Adams, Frémont left Billings to focus on Britain while he returned to France, where he began seeking arms to purchase and signed several contracts. The preference of army officials was for American-made weapons, but there were few to be had in spring 1861, and army stores were quickly cleaned out as governors scrambled to supply their new recruits. European arms would play a crucial role in the first months of the war, and Frémont, with no authority or official brief, wanted to make sure the Federal forces would get their share.

In typical Frémont fashion, he went about this task in an eccentric way, enlisting an antiquarian bookseller from Vermont. Henry Stevens was also a cousin of Frederick Billings and a close friend of James Buchanan (who was godfather to Stevens's son Henry Jr.). Frémont had first crossed paths with Stevens in 1852, when he and Jessie visited Europe to accept the Founders Medal from the Royal Geographical Society, and again in 1860, when Frémont bid unsuccessfully on the library of scientist and polymath Alexander von Humboldt, one of Frémont's heroes and role models.[47]

With no government money in hand and no official sanction to act on behalf of Washington, Frémont began arranging purchases, in some cases by promising his own funds as security, with Stevens and Billings acting as agents. British, French, Italian, and Austrian arms makers were busy working to exploit the American market and were happy to have an active buyer from the North.

The South was already engaged. These arms were not always of the highest quality or modern design. Frémont purchased ten thousand rifles in France and ordered cannon and shells in England. Snobby Englishmen called Stevens "the Yankee peddler without a shop," but he got the job done. Of the $75,000 eventually provided by Adams for purchases in the United Kingdom, Stevens spent $71,000. (Stevens did fail to obtain a cache of Austrian swords Frémont had requested because Adams thought it a waste of money and refused to sign off.[48])

Frémont took Adams's advice and met with Dayton, who gave Frémont a letter for Adams urging that the London-based minister do something but committed to nothing himself. Dayton then reported to Seward that he was being inundated with requests from French officers seeking appointments in the Union Army: "I have had many applications . . . by foreigners for service as officers in the army of the United States, and I understand from one of the former secretaries of the legation that many applications were made at the office of the legation before I came. . . . To these applications I have said that our service was open to volunteers, but I had no authority to commit the government to appointments; that, in fact, we needed arms rather than men." But he was hesitant to move on that score without Adams's concurrence, and Adams was just as hesitant to move without Dayton's. That diplomatic reticence kept Frémont bouncing between the two capitals.[49]

As Frémont moved back and forth, he found himself joining a group of loyal unionists for a festive breakfast at the Hotel de Louvre in the French capital on May 29. At tables "loaded with plate, cutglass, flowers and other objects recreative to the eye" were seated nearly two hundred guests, including Maria DeHart Mayo Scott, wife of Gen. Winfield Scott, commander of all U.S. forces.[50]

As was the case nearly everywhere, war was the main topic. Frémont was asked to say a few words, as were Dayton and fellow diplomats Cassius Clay and Anson Burlingame, who introduced Frémont as "casting from him the urgent claims of his private affairs, almost without warning and notice, determined to fly to the defence of the flag he has done so much to exalt. . . . We know what will follow where he goes before, for 'born and nursed in danger's path, he's tried her worst.' We know his future will be as bright as his past, and that he will enjoy a soldier's triumph or the sweet tranquility of an honored soldier's grave. And now all hail Frémont, and farewell!" Frémont thanked Burlingame and his hosts and then noted, "A few days back our honored flag was trailing in the dust at the foot of an insolent foe; at present its stars are refulgent from a thousand heights, swarming with brave hearts and strong arms in its defense." He praised France's history of cooperation in the enterprise of American freedom but made no appeal for foreign help in the latest war. Rather, he said, "we are willing to work out our own destiny, and make our own history." Then, in an eloquence rare for him, Frémont assured his audience, "Before this struggle closes, the world will recognize that enlightened liberty is self-sustaining, and that a people who have once fully enjoyed its blessings will never consent to part with them." Clenching his chair tightly and making no gestures, he then appealed to his dissatisfied countrymen: "We have deprecated this war, fratricidal and abominable; most gladly would we welcome back our people, if they would return to their allegiance. We would bury, deep as the ocean, the hasty anger which their parricidal conduct provoked. But they must return at once to their allegiance. We shall not permit them to dishonor our flag, and desecrate our sacred graves." This statement brought a cheer from the crowd, and he rose to a stirring peroration. "They cannot be permitted to dismember our country and destroy our nationality," which brought more cheers. "We shall maintain these in their fullest integrity, in the face of every evil, and at every hazard. Above every consideration is our country," he said, invoking Daniel Webster, "as we have learned to love it—one and indivisible—now and forever, and so we will maintain it; we will do our duty loyally, and we will make no compromise with treason, and no surrender to rebelling." Long and loud cheering escorted Frémont off the stage. His brief remarks were "the most earnestly applauded, the least rhetorical, and the most effective of them all," according to the *New York Tribune*. Another journalist reported, "He made quite a moderate speech. He regretted this fanatical war but felt confident that it would end in the triumph of truth and justice." The focus was on the Union, with nary a word about slavery. The next day, Lincoln appointed Frémont, pending Senate approval, to be a major general in the regular army.[51]

As Frémont began finalizing plans for his departure, he would be joining a considerable exodus. Adams noted on May 25 that, with hostilities underway, a "great number of American[s] are returning" to the states from Britain. Before departing for home, though, Frémont had more business to conduct with Adams. He wrote to Francis P. Blair that he had "fully intended to sail for New York on the *Asia* tomorrow [May 25] but under all the information I can obtain I judge that a supply of efficient arms would be valuable to our cause just now, and I have decided to remain a short time longer with the object of bringing them with me." He also asked Blair to explain to Lincoln the cause of his delay in returning to take up whatever command awaited him. "Pray don't let these few weeks operate prejudicially to me," he implored his sponsor. But a few more weeks it would be. The arms deals could not be closed quickly enough for Frémont to personally escort his purchases back to the States, so he left the closing in the hands of Stevens and Billings. But he did pin Adams down. Their meeting on June 4 sealed the deal for Frémont's self-appointed military mission and secured government funding for his purchases, pending Dayton's assent. It also offered a glimpse of how he would handle lines of authority for the rest of the war: shoot first and ask questions later.[52]

Although Adams wrote to his son, "My position here thus far has not been difficult or painful," he confided to his diary:

> The most difficult and troublesome of my undertaking I have attempted is that of assisting Colonel Frémont to obtain arms and ammunition to carry with him to America. He has no means of raising money and desires me to help him with credit. To this end he brought a letter from Mr Dayton which urged me to do something. This something Colonel Frémont is attempting to stretch up to two hundred thousand dollars. And on enquiry I find that he has been making contracts in Paris without going near Mr. Dayton . . . even though he knows that I had made Mr. Dayton's cooperation in the engagement a condition precedent to all movement. He came to me today with his bills, and I frankly told him that I should be obliged to send a letter to Mr. Dayton first, and await his assent to the signature of the bills.[53]

It took three days to get a response from Dayton, who offered his approval and encouragement but no money. Dayton "seems to fear taking the responsibility," the U.S. ambassador to Belgium, Henry Shelton Sanford, told Seward. Sanford grew so frustrated that Frémont had not been commissioned to purchase arms that he expressed a desire to buy up all of Belgium's excess supply and ship them to the United States on his own authority. Adams might have taken Dayton's reticence as a sign—Dayton knew Frémont better than Adams did. But the patriot in Adams, who shared some of Sanford's frustration, overcame the cynic. On June 7, the same day Parliament decided not to debate the issue of recognizing the Confederacy, Adams reported, "Colonel Frémont and Mr Billings called today, and I arranged with them the amount of the liability to be incurred." It came to $75,000 for the English arms and $125,000 for the French rifles, financed by the famous Barings Brothers banking house, and the amount left Adams "not a little uneasy touching the transaction."[54]

As well he might be, considering the private nature of the purchases and, unbeknownst to Adams, the slapdash way in which Frémont frequently conducted his financial affairs. But there was a war on, and all parties concerned felt it to be an absolute necessity to obtain the arms and get them to America as quickly as possible. Whatever Adams actually thought of Frémont—he claimed to repose "great confidence in the capacity and the energy" of the soon-to-be general—he recognized the accuracy of a later statement by a Confederate arms buyer. "Any army officer, fit for such a mission as that of buying arms for a great Government at the outbreak of a war, would have acted, if necessary, without instructions, and secured everything he could find in the line of essentials, especially arms," the southern agent wrote. That's precisely what Frémont did, cost be damned, and it's how he would continue to operate throughout the rest of 1861.[55]

Adams, who admitted to exceeding his authority in approving the purchases, and Frémont, who was bound by no authority other than his own flexible conscience, felt that way not only because the Union Army needed the supplies but also because agents for their enemies were active, despite the certainty of Dayton and others that the South had not yet made any effective moves in Europe.

"I think I may say with some confidence that all the efforts of the agents of the confederates on this side of the channel have thus far been abortive," Dayton over-optimistically reported to Seward at this time. "They have no encouragement to their hopes of recognition. They have met with no success in their attempts to negotiate a loan. I do not believe they have got any considerable supply of arms, and I think that we know substantially *what they have done* and are *attempting to do*." On European recognition of the Confederate government, Dayton proved correct; on the South's acquisition of credit and military stores, he was dead wrong, and Frémont was right. "The agents for the Seceders are very active here," Frémont told Blair in May. And when he assessed those who had helped him on his quest for arms, Adams and Sanford were praised while Dayton was conspicuous by his absence. As early as February, a former West Pointer, Maj. Caleb Huse, had been dispatched to Europe in search of arms for the rebels. On June 4, the same day Frémont met with Adams to discuss the U.S. government paying for his purchases, Confederate agent James D. Bulloch arrived in England and quickly established a relationship with a Liverpool banking house, Fraser, Trenholm & Co., which had offices in Charleston and New York. The firm provided considerable credit with which the South purchased arms, camp supplies, naval stores, and even ships.[56]

The arms of Europe were more important to the Confederates than to the Federals, as Massachusetts Democratic politician and diplomat Caleb Cushing impressed on Huse when the two bumped into each other in New York as Huse prepared to sail for Europe in the late spring of 1861. "The money is all in the North," Cushing told Huse, a fellow Bay State native who, like William Tecumseh Sherman, had taken a leadership position at a military training institute in the South after leaving the army. Unlike Sherman, Huse had sided with his new home state of Alabama. "The manufactories are all in the North; the ships are all in the North; the arms and arsenals are all in the North; the arsenals of Europe are within ten days of New York, and they will be open to the United States Government, and closed to the South; and the Southern ports will be blockaded."[57]

Cushing's warning did not deter the Confederate arms merchant, who would prove quite effective in defying it, aided by (among others) a coterie of former U.S. Navy officers who had defected southward. In some cases, arms manufacturers were supplying both North and South, and Huse had been given carte blanche—a phrase that would later come to haunt Frémont—by President Jefferson Davis to do whatever was necessary to achieve his objective. And, despite Dayton's confidence, the Confederates were well informed about what Frémont and other northern agents (official and unofficial) were up to. They also ran a successful counterespionage network that effectively prevented northern efforts to stop or intercept supplies bound for the South.[58]

The federal government didn't get around to appointing an official agent to purchase arms in Europe until the end of July. Col. George Schuyler was empowered to spend "such amounts as may be necessary," granted discretion "to make such purchases of arms as you may deem advisable upon the very lowest terms compatible with the earliest possible delivery," and urged to keep meticulous records of those purchases, which would be arranged through Barings.[59]

The European arms race would continue for some time, but it would go on without Frémont. In a brief piece about Frémont's purchase of weapons in Europe, the *Christian Recorder* was already looking toward a time when the antislavery hero of the first Republican presidential campaign would put those arms to use in the cause of freedom. "Would not the name of the gallant leader of the Republican forces in 1856, of the path-finder of empire, rally around his standard a larger, more energetic and determined body of men than any other one man in the United States could raise?" the newspaper asked. "Col. Frémont has received, within a few weeks past, scores of letters from friends, acquaintances, and strangers, urging him to come, and he has replied to them that his heart and soul is in the cause of his country, and that he is ready to sacrifice time, money, and life, if need be, in her behalf."[60]

The fiscal efficacy of Frémont's purchases and the quality of the arms obtained would eventually come into question. But Cameron and Lincoln, like Frémont, would both approve the purchase of inferior or defective weapons and sign off on exorbitant prices because all recognized the urgency. In response to

Lincoln's April call for seventy-five thousand troops, states were sending men to Washington, but many were marching without arms. As the historian of the Army Ordinance Bureau noted, "Whatever the critical evaluation of these foreign arms, it must be remembered that they filled a void which could not have been filled in any other way." They allowed troops to be armed and provided a stopgap until U.S. arms manufacturers could ramp up production.[61]

Having failed in his original mission of obtaining funding to rescue his investment in Las Mariposas, Frémont left Europe confident he had succeeded in a far more important endeavor: arming the soldiers he would be commanding. As he had told an acquaintance in Europe, "There is nothing I should like better than a fine regiment of active men to stand under the American flag at Richmond and Norfolk, and if necessary march to New Orleans." But before Richmond, Norfolk, or New Orleans would come Boston. On June 27, Frémont sailed into the harbor aboard the steamship *Europa* and then proceeded southward toward a reunion with Jessie and a fateful meeting with Lincoln.[62]

"A SORT OF ROMANTIC HALO"

Thousands of miles to the west, Jessie was making her own preparations to pack up the home she loved at Black Point and to leave friends she adored and who adored her. John had written from London that he would soon be returning and that he expected to get a high field command. He asked Jessie to join him if she could "risk the rebel cruisers in the Gulf." Unlike many others who forecast a quick end to the rebellion, Frémont expected the war to last for years and did not want to be separated from his wife for that long, assuming "he would be in it to the end."[63]

For Jessie, it was a heady time, though not without its sorrows. California had a sizable southern population that was agitating for secession. The governor made noises about leaving both North and South behind and establishing a new Californian republic. Into the ferment stepped Jessie's close friend Thomas Starr King.

John, who was not known for lavishing praise or waxing sentimental, observed of the conversations between Jessie and Bret Harte, "When we heard the two talking together, their low well-modulated voices rising and falling, it was beautiful. When to them was added the deep and vibrant tone of King's voice, it was a trio as good as music." King now meant to lend his vibrant tones to the cause of the Union—thus, both of the men closest to Jessie were doing their part for the cause.[64]

Even before the firing on Fort Sumter, King was mustering pro-Union Californians in support of the government. On February 22, two days after Frémont met with Lincoln in New York, King addressed a rally of a thousand people in San Francisco where he "pledged California to a northern republic, and to a flag that should have no treacherous threads of cotton in its warp, and the house came down like thunder." Jessie told him that "she hadn't been stirred and fed so in years." He made similar speeches in Marysville and Stockton. At a May 11 rally, twenty-five thousand thronged the city's streets. "We are getting California safe out of southern hands," he wrote. A week later, the state legislature voted to attach California to the cause of the Union, "against foreign or domestic foes." King would continue throughout the summer, after Jessie's departure. His commitment to defending the Union through oratory would force him to miss a deer-hunting trip to Oregon that he and Baker had planned during a salon session at the Frémonts'. By that time, Baker would also be otherwise engaged.[65]

Jessie Frémont searched for ways to contribute as well. "The fear of what may be in store for us all if this cloud of civil war takes shape," she had written early in the year, "makes me restless & I am unfortunate in not being able to live more away from myself just now."[66]

In John's absence and with King traveling, she was keeping to herself more than usual. At Black Point she brought Harte closer into her confidence to fill the gap. And she jokingly chided King for being "a negligent pastor" for not checking in on a member of his flock who had not occupied her pew for a month. The Episcopalian Frémonts had purchased a pew in King's First Unitarian Church on Stockton Street, a serious step considering the grief the couple had taken about being closet Catholics during the 1856 campaign.[67]

With Lincoln now inaugurated, Jessie expressed continuing anxiety about what was coming next. "Our movements are so uncertain that it is unsatisfactory to write of ourselves," she wrote to Lizzie Lee, noting that she had no concrete idea when her husband would be back in the United States.[68]

Compounding her sorrow was the case of Albert Lea, who had been with the family for years. Lea's mother was a free black woman who had worked for the Bentons. Lea had accompanied Frémont on his last western expedition and remained attached to the family at the Las Mariposas home in Bear Valley, where he had taught Frank and Charley how to ride horses bareback. In July 1859, while the Frémonts were at Las Mariposas, Lea had killed his estranged wife, Meline Delphine Agnes Lee, shooting her in the head on a San Francisco street. He was convicted in October 1859 and sentenced to hang. The facts of the killing were undisputed. But the Frémonts worked with local attorneys to get a retrial, arguing that Lea was temporarily insane. They persuaded a judge to retry Lea, but he was just as quickly convicted again. This second jury recommended mercy in the form of a life sentence, but Lea was again sentenced to hang. An appeal to Irish-born Democratic governor John Downey for clemency proved fruitless. The hanging was scheduled for March 1, 1861.[69]

Just days before the scheduled execution, the *Daily Alta California* ran a story about the case that incensed Jessie, and she took up her pen to respond. Among other things, the paper had referred to Lea as John's "body servant," implying a master-servant relationship that Jessie vehemently objected to, as well as to the less embarrassing implication that Frémont needed a "valet" in the wilds of the Rocky Mountains. She recounted Lea's mother's long years of service to her father and Lea's "nerve and loyalty" shown to Frémont during the 1853 journey. But six years later, she wrote, "so great a change took place in Lea, that the servants and family watched him with concern. From an active healthy manner and walk he became silent and pre-occupied, staying apart, eating, and, at last, even cooking for himself, at a distance from the house. Finally he left Bear Valley, and when the news of the murder reached there, there was an instant expression that 'Lea was mad.'" Jessie blamed the machinations of Lea's mother-in-law for his altered personality. Disappointed in her daughter's choice, she "tried to make moves with two human beings full of passions, as though they were figures on a chess-board."[70]

In her response, Jessie did not ask for the execution to be set aside or even postponed. "His sincere, manly penitence is unmistakable," she wrote. "The mere privilege of retaining the breath of life, when all that makes life useful or desirable, is lost, is never so great a boon that it should be begged for or clung to." When she visited him in his last hours, Lea remained stoic. "No knightly cavalier going to the block for his king & his cause ever had a more truly noble aspect," she told Lizzie Lee.[71]

The paper gave Lea's mother-in-law, Maria Pallier, the opportunity to rebut, and the public involvement of women—especially a free black woman—in a case as sordid as the Lea murder caused a bit of a stir all its own, with one of Frémont's business partners being drawn into it. "You probably saw the controversy between Mrs. Frémont & Mr. Lea's wife's mother in the papers," a local relative wrote to Mariposa part-owner Trenor Park. "It may lead to something serious, as they are both fighting cusses."[72]

But it led to nothing more. On March 1, a small cluster of spectators gathered outside the prison yard, but a police cordon kept them at bay. Many more gathered on nearby rooftops and at windows to peer down into the yard. About seventy-five ticketholders were allowed in to watch the spectacle. Lea, dressed in black and lost in prayer, removed his hat as he moved toward the noose. The death warrant was read, and he looked up to address those gathered in the yard "in a firm and loud voice, expressing his deep love for his murdered wife," the *Daily Alta California* reported, and thanking the sheriff and prison staff for their tender care. When Lea was done, a minister recited "an impressive prayer . . . the prisoner's arms were pinioned, the noose adjusted, the black cap hid his features, and Albert Lea suffered the extreme penalty of the law—death by hanging."[73]

In the end, Lea took his execution better than Jessie did. She felt certain that race and politics played a part in Downey's refusal to grant Lea a pardon. "His execution could not have taken place where the executive was unprejudiced," she wrote Lizzie Lee. "But Irish & extreme southern principles were the determining powers & nothing could avail." Jessie was not alone in her sentiment. In a turnout unheard of for a black man in San Francisco in those years, more than a thousand mourners attended Lea's Masonic funeral.[74]

Jessie resumed waiting for word from her husband. News of Sumter reached San Francisco on April 25. During a carriage ride on Russian Hill a few days later, her horses bolted, and she was thrown into the street, landing on her head. She was restricted to bed for several weeks, suffering back and neck pain. With no word yet from John, she relied on King to keep her up to date on the state of things as he popped back into town during his tour of Union rallies. In June, a letter finally came from John asking her to meet him in New York. With an arm and a foot still in splints, she spent the next eight, hectic days packing, making travel arrangements, and bidding farewell to friends. To them, she revealed her determination that when she and John were reunited, it would not be merely to see him off to his next assignment. "We go to join Mr. Frémont & I will be with him everywhere—I will," she wrote one.[75]

Before hearing from John, she had appealed to Edward Beale, whom Lincoln had named surveyor general of California and Nevada, to find a place for Harte that would not be too onerous, leaving him time to write. Beale happily obliged, and Harte was effusive in his thanks to his "Fairy Godmother." Once she knew she was leaving, Jessie rented the house at Black Point to Beale, who also bought most of the accoutrements—furniture, horses, and carriage.[76]

Sailing was set for June 21 aboard the *Sonora*. King went to the boat to see her and the children off. Their friendship had become so close that within months of King's arrival, he had become, for her, "new life in a literary way . . . so clever & charming in conversation." And now, after little more than a year, they were parting. He presented her with a bouquet of long-stemmed English violets, her favorite flower and signature color, and a book of essays by his friend Ralph Waldo Emerson. In tears they said their final good-byes. Their correspondence would continue, but they would never meet again.[77]

In addition to its passengers and crew, the steamer carried a fresh batch of recruits for the Union Army and more than $1 million in California gold bound for eastern markets. The Pacific passage from San Francisco to Panama proved uneventful, though Jessie noted that "extra care was taken" to safeguard the gold as it was transported across the isthmus by railroad. Once on the Atlantic side, though, the captain of the aptly named *North Star* took precautions against the possibility of Confederate depredations. Dinner was served early, and lights were extinguished after sunset. As she and her children headed for their rendezvous with husband and father across the vast expanse of water, "silence and darkness were the rule."[78]

As the ship steamed past Cape Hatteras, North Carolina, "a handsome swift sail vessel," the five-gun privateer *Jeff Davis*, came after them. "It was a sparkling cold and windy day," Jessie remembered, "and we had the out-of-date sensations described in pirate stories as the wind now helped, now hindered our pursuer; but the wind of the North"—it's not clear whether this reference was intended literally or figuratively—"was our ally, and we outran her before night; and never were the twin lights of Sandy Hook so welcome." They had reached New York—and Frémont, who had been kept apprised of the chase and had confidently suggested the rebels might be in more danger from Jessie than the other way around.[79]

Frémont would later describe the "great confusion and indecision in affairs" of those early days of the conflict, when, as he saw it, "the people in power were slow to realize the actuality of war; it was long before they realized its magnitude." He must have wondered whether they would figure it out in time. His actions in Europe had been met with a considerable degree of official skepticism, although they proved highly popular among the northern public, adding to his already stellar reputation as a patriotic man of action, almost Jacksonian in stature. For a man who was known to have never commanded more than a few hundred soldiers in combat (and that dubiously), the people reposed a remarkable amount of martial confidence in him. It was a mark of the respect that accompanied his fame, as well as the emotional investment the antislavery movement had made in the 1856 campaign. But in truth, no one really knew whether Frémont was qualified for the position he was about to be handed.[80]

The *Christian Recorder*, an African American newspaper, harbored no doubts: "Frémont's appointment will be greeted with enthusiasm by our army of northern volunteers, many of whom, four years ago, fought a bloodless but valorous fight under his banner."[81]

The white press was scarcely less enthusiastic. "The appointments of Colonel Frémont and ex-Governor Banks as Major-Generals are commented upon, and generally approved. With veterans like General Scott to counsel, and men like Mansfield, McDowell, McClelland, Butler, Dix, Banks and Frémont to execute, this war will be sooner closed," *Frank Leslie's Weekly* opined.[82]

Even the *New York Herald*, not known for its friendliness to Republicans, insisted that Frémont be recalled at once from Europe "and appointed to a high command. He is an officer of great military ability, and his services would be invaluable at the present moment." He would, the *Herald* suggested, "make himself the Garibaldi of this campaign. . . . [H]e will rally to his standard more men than any other man in the world could do. . . . [H]e is one of the great men of the age." A few months earlier, the paper had been saying nice things about secessionists. Now it said of Frémont, "Put him at the head of an army of 100,000 men, and Jeff Davis and his scoundrel crew will go up higher than old Haman did."[83]

Along the same lines, John Hay, Lincoln's private secretary, laid it on thick in an anonymous dispatch that ran in the *Illinois State Journal*. Frémont, Hay wrote, "is a man in every way qualified for the discharge of the duties of his responsible office. He is just such a person as Western men will idolize and follow through every danger to death or victory. He is upright, brave, generous, enterprising, learned and eminently practical." Hay assured doubters, if there were any, that "before he has been a month at the head of his Division, both officers and men will learn to place implicit confidence in him." The officers and men mostly did. The politicians, including Hay and his boss, were another story.[84]

Gustave Koerner, an Illinois politician and Frémont supporter who would briefly serve on the general's staff, wrote, "There was a sort of romantic halo about him," although Koerner also perceptively noted that Frémont "had very little knowledge of the nature of men."[85]

That lack of knowledge would play a crucial role in the events to come. The "great confusion and indecision in affairs" was fated to continue for some time. But about one thing, no confusion remained. War had come, and the Frémonts were in it.

Chapter Two

"Making bricks without straw"

WHILE FRÉMONT WAS FOCUSED ON EUROPE, FRANK BLAIR, THE ONLY BOR-der-state Republican in Congress, was working assiduously in Missouri to save the Show Me State for the Union—and, as a Republican of convenience, to save his own political existence. Blair, once a slave owner, might have been William Seward's running mate if the New Yorker had prevailed at the Chicago convention that nominated Lincoln. Seward had once called him "the man of the West of the age." Instead, he was a militia colonel striving to fend off a governor with rebel sympathies.[1]

"The Secessionists are making a great rush at Missouri but . . . Frank has his ship fixed to ride out this storm & has at his command too many neighbors to make it practicable—in that State," sister Lizzie Lee wrote confidently to her husband in early January.[2]

A man of "arbitrary temperament," a heavy smoker and drinker who usually carried a pistol and had once been indicted for issuing a challenge to a duel, Blair had hazel eyes, light hair, a high forehead, and none of the cadaverous look of his father. "He combines in himself more inconsistencies than fall to the lot of most men," journalist Noah Brooks wrote. The younger Blair sported a "sour, cynical face" and wore a diabolical-looking droopy mustache that would blossom into a full beard during the war. An acquaintance described Blair as "an interesting, picturesque character . . . a man of very rare physical charm, a noticeable figure in any group." Another noted that he was "a politician first, last and all the time." Like Frémont, he had encountered Stephen Watts Kearny in the Mexican War, though rather more happily. While Frémont was stirring up trouble in California, Blair was helping write New Mexico's new constitution. These two temperamentally different but equally unpredictable men would soon collide in Missouri, with fateful consequences for Frémont.[3]

That Blair was a politician through and through was an opinion shared by a fellow St. Louis resident who observed Blair up close in the city as well as in the field later in the war. William Tecumseh Sherman said Blair was a man of "great courage, and talent" but a politician "by nature, and experience." Sherman confided to his brother, Ohio senator John Sherman, "Blair is regarded here as Lincolns Vice Roy, and I doubt the wisdom of the choice."[4]

A southern sympathizer escaping from St. Louis later in that first year of the war might have summed up the general feeling of those in opposition: "The idea of soon being from under the rule of Frank Blair puts us all in the best spirits imaginable."[5]

Blair's counterpoint in Missouri was the governor, Clairborne Fox Jackson, who had been elected the previous August and took office on January 3, 1861. If the Missouri of Jessie Benton Frémont's father was relentlessly western, Jackson's Missouri was decidedly southern, a sentiment he revealed in his inaugural address. "The destiny of the slave-holding States of this Union is one and the same," he told an enthusiastic crowd in Jefferson City. "So long as a State continues to maintain slavery within her limits, it is impossible to separate her fate from that of her sister States who have the same social organization." He called for the election of delegates to a convention to consider secession.[6]

Blair saw Jackson for what he was: a closet secessionist who had one hand on the doorknob ready to exit. When Lt. Gov. Thomas Reynolds made a speech in St. Louis calling for cooperation with the seceding states, Blair moved to turn the Wide Awakes, a pro-Lincoln presidential campaign group, into a miliary force, rechristened the Home Guard. He also organized a Union Committee of Safety, made up of prominent pro-Union St. Louis residents. Four of the members, including Blair, were slaveholders. And he got to work drilling the Home Guard. On January 29, Kansas entered the Union. Missouri was now surrounded on three sides by free states. On February 6, at Montgomery Blair's request, anti-slavery firebrand Col. Nathaniel Lyon reported for duty at the St. Louis Arsenal with a company of eighty men. Just a few days earlier, Lyon had written, "It is no longer useful to appeal to reason, but to the sword."[7]

Fearing southern sympathizers would loot the cache of arms, Lyon asked Gen. David Hunter on February 9 to intercede with Lincoln to give him command of the arsenal. Hunter, who was riding with Lincoln on the train from Springfield to Washington at the time, did as he was asked, but Winfield Scott scotched the idea. So, Blair went to Washington to lobby in person. That worked. Thus began three months of plotting by Lyon and Blair against Gen. William S. Harney—commander of the Department of the West, headquartered in St.

Louis—and others, employing the Blairs' political connections in such a blatant manner that Thomas Hart Benton's past intercessions on behalf of Frémont paled by comparison.[8]

Per the governor's call in his inaugural address, elections were held on February 18 for delegates to a convention to "consider the existing relations between the government of the United States, the people and governments of the different States, and the government and people of the State of Missouri." That same day in Montgomery, Alabama, Jefferson Davis delivered his inaugural address as provisional president of the Confederate States of America.[9]

The Missouri state convention convened ten days later, with a four-to-one majority of unionists, though they were divided between antislavery, or "unconditional unionists," and pro-slavery, or "conditional unionists." On March 19, the convention voted overwhelmingly to remain in the Union. But it was most assuredly a conditional unionism. At about the same time, Lincoln put Lyon in charge of the St. Louis Arsenal. If Blair and Lyon had not heightened the divisions in the city, their aggressive actions in defense of the Union had made stark the divisions that already existed.

After the attack on Fort Sumter, Lincoln issued a call for seventy-five thousand volunteers, with each state apportioned a percentage based on population. Missouri's quota was 3,123 men. When Jackson received notice from the War Department, he was swift and certain in his response. "There can be, I apprehend, no doubt but the men are intended to form a part of the President's army to make war upon the people of the seceded States," Jackson wrote to Secretary of War Simon Cameron. "Your requisition, in my judgment, is illegal, unconstitutional, and revolutionary in its object, inhuman and diabolical, and cannot be complied with. Not one man will the state of Missouri furnish to carry on any such unholy crusade." The Berthold mansion at Fifth and Pine Streets, once the headquarters of the state Democratic Party, became the chief Confederate recruiting depot and training site for secessionists organized into quasi-military companies called "Minute Men." At the same time, Blair's pro-Union Home Guard and German American groups organized regular drill and target-practice sessions.[10]

Blair was back in St. Louis on April 17. Two days later he wrote his brother, Montgomery, asking that General Harney be relieved of command. He believed the slaveholding Tennessean was too reticent about confronting the rebels in St. Louis, and he was probably right. Harney thought using caution and compromise was the best way to preserve both the peace and the Union. Some (though not Blair) thought Harney disloyal, a charge the grizzled veteran vehemently denied. "The flag, whose glories I have witnessed, shall never be forsaken by me while I can strike a blow in its defense," he wrote to a St. Louis friend. When the next blow was struck, on April 20, it was not by Harney but on the other side of the state, where an armed rebel militia took over the undermanned Liberty Arsenal, seizing sixteen field guns with several hundred rounds of shot, about twenty-five hundred small arms, hundreds of sabers, and more than ten thousand pounds of powder.[11]

One day later came word that Blair's request had been granted. Harney was relieved of command. Blair offered the post to Sherman, who turned it down, citing economic necessity. Sherman also confessed to his brother that he harbored lingering anger over Blair's opposition to his getting a Treasury Department position. Beginning in January 1861, Sherman had lobbied his brother for a Treasury job in St. Louis, where a brother-in-law, Charles Ewing, was an attorney, despite his expectation that "Missouri will be a scene of strife." Frank Blair had someone else he wanted in the St. Louis subtreasury and opposed Sherman's appointment, which went to Blair's candidate. "I would starve and see my family want rather than ask Frank Blair, or any of the Blairs, whom I Know to be a selfish and unscrupulous set of ____." He also turned down Montgomery Blair's consolation prize of an assistant secretaryship at the War Department. Still, he promised his senator brother that he would "be prudent & quarrel with no one much less the Blairs."[12]

The command fell to Lyon, who had served with Harney in the Mexican War and at Fort Scott, Kansas. Lincoln endorsed the move. "It is revolutionary times," he wrote in a note appended to Cameron's order to Lyon, "and therefore I do not object to the irregularity of this." The post surgeon at Fort Riley, Kansas, described Lyon as "intolerant of opposition, unmindful of the many obligatory courtesies of life, prone to inject the most unpopular opinions at times and places when he knew they would be unwelcome, and enforcing them with all the bitterness and vehemence of which he was capable; easily aroused to a degree of anger that was almost insane in its manifestations; narrow-minded; prejudiced, mentally unbalanced, and yet with all this, honest to the core, intelligent, well-read," and "one to trust in emergencies with absolute confidence." He and Blair were two peas in a pod.[13]

Governor Jackson's call-up of the militia on May 3 proved a turning point. Pro- and anti-Union forces had been organizing rallies and speeches across the state since the fall of Sumter. Jackson's move to activate the militia on behalf of the rebels turned up the heat even more. At one such gathering in Buffalo, thirty-five miles north of Springfield in the southwestern part of the state, a local volunteer recalled a veteran of the War of 1812 who, "though a slave owner . . . was as true as steel to the Union, and . . . for a few moments, he poured forth a torrent of patriotic eloquence that I never heard surpassed. . . . As the old hero hobbled to his place, several hundred men waved their hats, hurrahed for the Union, and formed in a long line by his side." Competing demonstrations on behalf of southern nationhood took place across the state.[14]

After his dismissal in April, Harney had traveled to Washington to make a case for reinstatement. His lobbying would prove temporarily successful, but success would come too late to avoid bloodshed in St. Louis. Jackson's militia order and the civil turmoil were enough to set the primer, but it was the order for Harney's reinstatement to command that lit the fuse.

On April 26, Sherman wrote to another brother-in-law, Thomas Ewing Jr., "Frank Blair is determined to push things to the bitter end, and if violence occurs here I shall feel disposed to trace it to him." Under Jackson's call-up order, militia units were to gather on the western outskirts of St. Louis at the newly christened Camp Jackson, described as "not much of a military installation, but . . . a symbolic threat to the Union in Missouri." Blair and Lyon were determined to squelch that threat.[15]

In January, southern sympathizers had seized a cache of arms from the Baton Rouge Arsenal, a move that Sherman (then superintendent of the Louisiana State Seminary of Learning and Military Academy) called "a declaration of war." Declaration of war or not, Sherman allowed the arms to be stored at the academy until they were shipped north. They arrived in St. Louis on May 8 via steamer. Rebels moved part of the stash to Jefferson City by boat. The remainder was stored at Camp Jackson.[16]

Lyon anticipated a move by the forces at Camp Jackson against the St. Louis Arsenal's fifty-six acres. Sloping down to the Mississippi and bounded on the west and south by hills, the facility was susceptible to artillery fire. Lyon bolstered the three-story building—protected by a ten-foot-by-three-foot limestone wall surrounding it on three sides, a plank fence and water gate on the river side, and a single gated entrance on Carondelet Street—with batteries and earthworks. The arsenal held the largest cache of Federal arms west of the Mississippi and in the slave states, with sixty thousand Springfield and Enfield rifles, ninety thousand pounds of powder, one and a half million cartridges, forty artillery pieces, and the machinery necessary to make both arms and ammunition. It was defended by about six hundred regulars and fifteen hundred volunteers, "not one of whom can speak English," Sherman exaggerated in referring to those he called Blair's "lager beer friends." If it fell into rebel hands as the Baton Rouge

Arsenal had, the blow to the Union force in Missouri would be incalculable. On top of the added fortifications, Lyon was able to secretly move some of the cache across the river into Illinois, out of the reach of the rebel troops commanded by Gen. David M. Frost, a native New Yorker and West Point classmate of Lyon. That action should have negated the need for any immediate move against Camp Jackson. But Lyon had other ideas.[17]

In an attempt to figure out what the militia was up to, Lyon donned a black gown, veil, and bonnet owned by Blair's mother-in-law, hid two pistols in the folds of the dress, and reconnoitered the camp by carriage on May 9. Prone to alarm in any case, Lyon, seeing crates bearing the weapons stolen from the Baton Rouge Arsenal, became alarmed enough that he was determined to attack. When he found out later that night that Harney had been reinstated, Lyon decided not to wait. He would assault Camp Jackson before Harney could get back to St. Louis and stop him.[18]

It rained hard overnight, dampening the six miles of city streets between the arsenal and Camp Jackson but not Lyon's ardor. Ulysses S. Grant, who was in the city that day, reported, "Union troops marching out to the secession encampment to break it up. I very much fear bloodshed," although he had written to his father and wife in recent days that he believed the war would be short. But when Lyon and Blair's men reached Camp Jackson on May 10, they met no resistance. Lyon's men outnumbered the militia ten to one, and Frost surrendered without a fight. The easy surrender surprised Lyon, and he wasn't immediately prepared to move prisoners. The hour-and-a-half delay in organizing the surrender and disarming of the 689 prisoners allowed time for a crowd of civilians to gather. Many of them brought guns. Picnickers sitting on the hills west of the camp watched to see what would happen next.[19]

What they saw and heard were crowds in the streets shouting, "Hurrah for Jeff Davis" and "Damn the Dutch," among other epithets. "Men, women, and children cursed and abused us for everything they could think of," one of Lyon's troopers reported. At first dirt clods and rocks were thrown. Suddenly shots were fired. Most accounts say the first shots came from the mob, not the troops. But the Home Guard instantly responded, and twenty-eight people were killed, with dozens more wounded.[20]

Harney returned to St. Louis the next day. Confronted by city leaders demanding Lyon's head and Blair insisting that Lyon stay put, the general had little choice but to side with the man who had Lincoln's ear. "The past cannot be recalled," he said. "I can only deal with the present and the future."[21]

The operation was a tactical success but a strategic failure. The *Missouri Republican*, the city's main Democratic newspaper despite the name, blamed the Camp Jackson affair on the "ambition, self-will, and domineering spirit of Francis P. Blair, Jr., and his political confederates." Contemporaries called the attack the "coup d'tat at St. Louis" and considered it the "greatest military blunder of the Civil War." Sherman, who at that time was in daily contact with Blair, said "this event will be used at Jefferson City to precipitate secession for it was a direct attack on State authority." Historian William E. Parrish called the Camp Jackson affair "a colossal blunder," arguing that it strengthened secessionist sentiment, turning winter unionists like former governor Sterling Price, who had served with Blair in New Mexico, into spring secessionists. While these judgments are in some sense valid, the reality was that Missouri was going to be fought over in any case. Lyon correctly judged that it was better to secure the arsenal, the arms, and the city at the beginning than to have to recover them later.[22]

Blair wanted Harney gone, but Lincoln vacillated for a month. Even when he finally empowered Blair to move against Harney, he hesitated. Citing his removal order, he wrote to Blair, "I was not quite satisfied with the order when it was made, though on the whole I thought it best to make it; but since then I have become more doubtful of its propriety." He wouldn't countermand the order but asked Blair to "withhold it, unless in your judgement the necessity to the contrary is very urgent." Blair got the same advice from his father. Lincoln also offered some reasons to keep Harney in place and then closed with permission: "Still, if in your judgment, it is *indispensable* let it be so." Lincoln wrote the letter on May 18, and Blair received it on May 20. It would not take him long to decide what to do with the authority the president had given him.[23]

The day after Blair got Lincoln's permission to fire Harney, the commanding general announced a deal with Sterling Price, commander of the Missouri State Guard, recognizing Missouri's so-called neutrality and dividing responsibility for keeping the peace between Harney in St. Louis and Price everywhere else in the state. Harney promised to use only regular troops—rather than itchy-fingered, undertrained volunteers—to keep the peace.

Sherman called it a "cheap victory," but Price and Jackson had little interest in keeping the peace and fewer means with which to do so. Lyon began sending out detachments to arrest secessionists and in the middle of May nabbed small groups in Potosi, Hillsboro, and Ironton south of St. Louis. "Lyon is . . . so full of vim that he would be marching upon Jefferson City had he his own way," Sherman presciently predicted. As the city was flooded with reports of rebel attacks on loyal citizens, unionists protested the Harney-Price agreement, and Lincoln—via Adjutant General Lorenzo Thomas—prodded Harney to "[put] a stop to them summarily by the force under your command." When Harney still refused to act, Blair did. On May 30, he delivered the news to Harney. He was out, and Lyon was in. At the urging of Attorney General Edward Bates, a Missourian, the state was added to the Department of the Ohio under Gen. George B. McClellan on June 6, though Lyon didn't find out for another two weeks.[24]

Now the moderates who had supported Harney appealed to Blair and Lyon to show restraint. Acquiescing for the moment, Blair arranged a meeting for June 11 at the Planter's House in St. Louis, where he had once heard Charles Dickens lecture. The meeting included himself, Lyon, Jackson, and Price. Blair and Price had a history, reaching back to the time they feuded in Santa Fe during the Mexican War, when Price was an army commander and Blair was the territory's attorney general. Their latest encounter went no better. After four hours of fruitless back-and-forth, Lyon had heard enough. Rising with a flourish, he ended the meeting by declaring, "This means war," ordering Jackson and Price out of the city, and stomping out of the room, his saber literally rattling.[25]

Price headed for western Missouri. Jackson returned to Jefferson City, where he cut the telegraph lines and burned the Missouri River bridges. Lyon quickly followed in pursuit, and Jackson fled the city on June 14, leaving it to Lyon without a battle. Lyon's plan after seizing the capital was to secure the river and railroads to divide secessionists in the northern and southern parts of the state and then move southwest to clear Missouri of State Guard troops and any Confederate forces that might enter the state. Lyon followed Jackson northwest in sweltering weather. "The sun poured down his heat upon us, as if we were human flapjacks," one trooper reported. On June 17 at Boonville, around fifty miles up the Missouri River from Jefferson City, Lyon's troops routed the state militia, which withdrew to the south.[26]

The Battle of Boonville, small as it was, brought national attention to the war in Missouri. The *New York Times* praised Lyon as "evidently the right man in the right place." Had he stopped at Boonville, Lyon would have been hailed as the conquering hero of Missouri. More than that, the state had effectively been secured, even with the rebels in control of the southwest, from which they posed no threat to Union control. The Missouri River, as Jackson's aide-de-camp noted, was now a "Federal highway from its source to its mouth."[27]

Once Lyon found out on June 18 that Missouri had been added to the Department of the Ohio, the Blair brothers began lobbying Winfield Scott and Attorney General Bates to create a separate Western Department. McClellan put up no protest; he didn't want Missouri anyway. But the conditional unionists of Missouri, led by Bates, considered Lyon too rash and too antislavery for overall command; Frank Blair considered him too valuable in the field to be locked up at headquarters shuffling paper. Frémont was the logical choice.[28]

Meanwhile, the fighting continued. At Carthage on July 5, Franz Sigel missed the opportunity to keep Price from uniting with Confederate forces from Arkansas under Ben McCulloch, a testy Texas Ranger with little regard for Missouri militia troops. With the sitting governor in armed rebellion and chased to the far western side of the state, the state convention reconvened and on July 22 elected former state supreme court judge Hamilton Gamble provisional governor and tentatively scheduled elections for the following year. With a unionist (though pro-slavery) governor now in place in Jefferson City, Frémont should have had an ally he could work with to keep Missouri tethered to the North.

"I HAVE GIVEN YOU CARTE BLANCHE"

Having arrived in Boston on June 27, Frémont wasted no time heading south. He arrived the next day to find Washington a much-changed place from the days when he was a senator and sometimes visitor. "Such liveliness, rushing, and shoving on the once so empty Pennsylvania Street, where before one could have been robbed in broad daylight by thieves and no one would have seen it," reported a German correspondent from St. Louis.[29]

After the fall of Sumter and Lincoln's call for seventy-five thousand volunteers, the president worried about the capital's safety. Only two thousand troops were stationed there, and Lincoln was reluctant to activate the District of Columbia militia for fear it would prove disloyal. But concerns about a rebel attack eased with the arrival of the 7th New York on April 25, and thousands more troops followed that first wave. In late May, Federal troops crossed the Potomac and occupied Alexandria and the Arlington heights, overlooking the city. By July, worries about a Confederate invasion had diminished as the city became an armed camp with troops scattered all over the district—on the grounds of the Capitol, at the Patent Office, even in the hallways of the Willard Hotel at 14th and F Streets, two blocks from the White House.

Like Lincoln before him and hundreds of generals who would follow, Frémont checked in at the Willard, his arrival causing "something of a rush to the register to get a sight of his autograph." The *New York Herald* reported, "Major General John C. Frémont . . . will be appointed to the Department of Virginia, now commanded by Brigadier General McDowell. This we believe has not been definitely decided upon." And indeed it had not. The source for that story might have been Treasury Secretary Salmon Chase, who had lobbied without success for Frémont to be posted in the East. There can be no doubt, as Lincoln would later say, that it was the Blairs who "mainly induced me to make him a major general and send him to Missouri."[30]

On June 29, after breakfast with the Blairs at Silver Spring, Frémont joined Lincoln at a cabinet meeting that also included Generals Winfield Scott, Irvin McDowell, Montgomery Meigs, Joseph Mansfield, and Daniel Tyler. McDowell presented his plan to move against Manassas. Several attendees expressed concerns about the ability of Maj. Gen. Robert Patterson, who was almost seventy, to keep Confederate general Joseph E. Johnston from moving south from Harpers Ferry to bolster the forces under P. G. T. Beauregard near Manassas. Following the cabinet meeting, Frémont was "closeted" for the rest of the day with Cameron and Frank Blair. Blair would not have been there to talk about Virginia. The next night, Frémont was back at Silver Spring, joined again by Cameron and the younger Blair. In this case, Cameron was an invited guest, but when Frémont arrived unexpectedly, another place was set. Every indication was that Frémont was headed west. "We shall not be able to indulge ourselves in burning Richmond," Jessie would write. The Blairs were enthusiastic. "The genius and energy of this remarkable man would soon astonish the country," declared Montgomery Blair, who now resided in Maryland but had served as U.S. attorney and mayor of St. Louis in the 1840s.[31]

The Silver Spring meetings were followed by speeches at Blair House by Frank Blair and three others on July 1. "They proclaimed that the country wanted action! Action," the *National Republican* reported, "that the universal cry was Frémont! And meet the enemy, strategy or no strategy."[32]

The next day, Frémont met with Lincoln at the White House, where they discussed the broad strokes of Frémont's duties: securing Missouri sufficiently to permit its use as a base to descend the Mississippi, one movement on which Frémont, Lincoln, and commanding general Winfield Scott all seemed to agree. "Who held the Mississippi would hold the country by the heart," Frémont believed, and his superiors concurred. The Department of the West encompassed Illinois, Missouri, and all U.S. territory to the Rocky Mountains—an enormous swath, with more possibly in the offing. "For reasons not wholly military," Frémont wrote, "the President reserved the State of Kentucky, but assured me that so soon as I had succeeded in raising and organizing an army for the descent of the Mississippi river, he would extend my command over that State and the left bank of the Mississippi," an exclusion that would be only partially remedied in the heat of battle.[33]

While still in Europe, Frémont had told friends, "If I take a command I must be allowed a wide margin, and be hampered as little as possible by the slow and tedious routine of government." Lincoln seemed ready to acquiesce in those terms. Lincoln and Frémont talked at some length about the campaign ahead, with Lincoln doing most of the asking and Frémont the answering. At the conclusion, they walked down the stairs of the portico together, and Frémont asked the commander in chief whether he had any last words of advice. "No," Lincoln told him. "I have given you carte blanche. You must use your own judgment and do the best you can." Frémont would take those words to heart. Lincoln would live to regret them.[34]

The day after meeting with Frémont, Lincoln and Seward met with Cameron to issue General Orders No. 40 officially creating the Department of the West and to assign the new major general to command it. The appointment of Frémont, like that of other political generals such as Benjamin Butler, Nathaniel Banks, John McClernand, Daniel Sickles, Carl Schurz, and even Frank Blair, would prove to be a net loss for Lincoln and the country. Lincoln believed he needed to appease various political constituencies—especially Democrats—and handing out senior military positions to leaders of those constituencies was one way to do it. Most would prove to be ineffective in the field; some would be downright damaging to the cause. Everything is a trade-off, as the president surely understood, but Lincoln can't escape responsibility for placing these men, including Frémont, in command.[35]

Frémont was something of a hybrid—a politician who had a military record, although not much of one, but who was not a graduate of the U.S. Military Academy. He and Jessie had always felt looked down on by West Pointers, going back to Frémont's days in the Corps of Topographical Engineers and the behavior of Gen. Stephen Watts Kearny during Frémont's court-martial arising from his actions in California before and during the Mexican War. Now he had a senior command that made him one of the highest-ranking officers in the army, and the regular army officer corps didn't much like it. "There is great jealousy in giving Frémont an extensive command," Elizabeth Blair Lee reported to her husband a week after the appointment became official.[36]

Frémont wasn't the only target of the West Point clique. His fellow politician major general, Nathaniel Banks, a former speaker of the House who had helped engineer Frémont's presidential nomination in 1856, was treated just as disdainfully. Whether it was jealousy or simply a belief that volunteer commanders were not up to snuff, William Tecumseh Sherman suggested to his brother-in-law that the "appointment of [John] Pope, [Andrew] Reeder,

Banks, Frémont &c. will afford to [Braxton] Bragg & [Jefferson] Davis & [P. G. T.] Beauregard the liveliest pleasure," lumping the politically connected West Pointer Pope with the politicians. Sherman expressed a similar sentiment to his foster father, bemoaning that, with such generals, "nothing but good luck, or the mere force of numbers will extricate us from Calamitous results." Of course, the Confederates faced the same conundrum. West Point Confederate Thomas J. "Stonewall" Jackson claimed, "The great interests of the country are being sacrificed by appointing incompetent officers. I wish that if such appointments are continued, that the President would come in the field and command them, and not throw the responsibility upon me of defending the District when he throws such obstacles in my way."[37]

Frémont would cross paths soon enough with Sherman and Jackson. But as far as he was concerned, the most important officer in the military was not a West Point general but a volatile colonel of a unit of Missouri volunteers. Frank Blair had returned to Washington from Missouri after the Battle of Boonville to take his seat in the special session of Congress that convened July 4. He made a bid to become Speaker of the House, but the post went to Galusha Grow, a onetime Democrat from Pennsylvania. Instead, Blair was named chairman of the House Military Affairs Committee, the post held in the Senate for years by Thomas Hart Benton. But the restless Blair would not be limited by politics. He would continue to float between Congress and the field for the rest of the war, serving under Sherman, doing Lincoln's bidding, looking out for the Blair family's interests, and bird-dogging Frémont.

Frémont had early and strong support for a senior command from Francis P. Blair. Frank had offered the command to Sherman, who turned it down, and then wanted to keep Gen. Nathaniel Lyon, a West Pointer (eleventh of fifty-two in the Class of 1841), in charge in Missouri, perhaps even while he operated in the field. Lyon had proved an effective ally through early 1861 in Blair's efforts to sustain Missouri for the Union. But Lyon's lack of seniority and reputation as a hothead worked against him. So Frank, like the other Blairs, was happy to settle for Frémont, whom they all saw as an ally and perhaps as something of a cipher they believed they could manipulate to their advantage. That would prove a grave miscalculation. At a moment when Missouri was desperate for the art of subtle diplomacy, its wartime politics would be dominated by the volatile trio of Frank Blair, Nathaniel Lyon, and John C. Frémont. All were stubborn, self-assured to the point of arrogance, and defiant of authority. Together they promised to make an already explosive situation worse, in whatever order of rank.

"I go immediately to the West"

Before heading for New York, Frémont stopped in Baltimore to meet Nathaniel Banks, who commanded the military district that included hostile Baltimore, where some of the first Union troops bound for Washington had been attacked in April. Then, accompanied by Cameron, Adjutant General Lorenzo Thomas, and a bevy of engineers, he took a steamer down the Chesapeake to inspect the works at Fortress Monroe on the Virginia coast.[38]

When Frémont reached New York, he met with Henry Stevens's brother, Simon, who handled the family's book business in the city, and arranged to process the shipments of arms coming from Liverpool and Southampton and have them forwarded to the West. That included a 24-pounder cannon, 50 casks of 24-pound solid shot, 50 24-pound shells, 204 cases of artillery shells, 2,500 French rifles, 450 French revolvers, 102,000 cartouches (for stamping rifles), and 2 million percussion caps. Not all the weapons Frémont had worked so assiduously to procure would end up under his command. Frémont also invited Stevens to join his staff, an appointment Stevens (who had no military experience) politely declined.[39]

Even those few arms Frémont had been able to procure while in Washington slipped through his fingers. He complained to the army bureaucracy about his order for seven thousand rifles being countermanded but got little satisfaction. Instead, he was sent begging to multiple posts and arsenals to scrape together enough weapons to fit out about twenty-three thousand men. He then had to arrange to have those arms gathered, packed, and shipped off to St. Louis, all with no help from Washington and as yet only a skeleton staff. Critics would later condemn Frémont for lingering in New York for three weeks before departing to St. Louis, but that time was well spent securing arms for the troops he would soon command.[40]

Frémont had been in the city less than a week when he returned to Washington for a quick overnight visit and a trip to the White House, where he met Orville Hickman Browning, Illinois's new senator. Browning lived in Quincy, just across the Mississippi River from Missouri. The two had only a brief chat about the deployment of Illinois troops, but Browning would prove an ally later, when Frémont needed one most. Frémont also met with commanding general Winfield Scott, likely relaying to Scott the details of his meeting with Lincoln and possibly his encounter with the general's wife in Paris. They likely discussed the formation of Frémont's staff and the broad outlines of a western strategy.[41]

Shortly after the fall of Fort Sumter, Scott had devised what came to be known as the "Anaconda Plan." The old general envisioned a tight blockade of southern ports, combined with a movement down the Mississippi to cut the Confederacy in two, slowly squeezing the life out of the rebellion, with the aid of internal dissent from what he believed was strong but silent unionist sentiment in the South, a belief shared by Lincoln. Any movement down the Mississippi would fall under the auspices of Frémont as commanding general in the West.

The U.S. Army had about seventeen thousand men, not nearly enough in cooperation with the navy to accomplish Scott's agenda. He was supportive of the president's proposal to increase the size of the regular army—indeed, he believed Lincoln's plan to boost the army by about twenty-two thousand men and the navy by eighteen thousand would prove inadequate. But Scott was no fan of volunteers. His experiences in the War of 1812, the Seminole War, and the Mexican War had taught him that volunteer troops were too undisciplined. If he had his way, this war would be fought with regular troops recruited, trained, and commanded by regular officers. It soon became apparent that Scott was not going to get his way on either front. In his message to Congress, which convened in special session on July 4, Lincoln asked for an additional four hundred thousand men, raised largely by the states. The war would be fought with volunteers, and those volunteers would be expected to fight, not stand at post while the navy squeezed the rebels to death.

At this point, both Lincoln and Seward clung to the hope that this massive show of force might mean the war could be short, that one solid blow on the rebels' heads might bring them to their senses and back into the Union. Scott didn't believe that, and neither did Frémont, who was devising his own plan of attack, which, like Scott's, involved a movement down the Mississippi. How much of that thinking he shared with the commanding general at their July meeting is unknown. But he would make it clear to his superiors quickly enough.

Lincoln rejected Scott's plan as politically infeasible. The North was aroused, and it would not countenance the long periods of inaction contemplated by the Anaconda Plan. As the speakers at the Blair House on July 1 had said, "On to Richmond" was the cry, with or without a concrete plan, and a slow death by blockade would not suffice. Newspapers across the country clamored for action. Still, Lincoln was cautious, and even some in his own house seemed skeptical, with Montgomery Blair deriding "the dilatory policy of the Administration" of which he was a part. Lincoln soon pushed his generals to act, but at this point he had no conception of how difficult it would be over the next year to get his senior military commanders—including, but certainly not limited to, Frémont—to do his bidding.[42]

On July 12, Frémont was back at his New York headquarters at the Astor House accompanied by his newly installed chief of staff, Brig. Gen. Alexander Asboth, a civil engineer who had fought in Hungary with Louis Kossuth and then emigrated to the United States in 1851 like so many other of the failed European revolutionaries of 1848.[43]

Having won the chase against the Confederate cutter, Jessie and the children arrived in New York on the evening of July 13. Frémont, attired in a "long unused uniform" from his army days of the 1840s, motored into the harbor aboard a quarantine boat to meet them. But after the excitement of her triumphant arrival, Jessie skulked around looking to be useful. Her husband was extraordinarily busy, with "stacks and stacks not only of bayonetted muskets to examine but of work of all sorts," she reported to Thomas Starr King. "We have really had no chance to have a talk." But after so many lean emotional years, she had learned some patience. "I haunt around taking my chances of a word—sometimes it is only a look—but after the hungry yearning of that far off blank life at Black Point it is enough."[44]

In addition to dealing with the European arms orders and putting together a staff, Frémont tended to the more ceremonial side of his job. On July 16, he met at the Astor House with a newly organizing German regiment, the 46th New York Volunteers, that bore the name Frémont Rifles. The commander was Col. Rudolph Rosa, but his second, Lt. Col. Germain Metternich, like many of Frémont's nascent staff, had fought in the European uprisings of 1848 before emigrating to the United States two years later. Frémont "expressed himself well satisfied" with the unit and promised to help them get accepted into the army.[45]

While Frémont lingered in New York, the Missourians were getting antsy. On July 18, Gen. Nathaniel Lyon alerted Frank Blair regarding his and the state's "perilous condition," and Montgomery Blair forwarded that information to Frémont, who was wrapping up his business. Frémont also received word from Scott that same day telling him to proceed on to St. Louis without another trip to Washington because the commanding general had "no particular instructions for you at present." With that, "I go immediately to the west," Frémont assured Ohio governor William Dennison on July 20. The next day he told Illinois congressman Owen Lovejoy, who would later briefly serve on Frémont's staff, "I am doing my best to get off this afternoon," explaining that part of the delay was due to Cameron's objections to his staff appointments. "He thinks that I ought to get along with three," Frémont complained.[46]

One more bit of political drama would play out before Frémont reached Missouri. The day Frémont wrote to Lovejoy, Union forces were defeated at

Manassas. In the wake of this political and military embarrassment, the conservative press tried to stir up a mini-revolt against Seward, Chase, Cameron, and other "rabid anti-slavery Republicans" in the administration. They pushed Frémont, once again, as secretary of war. Lincoln ignored the controversy, and so did Frémont. After telegraphing Scott for any last-minute instructions and being told he had none, Frémont boarded a train for St. Louis. John, Jessie, and the children took the quieter route through New Jersey and Pennsylvania rather than northward toward Buffalo, hoping to avoid the crush of his celebrity. What they ran into instead was news of the disaster at Bull Run and an inkling of the troubles that lay ahead of them. "As we passed through Altoona," Lily remembered, "we were overwhelmed with the news of the defeat of our forces" at Manassas. "In Ohio & all the way we met western troops on their way to the Potomac," Jessie wrote, "the western waters left to defend themselves as best they might."[47]

As the Frémonts traveled westward, news of Bull Run had also reached Missouri, where Col. John A. Palmer, a friend of both Frémont and Lincoln, on July 24 anticipated "a large increase of courage if not numbers in the rebels" in response to the Confederate victory in Virginia. He suggested arming the locals. Palmer's letter was forwarded to Lincoln, who sent it on to Frémont, who arrived in St. Louis on July 25. Responding to Lincoln a few days later on behalf of her husband, Jessie wrote, "The plan suggested by Col. Palmer is about what Genl. Frémont has been doing since arriving in Missouri."[48]

"IMPOSSIBLE NOW TO GET ANY ATTENTION TO MISSOURI"

"He has aged greatly since the great campaign of 1856, and gray now predominates in his hair and beard," a correspondent for the *Anzeiger des Westens* reported on Frémont's arrival. "Otherwise he is strong and possessed of his usual iron energy." The *Missouri Democrat*, founded in 1853 as Benton's mouthpiece but taken over by Blair and his allies in 1857, also warmly welcomed Frémont. The paper had become the voice of the unionist antislavery cause in Missouri, opposed equally to the extension of slavery and to immediate abolition but in support of gradual emancipation and the colonization of free blacks. The consensus among the city's pro-Union leadership was that Frémont "was certainly the most welcome Commander to all progressive elements in the new Department."[49]

As warmly as the Frémonts were greeted, war had turned St. Louis into something of an alien landscape for Jessie. "Everything was changed. There was no life on the river; the many steamboats were laid up at their wharves, their fires out, the singing, cheery crews gone—they, empty, swaying idly with the current. As we drove through the deserted streets we saw only closed shutters to warehouses and business places; the wheels and the horses' hoofs echoed loud and harsh as when one drives through the silent streets late in the night." Drawing on intelligence from family retainers, Elizabeth Blair Lee noted the same dynamic. "Commerce is in St. Louis as every where else defunct," she wrote to her husband just a couple weeks before the Frémonts arrived. A French visitor observed that in "the deserted and poorly lit streets, we saw no stores and no bars open." Jessie noted not just a lack of industry but also a rebel atmosphere. "It was a hostile city and showed itself as such." Comparing her childhood home to the Mariposa camp, she found "such discord, such dangers and such malice, envy and all uncharitableness, that the Sierra life with its mining riot, the Indian troubles, all the things that seemed hard to bear there were light by comparison."[50]

Because the city was so thick with southern sympathizers, Jessie and Lily had a hard time even finding a spot for the "war sewing circle" they organized, "until a German woman opened her home for the cause." The hastily organized Frémont Relief Society eventually joined forces with the St. Louis Ladies Union Aid Society, which was founded just before the Frémonts arrived. The pro-Union women would parade their knitting in proud red, white, and blue through the streets as they traveled between their homes and the circle's headquarters. Apparently Lily was no seamstress at that stage. "After I had presented my quota of knitted sock, I was told that they would do for hospital use, for as no two were of the same size, they would be suitable only for men who had lost a leg." Over the next several months, Lily's socks would not go to waste. The sewing circle also sewed uniforms of different colors because they used what cloth was at hand; this practice would cause a grave problem at a key moment when southerners were mistaken for an Iowa unit that wore gray at the Battle of Wilson's Creek.[51]

Even discounting the effects of wartime strictures, St. Louis had changed considerably since Jessie had last lived there decades earlier. Between 1840 and 1850, immigration from southern states had outdistanced that from the North by almost three to one. But in the 1850s, an influx of New England businessmen and German immigrants had bolstered the city's antislavery ranks and added to its already multicultural air, bringing a touch of Teutonic industry to the French and Spanish influences of the fur-trading center's early years. Immigration and an evolving economy had driven down the percentage of the population that was enslaved from 17.7 percent in 1839 to 9.7 percent by 1860.[52]

That year, there were 88,487 German immigrants in Missouri, more than 50,000 of those in St. Louis, where half the population was foreign-born. Many were highly educated professionals who had fled the revolutions of 1830 and 1848—college professors, lawyers, engineers, and successful merchants. A native press bloomed, led by the *Anzeiger des Westens*, the first German-language newspaper in the state. Its editor, Charles Bernays, became a good friend of Lincoln, who had once owned a German-language paper in Illinois.[53]

The river and the railroad connected St. Louis to the North economically and culturally in a way that much of the state was not, further weakening the city's cultural attachment to slavery. "St. Louis has the character of a city of a free state, a virtual enclave in this region of slavery," reported the German-language *Mississippi Blatter*. Sherman suggested in mid-May that "St. Louis is past the worst, and that whatever Confusion occurs will be along the Missouri & lines of travel." But there remained in St. Louis and across the state—especially in the fertile farmland along the Missouri River noted by Sherman—a substantial pro-slavery minority that wished to join the Confederacy. A journalist had noted in the month before Frémont took command, "Missourians believe very generally that we came here to steal their niggers, hang the men and ravish the women."[54]

Frémont established his headquarters at the Chouteau Avenue mansion of Jessie's cousin, Sarah Benton Brant, charging the $500 monthly rent to the War Department. Widow Brant was living in France. "More than ever it seemed home now," Jessie wrote, an "ark with some household gods still left in it." The elaborate quarters became a point of contention later, but the headquarters was no more splendiferous than the three-story Charles Wilkes mansion on Jackson Square in Washington where George McClellan established his headquarters, close to both the War Department and the White House, taking up multiple floors and providing room for dozens of staff and subalterns.[55]

In Jessie's ark, husband and wife had offices next to each other, where Frémont often worked from 5:00 a.m. until midnight. The basement served as the reception area and armory. The first floor included a telegraph office, a small printing press, and offices for most of Frémont's staff. Jessie and John lived on the second and third floors with the senior staff.[56]

Jessie Frémont had been in St. Louis all of two days when she began lobbying her husband to return to Washington as his representative to appeal directly to Lincoln. She simply couldn't believe that the president, "a western man and not grown in red tape," would leave the West defenseless if he knew the true state of things, and she aimed to inform him. "I have begged Mr. Frémont to let me go on & tell him how things are here," she wrote to Elizabeth Blair Lee. "It's making bricks without straw out here & mere human power can't draw order out of chaos by force of will alone." But, fearful for her health after all the recent travels—and worried that he couldn't get along without her—Frémont demurred on the offer. But she wasn't giving up. "Don't be surprised if you see me some day at Silver Spring. I will obey a higher law than my dear chief's and open out the view to the M[ississi]ppi. It seems to stop now at the Potomac."[57]

The urgency of this letter would soon be coupled with poignancy. It would be the last letter Jessie would write to "My dear Lizzie" for more than twenty years.

Others besides Jessie had noticed the paucity of attention paid to the West. "In the distribution of the money necessary to carry on the war for the Union, it looks a little as though the West is to be overlooked," the *Chicago Daily Democrat* reported. "But in braving the burdens and making the sacrifices necessary to sustain the cause, we will have to bear our full share."[58]

Officialdom made it clear there would be little (if any) help while Washington felt besieged by Virginia Confederates. Montgomery Blair cabled Frémont on the day he arrived in town: "I have two telegrams from you, but find it impossible now to get any attention to Missouri or western matters from the authorities here," the Judge wrote to the General. "You will have to do the best you can, and take all needful responsibility, to defend and protect the people over whom you are specially set."[59]

Before Frémont could deal with what he wasn't getting from Washington, urgent business awaited 150 miles down the Mississippi. On July 19, Assistant Adjutant General Chester Harding telegraphed Frémont, who at that point was still in New York, about the "extremely dangerous" situation at Cairo, Illinois, and Bird's Point, opposite Cairo on the Missouri side of the strategic point at the confluence of the Ohio and Mississippi Rivers. Frémont received a similar message from Brig. Gen. Benjamin Prentiss, the commander at Cairo, who had only about six hundred men available. Two days after the defeat at Manassas, Lincoln prepared a memorandum urging Frémont to "push forward his organization, and operations in the West as rapidly as possible, giving rather special attention to Missouri," but also calling for "a joint movement from Cairo on Memphis." Then, on July 28, Confederate general Gideon Pillow occupied New Madrid, Missouri, fifty miles overland from Cairo (though somewhat farther via the river), a move that "only prompted greater haste for Frémont's Cairo expedition," a St. Louis resident reported. The commanding general arrived at the confluence on August 2 trailed by a fleet of eight steamboats carrying about four thousand men. He was greeted by enthusiastic cheers as his flagship, the *City of Alton*, fired a salute that was answered from shore.[60]

Unbeknownst to Frémont, he had a stowaway on his flagship. Not wanting to be left behind on the first big adventure of the new command, Jessie had hidden herself in the stateroom until they were far enough down the river that it would have been impractical to send her back. Frémont was surprised and annoyed when she showed up in his cabin. Wearing John's socks and underwear because she had not stashed a change of clothes, she made herself useful dealing with the awful sanitary conditions. A report from the U.S. Sanitary Commission issued a few weeks before Frémont's arrival noted that the "camp police of Cairo was not good; the men being shockingly remiss in the use of the sinks, which are badly situated and poorly constructed. . . . [T]he camp showed a great deal of garbage and waste water lying about. The officers complained bitterly of the carelessness of the men in all these respects." The swampy confluence was rife with fever and dysentery, and the commander, Benjamin Prentiss, was just now recovering from a bout of sunstroke. Jessie busied herself organizing some of the boats as floating hospitals for the men laid low by the heat, which one officer described as "excessively oppressive."[61]

Taking stock of the situation in Cairo and elsewhere in his department, Frémont reported to Lincoln, "I have found this command in disorder, nearly every county in an insurrectionary condition, and the enemy advancing in force by different points of the southern frontier." Short of men, arms, and guidance, Frémont had to make a decision: reinforce the strategic site of Cairo against a threatening Confederate army fifty miles away or send more troops to Lyon as he followed a Missouri militia moving westward to rendezvous with another Confederate army moving up from Arkansas. Frémont made the logical—and correct—choice. In June, Lyon had recommended reinforcement of Cairo, recognizing its significance. Both the president and General Scott had emphasized the importance of a movement down the Mississippi, echoing Frémont's own plans. Even Stephen A. Douglas had recognized the significance of Cairo, listing it as one of three key points to be reinforced when he met with Lincoln on April 14 in the wake of Sumter. There could be no movement southward if the Mississippi was not secure and no secure Mississippi without a secure confluence with the Ohio. Lyon would have to wait. But waiting was one thing Nathaniel Lyon was not interested in. Frémont's journey to Cairo did not spare him from Lyon's repeated calls for reinforcements. The day Frémont arrived, he received yet another appeal. "General Lyon wants soldiers—soldiers—soldiers!" Assistant

Adjutant General John Kelton telegraphed from St. Louis. When Frémont returned to the city on August 4, more appeals from Lyon would greet him.[62]

"DESTITUTE OF EVERYTHING REQUIRED FOR THEIR USE"

Frémont dueled with Cameron about the size of his staff. The secretary thought he could get by with three. Frémont thought that was far too few to manage a department stretching from the Mississippi to the Rockies. That staff was chiefly composed of Hungarian and Italian refugees with military experience. Frémont was not plugged into the West Point pipeline and could not readily draw on the academy's old boy network. One West Point product who served as a general in the Civil War remembered that his fellow academy graduates viewed Frémont as "vanity incarnate." Frémont had to look elsewhere to fill his staff. Typically, he looked to outsiders like himself. And his international fame helped attract dashing European officers with little regard for American military decorum.[63]

A sizable group of foreign officers served in the multicultural city of St. Louis. Most were German. But about three thousand Hungarians lived in the United States in 1860, most of whom were refugees from the 1848 revolutions, and a number ended up on Frémont's staff. Lincoln himself had joined with fellow citizens of Springfield in 1849 to produce a resolution of sympathy with the cause of Hungarian freedom. Immigrant St. Louis also included sizable communities of Bohemians, Swiss, French, and Poles.[64]

As with most organizations of any size, the reliability of Frémont's staff ran the gamut from highly competent through middlingly inefficient to downright corrupt. Brig. Gen. Alexander Asboth, his chief of staff, was another Hungarian, a civil engineer who fought with Kossuth and came to the United States in 1851. Topographical officer Col. John Fiala had been an early activist in organizing Germans in St. Louis into Home Guard units and had been part of the capture of Camp Jackson. A railroad construction engineer, Fiala helped guide construction of the fortifications in and around St. Louis. Col. Albert Anzelm joined the staff as Frémont's adjutant and would later become chief of staff. Col. Gustave Wagner, an engineer and ordinance officer of Czech ancestry who fought with the Hungarians in 1848–1849, served under Frémont until he was detailed to Grant's command.[65]

Frémont's Body Guard, a 150-strong cavalry unit, was commanded by Charles Zagonyi, a dashing veteran of the Hungarian Revolution who had come to the United States in 1851 via Turkey and England. He had volunteered in April 1861 but was rejected by a New York regiment. Asboth invited him to come west and introduced him to Frémont. Zagonyi chose the officers for the Body Guard; most were American, with only three foreign-born. He also designed the uniforms—dark blue coats, pants, and hats. While they were not especially flamboyant compared with some European armies, they seemed so to many ill-clad Missourians and stuck in the craw of quite a few envious regular army officers.[66]

Seven other Hungarians and three Italians, plus a floating contingent of American officers, were also part of the group. Gustave Koerner described the staff as "a curiosity" and guessed that its twenty-eight members were enough for a man commanding one hundred thousand troops. "Some of the officers of that staff were unknown to our service, as for instance, the 'commander of the body guard,' the 'musical director,' the 'adletus to the chief of staff,' (an Austrian denomination), and a 'director of transportation,' there being already a quartermaster-general and an assistant quartermaster-general on the staff, whose business was transportation. A 'military registrator and expeditor' (no one knew what this meant), a 'postal director,' a 'police director,' and two private secretaries, fifteen aides-de-camp," which would come to include politicians such as Koerner (the only German) and Lovejoy as volunteers working without pay. Koerner judged most of the staff already stationed in St. Louis on Frémont's arrival—which included the troublesome and corrupt quartermaster Maj. Justus McKinstry—to be highly competent. History does not bear out Koerner's judgment in this case. Frémont's staff was colorful and loyal, but it failed in its primary function of helping the commanding officer achieve success. Much of the responsibility for that failure rests with the man who selected them.[67]

The region these men were charged with defending had been in a state of violent turmoil for the past six months. Montgomery Blair assured Frémont in mid-July that Lincoln was "going in person to the War Department to arrange matters for you." If he did, the trip yielded nothing to speak of.[68]

The historian of the Ordinance Bureau has noted that favoritism and state interest were determining factors in who got weapons and, just as important, who got the good ones. As secretary of war, Cameron "clearly favored the Pennsylvania troops with good rifled arms," although Frémont was able to use "the prestige of his name and his wife's family name" to have his appeals heard. And while Frémont was complaining about not being able to arm his men, Sherman in Ohio was complaining that Frémont and McClellan were sucking up all the supply.[69]

Both Frémont and McKinstry understood themselves to be on an island and empowered to deal with circumstances as they saw fit because the authorities in Washington were too busy worrying about the war in the East. "A few weeks sufficed to crowd the city and the arsenal with new levies, who were entirely unequipped and for whose unexpected necessities no preparations had been made," was how McKinstry summed up the situation. "I was destitute of everything required for their use." Troops in other states were outfitted by their state governments, and some of them were beginning to make their way to Missouri. That was not an option in the first weeks of the war because the pro-southern state government refused to cooperate with Washington. As Frémont quickly "collected a force that was enormous in comparison with the resources of the Department," he and his quartermaster moved with alacrity to address the situation. Their insistence that they were empowered to act in the absence of aid from Washington would create, arm, and outfit an army, but the workarounds they devised to accomplish this task would also contribute to their undoing.[70]

That included, in Frémont's first days, the necessity of collecting funds to make such purchases. This process often involved forced loans—in effect, confiscation—of the deposits of local banks and, as Frémont reported to Lincoln, sending troops to collect Treasury Department funds that the paymaster refused to disburse. Another step McKinstry took was to enlist brokers to secure deals for the needed goods—horses, mules, tents, canteens—with their own cash or putting their own credit to work, without the time-consuming process of putting orders out to bid and waiting for the government to deliver the money to pay for them. In return, they would receive "the promise of a fair mercantile profit as their compensation" for moving fast and assuming the risk.[71]

It was an enormous undertaking. From scratch, with barely a dollar in hand, they had to equip and arm twenty-three infantry regiments, three cavalry regiments, and one artillery regiment. And all of it needed to be done in a few weeks, because the enemy was on the move. The quartermaster general told Frémont and McKinstry it couldn't be done—at least not in the time frame they were considering. But he had also told McKinstry "that while economy is right, there be no room left for charging the failure of any military movement upon want of promptness and efficiency in the Quartermaster's Department." Like Lincoln's "carte blanche" to Frémont, this grant of authority would soon be forgotten by those who issued it. Extensive communications with Assistant Quartermaster General Charles Thomas in Philadelphia support McKinstry's contention that he got little help from back east in terms of acquiring needed supplies but was empowered to "furnish the regular supplies of camp equipage" by his own devices. In that spirit, Frémont ordered McKinstry "to take immediate steps to furnish the articles called for, in the most expeditious manner." And that's what McKinstry did, while ensuring that he profited from the exchange.

In the opinion of fellow staff member and Illinois politician Gustave Koerner, "a great deal of the dissatisfaction with Frémont was owing to McKinstry."[72]

Treasury Secretary Salmon Chase was a Frémont supporter. Shortly after the general arrived in St. Louis, Chase wrote to him that the "energy wh. you are displaying is admirable, and excites the best hopes, of the entire fulfillment of wh. I am very sanguine." At the same time, he offered Frémont some advice: "Let me, however, take the privilege of a frd., as well as perform the duty of a Secy. of the Treasy., in urging you not to allow the pressure of yr. other cares to withdraw yr. attention from the expenditures of the Army under yr. command, and in yr. Dept." He pointed to "the disgust created by fraud or exorbitance in Contracts" that was already rife elsewhere, and he warned Frémont to remain vigilant. It was a reminder that Frémont, with some justification, would largely ignore. His position more closely resembled that taken by the *Chicago Tribune*: "What may be saved by procrastination will be five fold lost by delay to the country at large."[73]

Frémont was scrambling now because the preparations he had made in Europe in the spring were not paying dividends—or, at least, others were reaping the rewards. Most of the weapons Frémont had bought with his own money in Europe were appropriated by the federal government and sent to Virginia, or they were delayed in Europe by diplomatic wrangling that Frémont's lawyer, Frederick Billings, blamed largely on Charles Francis Adams. "Mr. Adams & Mr. Dayton both requested me to oversee this purchase of the French rifles—I had half a mind to refuse—because they would not treat you properly—but as I thought then my rifles would go right to you, (though they will ship them to Secy. of War) . . . and the matter requires great care & delicacy, I consented. . . . You should have had the Dept. send special instructions to Adams & Dayton to pay yr. orders—The whole difficulty comes from a little want of precision," a common Frémont fault. Few—perhaps none—of those arms made it to Missouri.[74]

Frémont reasoned with some justification that St. Louis, as an island of freedom in a sea of slavery, was worth defending to the hilt as a military, economic, psychological, and moral necessity. Indeed, the city would remain under the threat of rebel attack well into 1864.

Lt. Col. Franz Hassendeubel, a native of the Palatinate who came to America in 1842, supervised the building of ten forts around St. Louis for Frémont in autumn 1861. In addition to the construction of new facilities, considerable repair work was needed on existing ones. Jefferson Barracks, the primary living quarters for soldiers located ten miles south of downtown St. Louis, had been built in 1826. Covering seventeen hundred acres, it was the largest post in the

West. And it was "rapidly falling into a dilapidated state," the U.S. Sanitary Commission reported in July. The "present aspect of the barracks is disgraceful." An inspection of the Marine Hospital in St. Louis found the "beds all dirty and disgusting."[75]

Jessie enlisted the help of Dorothea Dix, the superintendent of army nurses, to help clean up and reorganize the medical facilities. Mrs. Frémont concluded, backed by leading citizens of St. Louis, that, as with arms, the department could not depend on those back east. Instead of relying on the U.S. Sanitary Commission, they would create their own. Six weeks after Frémont's arrival, the Western Sanitary Commission was born. "Frémont has stirred up things in St. Louis & given new life there—spending money there in employing the people there to minister to the wants of the Army," Elizabeth Blair Lee noted, viewing military spending as economic stimulus. "The local effect has been 'fine—' Frémont has plenary powers in the West—& plenty of money & if he & Frank cant take care of Missouri I am mistaken in the men."[76]

Frémont inherited a situation that was inherently hostile and had been made more so by the actions of Frank Blair and Nathaniel Lyon. He had secured the strategic river junction at Cairo, begun building fortifications and a river navy, and upgraded living quarters and medical facilities. The opening of Benton Barracks on September 16 was indicative of his progress. He had also brought a halt to Confederate recruiting in St. Louis, if not elsewhere in the state. And he had secured the Iron Mountain and Pacific railroads north, west, and south of St. Louis, essential to any future troop movements. "When Gen. Frémont came to St. Louis, the cause of the Union, though gallantly defended, was the unpopular cause," John Hay wrote anonymously in the New York World. "Frémont and his heroic wife have brought loyalty into vogue, and have made treason not only criminal, but what is far worse, vulgar." Volunteers from across the Old Northwest appealed to serve with the "gallant pathfinder."[77]

But the Pathfinder had failed to make clear any military path away from the Mississippi. Lyon was marching across the state toward an uncertain fate in search of an uncertain foe. Neighbors were at war with each other. And despite enormous effort, the army remained undermanned, underarmed, and underprovisioned. Many of the troops were ninety-day men whose enlistments were coming to an end, and many of those had not been paid. Frémont took the unusual step of personally guaranteeing the pay of ten thousand men if they would remain in uniform for a fourth month. Lincoln had to make strategic decisions about disposition of forces across an eighteen-hundred-mile front, depending on his own resources and men whose advice wasn't always the soundest. He needed help from Frémont. In Missouri, the strategic situation remained unfocused, and the commander on the spot was not doing enough to clarify it. Missouri had an antislavery military administration under Frémont and a pro-slavery conditional unionist civil administration under provisional governor Gamble, who had offered an amnesty—endorsed by Lincoln—to rebels in arms. Within a month, these circumstances would lead to the greatest crisis Frémont would face during the war and to a contest with the president that he couldn't hope to win. But before that, Missouri would be the scene of the second great battle of the war, following hard on the heels of the Union defeat at Manassas.[78]

Chapter Three

"If he fights, he will do it upon his own responsibility"

Lincoln took the defeat at Manassas with relative equanimity. He at first expressed confidence in Irvin McDowell, although Maj. Gen. George McClellan was quickly sent for. Fresh off some minor victories in western Virginia for which he claimed more than his share of the credit, the Young Napoleon arrived in Washington within days of the battle and, on July 26, was put in charge of what would soon become the Army of the Potomac.

It might have been otherwise if Lincoln had listened to the advice of Treasury Secretary Salmon Chase, who was already developing a reputation for sticking his nose into military matters. "Two weeks ago I urged the sending of Frémont to this command; and had it been done we should now have been rejoicing over a great victory," Chase wrote two days after the battle. It wasn't hindsight. He had been urging Lincoln to keep Frémont in the East for several weeks, to replace the sixty-nine-year-old Maj. Gen. Robert Patterson, who had failed to block Confederate general Joseph Johnston from reinforcing P. G. T. Beauregard at Manassas. Patterson was cashiered before the end of the month, which was little solace to Chase or to the defeated Union army that had skedaddled back to Washington. Chase followed up with a note to Frémont two weeks after Manassas, expressing further "regret that the suggestions wh. I ventured to make respecting yr. employment after yr. return [from Europe] were not adopted." The treasury secretary reassured Frémont, "Yr. services are of the highest value where you are, I do not doubt," but he continued to feel that had Frémont been in Virginia, "our army wd. now have been in possession of Manassas and the whole line of communication with W. Va." But Frémont remained in Missouri, where, Chase assured him, the "country expects great things from you . . . and I am confident will not be disappointed."[1]

Missouri's largest concentrations of slaveholders lived along a wide strip stretching east to west across the state along the Missouri River. This area was, not surprisingly, also a center of Confederate sympathy and rich recruiting ground for the pro-slavery Missouri Home Guard. Containing rebel sympathies, destroying the enemy's ability to recruit, and defeating the Confederate Army and the Missouri Home Guard in battle were the broad aims of Nathaniel Lyon's strategy.

When Lyon left Boonville, citizens turned out to cheer on his troops as they moved southwestward in pursuit of Sterling Price, who was attempting to unite his Home Guard with Confederates in Arkansas under former Texas Ranger Ben McCulloch. His movement involved three columns—one moving overland from St. Louis via Jefferson City, one by rail from St. Louis to the end of the line at Rolla, and the third southeastward from Fort Leavenworth, Kansas, uniting near Clinton, Missouri, about ninety miles north of Springfield. He hoped to intercept Price and keep McCulloch at bay. Lyon's plans, though, bore little relation to the actual capacity of his army to accomplish them. His force of about fifty-eight hundred men paled before the combined force of Price and McCulloch, although not nearly by as much as Lyon estimated.[2]

A large portion of Lyon's forces were ill equipped and ill fed. Some of the troops in the field were on one-third rations because of the lack of supplies and the want of transportation to move goods. For those shortcomings, Lyon blamed not Frémont but his quartermaster, Justus McKinstry. Like Lyon and Frémont, McKinstry had led a checkered army career. He had served with William Harney and Lyon in Mexico. He had been arrested multiple times, nearly been cashiered on more than one occasion, and earned a reputation for corruption that rivaled Simon Cameron's. Lyon had sat in judgment as an officer in one of McKinstry's court-martials. Over six feet tall, solidly built, with black hair, black eyes, and a thick black moustache, McKinstry looked "very much . . . like a high tragedian or the Big Villain in a melodrama"—a fair description of what he was about to become.[3]

On July 6, three weeks before Frémont's arrival in St. Louis, McClellan, in command of the Department of the Ohio, sent Lyon six Illinois regiments. He told Lyon that he couldn't spare any from Ohio or Indiana, and he ordered McKinstry to provide wagons and teams for them to move. "Distant as I am from Missouri—I can only say, General, that so long as it remains attached to my Dept, you may confidently rely upon my giving you all the support in my power."

But Missouri was already detached from McClellan's department, as he noted the same day in another letter, to Assistant Adjutant General E. D. Townsend, citing "newspaper reports . . . that my department is to be broken up." Lyon would now have to look to Frémont for support, though he was also capable of defying orders on his own. His ninety-day men's enlistments were up in late July and early August. When he got an order in mid-July detaching five companies of regulars from his service, he told Washington he would refuse to send the men away until the War Department responded to his calls for help. Cameron dropped the matter.[4]

Lyon had avoided dealing with McKinstry even before Frémont's arrival, choosing to house troops in private homes, in commercial buildings, and on the St. Louis Arsenal grounds rather than ask the quartermaster to requisition housing. He also refused to go through official channels to obtain draft animals. McKinstry, annoyed that Lyon had done an end run around him for supplies because he didn't trust the shifty quartermaster, now slow-walked supplies to the general as he inched southwestward. Supplies that were ordered just after Lyon left Boonville in mid-June were still sitting at the railhead in Rolla seven weeks later.[5]

"The want of supplies has crippled me so that I cannot move, and I do not know when I can," Lyon wrote to Chester Harding, a moderately famous portrait painter serving as Lyon's assistant adjutant in St. Louis. He asked Harding to beseech McClellan and the War Department as well as Frémont, whose arrival was at that point still more than a week away. Playing his trump card, Lyon implored Harding to "stir up Blair." Otherwise, he warned, "I must . . . abandon my position."[6]

Once Frémont made it to St. Louis, Lyon flooded the newly arrived commander with pleas for troops and supplies. Desperate for help and hearing nothing, Lyon dispatched two couriers to St. Louis to appeal to Frémont in person. Capt. John Cavender left camp on the day of Frémont's arrival, July 25, and John S. Phelps, the slaveholding unionist congressman from Springfield, a loyal island in southwestern Missouri, departed on July 27. Cavender met briefly with Frémont on the afternoon of July 26 and was asked to come back at 9:00 p.m. When he returned, he found the headquarters dark and shuttered. He tracked down Capt. John Kelton, Frémont's adjutant, who assured Cavender that a paymaster was on the way with two months' pay for the troops and that reinforcements would soon follow. Somewhat reassured, Cavender left St. Louis the next day to report back to Lyon. He told the general that Frémont had displayed a "shocking indifference" to the army's plight. Despite Kelton's assurances, neither the pay nor the reinforcements arrived. Phelps followed Cavender into town and described Lyon's predicament to Frémont, suggesting that withdrawing was just as dangerous as fighting. Staying in place and doing nothing was not an option because enlistments of the ninety-day men were about to expire, and all their regiments would have to be replaced, although Lyon believed many would stay if they could be paid. He also told Frémont what the general already knew: "Orders from General Scott strip the entire West of regular forces, and increase the chance of sacrificing it." Frémont downplayed Lyon's predicament. He felt certain that Price's and McCulloch's forces were nowhere near as large as Lyon feared, and in this respect Frémont was correct. In his confidence that "Lyon could take care of himself," he proved less a prophet. His message to Phelps as well as all others lobbying on Lyon's behalf was that, for the immediate future, Cairo would take precedence over southwestern Missouri, and Lyon would have to "do the best he could." Confronted with the facts of the situation, an unhappy Phelps did not report back to Lyon. He headed to Washington to complain to Frank Blair, who took his concerns to Lincoln. The president, worried how it might look politically to abandon a unionist stronghold like Springfield, overrode the strategic decision of the commander in the department and ordered Cameron to send Lyon more men. The units he had in mind were made up of locally raised troops but were, as Lincoln noted, "not yet organized," so they would not be available for weeks and perhaps months. The rashness of Lyon's next move would render Lincoln's politically motivated intercession militarily moot.[7]

Events were piling up on Frémont. Brig. Gen. Samuel R. Curtis arrived in St. Louis on August 5. He found Frémont "excited and perplexed" and confessed to his wife that "things look a little squally." Curtis was a West Pointer and Iowa congressman who had resigned his seat to take a Federal army commission. He would play a crucial role in Frémont's life over the next three months. He found Frémont "so busy he can hardly find time to speak even to his Generals but seems very cordial when we do meet." Curtis also expressed "great anxiety about Genl Lyons command." When Gen. Benjamin Prentiss visited St. Louis on August 8, Frémont expressed full confidence in his ability to defend Cairo but told Prentiss that he was "not so well pleased with some other generals he might mention." Frémont named no names, but it would be clear in a matter of days that he was referring to Lyon.[8]

"A SEVERE AND BLOODY CONFLICT"

A Home Guard officer who encountered Nathaniel Lyon in early August found him "very nervous from over-work and anxiety." And then there was the heat. "Men dropped in the ranks as if smitten by lightning," a journalist traveling with the army wrote. Tramping over "the poorest, rockiest, meanest, most God-forsaken country" was especially hard on men not used to such exertions. But even hardy veterans were not immune, including those "who went through the fiery rays of Mexico's sun during the war. . . . [A]ll confessed that they never had known anything comparable." It continued seemingly without end. "For several days past thermometer has been about 95. Some days as high as 107. It boils out ambition and enterprise rapidly," a member of the 13th Illinois recorded on August 3 near Rolla. By August 8, he noted two weeks without rain—"the criks are dry and the wells very low"—and temperatures still over one hundred degrees.[9]

Lyon estimated that Price and McCulloch put together would have about 30,000 men; the real number was closer to 13,500, still more than twice Lyon's force of 5,800 but nothing so overwhelming as Lyon's McClellan-like estimate. To make matters worse, the press echoed Lyon's wild overestimation of the enemy forces, claiming a "six-to-one" advantage for the rebels. Both his officers and his commanding general were urging Lyon to pull back. But, like Frémont, Lyon had spent much of his army career defying authority. He saw no reason to change at this late date.[10]

Lyon had done well enough at West Point that he had his choice of assignment. In selecting the infantry over the more prestigious cavalry or artillery, he gave an early indication that he wasn't playing by the same set of rules as everyone else. Lyon had been arrested by military authorities more than once, court-martialed for mistreatment of a prisoner, and passed over for promotion on multiple occasions. One of his soldiers said of Lyon, "To the men of his company he is a tyrant and every man hates the very sight of him." After he served under Harney in Florida at the tail end of the Seminole War, Lyon's career was revived by a sparkling performance in the Mexican War under Zachary Taylor. Most of his service in California at the end of the war was much less eventful than Frémont's. After the war, though, Lyon was involved in one of the most savage massacres in California history, when he led a company against a displaced Indian village at Clear Lake, about one hundred miles north of San Francisco, killing an estimated two hundred men, women, and children at what became known as Bloody Island.[11]

73

Stationed at Fort Riley at the height of Bleeding Kansas, he nearly fought a duel with an officer from South Carolina. Lyon's time in Kansas helped cement his already strong antislavery sentiments, though he was no proponent of equal rights, and he began to believe that he was an instrument in the hands of God, put in his position for some great reason. Like many white settlers in Bleeding Kansas, he saw slavery as bad for free white labor. A northern Democrat until 1856, he became a Republican at that point and supported Frémont's presidential campaign.

But Frémont would not support Lyon in this campaign. "If he fights, he will do it upon his own responsibility," he told one of Lyon's emissaries. The experience of Bull Run, where the perception was that unready and uncertain officers were pushed forward by overeager politicians, informed Frémont's caution when it came to Lyon's plans.[12]

Supplies reached Springfield from Rolla on August 6, providing full rations for the first time in two weeks. Morale improved accordingly, but the strategic outlook remained unchanged. Lyon convened a council of war on the afternoon of August 8 at which he told his senior commanders, "There is no prospect of our being reinforced at this point; our supply of provisions is running short; there is a superior force in front. . . . It is evident we must retreat." But he did not mean immediately. "Shall we endeavor to retreat without giving the enemy battle beforehand, and run the risk of having to fight every inch along our line of retreat, or shall we attack him in his position, and endeavor to hurt him so that he cannot follow us?" Lyon was "decidedly in favor of the latter plan," but his officers expressed reluctance, in part because many of their troops were exhausted and hungry following a long scouting expedition in the humid one-hundred-degree weather. Lyon agreed to wait for one day but remained committed to attack.[13]

A dispatch carrying Frémont's message to Lyon, written on August 6, arrived on the morning of August 9. According to John Schofield, Lyon's adjutant, Frémont told Lyon that if he "was not strong enough to maintain his position as far in advance of Springfield, he should fall back toward Rolla until reinforcements should meet him." But it was not an order to do so. Lyon tossed the communiqué aside and shouted, "God damn General Frémont! He is a worse enemy to me and the Union cause than Price and McCulloch and the whole damn tribe of rebels in this part of the State!" Lyon reported back to Frémont that he was "at present unable to determine whether I shall be able to maintain my ground or be forced to retire." In the event, he did neither. A reconnaissance force brought back intelligence confirming that Price and McCulloch had joined forces. Lyon reasoned that staying put was no longer tenable and retreating was at least as dangerous as advancing. He called another council of war, and again his officers urged a retreat—as councils of war almost always do—to the railhead at Rolla or to Fort Scott on the Kansas state line. Lyon acknowledged the logic of their position but argued again that first damaging the enemy would make any eventual retreat easier. He also argued that retreat would leave the unionists of Springfield at the mercy of rebel troops and disloyal neighbors and that running away in the face of the enemy "might seriously damage the prestige of the national arms." Others would later take a similar view. A major in the Home Guard argued, "Tens of thousands of brave, but then wavering men, who finally became good Union soldiers, would have gone to the other side" if Lyon had withdrawn. But Lyon's insistence that he was an instrument of God left some army colleagues wondering about his sanity. Schofield worried that Lyon "could not take the cool, soldierly view of the situation."[14]

Lyon's decision to attack defied logic, the opinions of his officers, the desire (although not the orders) of his commander, and his own misguided notion of what was in front of him. Outnumbered as he was two and a half to one, his better chance at victory lay in a retreat to Rolla, where he could be resupplied and reinforced. If the rebels pursued him, he could fight on ground of his choosing. And Lyon believed he was outnumbered five to one, odds that should have made any attack out of the question. Nevertheless, on August 10, he launched the second major battle of the Civil War.

With that attack, Lyon moved from rash to reckless. At the suggestion of Franz Sigel, hero of the St. Louis German community, Lyon divided his outnumbered force, sending Sigel on a flanking movement designed to surprise the rebels from two directions. Whether this decision stemmed from exhaustion, or fear of Sigel's popularity with the German troops, or a belief that it was their best option militarily is a moot point. It was the sort of audacious move that Confederate generals Robert E. Lee and Thomas J. "Stonewall" Jackson would put to effective use later in the war. But Lyon was no Lee, and Sigel was no Stonewall. And their troops, while possessing more military training than many did this early in the war, were not the hardened warriors that the Army of Northern Virginia would boast in 1862 and 1863. They were inexperienced and exhausted.

The armies that collided at Wilson's Creek were representative of the conflict in Missouri and the challenges facing Frémont or anyone else trying to secure the state. Both armies included men from North and South and from multiple foreign countries. Both included slaveholders. Some had brought their slaves with them on campaign. The northern army included abolitionists; the southern army included men who were too poor to own much of anything, let alone a slave. Some northern soldiers helped slaves escape. Others returned escapees to their masters. Some officers in the rebel army had been state convention delegates who opposed secession. Others were enthusiastic secessionists from the start. Five future governors of Arkansas fought in the battle, including one on the Union side.[15]

Before Antietam or Gettysburg, the battle at Wilson's Creek was the first invasion of the United States by the Confederacy, led by the Tennessee-born McCulloch, who had fought in the Texas War of Independence, the Mexican War, and the Indian Wars and dug for gold in California. Sterling Price had a "tendency to quarrel," according to his biographer. He deferred reluctantly to McCulloch, who in those early days of the war was the only Confederate general who was not a West Pointer. But McCulloch was hesitant to attack. Just as Lyon repeatedly complained to Washington about the lack of arms and provisions, McCulloch complained to Richmond. Neither got satisfaction. McCulloch also complained incessantly about the condition, training, and lack of discipline among Price's Missouri troops, which he said were "badly organized, badly armed," with "no concert of action among them, and will not be [organized] until a competent military man is put in command of the entire force." Price was not that man, in McCulloch's eyes. He agreed to attack only after Price threatened to detach his Missourians and attack Lyon without McCulloch's Confederates or Arkansas state troops. Before that could happen, Lyon would beat him to the punch.[16]

Neither army was in especially good shape to fight—unpaid, underfed, uniforms in tatters, shoes disintegrating, suffering from illnesses caused by poor diet and exposure to extreme weather. Sigel's flanking maneuver proved disastrous when he mistook an attacking Louisiana force for friendly Iowans who were outfitted in gray. As they marched into battle, Lyon had forty-three hundred men and ten guns. Sigel had about twenty-two hundred. Lyon left twelve hundred men and one section of artillery behind to guard Springfield. Outnumbered and ignorant of what was happening to Sigel, Lyon was wounded twice and then killed in a desperate charge toward the end of the fighting. The northern army retreated to Springfield, leaving hundreds of dead and wounded on the field.

Wilson's Creek, a battle that should not have been fought, was another disaster for the North, renewing the humiliation of Manassas, fought just three weeks earlier. Sterling Price called the battle "a severe and bloody conflict," and so it was for both sides. The Federals lost an estimated 285 killed, 873 wounded, and 186 missing, a casualty rate of almost one in four. The Confederates suffered

277 dead and 945 wounded, a rate about half that of the Union army. But even beyond the dead and wounded, this loss following so closely on the heels of the defeat at Manassas was a psychological blow to the North and raised questions about the efficacy of Frémont's command.[17]

After the fighting ended, the rumors began, with an assist from Frémont, who reported Price and McCulloch both killed in his first brief telegraphic report to Washington. That misinformation would be cleared up quickly, but Frémont would not send a full report until the end of the month. By then, it was clear to all, if it hadn't been before, that "the slaughter . . . convinces our boys that this war is no boys play."[18]

The Confederates, worn down and with their senior commanders arguing among themselves, were in no condition to pursue the retreating enemy. The three prongs of the southern army would soon break into their constituent pieces and go their own ways. Despite the defeat, Sigel managed to carry $250,000 in specie from the Springfield Bank off the battlefield. Along with the money came 721 wounded who were taken from Springfield to the terminal of the Southwest Branch of the Pacific Railroad at Rolla, 110 miles in rickety ambulances and springless army wagons, over rough roads, arriving on August 17. From there, it was on to St. Louis by train. Barely any preparations had been made, and when the first hundred or so men arrived late at night on August 18, most had had nothing to eat for at least ten hours, and many had undressed wounds. Their uniforms were soaked with blood, and there were no clean clothes to change into. Helped off the train, they were transferred to furniture carts, and volunteers toted them the last three miles to the New House of Refuge Hospital, just south of the city. They found little comfort there. It had opened only four days before the battle and was ill equipped for the task, having "neither stoves, nor bedsteads, nor beds, nor bedding, nor food, nor nurses, nor any thing prepared," including food.[19]

The surgeons enlisted neighbors to scare up some grub, but most men had to lie on the floor for lack of beds. As hundreds more poured in, accoutrements finally began to arrive. Men were moved from the floor to beds, and, by the end of August, the facility began to have the semblance of a real hospital. Other hospitals in the city were made available as well, but they filled up quickly as hundreds more men arrived at the 14th Street train station.[20]

Four days after the battle, Connecticut governor William Buckingham asked Missouri governor Hamilton Gamble to "have the body of General Lyon preserved for transportation to this state." After a circuitous journey that included a stay in Congressman Phelps's icehouse and a brief burial in a cornfield,

Lyon's disinterred remains arrived in St. Louis by train on the evening of August 26. They were taken to Frémont's headquarters, where they lay in repose for two days. Thousands passed by to see the fallen hero's casket. Frémont's special order praised Lyon's "prowess and undying devotion to duty." Frank Blair, who had rushed to St. Louis from Washington following the battle, joined the train that carried Lyon's remains to Connecticut.[21]

Lyon, the first Union general to die in battle, might not have been the most significant casualty as far as Frémont's future was concerned. Cary Gratz, a cousin of the Blairs, was also killed at Wilson's Creek. Frank Blair was born in the Gratz home in Lexington, Kentucky, and the death of this "very dear kinsman" would feed the family's budding disillusionment with Frémont even more than Lyon's death.[22]

In the wake of defeat, Francis Preston Blair laid out in a letter to "My Dear Jessie" his expectations that the Frémonts would do his bidding. He was not subtle: "I shall expect you to exert your utmost influence to carry my points." In the familiar tone they had long shared, the elder Blair assured her he would "let you have what your father called 'the inside view of things' at Washington and you must make me up 'Ceasars commentaries of the civil war' in Missouri." His first demand was to have Frank made a brigadier general of state militia. This position would give him a senior command while permitting him to retain his seat in Congress, which accepting an appointment in the Federal army would prohibit. Lyon's death made Frank's appointment even more important. Knowing his audience, Blair appealed to the vainglory in both Frémonts, hailing the war in Missouri as a cause "to ennoble in History the man who gains a triumph and the country which is to be aggrandized by it. To be the chief to conduct to such results, is a superiority rashly more eminent than that at which we arrived in 1856." Blair also offered a piece of sound advice: "In these revolutionary times energy and promptitude & enthusiasm guided by intelligence must take the place of slow routine." It was advice Frémont might have profited by had he applied those virtues in a different direction than the one he chose. He did, however, ask the governor to commission Frank (then a colonel) as a brigadier general of state volunteers, citing a "want of superior officers to whom important trusts may be confided." Gamble refused, asserting that he did not have the authority to make such an appointment, and recommended Lincoln handle it, which he did.[23]

Attorney General Edward Bates was also handing out advice, urging Governor Gamble, his brother-in-law, to "cooperate heartily with the Federal powers, whether you exactly approve of everything done or not." With the city swamped with wounded, an army demoralized by defeat, and a threat of attack from west and south, Frémont declared martial law on August 14 in St. Louis (an action Gamble most certainly did not approve of), and he appointed the dubious quartermaster, Justus McKinstry, as provost marshal in charge of policing the city and county.[24]

Secretary of War Simon Cameron had empowered Frank Blair to declare martial law back in May, an authority Blair never used. Now that Frémont had, coupled with the defeat at Wilson's Creek, Washington was stirred to act. On August 15, Lincoln wired Frémont, "The War Department has notified all Governors you designate to forward all available forces." The next day, Montgomery Blair wired, "Every available man and all the money in the public chest have been sent. We will send more money immediately. . . . Let our fellows cheer up; all will be well." Frémont wasn't entirely reassured by these guarantees. He wrote to Henry Stevens and Frederick Billings on August 17, urging them to "hurry up any and all" of the arms he had ordered in Europe for which they were acting as agents. "Don't, pray, wait for all, if there is delay, but send each 1000 as it can be got ready." Within days, he ordered Ulysses S. Grant (whom Frémont had given his first combat command of the war) to send detachments from Jefferson City to Lexington, Liberty, and Paris to seize the deposits of the Farmer's Bank, which was suspected of disloyalty.[25]

The same day that the postmaster general assured Frémont that all would be well, the victorious Ben McCulloch issued his own proclamation to the people of the state: "Missouri must be allowed to choose her own destiny; no oaths binding your consciences will be administered. I have driven the enemy from among you. The time has now arrived for the people of the State to act; you cannot longer procrastinate. Missouri must now take her position, be it North or South." Frémont would soon respond with a proclamation of his own that would not decide the question for Missouri but would play a significant role in changing the nature of the war.[26]

"Select, fit up and furnish suitable buildings"

The army's unpreparedness in dealing with the casualties from Wilson's Creek also prompted Frémont to respond. An early chronicler of the Western Sanitary Commission wrote, "The necessity for it was both sudden and unexpected." It might have been sudden, but it shouldn't have been unexpected. A volunteer in the 24th Missouri Infantry recalled the "water at Benton Barracks was bad, and malarial fevers, diarrhea, and cholera-morbus prevailed among the men." Frémont had witnessed the unsanitary conditions at Cairo and Bird's Point. A doctor with the U.S. Sanitary Commission had been sent west in the first week of August to offer advice. In the wake of Wilson's Creek, the need became even more obvious.[27]

Reverend William Greenleaf Eliot, a native New Englander, was pastor of the Unitarian Church of the Messiah, the house of worship for many of St. Louis's elite. Shortly after the war started, Eliot organized the St. Louis Provident Society, a clearinghouse for the city's many charities. In late August, he went to Jessie with a plan to improve the hospital situation in the city. Jessie had already written to Dorothea Dix, asking her to come to St. Louis to assess the situation. Dix, whom Jessie had befriended in Washington in the 1850s, endorsed Eliot's plan for an independent western commission. The U.S. Sanitary Commission, created in the third month of the war with official sanction from the president and the War Department, sent a representative to St. Louis to discuss bringing the western theater under its umbrella. Frémont heard them out but predictably opted for Eliot's independent proposal. On September 5, he issued General Orders No. 159, establishing the Western Sanitary Commission "with a view to the health and comfort of the Volunteer Troops in and near the City of St. Louis" and empowering it to "select, fit up and furnish suitable buildings for Army and Brigade Hospitals, in such places and in such manner as circumstances require." The words were Eliot's, the handwriting Jessie Frémont's, and the signature John's.[28]

The four men who joined Eliot on the commission were all members of his church, and all but one were native New Englanders. The fifth was a former slaveowner from Tennessee. Their first task was to find a site for a much larger hospital than the city now had, to accommodate up to five hundred patients. A five-story building in the heart of the city, at the corner of 5th and Chestnut Streets, was rented and quickly prepared. It opened on September 10 and just as quickly filled.[29]

The Western Sanitary Commission set up its headquarters in this new facility, dubbed City General Hospital. Over the next two months, the organization opened an additional five hospitals across the city. As the war in Missouri intensified, bringing fresh batches of wounded to St. Louis, Frémont ordered the commission to set up a pair of railroad cars with medical facilities, "probably the first hospital cars prepared and furnished as such in the United States," a historian of the Western Sanitary Commission noted. Those trains would then deposit wounded at a makeshift receiving hospital set up right at the station, also a first that was widely emulated in other theaters of war. The commission also established a 160-bed hospital to handle measles patients, set up a smallpox ward at the existing City Quarantine Grounds, and built a convalescent center for one thousand wounded at Benton Barracks.[30]

The U.S. Sanitary Commission, under the guidance of another Unitarian minister, Henry Bellows, belittled and resented the upstart western organization. It also had big hitters from East Coast cities on its board, and they argued—in the name of efficiency, of course—that the Western Sanitary Commission needed to be brought under the national organization's umbrella. Bellows detailed J. S. Newberry, in charge of the U.S. Sanitary Commission's western department, to St. Louis to try to talk some sense into the upstarts. Bellows had a hint of what he was in for. He was a friend of Thomas Starr King, who had warned him that Mrs. Frémont was "sublime, and carries guns enough to be formidable to a whole Cabinet; a she-Merrimac, thoroughly sheathed and carrying fire in the genuine Benton furnaces." She acted as the go-between for her husband and Eliot.[31]

Backed by both Frémonts and Dix, Eliot stood his ground. He patiently explained the necessity of being able to respond quickly to circumstances without waiting for advice or assistance from the east. Frémont could certainly sympathize with that position. After Newberry left, Eliot headed to Washington to lobby his organization's case on his own. He met with Cameron and enlisted Bates. Montgomery Blair's place as a second Missourian in the cabinet didn't hurt in defending the Western Sanitary Commission's independence. The St. Louis–based commissioners promised cooperation with the U.S. Sanitary Commission but refused to be subsumed.[32]

The Western Sanitary Commission arose out of a military necessity and the justified belief that the western armies would get no more attention from medical professionals in the East than they had from military professionals. It also rested on Frémont's desire to maintain a modicum of independence and on Jessie's desire to contribute in concrete ways.

* * *

Franz Sigel arrived in St. Louis on August 27 from Wilson's Creek, via Rolla, and met with Frémont, Blair, and some of the general's staff. After the meeting, Sigel went to his house on Gratiot Street, where a late-night crowd gathered to serenade him. He gave a speech in English and German, urging unity in this moment of peril. Whatever had happened in the field, Sigel remained popular among his fellow Germans and apparently still had Frémont's confidence. The *Anzeiger des Westens* rallied on behalf of both. "Give a cheer for the men on whom our hopes for a happy future rest," the paper exulted. "Long live Frémont! Long live Sigel."[33]

In the northern part of the state, Brig. Gen. John Pope was optimistic that his plan to put locals in charge of subduing their rebellious neighbors would bear fruit but warned, "If the people of the Counties are not willing or not able to preserve peace among themselves and to prevent the open organization of military companies to make war, the military forces of the United States will perform the service." And he intended to charge them for it.[34]

Ulysses S. Grant, operating in the middle of the state, feared that "the country West of here will be left in a starving condition for next Winter. Families are being driven away in great numbers for their Union sentiments, leaving behind farms, crops, stock, and all." Rebel sympathizers were swooping in and carrying it all away. Samuel Curtis, the congressman turned general from Iowa, reported to his wife, "While I am everywhere trying make excuses for our Government I confess it is humiliating to see how destitute we now are when the enemy is at our very doors."[35]

At this point, Frank Blair remained conditionally supportive of Frémont, writing to brother Montgomery on August 24 of his hope "that General Frémont be clothed with power to do just as he pleases & have all the money he wants and that he be held responsible for results." That same day, Montgomery—who was blaming Lincoln (and, by implication, Winfield Scott), not Frémont—wrote the general about the president, "He is of the whig school, and that brings him naturally not only to incline to the feeble policy of whigs, but to give his confidence to such advisers." The Blairs' confidence in Frémont began to fade soon after. Just five days later, Frank confided, "I am beginning to lose my confidence in Frémont's capacity. He seems to occupy himself with trifles and does not grasp the great points of the business." There were rumblings elsewhere as well. "I cannot help feeling disposed to join in the general clammer against the Commander in chief who ought to admonish his Generals everywhere against such detachments," Samuel Curtis complained of the late Lyon's decision to divide his army in two. But, of course, Lyon had ignored Frémont's admonishment not to attack at all.[36]

There was some truth in Frank Blair's assessment of Frémont (and in Montgomery's of Lincoln), but it was also true that Frémont and Blair had differing ideas about exactly what the "great points of the business" were—and on those, Lincoln agreed with Blair, not Frémont. On August 26, the president countermanded Frémont's order to bring a Kentuckian, Col. Lovell H. Rousseau, to St. Louis. Rousseau, who had served in the state legislatures of both his home state and Indiana, was an experienced officer, having served in the Mexican War. He had played a crucial role in organizing and recruiting pro-Union companies in southern Indiana and the Bluegrass State, and he might have been invaluable to Frémont in organizing the massive new army taking shape in Missouri. "Intelligent gentlemen at Louisville"—including Lincoln's longtime friends James and Joshua Speed—"say the presence of Rousseau's regiment is needed there," the president explained. "Pardon us for countermanding your order to him to join your department." To Frémont, Lincoln's reversal was just one more piece of evidence that the West was being neglected. It should have been a signal that the "carte blanche" Frémont believed he had been given would not be quite so blanche as he had supposed. But transferring an officer from one command to another was relatively unimportant. Frémont's authority to act was about to be tested on an infinitely more significant issue.[37]

CHAPTER FOUR

"To strike at cause as well as consequence"

On July 4, Congress convened in special session to endorse Lincoln's actions following the attack on Fort Sumter and to consider legislation necessary to carry on the war. In his message to Congress, the president justified the steps he had taken, explained why be believed secession was unconstitutional, and asked lawmakers to "give the legal means for making this contest a short, and decisive one." He also asked for an army of four hundred thousand men and $400 million to pay for it. Lincoln would get the money and the men (Frank Blair, as chairman of the House Military Affairs Committee, pushed the former number up to five hundred thousand). But Lincoln also got a House committee, chaired by Charles Van Wyck of New York, to investigate army procurement practices, which would prove a thorn in the sides of both Frémont and the Lincoln administration. In the 6,261 words of Lincoln's message, the word "slave" appears but once, in a reference to "the States commonly called slave States." There was not so much as a nod toward emancipation.[1]

Congress met for nearly five weeks, though some members at first wondered whether it needed to hang around that long. Lincoln's Illinois ally, Owen Lovejoy, wrote on July 14 that he thought the session might be over in a few days. But as the northern army began moving, first toward the enemy and then in retreat back to Washington, Congress found plenty to do. It also found things not to do, rejecting a resolution urging the army to "speedily advance" because it was deemed unnecessary, as the army was preparing to move, and because it "would imply a censure of the commanding Gen.," wrote Illinois senator Lyman Trumbull, a onetime rival and sometime ally of Lincoln but not a close friend. "The disinclination to do anything which may look like censure of the administration, or a want of confidence in the infallibility of Gen. Scott is such that it seems to control the majority."[2]

After Manassas, Kentucky congressman John Crittenden, with Tennessee senator Andrew Johnson, introduced resolutions in each chamber intended to define the purpose of the war. The Crittenden-Johnson Resolution asserted as resolved "that this war is not waged . . . in any spirit of oppression, or for any purpose of conquest or subjugation, or purpose of overthrowing or interfering with the rights or established institutions of those States, but to defend and maintain the supremacy of the Constitution, and to preserve the Union with all the dignity, equality, and rights of the several States unimpaired; and that as soon as these objects are accomplished the war ought to cease." As Lincoln had stressed in his message to Congress, this was a war to preserve the Union, not to end slavery.[3]

The last of Crittenden's four Senate terms had ended with the 36th Congress. Like his Kentucky mentor Henry Clay, he consistently sought compromise. He served as a delegate to the forlorn peace conference held at the Willard Hotel during the secession winter. When that effort failed, he unsuccessfully proposed a package of constitutional amendments designed to appease the South. When that also failed, he went home and won election to the House. In an earlier life, Crittenden's Washington home had been a refuge for John C. Frémont and Jessie Benton—the eloping couple were married at the Crittenden house in 1841. Now Crittenden, with a son in each army, looked desperately for a way to limit the bloodshed. He believed a conciliatory attitude toward the wayward sister states was the best path.

Critics of Crittenden held him up as a relic. "But for the indignity which would be offered his constituents thereby, the members of the next Congress might properly box up Mr. Crittenden in a glass case, and hand him down to other generations, as a specimen of the Compromisers of 1861," one newspaper opined. "His days of usefulness are gone, if any such he ever had." To abolitionist congressman George W. Julian of Indiana, the Crittenden-Johnson Resolution "seemed like an apology for the war, and a most ill-timed revival of the policy of conciliation."[4]

That seemed to be a minority opinion. The House passed its version of Crittenden's resolution 119–2, and the Senate passed Johnson's 30–5. Significantly, the only Republican senator to oppose the resolution was Trumbull, who had pushed for the resolution urging the army to speedily advance. For Lincoln and the majority of Congress, the sole purpose of the war was the preservation of the Union. But almost from the moment northern soldiers moved onto southern soil, the effect of the war was emancipation. On May 23, 1861, a mere six weeks after the fall of Fort Sumter, three Virginia slaves made off with a boat at Sewall's Point on the northern edge of Norfolk and rowed across Hampton Roads to Fortress Monroe. The next day, the voters of Virginia endorsed the state convention's ordinance of secession.[5]

Gen. Benjamin Butler, a Massachusetts Democrat and onetime law partner of Martin Van Buren, was one of those political generals Lincoln had appointed. In command at Fort Monroe, he knew the Confederates were using slave labor to build fortifications, and he had no intention of sending the three men back to aid the enemy. When an agent for their owner came calling to collect his "property," Butler handed him a receipt instead, promising the men would be returned when the war was over. To demands that he must abide by the Fugitive Slave Act, Butler pointed out that Virginia had just seceded from the Union; it was no longer a state and therefore no longer covered by the law. But he needed a rationale for keeping them, and he found one in the laws of war. "Property of whatever nature, used or capable of being used for warlike purposes, and especially when being so used, may be captured and held either on sea or on shore as property contraband of war," he reasoned. "Whether there may be property in human beings is a question upon which some of us might doubt, but the rebels cannot take the negative."[6]

Butler wrote to Washington for instructions, and the cabinet gave his action a thumbs-up. Word spread quickly. Wherever they could, slaves began flooding toward Union lines. Within days, the *New York Times* reported, "Slaves are running away from their masters in troops."

Many had foreseen this outcome. Writing to abolitionist Wendell Phillips back in February, Lincoln's law partner, William Herndon, predicted that "disunion is Freedom to the slave." Lincoln himself had warned southerners in an 1859 speech in Cincinnati, across the Ohio from Kentucky, that, in the event of secession or war, the North would be "under no obligation whatever to return those specimens of your moveable property that come hither."[7]

Now that the exodus had begun, Congress felt it necessary to go beyond Butler's ad hoc policy. Lyman Trumbull, who had won election to the Senate in 1855 by defeating Lincoln, led the way. A strong proponent of congressional war powers, he had no intention of leaving the conduct of the war to the president and the generals. Trumbull reasoned that anywhere civilian authority had broken down, the military could fill the legal vacuum without recourse to traditional due process limits. If a soldier is empowered to kill the enemy and not be arrested, then, surely, he could also seize their property. He wanted Congress to codify that reasoning. Since Trumbull and other antislavery advocates refused to acknowledge that those held in bondage were property, they made the case that the "property" being seized was the slaves' labor, not the slaves themselves. "The bayonets of our brave soldiers are the 'due process of law' authorized by the Constitution to put down this wicked rebellion," he argued.[8]

On July 20, a day before Manassas, Trumbull offered an amendment to a bill that had just been reported out of the Senate Judiciary Committee, of which he was chairman. The amendment, in language that studiously avoided use of the term "slave" (reflecting the Constitution), stated, "That whenever any person claiming to be entitled to the service or labor of any other person, under the laws of any State, shall employ such person in aiding or promoting any insurrection, or in resisting the laws of the United States, or shall permit or suffer him to be so employed, he shall forfeit all rights to such service or labor, and the person whose labor or service is thus claimed shall be henceforth discharged therefrom." Border-state members objected to the discharge language, considering it "wholesale emancipation." The House amended the bill to remove the final clause and sent the measure back to the Senate on August 3. Two days later, the Senate cleared the measure for the president's signature. One congressman called it "the first law since the organization of the Federal Government by which a slave could acquire his freedom." The first legislative step on the road to emancipation had been taken.[9]

When the Senate sent Lincoln the bill, the president wavered. He feared it violated both Fifth Amendment due process protections and Article III guarantees against bills of attainder. He also had political concerns about its effect on loyal slaveholders in the border states, particularly Kentucky. But he set those reservations aside after some lobbying by members of Congress and signed the bill into law on August 6.[10]

Two days later, in a note to Ben Butler, Secretary of War Simon Cameron detailed how the new law should be enforced. While stressing that "the war now prosecuted on the part of the Federal Government is a war for the Union," he also wrote that the Confiscation Act "declares that if persons held to service shall be employed in hostility to the United States the right to their services shall be forfeited and such persons shall be discharged therefrom." That's not what the law said, the clause on "discharge" having been excised. But Cameron's order effectively put it back in, at least for disloyal owners. Loyal owners would also forfeit their property under Cameron's order. The final disposition of their slaves was left to be sorted out by Congress or the courts "upon the return of peace."[11]

Lincoln would not alter Cameron's order until he issued the Emancipation Proclamation, but at this point he remained a somewhat reluctant emancipator. In his July 4 message to Congress, Lincoln had asserted, "It may well be questioned whether there is, to-day, a majority of the legally qualified voters of any state, except perhaps South Carolina, in favor of disunion." This belief in the tenacity of unionism in the South was the foundation of Lincoln's pursuit of conciliation and the justification for fighting what came to be known as "soft war." As historian Elizabeth R. Varon wrote, for Lincoln, "the premise of the Union war was that white Southerners could be redeemed."[12]

In this pursuit, Lincoln had allies in William Seward and Edward Bates. While Lincoln was still putting his team together in December 1860, Seward had suggested to Thurlow Weed, "If Southern members will be for once cautious and forbearing; if we can keep peace and quiet for a time, the temper will be favorable on both sides to consultation." Missourian Bates had suggested leaking news of his appointment as attorney general to foment good feeling in the border states, a proposal Lincoln endorsed. Sumter changed the views of neither man.[13]

One goal of conciliationists and hard-war advocates was the same: persuade southerners to give up the dream of a separate country and return to the Union. The question was whether that goal would be accomplished with honey or vinegar. Lincoln's top general, Winfield Scott, who had conducted a soft war toward Mexican civilians, and those who had served under him as junior officers, such as George McClellan, endorsed the former. Frémont and some of the other political generals—particularly Butler—had a clearer sense of the politics of the war than did these West Pointers, even as they fumbled their military response to it.[14]

Frémont had fought in a different theater in the Mexican War than Scott and McClellan and held a different view of the current conflict. In his stirring oration in May to the Americans in Paris, Frémont, too, had focused on preserving the Union and paid no heed to emancipation. His actual record on the issue was scant and not all that inspiring. As a Democratic senator, he had supported ending the slave trade in Washington, DC, but opposed emancipation in the district. As a presidential candidate, he endorsed the 1856 Republican platform that called for no extension of slavery into new territory but accepted the political consensus that the federal government could do nothing about slavery where it existed. In Paris, he had declared, "Most gladly would we welcome back our people, if they would return to their allegiance." It now seemed clear to Frémont that was not going to happen. One month in Missouri had hardened his attitude toward both rebellion and slavery. Ulysses S. Grant had gone through a similar evolution in southeastern Missouri. John Pope had always supported harsh measures. The commanders' attitudes were reflected on the ground, where soldiers and civilians were already practicing hard war of a kind not seen in other theaters (and, in an exception to his general rule in the first months of the war, tacitly endorsed by Lincoln via Blair, whose tough response in early 1861 had not caused the bitter division in Missouri but merely revealed it sooner than in other states). Frémont had an ally in Trumbull, author of the Confiscation Act. On the last day of the month, Trumbull wrote a grumbling letter in which he expressed fear that "the men at the head of affairs do not realize our condition & are not equal to the occasion. The war must be conducted on different principles or it will never end, except in a dismemberment of the Union & the humiliation of the North." And he praised Frémont's efforts in Missouri: "Frémont has done more in organizing & getting together an efficient army in four weeks than had previously been done in four months, & this, too, without means. He has had to assume responsibility, act without orders, & even borrow money to get along." Now Frémont would join those efforts to Trumbull's Confiscation Act to conduct the war on "different principles."[15]

"THEIR SLAVES . . . ARE HEREBY DECLARED FREEMEN"

On August 30, Brig. Gen. Ulysses S. Grant wrote to Western Department Assistant Adjutant General John Kelton from Cape Girardeau, 115 miles south of St. Louis, that "a number of contrabands in the shape of negroes are being employed apparently much to their satisfaction." Having adopted Butler's terminology, Grant informed Kelton that he would "make inquiry how they came here, and if the fact has not been previously reported ask instructions."[16]

That same day, demonstrating that Frémont was still in the Blairs' good graces, Montgomery telegraphed Frémont to be on the "lookout for your share" of one hundred new officers approved for service in volunteer regiments. The years of close friendship and the days of such comity were about to come to an end. To some abolitionists, Frank Blair's election to Congress in 1856 had been a portent of an emancipated border, although Blair utterly rejected the immediacy of the abolitionist movement. He was, in journalist Noah Brooks's phrase, a "gradual (very gradual) emancipationist." Frémont's and Blair's visions of what emancipation would look like were worlds apart.[17]

After the special congressional session ended, Blair returned to St. Louis. While he occasionally met with Frémont, the two men's duties did not allow for much camaraderie. Walled up behind a loyal staff, Frémont spent most of his eighteen-hour days working alone or consulting with his wife and a few trusted aides. When, at the end of August, he decided to expand martial law statewide and take a monumental step toward emancipation, it was a solitary affair. Frémont later told Lincoln he acted "without consultation or advice with any one" and spent the night of August 29 alone working on the text. For Frémont, such a heedless act was perfectly believable. Not only had he not consulted or informed Lincoln, but he also hadn't told Blair or Governor Hamilton Gamble, whose authority he was usurping via the martial law declaration. (The governor had been inundated with complaints about "abolitionists" taking over militia units. In response, on August 5, he had issued a statement declaring, "No countenance will be afforded to any scheme or to any conduct calculated in any degree to interfere with the institution of slavery existing in the State. To the very utmost extent of my Executive power, that institution will be protected.") On August 30, Frémont shared his decision with Jessie and Capt. Edward M. Davis, a family friend serving as assistant quartermaster. Davis was a Quaker who had set aside his pacifism to accept an army commission and the son-in-law of women's rights advocate Lucretia Mott. Both listeners were enthusiastic, but Davis told Frémont that Lincoln would never let the emancipation provision stand. Frémont waved away Davis's warning and had the proclamation printed and distributed that day. Davis alerted fellow abolitionist Sydney Howard Gay, an editor at the *New York Tribune*, who published it on August 31.[18]

The chaotic situation in Missouri clearly justified a declaration of martial law. Lincoln had recognized this fact as far back as April, when he empowered Frank Blair to take the step in St. Louis if he felt it necessary. Blair had demurred. Frémont did not. "Circumstances, in my judgment, of sufficient urgency render it necessary that the commanding general of this department should assume the administrative powers of the State," he began. "Its disorganized condition, the helplessness of the civil authority, the total insecurity of life, and the devastation of property by bands of murderers and marauders, who infest nearly every county of the State, and avail themselves of the public misfortunes and the vicinity of a hostile force to gratify private and neighborhood vengeance, and who find an enemy wherever they find plunder, finally demand the severest measures to repress the daily increasing crimes and outrages which are driving off the inhabitants and ruining the State." Citing both "the public safety and the success of our arms," Frémont, who had placed St. Louis under martial law two weeks earlier, "established martial law throughout the State of Missouri." Anyone captured with arms would be tried by court-martial and shot on conviction. Missouri, though still in the Union, was now effectively under Federal occupation. The personal property of anyone in rebellion would be confiscated, and, the kicker, "their slaves, if any they have, are hereby declared freemen."[19]

Frémont justified emancipation as a military necessity, "to place in the hands of the military authorities the power to give instantaneous effect to existing laws, and to supply such deficiencies as the conditions of war demand."[20]

The martial law declaration was popular in some quarters. *Anzeiger des Westens* endorsed "summary punishment, including execution for spies and other cohorts of rebels." New York diarist George Templeton Strong called it "war in earnest, at last." There was some doubt about whether it would have much effect, though. Gen. Samuel Curtis, an Iowa congressman commanding at Jefferson Barracks, worried, "Under the order restricting the military action in carrying it out I do not think it can make much show." This was because Frémont had ordered, "The law will be administered by the civil officers in the usual manner, and with their customary authority, while the same can be peaceably exercised." Curtis had little faith that Missouri's courts would hold rebels' feet to the fire. For all its shortcomings, no subsequent commander in Missouri over the next four years sought to revoke the martial law declaration.[21]

But, as Curtis noted, it was not martial law but "the abolition Clause [that would] make more noise than any thing," although it met with his "cordial approval." Many shared these sentiments. Frémont's proclamation was "the inevitable result of the rebel war," according to the *New York Times*. Jessie contended that "Frémont's order struck the first blow for freedom for the slave, and declared war on slavery as well as on secession." Whatever other effects it had, the order inspired abolitionists and antislavery advocates in the North, giving them greater cause to believe in the mission of the war.[22]

"Are you not greatly cheered by Frémont's Proclamation? Is it not 'the beginning of the end,' and is not the end near?" abolitionist William Lloyd Garrison asked fellow movement leader Gerrit Smith.[23]

James Bowen, president of the New York City Board of Police Commissioners and later provost marshal in New Orleans, wrote to John Bigelow, a Frémont supporter in 1856 who had since soured on the Pathfinder, that it was "wonderful to see the general approval of the act. . . . I have not yet seen the man either democrat or republican who doubts its wisdom." Plenty would soon appear.[24]

Official Washington, as officialdom generally is, was a bit more wary. Treasury Secretary Salmon Chase, who had labored in the antislavery cause as long as anyone in power, took a cautious approach. He was inundated with letters protesting the proclamation but defended it in legalistic terms, suggesting that the outcome would rest on the battlefield. "My own judgment is that it is capable of a fair construction wh. will restrict its effect to the simple recognition &

enforcement" of the Confiscation Act, enacted three and half weeks earlier. "It is by no means likely that Genl. F------ intended it shd. have any more." He was confident that "there is no occasion for alarm." But he also made a prediction: "shd. this war be prolonged . . . a fatal result to Slavery will be well nigh inevitable."[25]

But would it? Even if Chase was right about the states in rebellion, the loyal slaveholding states were a different matter. Missouri (and Kentucky) had pro-slavery governors and vociferous and volatile slave-owning elites. Considering Frank Blair's reputation for defying authority, it was likely that Frémont's tendency toward insubordination was an attraction rather than a deterrent in Blair's initial recommendation of him to Lincoln. Blair and Frémont were kindred spirits in some ways, but they had different political goals and disparate views of slavery. Still, Frank endorsed the substance of Frémont's proclamation, telling Montgomery it was "the best thing of the kind that has been issued," but he qualified that endorsement by suggesting the edict "should have been issued when he first came when he had the power to enforce it & the enemy no power to retaliate." Whether Frémont—undermanned, undergunned, and wholly disorganized—had the means at hand to enforce emancipation a month earlier is a dubious contention, given that he didn't have it a month later.[26]

How Frémont planned to enforce the proclamation was left up in the air, other than his reliance on civil courts. But it was clear that Lincoln's reading of the Confiscation Act was too narrow for Frémont's purposes. The law targeted those "employed in or upon any fort, navy yard, dock, armory, ship, entrenchment, or in any military or naval service whatsoever." In Lincoln's view, that did not encompass field hands working the land or guarding the homestead. But to Frémont and many others, every slave, no matter how far removed from the scene of fighting, was aiding the Confederate cause. Every slave planting corn was feeding a Confederate soldier. Every slave picking cotton was providing hard currency to a Confederacy starved of it. Every slave tending the home fires was replacing a Confederate soldier who did not have to be at home to tend them himself. As Jessie put it, "He determined to force the rebel sympathizers, who did not join the rebel armies as soldiers, to remain at home, and to make them feel that there was a penalty for rebellion, and for aiding those who were in rebellion."[27]

"A spirit of caution and not of censure"

Jessie had once perceptively written to her husband, "I think we share a dislike to being scrutinized." It was an astute observation, and it helps explain why

Frémont was so at home in the lonely wilderness and so lost in the sea of politics. Their tolerance for scrutiny was about to be tested as it had never been before.[28]

On August 5, Kentucky unionists scored an impressive victory, sweeping eight of nine congressional seats. But Joseph Holt, a Kentucky lawyer and newspaper editor who had served briefly as secretary of war at the end of the James Buchanan administration, told Lincoln, "In defiance of the overwhelming popular vote just cast, the traitors in that state are preparing to carry her out of the Union by a coup de main." Now, he worried, Frémont's proclamation might raise questions about "the power & fervor of the loyalty of Kentucky."[29]

Holt's was a voice Lincoln respected, and he was hearing similar sentiments from other Kentuckians. Robert Anderson, the hero of Sumter, said Frémont's proclamation was "producing most disastrous results in this State, and that it is the opinion of many of our wisest and soundest men that if this is not immediately disavowed, and annulled, Kentucky will be lost to the Union."[30]

Joshua Speed, one of Lincoln's oldest and dearest friends, also weighed in. "Our Constitution & laws both prohibit the emancipation of slaves among us—even in small numbers—If a military commander can turn them loose by the thousand by mere proclamation—It will be a most difficult matter to get our people to submit to it," he wrote Lincoln on September 1. He also raised the specter of slave insurrection, believing that the proclamation would inspire the enslaved to revolt. Without waiting for a reply, he wrote more alarmist nonsense two days later: "I have been so much distressed since reading, that (to us and to the union cause) foolish proclamation of Frémont, that I have been unable to eat or sleep—It will crush out every vestige of a union party in the state."[31]

Lincoln would soon enough reassure Speed, Holt, and other Kentuckians. In doing so, he might have reiterated to Speed something that he had said six years earlier regarding slavery: "You ought rather to appreciate how much the great body of the Northern people do crucify their feelings, in order to maintain their loyalty to the constitution and the Union." Six years later, Lincoln seemed to be ignoring his own advice. He had his own legitimate concerns about politics, presidential power, and the border states, but he would presently give short shrift to the feelings about slavery held by "the great body of the Northern people."[32]

Those northern people were coming out in force behind emancipation. "Frémont's proclamation has made a stir," Capt. Robert Gould Shaw wrote to his mother on September 5. Frémont knew the Shaws, who were prominent abolitionists in Massachusetts. He attended the wedding of Captain Shaw's sister in 1856, when Francis and Sarah Shaw were supporting his campaign for the presidency. Shaw admired Frémont and harbored as a "very desirable" hope the possibility of leaving his Virginia posting to join the general's staff in Missouri. "I hope he will not be interfered with by the Government and that the other Generals will follow his example."[33]

John L. Scripps, editor of the *Chicago Tribune*, postmaster of Chicago, and author of Lincoln's 1860 campaign biography, told his benefactor that even while "admitting that the loyal men of Kentucky had the right to object" to Frémont's proclamation, it had "stirred the hearts of the people, as they had not been stirred before since the beginning of the war." And he wondered "whether it is not better to make it satisfactory to the latter, and even if slightly distasteful to the former."[34]

Longtime abolitionist leader Gerrit Smith wrote to Lincoln that the "North will perceive that Frémont has done the right thing, and will demand that it be done elsewhere." Smith also suggested to Lincoln that a full secession by all the slaveholding states would have made his task simpler and the war shorter. "Had all the slave States seceded and all the slaveholders sanctioned the secession, the war would have been over ere this time," he wrote. "Immediately on its breaking out you would have given to the rebellion its death-blow by your proclamation, inviting to our standard all the people of those States. Not only would it have been in your heart to do so—but it would have been in every true Northern heart to have you do so." Lincoln's preoccupation with "conciliating loyal slaveholders" was a mistake, and now Frémont had presented him with the opportunity to rectify it.[35]

Lincoln chose not to do so. Time would soon prove the concerns of Lincoln and such Kentuckians as Holt, Speed, and Anderson to be overblown. In September 1861, however, the president was inclined to address them. Five months into the war, he was still acting more out of caution than boldness. "It would do no good to go ahead any faster than the country would follow," he told a friend of Charles Sumner. "I think Sumner and the rest of you would upset our applecart altogether if you had your way. . . . This thunderbolt will keep." Lincoln might have been right in his analysis of the weakness of Kentucky's commitment to the Union, or he might have been wrong. But, as historian James McPherson wrote, Lincoln believed "he could not take the risk at this stage of the war." Three days after the proclamation was issued, Lincoln responded to Frémont.[36]

"Two points in your proclamation of August 30th give me some anxiety," he began. "First, should you shoot a man, according to the proclamation, the Confederates would very certainly shoot our best man in their hands in retaliation; and so, man for man, indefinitely. It is therefore my order that you allow no man to be shot, under the proclamation, without first having my approbation or consent." And, indeed, on hearing of Frémont's order, Confederate brigadier general M. Jeff Thompson, operating in southeast Missouri, issued his own proclamation in which he promised, "For every member of the Missouri State Guard or soldier of our allies the armies of the Confederate States who shall be put to death in pursuance of said order of General Frémont I will hang, draw and quarter a minion of said Abraham Lincoln." If the Union began executing rebels, Thompson declared, "I intend to exceed General Frémont in his excesses and will make all tories that come in my reach rue the day that a different policy was adopted by their leaders."[37]

Thompson did not address emancipation. Lincoln did. "I think there is great danger that the closing paragraph, in relation to the confiscation of property, and the liberating slaves of traiterous owners, will alarm our Southern Union friends, and turn them against us—perhaps ruin our rather fair prospect for Kentucky." Here, again, Lincoln made a political/military argument, not a constitutional or civil/military argument. Lincoln wasn't worried that Kentucky would secede because Frémont didn't follow the chain of command; he was worried about the effect of emancipation. But he did not order Frémont to rescind the proclamation. Rather, he asked him "as of your own motion" to "modify that paragraph so as to conform to" the relevant portions of the Confiscation Act. He assured Frémont, "This letter is written in a spirit of caution and not of censure."[38]

By asking Frémont to bring his proclamation in line with the Confiscation Act, which was intended to apply to the states in rebellion, the president indicated he was going to treat the law as applying to places in slaveholding states still in the Union where there was considerable anti-Union feeling. That was a small step forward for emancipation even if Frémont's broad order ended up falling.[39]

Less welcome (had Frémont known about it) was another step Lincoln took, this one indicating he was already seriously considering removing Frémont from command. On September 5, the president felt out Gen. Winfield Scott regarding the possibility of sending Maj. Gen. David Hunter to Missouri to act as a guiding force for Frémont and—although he likely did not share this point with Scott—a spy for the administration. Scott pointed out that Hunter was too high a grade to serve as an aide to Frémont, something Lincoln almost certainly knew, which lends credence to the notion that he was preparing to replace the western commander. As an alternative, Scott recommended Brig. Gen. George Stoneman, who Scott believed had the crucial qualities for such an undertaking: "youth, vigor, intelligence discretion, firmness, conciliatory manners," and, unusual for a West Pointer, the quality of being "perhaps the only one of high rank in the entire army who is on tolerable terms with Frémont unless Hunter be a second exception." And one more thing, Scott advised Lincoln: "Among [Stoneman's] rare merits, is this crowning one: to do his country proportionate service, he is always willing to go from the most agreeable to the most disagreeable, post & duty." McClellan wanted to keep Stoneman and recommended Ethan Allen Hitchcock, who was already in St. Louis. Either would have sufficed for the advisory role. But Lincoln didn't know Stoneman as he knew Hunter, a political ally who had traveled on the train to Washington with Lincoln in February. Hitchcock was sixty-three years old, making him an unlikely candidate to take command. Lincoln wanted someone he was closer with to handle the spying part and someone of a sufficiently high rank and stamina to take over if it came to that.[40]

Four days after meeting with Scott, Lincoln asked Hunter to go to Missouri. "Gen. Frémont needs assistance which it is difficult to give him: He is losing the confidence of men near him, whose support any man in his position must have to be successful," Lincoln wrote. "His cardinal mistake is that he isolates himself, & allows nobody to see him; and by which he does not know what is going on in the very matter he is dealing with. He needs to have, by his side, a man of large experience. Will you not, for me, take that place? Your rank is one grade too high to be ordered to it; but will you not serve the country, and oblige me, by taking it voluntarily?" Hunter, reading between the lines, happily obliged.[41]

Ignorant of these machinations, Frémont responded to Lincoln on September 5. He began by explaining that he had not kept Lincoln as fully informed as he might otherwise have done because events were changing so quickly in Missouri that he feared he would be constantly sending contradictory messages. He also worried that so much was happening that a full accounting would take up too much of the president's time. "Trusting to have your confidence I have been leaving it to events themselves to show you whether or not I was shaping affairs here according to your ideas," he explained. As for the proclamation, Frémont was "perfectly willing to receive the amount of censure which should be thought due if I had made a false step." Harking back to Lincoln's granting of "carte blanche" following his appointment, Frémont insisted that martial law and emancipation were "as much a movement in the war as a battle is, and in going with these I shall have to act according to my judgement of the ground before me, as I did on this occasion." And then came the kicker. If Lincoln thought otherwise, "I have to ask that you will openly direct me to make the correction. The implied censure will be received by me as a soldier always should the reprimand of his chief. If I were to retract of my own accord it would imply that I myself thought it wrong and that I had acted without the reflection which the gravity of the point demanded. But I did not do so. I acted with full deliberation and upon the certain conviction that it was a measure right and necessary, and I think so still." As he had told Lincoln's friend, Senator Orville Hickman Browning, who was in St. Louis that week, "he would adhere firmly to his proclamation and carry out the policy he commenced." To carry that message to the president, he appointed Jessie to deliver a copy of the letter to Washington. If Lincoln wanted the emancipation order overturned, he would have to do it himself, in a one-on-one audience with the general's wife.[42]

"QUITE A FEMALE POLITICIAN"

Jessie Benton Frémont had her critics, but the German press was not among them. "Mrs. Lincoln's Movements—this is all we are reading in the papers from back East," snarled the *Anzeiger des Westens*. "The devil take Mrs. Lincoln's movements. With all due respect to the ladies, and particularly to the president's wife, if she will not be like Mrs. Frémont and actually work personally with her husband for the great cause of the nation, then it would be better if she never made herself the subject of conversation."[43]

Jessie had been looking for a chance to return to Washington to make her husband's case almost from the moment of their arrival in St. Louis. Now she had the opportunity. Frémont was swamped with work and visitors. Dorothea Dix had arrived to discuss her role in building up the Western Sanitary Commission using female nurses. Prince Napoleon, cousin of Napoleon III, was in town as part of a tour of the United States, and Frémont had orders from Washington to tend to him "with proper ceremony," which he did with great fanfare. It was routine for Jessie to act in John's stead, and the couple thought nothing of doing it in this instance. "General Frémont had no idea but that I, always in constant intimate friendship with my Father and himself and previous Presidents would not be accepted as qualified to speak and answer for him as formerly. Mr. Frémont judged women as he had been fortunate enough to know them, helping in council as well as home."[44]

Frémont sent the original of his response to Lincoln via the messenger who had brought Lincoln's letter to him. But in typical Frémont fashion, he had little trust in the secrecy or the alacrity of the messenger. So he asked Jessie to go, to deliver the letter "into the President's hand, and to answer—as he knew I could," she wrote, "questions rising from it." Accompanied by her maid, she boarded a train on the evening of September 8, confident she could persuade Lincoln of the justice of her husband's cause. She did not know that Frank Blair had beaten her to the punch.[45]

On September 1, one day before Lincoln penned his response to Frémont, Frank Blair confided to his brother Montgomery his doubts about Frémont's performance. "Men coming here to give information are not allowed to approach him and go away in disgust," he wrote.

> I have felt it my duty to tell him what they say and he throws himself behind the reports of his officers who are trying to prevaricate & shield themselves for neglect of duty and he still clings to them & refuses to see for himself. . . . He talks of the vigor he is going to use, but I can see none of it, and I fear it will turn out to be some rash & inconsiderate move adopted in haste to make head against a formidable force which could not have accumulated except through gross & inexcusable negligence.

Then Blair issued a cry from the heart. "Oh! for one hour of our dead Lyon," he wailed, going on to insist that Nathaniel Lyon would have lived and prevailed if Frémont had reinforced him instead of Cairo. He also noted "the active want of discipline in the camps around & about St. Louis," calling the situation "a rehearsal of the state of affairs in Washington before the fight at Manassas," which he feared would lead to "similar results."[46]

Because "you and I are both in some sort responsible for Frémonts appointment and for his being placed in command of this Department," Blair felt a special necessity to "speak out openly about these matters." But he wasn't speaking out openly. He was writing a letter to his brother, using his position to ensure that the letter made its way to the president and, in the process, violating the military chain of command. And little wonder, since what he suggested was the overthrow of his commanding officer. "My decided opinion is that he should be relieved of his command and a man of ability put in his place—The sooner it is done the better," Frank wrote. He included a disclaimer, telling Montgomery that if he disagreed with his assessment, he could burn the letter, put it down to Frank being an alarmist, and ignore his recommendation. He also tepidly endorsed the emancipation order but did not see that as relevant to the current crisis. "Either the Government has failed to support Frémont as he should have been or he has failed to apply the means at his disposal," he wrote, not considering that both suppositions might be true.[47]

Frank's endorsement of Frémont's proclamation came with considerable strings. His long history of racism—severe among northern men even for the times—went back to his days living in frontier New Mexico, where he confessed to "getting tired of Indians & Mexicans, especially the latter, such a lying, thieving, treacherous, cowardly, bragging & depraved race of people."[48]

Even more than Lincoln, he was a strong proponent of colonization, arguing, "Free blacks hold a place in this country which cannot be maintained. Those who have fled to the North are most unwelcome visitors. The strong repugnance of the free white laborer to be yoked with the negro refugee, breeds an enmity between races, which must end in the expulsion of the latter."[49]

Montgomery shared Frank's letter with Lincoln, as Frank had intended. The president had the Blairs' version of events in his head as Jessie Frémont headed eastward. With no sleeper available, she sat up the nights of September 8 and 9 in the hot, crowded car, arriving in Washington in the early evening of September 10. Two allies met her at the Willard Hotel: New York judge Edward Cowles and Frémont's lawyer, Frederick Billings. She sent her card to the White House, informing the president that she had a letter for him from Frémont and asking when she could come to deliver it. After a short period, the messenger returned: Lincoln would meet with her right away.[50]

She had planned to take a bath and go to bed. Cowles thought that was a good idea. The meeting, he told her, could wait until morning. It was nearly 9:00 p.m. She was worn out from the long train ride and was wearing the same dress she'd had on for three days because her bags had not reached the hotel. But she felt the meeting could not wait. Joined by Cowles, she walked the two blocks from the Willard to the White House. Expecting to see Lincoln immediately— he had written "Now, at once" in response to her request for a meeting—they were instead shown into the Red Room, where they cooled their heels for "some time," according to Jessie's account.[51]

Lincoln entered the room silently and bowed. Jessie introduced Cowles, but the president remained mute. She then handed him the letter, explaining that her husband had felt the contents so important that he had sent her to answer any questions Lincoln might have. "At this he smiled with an expression that was not agreeable," she wrote, and moved closer to a chandelier so he could see to read. He did not offer her a seat, so she pulled a chair out on her own and slumped tiredly into it. Cowles retreated to the doorway, leaving her alone with Lincoln.

When Lincoln finished reading the letter, he pulled up a chair next to her and sat down. "I have written to the General and he knows what I want done," he said.

She repeated that she was there to explain the situation more fully. "The General feels he is at the great disadvantage of being perhaps opposed by people in whom you have every confidence," she said.

"What do you mean?" Lincoln asked. "Persons of differing views?"

"The General's conviction is that it will be long and dreadful work to conquer by arms alone, that there must be other consideration to get us the support of foreign countries," she said. As Lincoln knew, she continued, "we were on the eve of England, France and Spain recognizing the South; they were anxious for a pretext to do so; England on account of her cotton interests, and France because the Emperor dislikes us."

"You are quite a female politician," Lincoln responded.

At that, Jessie's confidence dissolved. "I felt the sneering tone and saw there was a foregone decision against all listening," she wrote.

Then Lincoln stated, "The General ought not to have done it; he never would have done it if he had consulted Frank Blair; I sent Frank there to advise him and to keep me advised about the work, the true condition of things then, and how they were going." Jessie perceived a rising anger. "Frank never would have let him do it—the General should never have dragged the negro into the war," he told her, as if the Negro was not from the beginning at the very heart of the war. "It is a war for a great national object and the negro has nothing to do with it."

"Then there is no use to say more, except that we were not aware that Frank Blair represented you—he did not do so openly," Jessie replied.

When, she asked resignedly, could she expect his answer? Tomorrow or the next day, Lincoln told her. She said she would come back to the White House to get it. Lincoln asked where she was staying and then said he would send it to her at Willard's. And they parted.

Walking back to the hotel, Cowles told her matter-of-factly, "Mrs. Frémont, the General has no further part in this war." If the Frémonts still had no hint up to this point that Frank Blair (and perhaps other Blairs) had begun to turn against them, Lincoln had revealed it for certain.

Lincoln's version of the meeting runs along the same general lines, but there are significant differences, particularly in what is left unsaid by each storyteller. In a conversation more than two years later with John Hay, John Nicolay, Norman Judd, and Interior Secretary John P. Usher, Lincoln claimed that Jessie insisted on seeing him at midnight "and taxed me so violently with many things that I had to exercise all the awkward tact I have to avoid quarrelling with her." Jessie perceived little, if any, tact. It's possible she left out of her account some of her own assertions, as Lincoln implies that more was exchanged between them than she included. "She surprised me by asking why their enemy Monty Blair had been sent to Missouri," Lincoln said, although that claim does not mesh with the Frémonts not yet knowing of Frank's letter. Most seriously, Lincoln said, "she more than once intimated that if Gen Frémont should conclude to try conclusions with me he could set up for himself." At that point Judd weighed in, suggesting it was "pretty clearly proven that Frémont had at that time concluded that the Union was definitely destroyed and that he should set up an independent Government as soon as he took Memphis and organized his army."[52]

Frémont's proclamation was "a severe trial" to Lincoln, according to the man who met with the president after Jessie left. Josiah Bushnell Grinnell, an Iowa politician who would later be elected to Congress, reported Lincoln as saying, "Not an hour ago, a woman, a lady of high blood, came here, opening her case with mild expostulation, but left in anger flaunting her handkerchief before my face, and saying 'Sir, the general will try titles with you. He is a man and I am his wife.'" After confessing that it was "the daughter of old Bullion," Lincoln noted "how her eye flashed."[53]

Grinnell's testimony seems to confirm Jessie's version of the timing—closer to 9:00 p.m. than to midnight. Surely Lincoln was not entertaining a minor politician at 2:00 a.m. after a trying meeting with Jessie Frémont. But Grinnell's reference to trying titles comports with Lincoln's version on that score. Perhaps "midnight" was Lincoln (or Hay) exaggerating for effect. It is possible that Jessie, at the end of three exhausting days and in response to Lincoln's dismissive attitude, might have alluded to the possibility of an independent West under Frémont in the event the war was lost (although Frémont certainly never did). And it's understandable why she would want to leave that detail out of a memoir.

The Blairs were operating under the same paranoiac assumption—that somehow Frémont was planning to "set up for himself" in the far-off wilds of Missouri. "I see Jessie is at Washington but I have not had a line from there for near a week & I expect Frémont is [in] a peck of trouble about his proclamation," Lizzie wrote on September 12, as Jessie was confronting Lincoln. To get a read on the situation, Francis Preston Blair paid a visit the next day to the Willard to meet with his once "dear Jessie." Jessie had previously told Lizzie, "You are my confessional." When Jessie met with Blair, it proved to be both confession and interrogation.[54]

A "very angry" Blair started right in on her. "Well, who would have expected you to do such a thing as this, to come here and find fault with the President," he said, eliciting a laugh from Jessie, who thought he must be joking. It was clear immediately that he was not. In a confrontation that lasted almost three hours, Blair listed all the services the family had done the Frémonts over the years—promoting John's fame as an explorer, Montgomery giving him legal assistance, Frank pushing to give him the western command. "She bridled up at this & put on a very *high* look," the senior Blair reported. He complained of her "ingratitude . . . to all who have contributed to put them in a position to make their jealousy oppressive."[55]

The heart of the matter for Blair, however, was that "they hate & fear Frank & are also hostile to everybody in the administration who is supposed to stand between them & imperial power which is they think to be clutched as easily as martial law by proclamation." He suggested Jessie was trying to play the part of Catherine the Great, to which Jessie responded, "Not Catherine but Josephine." He responded, "You are too imperious for her & too ungrateful for me—You have never made any return for services & you never shall." To Jessie, Blair had always been "Father Blair." Now he was saying that the lifetime of friendship between the two families had been merely transactional on the part of the Blairs. Jessie was no longer willing to pay the Blairs the deference they believed they deserved. "So I quit her," Blair reported to Lizzie.[56]

In his heated state, Blair revealed information confirming that Frank was indeed acting on behalf of Lincoln, that letters he had written critical of Frémont had been shared with the president, and that Montgomery Blair and Quartermaster General Montgomery Meigs were being sent to St. Louis to investigate the department. Along with the outcome of the meeting with Lincoln, this was intelligence Jessie needed to share with John as soon as possible.

On September 11, she telegraphed him that Meigs and Blair "leave this morning for St. Louis to investigate the Department." That bit of news had been leaked to the press, so Frémont might have already seen it. "Things evidently prejudged," she reported accurately. "Collateral issues and compromises will be attempted but the true contest is on the proclamation," she wrote, somewhat less accurately. And she warned him to "guard originals and have copies ready" of the proclamation and other crucial documents.[57]

Then she wrote to Lincoln, informing him that Blair senior had spilled the beans about Frank's letter "containing certain statements respecting Genl. Frémont and his military command in the Western Department" and about Lincoln's having dispatched Montgomery to St. Louis. She asked Lincoln to give her copies of Frank's letter and "any other communications, if any, which in your judgment have made that investigation necessary." In a second note, she asked when she could expect to get Lincoln's answer to Frémont's letter. She hoped to be on the evening train back to St. Louis, carrying it with her.[58]

On that score she was disappointed, although considering Lincoln's dismissive tone with her, she could not have been surprised. In a letter headed "Mrs. Genl. Frémont," he informed her that he had written that response and sent it by mail. Then he told her it was "not exactly correct" to say that he had sent Montgomery Blair "to examine into that Department and report." Blair was sent, Lincoln claimed, "to see and converse with Gen. Frémont as a friend." He also informed her that she would not get copies of Frank's letter. "I do not feel authorized to furnish you with copies of letters in my possession without the consent of the writers," he wrote. Lincoln also objected to any characterization of "being understood as acting in any hostility" toward Frémont.[59]

Lincoln's letter to John was more diplomatic than his exchanges with Jessie. "Assuming that you, upon the ground, could better judge of the necessities of your position than I could at this distance, on seeing your proclamation of August 30th I perceived no general objection to it," he wrote the commanding general. But "in relation to the confiscation of property and the liberation of slaves," Lincoln asserted, the order failed to conform with the Confiscation Act, which narrowly defined which classes of slaves were subject to confiscation and left to later dispensation their final status. "Hence I wrote you expressing my wish that that clause should be modified accordingly—Your answer, just received, expresses the preference on your part, that I should make an open order for the modification, which I very cheerfully do."[60]

That "cheerfully" was especially galling to abolitionists, who quickly jumped on Lincoln in support of Frémont. "The lawyer has prevailed over the warrior," Frederick Douglass complained.[61]

Writing to George L. Stearns, a Massachusetts abolitionist and industrialist who had financially supported John Brown's raid on Harpers Ferry, poet John Greenleaf Whittier wrote of the "duty and expediency of striking more directly at the real cause of the war. . . . If the present terrible struggle does not involve emancipation, partial or complete, it is at once the most wicked and the most ludicrous war ever waged. I hope the President has not undertaken to tie up the hands of Frémont. That would be worse for us than a score of Bull Runs."[62]

Whittier then took pen in hand to write his own ode to Frémont.

Thy error, Frémont, simply was to act
A brave man's part, without the statesman's tact,
And, taking counsel but of common sense,
To strike at cause as well as consequence.

In a jab at Lincoln's conciliationist tendencies, he continued,

It had been safer, doubtless, for the time,
To flatter treason, and avoid offence
To that Dark Power whose underlying crime
Heaves upward its perpetual turbulence.[63]

"One bugle note from Whittier's pen is worth at least ten thousand men," journalist Lydia Maria Child wrote.[64]

William Lloyd Garrison, editor of the *Liberator* and a founder of the American Anti-Slavery Society, worried about "a fresh development of pro-slavery malignity created by Frémont's proclamation of freedom to the slaves of the rebellious slaveholders in Missouri, which is rather heightened than mitigated by the President's interposing letter." He took special aim at the newspaper editors who were backing Lincoln's revocation of the emancipation order, writing, "Mr. Lincoln is so infatuated as to shape his course of policy in accordance with their wishes, and is thus unwittingly helping to prolong the war, and to render the result more and more doubtful!"[65]

Ohio senator Ben Wade wrote directly to Frémont. "The president may order a modification, but it is not in the power of Presidents nor their cabinets, to modify the effect of the noble sentiments of that proclamation upon the hearts of the people," he reassured the general.[66]

Charles Sumner excoriated Lincoln. "Our President is now a dictator, imperator, which you will," he exclaimed. "But how vain to have the power of a god and not to use it godlike."[67]

Black journalist Robert Hamilton wrote, "The reverse at Bull Run was a slight affair compared with the letter of Abraham Lincoln which hurls back into the hell of slavery the thousands in Missouri rightfully set free by the proclamation of Gen. Frémont." He accused Lincoln of giving the rebels "aid and comfort greater than they could have gained from any other earthly source."[68]

Many people who were not vocal radicals also objected to Lincoln's reversal of the emancipation order. A woman whose brother was serving in Missouri skipped legalisms but made the "military necessity" argument in a passionate plea to Lincoln. "Must we send our loved ones, to be shot down; butchered?" she asked, "and not use every means in our power to prevent it." Michigander Abner Williams suggested that "to fight Rebellion with one hand, & support Slavery, (its cause & strongest pillar,) with the other, is both unwise & criminal."[69]

Thomas H. Little, superintendent of the Wisconsin Institute for the Blind, told the president, "I have lived in the North & in the South, in the East & the West without contracting abolition principles; but in the midst of this war, I believe that I am only one of thousands who have changed views very much, & I just want to say that your letter to Gen. Frémont in regard to his proclamation will occasion great dissatisfaction to multitudes of us—Pray do not tie his hands if it be at all consistent with the public good. The people have great confidence in him."[70]

John Scripps sided with Frémont and used the president's own words to make the general's case. "As this war was made in behalf of slavery and in opposition to the government, so I have no expectations of seeing it ended until either slavery is exterminated or the government is destroyed. A peace short of the one result or the other will be but a suspension of hostilities—a postponement of the final and decisive struggle which, soon or late, must come. 'This Nation cannot endure part slave and part free,'" Scripps reminded the president.[71]

Carping from abolitionists like Garrison and Whittier was to be expected, and Lincoln gave it little consideration. But Senator Orville Hickman Browning, a fellow Illinois attorney and politico who was appointed to succeed Stephen A. Douglas in the Senate following the Little Giant's death in June, was a Kentucky-born old-line Whig, a Lincoln ally, and a frequent visitor to the White House during that first summer of the war. His critique could not be dismissed so blandly. Only a few weeks after Sumter fell, Browning had written to Lincoln about the emancipating effect of war. "Whenever our armies march into the Southern states, the negroes will, of course, flock to our standards—They will rise in rebellion, and strike a blow for emancipation from servitude, and to avenge the wrongs of ages. This is inevitable," he told the president, adding, "When they come we cannot repulse them—we cannot butcher them, we cannot send them back to bondage."[72]

Events had proven Browning correct. Now, in a remarkable series of letters between the two friends, they debated the legality and wisdom of Frémont's action and the merits of Lincoln's reversal, with the attorney Browning ably arguing Frémont's case more thoroughly than Frémont himself ever did or could.

On September 11, before Browning had learned of Lincoln's reversal, he told the president, "Frémont's proclamation was necessary, and will do good. It has the approval of all loyal citizens of the west and North West." At this point, Browning had heard only rumors "that the cabinet had disapproved it" but had dismissed them. "Such a step would disappoint and dishearten all loyal men who are fighting for the life of the Government," he wrote. And he endorsed

Frémont more generally, believing the general "competent to the command you have given him . . . pushing his measures with great vigor."[73]

Within days, though, Browning—along with the rest of the country— found out that Lincoln, not the cabinet, had in fact reversed Frémont's emancipation proclamation. And so he wrote again. "It is in no spirit of fault finding," he reassured the president, "that I say I greatly regret the order modifying Genl Frémont's proclamation," which "had the unqualified approval of every true friend of the Government within my knowledge." Supporters were disheartened, and rebels and traitors were pleased. "Are they to be at liberty to use every weapon to accomplish the overthrow of the government," Browning asked, "and are our hands to be so tied as to prevent the infliction of any injury upon them, or the successful resistance of their assaults? . . . Is a traitor's negro more sacred than his life? And is it true that the power which may dispose absolutely of the latter, is impotent to touch the former?"

That was the crux of the legal argument, which Browning would soon draw out in greater detail. But he didn't leave it there. As Lincoln was making both legal and political arguments, so did Browning. Lincoln's reversal, he warned, "is really filling the hearts of our friends with despondency." Responding to rumors that Frémont was to be relieved, Browning suggested that "coming upon the heels of the disapproval of the proclamation, it would be a most unfortunate step."

Browning reassured Lincoln that he remained a friend and supporter, but he closed with a warning about Lincoln's tendency toward soft war. "There has been too much tenderness towards traitors and rebels," he wrote. "We must strike them terrible blows, and strike them hard and quick, or the government will go hopelessly to pieces."[74]

Lincoln responded on September 22. Such a letter "coming from you, I confess it astonishes me," he began. He considered it odd that Browning "should object to my adhering to a law which you had assisted in making." But Browning had not objected to enforcement of the Confiscation Act. He had asserted that the power to emancipate rebels' slaves existed outside that legislation, in military necessity under the war power, as Frémont cited. Lincoln countered, calling the question of liberation and confiscation "purely political, and not within the range of military law, or necessity." A general may seize a farm or a fortification, but he could not decide what was to be done with that property for the rest of its existence. Once the war was over, civil authority would decide that question. "And the same is true of slaves," Lincoln continued. "If the General needs them, he can seize them and use them; but when the need is past, it is not for him to fix their permanent future condition—That must be settled according to laws made by law-makers." A general's assumption of that authority, Lincoln asserted, "is simply 'dictatorship.'"

Where Browning had argued that emancipation was essential to preserving the government, Lincoln argued that such an action would be "itself the surrender of the government—Can it be pretended that it is any longer the government of the U.S.—any government of constitution & laws,—wherein a General, or a President may make permanent rules of property by proclamation?" Congress might enact such a law, and Lincoln might sign it. But neither he as president nor Frémont as general could "seize and exercise the permanent legislative functions of the government."

But Lincoln went further. This was more than a constitutional question. It was also a matter of policy. He cited the concerns of Robert Anderson and other Kentuckians about the effect of the proclamation in that state. Lincoln's desire to fight a soft war combined with his belief that Kentucky, sitting astride great rivers and resting on the border between north and south, was the strategic key to the war. "To lose Kentucky is nearly the same as to lose the whole game," he wrote. "Kentucky gone, we can not hold Missouri, nor, as I think, Maryland. These all against us, and the job on our hands is too large for us. We would as well consent to separation at once, including the surrender of this capitol." This was a political/military justification, probably overwrought but defensible. It was not a high-minded constitutional argument about war powers and who could or should yield them.[75]

Lincoln reassured Browning "there has been no thought of removing Gen. Frémont on any ground connected with his proclamation" but hinted there might be other reasons for doing so. "I hope no real necessity for it exists on any ground," he concluded.[76]

If Lincoln thought this missive put the issue to bed with his friend, he was much mistaken. Just over a week later, an unpersuaded Browning sent the president "13 pages of fools cap" detailing a legal, political, and military defense of Frémont's proclamation.[77]

"I have been prompted to this course by a very sincere interest in your individual welfare, fame and fortunes as well as by a painfully intense anxiety for the maintenance of the Constitution and the Union, the restoration of the just authority of the government, and the triumph of as holy cause, in my judgment, as ever interested men's feelings, and enlisted their energies," Browning began. "I fear I have only annoyed you."

But he did not surrender on the point. Citing his friendship with Lincoln and his duty toward patriotism, Browning continued: "His proclamation in my opinion, embodies a true and important principle which the government cannot afford to abandon, and with your permission and with all deference to your opinions so clearly stated, I will venture a few suggestions in regard to it."

He started with the differing views the two of them had of the Confiscation Act and how Frémont's proclamation worked with it. He admitted that Lincoln's interpretation of the proclamation was "just, logical and conclusive, but either you have greatly misunderstood it, or I have."

"According to my understanding of it, it does not deal with the relations between the government and its citizens at all," Browning explained. "It does not deal with citizens, but with public enemies. It does not touch a legislative function but only declares a pre-existing law, and announces consequences which that law has already attached to given acts and which would follow as well without the proclamation as with it."

In Browning's view, Frémont's proclamation was "only a declaration of intention to live up to the laws of war, settled centuries ago by the consent of civilized mankind." The proclamation was not based on the Confiscation Act, nor was it in conflict with it. "Rebels and loyalists stand on the same platform before the statute," Browning argued, because its strictures were based on what the slaves were doing—war work versus, say, farm labor—rather than the status of their owners.

The proclamation relied not on the type of service provided but on the disloyalty of the slave master and was "in exact harmony" with the laws of war. Whatever case Lincoln or others wanted to make about the seceded states still being technically in the Union, Browning pointed out that as a matter of practical reality, they were not operating as states in the Union. Instead, "the Confederate States, and all who acknowledge allegiance to them, are public enemies. They are at war with the United States. Men taken in battle are held as prisoners; flags of truce pass between the hostile lines; intercourse is forbidden between certain States, and parts of States; and seaports are formally blockaded. These things constitute war, and all the rules of war apply, and all belligerent rights attach to the existing state of things." Lincoln had debated the blockade issue with his advisors earlier in the year, understood the implications, and decided that necessity required that action be taken. He was willing to accept the contradiction in that case but not in Frémont's.

Browning was asking him to reconsider, for the same reason of necessity. "Is there any question that the proclamation, carried into practical effect, would tend to our advantage by greatly weakening the enemy, and diminishing his ability to carry on the war and do us injury?"

Browning asserted that civil wars are governed by the same rules of war as conflicts between states, and so Frémont's proclamation "was not an excess of authority—was not in contravention of law—was not an invasion of any right of those to whom it related and upon whom it acted, of which they could rightfully complain."

Browning then became a prognosticator: "I do further think that it is a highly important and very valuable power which the government ought not to surrender and without the exercise of which this war can never be brought to a successful termination. I do not speak this in reference to slaves alone, but to all property. Can the war be prosecuted upon the understanding that all the property captured from the enemy is to be held for restoration to former owners when the war is over?"

That situation would create an absurd iniquity, Browning wrote. "The consequence will be that whilst they act upon the laws of war and plunder us, and confiscate all our property, and cripple and weaken us, our hands are so tied as to disable us from touching anything of theirs." Would Kentuckians object if "the proclamation had been limited to the confiscation of horses and cattle," he asked, "or would any one have supposed there was an excess or any abuse of power?"[78]

Browning's letter was a tour de force, but it made no impression on Lincoln. "There is a good deal of old Whig left in me yet," the president told Robert Winthrop, an old-line Whig who had supported the Constitutional Union ticket for president in 1860. Lincoln and Browning remained friendly for the time being, but the president never accepted Browning's reasoning as far as Frémont was concerned.[79]

While Frémont's supporters continued to appeal to Lincoln in private and made considerable noise in the public square, Lincoln had his supporters as well. "I am an abolitionist and so, I think, are you," Charles Francis Adams Jr. wrote to his father, the U.S. ambassador to the Court of St. James, "and so, I think, is Mr. Seward; but if he says the time has not yet come; that we must wait till the whole country has time to make the same advance that we have made within the last six months, till we can all move together with but one mind and one idea; then I say, let us wait. It will come."[80]

William Tecumseh Sherman worried, like Lincoln, about the military effect. "Frémonts Proclamation . . . makes our cause a hard one to sustain," he told his foster father.[81]

The Democratic press was especially harsh toward Frémont. "It is known that he is surrounded by a set of scamps and adventurers from California—a circumstance which in itself, certainly, does not argue much for his wisdom or strength of mind," the *New York Herald* opined. "Assuming that the charges are well founded, it is highly probable that they counselled him to issue his abolition proclamation in order to divert public attention by raising a new issue, and to gain popularity with the radical republicans at the expense of the government. Their object is to make him the next President of the whole United States, if possible; or, if the war should fail to restore the Union, to make him President of the Northern half of it; and if that cannot be accomplished to make him President of the West."[82]

Accusations that Frémont was setting himself up to run for president were inherently contradictory. The opponents of the proclamation in one breath claimed it would harm support for the war among most northerners and in the next asserted that the man who had devised it wanted to ride its popularity to the White House. He wanted both to become king of his own western empire and to be elected president of the United States. There is not a shred of evidence suggesting Frémont had electoral politics in mind when he issued the proclamation. He knew as well as anyone that the path to political success for a general lay in victory. He certainly wasn't acting like a man who had visions of presidential elections clouding his judgment. In 1856, he had lost considerable support because he refused to respond to allegations that he was a closet Catholic, arguing that there was nothing wrong with being a Catholic, so he would not stoop to respond to a nonsmear. Six weeks before he issued the emancipation order, the *New York Dispatch* had reported that Frémont had donated a plot of Mariposa land to build a Catholic church in that far-flung sector of the Archdiocese of San Francisco and "promised further aid when the building has commenced." It was a foolhardy move for anyone who might have been contemplating a future presidential race, and doubly so for Frémont, considering his history. Both the donation and the emancipation order were indicative of not only his lack of political acumen but also his lack of concern about normal political niceties. He wasn't a career politician and didn't think like one, making it difficult for the political class to assess his motives.[83]

If slavery was the cause of the war, then the logic of emancipation was determinative. What would be the use of a reconstituted Union with slavery intact, except to set the stage for another war? If northerners were reluctant to admit this fact, southerners had understood it for decades. Lincoln was dressing a political argument in a constitutional suit. The president had legitimate questions about the legality of Frémont's act, and he would continue to question the permanency of military emancipation until the end of his life, which is why he eventually pressed so hard to ensure freedom through the Thirteenth Amendment. But he ignored sound counsel to the contrary from Browning and others, at least in part because of his political concerns about the border states. That's why he spent so much time talking about the centrality of Kentucky to the Union cause and ignoring men like Frederick Douglass, who asked—quite justifiably—what the friendship of loyal slaveholders was worth if "there is a stronger bond existing between these loyal slaveholders and the slaveholding rebels, than subsists between the former and the Government."[84]

Lincoln would demonstrate within a matter of months that emancipation was justified by military necessity, just as Frémont said. As Browning argued, the president had the power to delegate his military authority on this question to commanders in the field (just as he delegated the authority to kill rebels). He chose not to do that in September 1861 for political reasons.

Lincoln stopped Frémont, but he had not stopped emancipation in Missouri. Even before the proclamation, Grant was gathering "contrabands" into his lines in the southeast. Illinois troops in the northeastern part of the state and Kansans in western Missouri were daily taking into their lines slaves owned by both disloyal and loyal Missourians. Some were already being enlisted and armed. Events were running ahead of the politicians and would continue to do so.[85]

Frémont understood something Lincoln either didn't understand or didn't want to admit: Garrison and the immediate abolitionists had been right all along that half measures would have no effect on slaveholders committed to preserving slavery at any cost. Lincoln had, for too long, overestimated unionist sentiment in the South. Now he was underestimating it in the border states. Benjamin Grierson, an officer serving under Frémont at Cairo, called it "a misconception of the true necessities of the hour—foolishly trying to conciliate rebels who were in arms, endeavoring by every means in their power to destroy the nation." He pointed the finger at Washington. The "weak and vacillating" politicians, and generals like Henry Halleck and McClellan, who wanted to turn soldiers into slavecatchers, failed to understand "that not only would the rebellion have to be put down, but that slavery, the real cause of the war, must necessarily be destroyed before peace could be restored."[86]

Frémont's inflated sense of his own destiny, buttressed by his wife, and his natural disposition to defy authority set him apart from those who could have been his allies. His status as the first Republican presidential candidate, bolstered by the Missouri emancipation order, had made him a symbol of a great movement. But there was little substance undergirding the symbolism. He was not a legal theoretician like Browning, nor a party builder like Chase, nor a policy advocate like Charles Sumner, nor an agitator like Wendell Phillips. He wasn't even a very good general. He simply had a hammer and tried to wield it. But slavery was not a nail. Slaveholders would not be pounded into submission by a single blow. Emancipation would not be accomplished by political declarations by Frémont, Lincoln, or anyone else. Freedom would be decided on the field of battle.

CHAPTER FIVE

"A blank page of our history waiting for Frémont's name"

WHEN JESSIE ARRIVED BACK IN ST. LOUIS, SHE WALKED INTO JOHN'S OFFICE TO find the two Montgomerys—Postmaster Blair and Quartermaster Meigs—bearing Lincoln's letter. Frémont had no choice but to follow Lincoln's direct order overturning emancipation and limiting his authority to execute prisoners, but he did not have to take Blair's advice. And once Jessie was finished briefing him on Lincoln's behavior toward her and her disagreeable meeting with Francis P. Blair, there was little chance he would. "Good faith is not a characteristic trait of the Blair family," journalist Noah Brooks observed, and that lack of good faith was on full display during this trip. On their way west, Montgomery Blair and Meigs had stopped in Chicago to deliver another letter from Lincoln to Maj. Gen. David Hunter, asking that officer to assist Frémont. Hunter joined them for the last leg of the trip. The trio arrived in St. Louis at midnight on September 12.[1]

Meigs began looking closely at the Western Department's contracts and accounts and found them a mess. Representatives of the Union Defense Committee of Chicago had told Meigs in August that agents of the quartermaster corps were buying horses in their city for $75 to $80 and reselling them to the government for as much as $110. This allegation added to a lengthening list of questionable contracting reports coming to Meigs's attention from the Department of the West. As far back as June, before Frémont had arrived in St. Louis, Meigs had warned Quartermaster Justus McKinstry to be diligent in providing public notice before letting contracts. Meigs understood that it was sometimes necessary to move swiftly and not always practical to wait for the lowest price to emerge. But McKinstry should strive to give even a day's notice whenever possible, and he was to keep Meigs informed when he deviated and why. John Schofield had also been sent to the city to examine the army's accounts. He reported similarly to Frank Blair that money was being spent with little attention to thrift or accurate accounting but also expressed sympathy for Frémont's position. "The general is charged with saving the country," he wrote. "The country will be very careful to approve his measures, and will judge his mistakes, if any, very tenderly if successful"—the implication being that victory would mean nearly any indiscretion could be overlooked, but failure would exact a price beyond the mere shame of defeat. Blair's role irritated Meigs, just as it did when Frémont worked through the family rather than the quartermaster's office, but there was little he could do about it as long as the Blairs were aligned with Frémont. Now that the alliance was threatened, Meigs had more power to act.[2]

With McKinstry under fire from Meigs and others, Frémont decided to axe him and telegraphed as much to Meigs while the quartermaster was on his way back to Washington. When he arrived and found the message, Meigs quickly appointed Maj. Robert Allen to replace McKinstry, whom Frémont then appointed provost marshal. Meigs instructed Allen to "leave no margin for profit in jobbing contracts," and he was to pay no contracts that had been signed before October 14 until a full investigation had taken place. And he was to pay none—of any date—that had been signed by McKinstry, whose assistants were summarily removed. Of course, he was to follow Frémont's orders as head of the department. "But he should be made aware with all respect and loyalty of the legal and other obligations, so that he can act with knowledge and be protected against errors arising from inexperience in the Regulations." If Frémont wanted to work around the regs, fine. But he would then bear the responsibility when congressional and executive investigators got around to reviewing his paperwork. Lincoln soon appointed a three-man Commission on the Debts of the Western Department to investigate Frémont's accounts, joining Charles Van Wyck's congressional committee's efforts (begun in July) to take a wider look into army purchasing. Within days of his appointment, Allen was begging the secretary of war for guidance on how to deal with the accounting mess left behind by McKinstry. "If the reckless expenditures in this department are not arrested by a stronger arm than mine," Allen wrote, "the Quartermaster's Department will be wrecked in Missouri alone."[3]

Blair and Meigs stayed a week in St. Louis. After his discussion with Frémont, Montgomery Blair met with his brother and then reported back to the president that Frémont "seems stupified & almost unconscious, & is doing absolutely nothing." That assessment contrasted with the reports of other visitors, including Lyman Trumbull and Orville Hickman Browning, who saw great energy and vigor in Frémont's command. Blair simply ignored contrary evidence. "I find but one opinion among the Union men of the State . . . & among the officers," he told Lincoln in an obvious exaggeration, "& that is that Frémont is unequal to the task of organizing the defences of the State." Meigs concurred. "I do not think he is fit for his place," he concluded. "He is prodigal of money; unscrupulous, surrounded by villains, inaccessible to the people and ambitious; should he see the opportunity he would not hesitate to play Aaron Burr." It was a reasonable assessment except for the conclusion. Meigs failed to see that the disorganized man he described as unfit for command could hardly be expected to have the wherewithal to set up an independent kingdom. These rumors proliferated among fretful politicians worried about Napoleons and Cromwells and would swirl around George McClellan and Joseph Hooker as well as Frémont. Such charges had more to do with the insecurities of the men in charge than any plots by the generals, which were altogether imaginary.[4]

Blair went on to rehash Wilson's Creek, blaming the defeat on Frémont's decision to reinforce Cairo rather than Nathaniel Lyon. That was off base, but his assessment off the feeble efforts of John Pope to resist rebel activities in northern Missouri, the threat to Lexington in the west, and the lack of specific orders to commanders in the field were on the nose. Frank, his brother said, had "endeavored to aid Frémont in good faith" but had ceased to offer counsel when he saw that Frémont was ignoring him. Montgomery laid it all at the feet of Frémont and his supposed political aspirations, recommending to Lincoln that "Meigs should be immediately put in command here." Putting Meigs in command was not what Lincoln had in mind. Hunter was now on the scene, though Frémont had dispatched him to Jefferson City to assume command of an as yet unformed wing of the army that Frémont would soon take into the field. Many of the troops were still at Rolla. Jessie would later contend that her husband's "power to command" was "virtually terminated at the time of this visit," which was not quite true. But it was the beginning of the end of Frémont's command in the West. The next rash step in the war between the Frémonts and the Blairs, which John would take at Jessie's urging, would prove decisive.[5]

"IT WAS IMPOSSIBLE . . . TO AVOID TAKING UP ARMS AGAINST SOMEBODY"

Frémont was not nearly so inactive as Montgomery Blair had conveyed to Lincoln, but shortages of arms and supplies hindered operations. Close to home, Frémont put Brig. Gen. Samuel R. Curtis in charge of drilling new recruits at Jefferson Barracks. Curtis, an 1831 West Point graduate who served in Mexico and Congress, took to the task with relish and good humor. "Jack Falstaffs Regiment was a dress parade compared to my command," he reported in mid-August. "Some have guns but none have uniforms, and many are destitute of shoes." Outfitting the army remained a problem into September. Even Ulysses Grant, who would become famous for going to war with the army he had, repeatedly wrote to Frémont and others seeking more arms, men, and money.[6]

The locals weren't helping much. On August 24, Governor Hamilton Gamble called for forty-two thousand volunteers; only six thousand enlisted. Montgomery Blair tried to lay the blame for this situation on "the clique into whose counsels F[rémont] has fallen," but the general retained considerable popularity, particularly in the German community. Gamble, like Lincoln, believed in conciliation. Lincoln would belatedly figure out that conciliation was a dead end. Gamble never did. Frémont wanted Gamble to appoint friendly commanders of volunteer regiments. Despite Frémont assuring him that congressional action overrode Gamble's concerns about his limited authority under state law, Gamble refused to act. He also hesitated to respond to Frémont's request that he replace the southern-leaning St. Louis police board, although he eventually acquiesced. The personality clash and divergent goals between the governor and the military commander would be resolved only with the removal of one or the other.[7]

While Frémont was applying to Washington and to midwestern governors for help, McClellan was trying to poach western troops. "I am told that Genl Frémont has some fifty thousand troops in the vicinity of St. Louis; if this is the case the safety of the nation requires that twenty five thousand of them be sent here without one day's delay," he whined to Secretary of War Simon Cameron. At this point, in mid-September 1861, McClellan had about eighty thousand troops at his disposal and no plan to use them anywhere. He claimed to be facing 170,000 rebels, a figure about twice their actual strength. His estimates of Frémont's strength were no better. Frémont did have roughly fifty-five thousand troops under his command, although only around seven thousand were "in the vicinity of St. Louis." The rest were spread far and wide across Missouri, Illinois, and Kentucky—and, unlike McClellan's troops, were actively engaging the enemy on multiple fronts. Nevertheless, Scott ordered five thousand regulars transferred from the Western Department to Virginia, to be replaced by a like number of raw volunteers from Illinois, Iowa, and Kansas. To Jessie, this decision was proof that the powers that be in Washington were deliberately sabotaging the war in the West. Frémont promptly shipped two thousand troops from St. Louis, two thousand from Kentucky, and one thousand from scattered other commands (including two regiments under Grant at Cairo) to Virginia. Asked why he simply sent the troops east, Frémont told a visiting congressman that to argue the case "would be insubordination, with which I have already been unjustly charged. The capital must be again in danger, and must be saved, even if Missouri fall[s] and I sacrifice myself."[8]

Having no better luck than Frémont in appealing to Lincoln for men, money, and arms, Gamble tried fellow Missourian Attorney General Edward Bates. "For God's sake get me arms for infantry & cavalry," he begged on September 17. "This is a most pressing emergency & will not brook delay. In Common justice, send the arms at once. I just heard today that 5 or 6 Regts have been ordered from Frémont's command to this place [Jefferson City]. And now, if arms are not sent to enable the true men to defend themselves, I shall conclude that Mo is to be abandoned to devastation & ruin." Bates passed along Gamble's plea, and Lincoln urged Cameron to act, if the War Department "can spare any for St. Louis." Only a few dozen small arms would be forthcoming.[9]

Montgomery Blair's concerns about the situation in northern Missouri were justified. Supplies moved north and west out of St. Louis on the Hannibal and St. Joseph and the North Missouri railroads and were distributed at Macon, where the two roads converged, making it a crucial junction to hold. "The Union cause in our section of the State is being greatly injured by the bad management of our military affairs," the president of the Hannibal and St. Joseph Railroad complained to the governor in mid-August. "The outrages on the people by the soldiery . . . are all causing Union men to leave." This was a criticism of Pope, which the railroad man conveyed to Frémont.[10]

Pope believed the enemy could be defeated in Missouri only by "making all engaged in [rebellion] suffer for every act of hostility committed." His plan was to hold the citizens financially responsible for damage caused by raiders. "As long as lawless parties of marauders were shielded by their neighbors and friends from punishment for these atrocious acts," it would be fruitless to try to interdict them militarily, he wrote. Pope ordered, "The population will be held responsible, and a levy of money or of property sufficient to cover the whole damage done will be at once made and collected." The order was met by howls of protest, but at first it helped deter attacks on the railroad, if not on their neighbors' farms, and other Federal officers followed his lead. When the locals refused to pay up, Pope sent the army to track down the guerillas, drawing more protests.[11]

In the southern part of the state, "There is a great deel of marching and counter-marching in this part of our troubled country without coming to blows," Grant complained at the end of August, although he was confident "they must follow however soon." Sure enough, on September 3, Lt. Gen. Leonidas Polk brought his army from Tennessee to occupy Columbus, Kentucky, saving Lincoln the problem of whether to move militarily against his native state. Tipped off by one of Frémont's scouts, the Confederate invasion gave Grant the opportunity to move against the rebel troops. Within days he was headed south with gunboats. On September 6, he spotted "numerous secession flags flying over" Paducah and "citizens in anticipation of the approach of the rebel army," which had begun moving northward. When Polk found out Grant was there, though, he turned back. Like Frémont's reinforcement of Cairo, Grant's quick action secured another strategic river junction—of the Tennessee and Ohio—that would prove decisive as he moved farther south in early 1862. Whatever plans Lincoln had for keeping Kentucky peacefully in the Union died with Polk's invasion. Kentucky would remain in the Union, but it would be fought over throughout the war, just as Missouri would be.[12]

In the west, where Montgomery Blair correctly surmised that the Federal armies were ceding control to the rebels, Sterling Price had gathered about twelve thousand men for a movement against a Union force of about twenty-seven hundred at Lexington under Col. James Mulligan. Local unionists were worried and made a written appeal to Frémont in the middle of August, just five days after Wilson's Creek: "As citizens of Lafayette County, & loyal to the Government of the United States, we respectfully represent to you that there is a great necessity for troops at this point. There is here but a very small number of soldiers all of whom—or nearly all are undrilled." After Price's initial attack on September 12 was stymied by stiff resistance from the little band, the Missourian settled in for a siege. Mulligan could have pulled out; he had a pair of steamboats docked on the Missouri ready to go. But he was sure he could hold out long enough for Frémont to send help. That proved a bad bet. Frémont was slow to order a concentration, and many of the troops that were supposed to gather were delayed by bad roads, bad weather, and delaying actions fought by determined rebels. Hunter asked Frémont for permission to gather up idle forces and move them to Warrensburg, two days' march south of Lexington, but Frémont refused. "I suppose it was considered a great piece of presumption on my part," Hunter wrote bitingly, "to make suggestions, when the Gen. was surrounded with such *distinguished* Hungarians." When Price intercepted a message that Samuel Sturgis was moving toward Lexington from Fort Leavenworth, he decided to move against Mulligan's men, who were tired, hungry, and nearly out of ammunition. When Price's troops came in force on September 19, the Union men at first held them off. But it was clear they couldn't do so for long, and Mulligan surrendered his command the next day. Historian William E. Parrish, a severe Frémont critic, noted that the "loss of Lexington, while not directly Frémont's fault, added to the already growing discontent with him in Missouri." Frémont's failure to monitor or anticipate Price's movements, and his tardy response to Mulligan's peril, constituted another entry on the debit side of Lincoln's ledger.[13]

Missouri was an active front in the war, with violence going on in virtually every corner of the state. Pope wrote, "It was impossible for any man living in the country, away from considerable towns, to avoid taking up arms against somebody." In a taste of the extremely violent irregular warfare that would come to western Missouri over the next four years, neighbors fought neighbors, and even uniformed troops engaged in terror. Schofield believed the violence in western Missouri was often a product of "old feuds, and involves very little, if at all, the question of Union or disunion." Whatever the cause, citizens appealed to the governor for help. "Please correct the many atrocities of the Home Guard Germans who have had a taste of blood and are terrorizing Missouri," one appeal read. Mistreatment by Union soldiers was driving Missourians into the arms of the rebels under deposed Governor Claiborne Jackson. Guerilla rosters were filled by formerly well-off citizens whose wealth had been lost when Frémont and his underlings confiscated the funds of banks to which these planters owed money. Left destitute and embittered, they took to bushwhacking. "Men are looking to Jackson's army as the only safety. They will go to him by the thousands unless the bloody hand is stayed." In relatively peaceful St. Louis, the commanding general was ensconced in his headquarters, trying to make sense of it all and decide what to do about it.[14]

"I HAVE BEEN SUSPECTING THAT FOR SOME TIME"

Benjamin Grierson, an acquaintance of Lincoln and a Jacksonville neighbor of Illinois governor Richard Yates, had encountered Frémont at Cairo and described him as "very approachable." Others, including Browning, also reported no problems getting in to see the general. A Pennsylvania friend of Simon Cameron's met Frémont and reported "a long & pleasant interview—found him ready & willing to furnish me any information I might desire." But that was far from the universal perception.[15]

The complaints started almost as soon as Frémont arrived. Writing to Montgomery Blair on August 4, Kentuckian John Howe reported, "Our friends who have visited the Courts of Europe say it is much easier to gain access to them than to the august presence of our Gen." When this complaint was registered, Frémont had been at post for one week, half of which he had spent at Cairo.[16]

A Col. Henry Charles de Alma was so incensed at being denied entry to the Brant mansion that he "forced his way into the headquarters at a few minutes before ten this evening in spite of the guard who endeavored to restrain him" and "used violent and insulting language, such as 'D-d body guard, Hungarian humbug,' 'you make yourself very big with your body guard' &c." De Alma was subsequently court-martialed. Blair, in a jab at Frémont, later recommended de Alma to Henry Halleck as a staff officer.[17]

Gamble met with Frémont on September 11 in hopes of clearing the air on cooperation between state and Federal troops. The next day, Frémont's judge advocate, R. M. Corwine, met with Gamble and assured the governor that Frémont wanted to set up another meeting. Two days later, Frémont left Gamble cooling his heels at the general's headquarters for an hour, after which the governor left and returned to Jefferson City.[18]

William Tecumseh Sherman, by contrast, had no trouble getting in to see Frémont, which he attributed to their earlier acquaintance in California. Once in the office, though, he wasn't happy with what he heard. He called Frémont "very communicative" but wrote his wife, "I could not discover that he was operating on any distinct plan but was assembling men of all kinds and materials, but whether he can Shape them into an army I don't know." And he was no fan of emancipation. "By proclamations and threats which there is no power to execute he has completed what Lyon began in alienating the support of all the moderate men of the city," the grumpy Sherman opined. "Missouri has had a hard time as between Lyon, Blair & Frémont."[19]

To stem the dissatisfaction, Frank Blair had suggested to Frémont that he set aside one hour a day to meet with anyone who showed up. It was a typically political idea from Blair. It carried symbolic value, but an hour would hardly suffice for the dozens of people who might show up at any given time demanding the general's attention and would simply lead to more dissatisfaction because of heightened expectations of access. Frémont rejected the idea, adding another layer to Blair's growing dissatisfaction with the commanding general.[20]

John Schofield had been the martyred Nathaniel Lyon's chief of staff at Wilson's Creek. Now back in St. Louis, Schofield was asked by Frank Blair to join him on a visit to Frémont. "All ingress by the main entrance appeared to be completely barred," Schofield wrote later. "But Blair had some magic word or sign by which we passed the sentinels at the basement door," and they gained entrance without difficulty. But what they found inside confounded both men. This was in the immediate aftermath of Wilson's Creek, and yet "no questions were asked, nor any mention made, of the bloody field from which I had just come." Instead, Frémont and the two men pored over maps as the general explained for more than an hour his plans for a movement across Missouri to the Arkansas River and by that route to the Mississippi. When the presentation was over, Blair and Schofield departed. They walked for a while without talking, until Blair turned to Schofield and asked, "Well, what do you think of him?" Schofield answered, "in words rather too strong to repeat in print, to the effect that my opinion as to his wisdom was the same as it had always been." Blair, fresh off the deaths of Lyon and Cary Gratz, replied, "I have been suspecting that for some time."[21]

A perceptive California acquaintance would later write about Frémont, "The more you consulted him the fonder you were of him, and the less you were convinced by what he said." But it was not just Frémont's lack of a serious plan of action, his remoteness, or (as Blair saw it) his focus on the wrong priorities. There was also a general sense of slackness in the command noted by others. From Jefferson City, Grant reported to headquarters, "Every place I have been thrown in command I have found . . . Commanders of Regts. & in many instances companies, give leavs of absence to their officers and men, in large numbers." Although he acted to reverse this practice, "I fear in many instances this is disregarded without my knowledge."[22]

The Frémonts had long had a certain paranoia about any sort of opposition or criticism from the regular army officer class, which included Schofield. They believed West Pointers disregarded Frémont because of his lack of academy training and favoritism from Thomas Hart Benton. The Frémonts were not alone in seeing a West Point conspiracy against them. One clever contemporary writer comparing the relative merits of McClellan, "a soldier educated at West Point," with Frémont, "a soldier educated at all points," found the academy version wanting. Although some of the criticisms leveled at John had merit, the Frémonts were probably right about being ostracized—just because you're paranoid doesn't mean they're not after you. And, as Frémont well knew, being a West Pointer did not guarantee wisdom or even loyalty: the Confederate Army was thick with former West Pointers. Frémont trusted his staff, and they were doing their job in keeping him insulated from people who likely were less interested in his success.[23]

The accusations of a lack of access likely hit home with Lincoln. He appreciated the value of what he called his "public-opinion baths" and was said to suffer from the opposite malady. "He is not good at dispatching business but lets every person use more time than he might if the interview were strictly limited to the real necessities of the case," journalist Noah Brooks observed of the president.

The image of an imperious general surrounded by parading foreigners, once placed in the public mind, was difficult to dislodge. Unfriendly reporters filled with a sense of their own importance couldn't conceive that Frémont might not share that opinion. Annoyed that Frémont wouldn't make time to see them, they filed snide commentary parodying his supposed isolation: "To gain heaven (here in St. Louis, especially); to gain speech with the man in the moon; to make love to the favorite of a Turkish harem; to wean a believer in Allah from predestination, or to instill maternal instincts into the bosom of a mule; are all thought to be difficult—yet in view of all these difficulties, that of obtaining an audience with FREMONT sinks into utter insignificance."[24]

"INSIDIOUS AND DISHONORABLE EFFORTS"

Frank Blair was not among those who had trouble gaining an audience with Frémont. But when it became clear that the general was ignoring his advice, Blair stopped going. He had friends in high places and didn't need Frémont to ensure that his ideas were given attention. Lincoln and Blair had worked together as early as 1857 to shift the political ground in Missouri toward anti-slavery. They had met in Springfield on multiple occasions and shared a conservative, antislavery border-state outlook, including support for the colonization of freed slaves. Blair had campaigned with Lincoln in central Illinois during his 1858 Senate race against Stephen A. Douglas. "Neither was an abolitionist. Neither was anti-slavery in the moral sense that inspired the northerners," one historian wrote. William Hyde, a reporter for the *Missouri Republican*, referred to Blair as "the universally recognized leader of the emancipation party" in Missouri and suggested that the "political career of Abraham Lincoln, from the time of the repeal of the Missouri Compromise, was patterned on this model." Lincoln and Blair were kindred spirits, ambitious politicians to the core. Frémont existed largely outside that world and felt ill at ease when forced into it. Whatever he had been before, the war had quickly made him an abolitionist. Lincoln had no real prior relationship with Frémont and did not share his emerging abolitionist outlook.[25]

Lincoln and Blair saw Missouri as a key test case for their ideas about gradual emancipation. Frémont was interposing himself and mucking up the works. Blair's growing opposition to Frémont had multiple triggers. Frémont as the leader of Missouri's growing radical Republican movement and his popularity with the German community would threaten Blair's political viability. Attorney General Edward Bates, a keen observer of Missouri's volatile politics, had foretold Blair's ultimate fate in a letter to Schuyler Colfax as far back as the

Republican convention in May 1860, where Blair had supported his candidacy. "I am grieved for Blair & other friends in this state, & cannot see, as yet, how they can maintain their status," Bates wrote in the wake of Lincoln's nomination. Frémont's dependence on California allies for major contract work, such as building fortifications and gunboats, had blocked Blair's allies from getting in on the booty; perhaps most important, Blair genuinely came to believe that Frémont was incompetent and would endanger the war effort. The September 1 letter to his brother might have been partly inspired by opposition to the immediacy of the emancipation order or by Frémont (and McKinstry) ignoring his demand for spoils, but that doesn't mean it wasn't a sincere cry from the heart. It just as certainly warranted the charges of insubordination and unbecoming conduct that Frémont would soon make public, despite the considerable irony of Frémont charging someone else with insubordination. Blair was a serving officer under Frémont, and he went outside the chain of command to level severe criticism of his commanding officer's conduct. He used family and political connections to do so, just as he had done to get Elizabeth Blair Lee's husband a preferential navy assignment.[26]

Although Frank Blair would later blame Lyon's death on Frémont for political reasons, the Blair family, including Frank, remained pro-Frémont in the weeks immediately following Wilson's Creek. But the situation was evolving, with Frank questioning Frémont's competence, and the emancipation order proved a turning point. Blair felt he could unfavorably compare Frémont's slowness to take the field with the alacrity with which he and Lyon had moved to save St. Louis and Missouri in the spring. It was not a fair comparison. Blair and Lyon were acting tactically on a small field, with the full force of the Blair political machine behind them; Frémont had to think strategically about the entire state and, indeed, the Western Department. But fairness was not uppermost in any Blair's mind at this point. On September 5, Elizabeth Blair Lee wrote of "a muss between Gamble & Frémont" and decided she "must hear from Frank" to get the details.[27]

Like Jessie Benton, politics was in Lizzie's blood. She, too, had been dandled on Andrew Jackson's knee, had fallen in love with a military officer native to the South—navy lieutenant Samuel Phillips Lee—faced parental opposition to her marriage, and endured long separations. However, their approaches to those romances revealed the differences in their temperaments. Jessie defied her parents and impulsively eloped. Lizzie patiently waited four years until her parents came around. While Jessie rode to the sound of the guns in St. Louis and later in Virginia, Lizzie fled north after Bull Run.

"'Tis my nature to believe the best until I know the worst," Lizzie had once written; yet she was now ready to believe the worst of one of her oldest and dearest friends. Like every other Blair, when Lizzie went in for a fight, she went in for a funeral.[28]

On September 16, Frémont had Frank Blair arrested, severing the last tie that had bound the families together for three decades. Frank's incarceration at the St. Louis Arsenal was "General Jessie's doing," Montgomery insisted. Lizzie was "grieved & cut to the heart by Frémont's treatment of Frank," she wrote the next day. Of John and Jessie, she now asked, "were there ever people who were so false to themselves & others[?] . . . I felt bitterly angry all day."[29]

"Information of such positive character has come to my knowledge implicating Col F P Blair Jr 1st Missouri Volunteers in insidious & dishonorable efforts to bring my authority into contempt with the Govt & to undermine my influence as an officer that I have ordered him in arrest & shall submit charges to you for his trial," Frémont telegraphed Assistant Adjutant General E. D. Townsend. He did not say what the information was, but it must have been based on Jessie's report of her meeting with Francis P. Blair, for at this point Frémont still had not seen Frank's September 1 letter. On September 19, Montgomery telegraphed Frémont offering to share the contents of that letter. "It is not unfriendly," the Judge insisted. "Release him." And for good measure, he chided his former legal client, "This is no time for strife except with the enemies of the country." In a strange irony, those words mirrored Jessie's message of September 12 after her unpleasant audience with Lincoln: "Attend only to the country's enemies," she told her husband. Montgomery was treading a thin line. He wanted to cool things down but still help his brother.[30]

The arrest was a political earthquake. The *Missouri Democrat*, of which Blair was still a part owner, abandoned him and sided with Frémont. Blair complained about unfair press coverage and sought allies who would relate his version of events to papers in New York and Washington. But even with local support, Frémont was outnumbered and outflanked. However justified, the arrest of Frank Blair was the worst mistake Frémont would ever make, and he had made many big ones. It sealed his fate, although the general didn't yet realize it.[31]

Lincoln came late to the party. It wasn't until September 27 that he told Winfield Scott to order Frémont to release Blair. By that time, Blair had been free for three days, having been granted his release on September 24 in response to Montgomery's plea. But incarceration had done nothing to change Frank's mind about Frémont, and his anger was stoked by Frémont's insistence that the arrest was inspired at least in part by Frank's use of family connections instead of military channels to register his complaints.

As if to rectify the accusation that he denied, Frank notified the adjutant general of his intention to file charges, accusing Frémont of neglect of duty, disobedience of orders, conduct unbecoming an officer and a gentleman, gross extravagance, waste, mismanagement and misapplication of public funds, and despotic and tyrannical conduct. Frémont ordered Blair back to his regiment, which was taking the field. Blair refused to go. So Frémont had Blair arrested on September 28 for a second time and had him locked away at Jefferson Barracks. This time, Lincoln did not hesitate to respond; within a day, Scott ordered Blair's release despite his blatantly disobeying a direct order from his commanding officer.[32]

Amid the turmoil over Blair's arrest, Lincoln considered calling Frémont to Washington for a face-to-face meeting. "The President desires to discuss certain matters of public business with you, personally," General Scott wrote on September 19. "Please place Major General Hunter, temporarily, in the Command of the Western Department of the army, & come hither without unnecessary delay." Lincoln then reconsidered, and Scott never sent the telegram. Lincoln met with Gen. John Wool—a seventy-seven-year-old veteran of the War of 1812 second only to Scott in seniority—to discuss lending Frémont a hand. When Wool replied that he would go to Missouri only if he were put in command, Lincoln turned elsewhere.[33]

"General Frémont is not to be removed—at least until he has had a full opportunity to retrieve his fortunes, or to ruin our state altogether and endanger our cause," Bates alerted Gamble on September 27. But the wheels were already turning. Lincoln wanted more firsthand information from sources that weren't related to or dependent on either of the interested parties. Seeking this knowledge, he sent Simon Cameron and Adjutant General Lorenzo Thomas to Missouri to find out what was going on. He asked Cameron to enlist Samuel Curtis, the former Iowa congressman and now general, to offer his evaluation of the situation. He also gave Cameron a written order for Frémont's dismissal, to be used at the secretary's discretion.[34]

Schofield, visiting the Blairs at Silver Spring, said, "Frémont has to act very vigorously to save himself. It is certainly risking matters some & yet it may be right to be patient." Lizzie saw in Lincoln's deliberation a lesson for her own cause. "Lincoln tho slow is a good true man & is doing a good work for his country & earning great renown for himself. His cool way of doing things will I hope teach the Blairs a lesson not to rush on at things or people so violently. I feel as if we were possessed about the Frémonts." Montgomery certainly appeared to be. "I confess I have never been so utterly deceived in my life in respect to a man's faculties," he wrote. And he held "Genl" Jessie responsible for Frank's arrest. "Frémont himself is too brave a man I believe to act in this way."[35]

It was beginning to look like Lincoln might be just as possessed about the Frémonts as the Blairs. On September 22, the president took the unusual step of giving his commanding general a tactical order to send a gunboat to Owensboro, Kentucky, adding, "Perhaps you had better order those in charge of the Ohio river to guard it vigilantly at all points." Neither the condescension nor the irony could have been lost on Frémont, who had done just that when he reinforced Cairo and was rewarded with criticism for choosing Cairo over Lyon. In early August, Jessie, writing on her husband's behalf, had snapped back to a suggestion from Lincoln that "the plan suggested . . . is about what Genl. Frémont has been doing since arriving in Missouri." But a more quiescent Frémont now simply told Lincoln that he had sent a gunboat to Owensboro and would "take measures to guard the Ohio."[36]

Blair had seen enough. "I cannot and will not serve under Frémont," he told Montgomery on October 1 after being sprung. "I have come to the conclusion, calmly and without passion, that those who are keeping Frémont in his place here, are guilty of the greatest crime which can be committed against the Government and the people." It was probably not his intention to indict Lincoln, but the man keeping Frémont in command was Blair's ally in the White House.[37]

"GEN. FRÉMONT HAS . . . STAKED HIS REPUTATION, AND HIS LIFE"

"I am taking the field myself & hope to destroy the enemy either before or after the junction of force under McCulloch," Frémont alerted Washington on September 23, while Frank Blair was still locked up at the St. Louis Arsenal. "Please notify the President immediately."[38]

Frémont knew the time had come to put up or shut up. He had lost the sponsorship of the Blairs and was rapidly losing the confidence of the president, even more than he knew. Investigators from the executive and legislative branches were bearing down on his command, and the president's envoys were on their way with more questions. One carried a tentative removal order. The loss of Lexington signaled a change in the military situation as well, emboldening disloyal elements across the state and encouraging guerillas to increase their activity.

While the details of these machinations were secret, the outline was not. The pro-Frémont German press was reporting in the middle of September that "an effort is being made by persons in the highest places to test public sentiment in order to prepare the ground for Frémont's removal." Lincoln had men in the field sending him reports, and he was closely following news coverage of Frémont's movements.[39]

"The President, poor man, is in great distress at the way things are going, without [as he supposes] power to change the current," Attorney General Bates wrote Governor Gamble. "He is an intelligent and virtuous man but immense mischief is caused by his lack of vim. . . . [H]e has no will, nobody is afraid of him."[40]

Thomas T. Gantt, a prominent St. Louis lawyer and political figure (and a West Pointer), also commiserated with Gamble about Frémont. "I have read with deep sympathy some of the letters you have addressed to Mr. Bates respecting the unhappy condition of Missouri, the misfortune she lies under in having so incapable a military commander, and the terrible consequences which may, and in all probability will, flow from leaving him in command."[41]

The capability of the military commander would now get a test in real time. Aide Gustave Koerner, an Illinois politician, told his wife as they departed, "Chaos reigns here. I will go with this expedition; and if things do not improve, I will resign." Edward Young Higbee, rector at Trinity Church and a New York friend of Frémont, was now "inclined to think him unequal to his great place."[42]

For all the political repercussions that resulted from the fall of Lexington, it brought no strategic advantage to the rebels. When Price marched south on September 29, desertions had left him only seven thousand troops, one-third of what he had immediately after the siege concluded, as local recruits returned to their homes rather than march away and leave their families to the tender mercies of invading Yankees.[43]

Frémont left St. Louis for the field on September 27, traveling with his staff and baggage on two railroad cars. The first stop was Herman, a German settlement about eighty miles west of St. Louis, where they enjoyed a meal of wine and sandwiches. Then it was another fifty miles on to Jefferson City, where they arrived late in the evening. It was so dark that the various parties got separated from one another climbing up the steep incline from the station. When they made it to town, some had to share a crowded room in a large house with some of the Body Guard, which had preceded them into town. Others were lodged in "a miserable tavern." Koerner and others expected to move out within a day or two, but Frémont told them to set up camp. There was not enough transportation available to move the army any farther west right away.[44]

Frémont, who had always taken genuine relish in being in the wild, expected his staff to share the joys of camp life with the men, not sleep in comfortable quarters in town. They set up tents on a bluff about a mile outside Jefferson City, "with a splendid view up and down the river and of the rich bottom-forests on the north side of the river." The weather was hot, but the ground was kept wet by regular evening thunderstorms, making life unpleasant for those who couldn't keep their tents dry.[45]

Jessie arrived on September 30 with Lily in tow. Frémont met her at the train station with his personal "bodyguard" and an infantry regiment. As their carriage pulled away from the station and rode through the capital city's main thoroughfare, a band played martial music. The band followed them to camp, where Jessie and Lily were quite a hit, and played late into the evening. "Nearly all the officers are in love with one or the other, or at least pretend to be," Koerner wrote to his wife. Jessie and Lily spent most of their day in camp with the general but spent nights in a nearby farmhouse.[46]

It was too much for some reporters, though accusations of "Oriental pomp" were denied by Frémont's supporters. "We have noticed no such pomp here in St. Louis," the *Anzeiger des Westens* reported. While acknowledging that some on his staff "wear the gold braid and the hats decorated with feathers," Frémont "keeps to a very simple manner." To criticisms of pomp for Jessie's reception in Jefferson City, one reporter for a German paper asked, "Were they supposed to receive her with a bad lantern and have her dragged on foot in the dirt and rain through dark streets?" noting that was how some of Frémont's staff were escorted into town by former lieutenant governor Thomas Price.[47]

The newspapers' endearing "our Jessie" of the 1856 campaign had been superseded by the mocking "General Jessie," a sign that Frémont's capital with the press was diminishing. However, Jessie contributed to the war effort despite the criticism. When a rebel-sympathizing chaplain was brought to Frémont's headquarters with information about the disposition of Price's forces to the west, "Frémont proved a very genial companion, but it was Mrs. Frémont who extracted from the chaplain what he had to tell."[48]

While in Jefferson City, Frémont appointed a commission to decide on the legitimacy of property seizures. Frémont's claims commission, tasked with deciding which Missourians were loyal and therefore entitled to payment for property seized by the army, consisted of Illinois congressman Owen Lovejoy, who had recently joined his staff as a volunteer; Illinois lieutenant governor Gustave Koerner; John A. Gurley, a minister and Ohio congressman; and former lieutenant governor Thomas Price. Judge advocate R. M. Corwine handled most of the disloyalty cases. Quite a few of the applicants were acquaintances of Price, at whose home the panel's sessions were held. Many of the accusations amounted to little more than "loud and disrespectful talk about Lincoln, to idle boastings in the streets and saloons, and to hurrahing for Jeff Davis." As a result, most appeals resulted in the return of the complainants' property.[49]

One reason Lovejoy, a strong Lincoln ally, wanted to join Frémont in Missouri was that he feared the war would come to Illinois if Missouri fell to the rebels. He also wanted to see how Missouri slaves were being liberated by the army. "Frémont will be pleased to receive you as one of his aids. Report to him," Cameron telegraphed in mid-August.[50]

Lovejoy was a founder of both the Liberty Party and the Illinois Republican Party and one of the few radicals with whom Lincoln got along well. Lincoln would later call him "the best friend I had in Congress." After taking several weeks to put his affairs in order, Lovejoy took the train to Quincy and caught a steamboat to St. Louis, arriving on September 27, quickly moving on to find Frémont in Jefferson City. Unlike some of Lincoln's other friends, he did not act as an agent for the president and offered no contemporaneous intelligence to the president on Frémont's activities. He was simply an observer with no expertise to offer. Frémont rarely took Lovejoy into his confidence but did note his "innocence" when it came to military matters.[51]

"We expect to leave in the morning," Lovejoy told his sons on October 6, "but I do not know where we shall go. I fear the enemy have run away & will not stay to fight. . . . I do not think we shall go much further as I think they will go to Arkansas." Lovejoy's assessment was correct on the essentials. Price, knowing he could not sustain himself alone in northwest Missouri, was moving southward for a link-up with Ben McCulloch near Springfield.[52]

Frémont knew where he was going but appeared to be in no hurry to get there—and, even if he had been, he didn't have the wagons he needed. "Gen. Frémont has, upon the issue of this campaign, staked his reputation, and his life, and he will not, in consequence, be apt to do anything hastily," one reporter predicted, stacking Frémont's slowness unfavorably against Lyon's "light, effectual movements," a comparison that ignored two salient points: first, Lyon was a field commander with considerably fewer command responsibilities than Frémont; second, Lyon's "light, effectual movements" ended up losing a battle and getting him killed.[53]

Such criticism was beginning to wear on Frémont. But on October 6, as Jessie described it, "the setting sun lit up the October colors of the trees and picked out the white tents covering the many hills." The mail had come, but Frémont couldn't bring himself to open it, expecting only more bad news. Then a staff officer brought Jessie a copy of the *New York Evening Post* that had just arrived, with the poem John Greenleaf Whittier dedicated to Frémont. "I read the words to the General and it was like David's harp of old," she wrote later to the poet. "His face lit up with such a different kind of look from the angry baffled resentful kind of face he had just had. His natural serenity came back & the whole tone of his mind was altered." Frémont took the paper and bent close to the fire to see.

> At length he said—"he speaks for posterity. I *knew* I was right. I want these words on my tombstone:—
>> God has spoken through thee
>> *Irrevocable*, the mighty words *Be free!*"
> "*Now* I can die for what I have done," Frémont said.[54]

In the first week of October, the force of more than thirty-seven thousand men was away from Jefferson City, spread across five commands: Hunter and Alexander Asboth at Tipton, Pope at Georgetown, Franz Sigel at Sedalia, and McKinstry at Syracuse. But Lovejoy's prediction that "the enemy have run away & will not stay to fight" was looking spot on. Transportation was a problem. To move toward the southwest, they left the railroad, and both wagons and mules were in short supply. So were passable roads. "Gen. Price has found in mud his savior," a reporter noted. "He should deify it, and hereafter worship it along with his other divinities that preside over bridge-burning and horse-stealing." Sterling Price was "75 miles ahead in the race," an officer wrote to his wife on October 13 from Tipton, thirty-five miles west of Jefferson City. And it appeared that Frémont had no prospect of catching up.[55]

But onward they moved, toward the southwest. A week later, Lovejoy was still pessimistic. "I fear I shall have to return without a battle," he wrote to his sister-in-law from Warsaw, about eighty miles north of Springfield, where Lyon and his army had come to grief two months earlier. Frémont, as one of Lincoln's St. Louis correspondents noted, had "the habit of contending with immense difficulties." But before Frémont could begin to consider how he might handle the difficulties in his front, he had to deal with those pursuing him from the rear.[56]

"I AM GREATLY PERPLEXED ABOUT GEN. FRÉMONT"

A week after Frémont led his army out of St. Louis, Senator Lyman Trumbull visited the city. "I spent yesterday in St. Louis & found a most deplorable state of things there," he reported to Lincoln. "The Western army is demoralized, ruined,

& I fear the Union irretrievably gone unless a remedy is speedily applied." The "ragged and half clad" men had no arms, and many were unpaid. "If the Government has not confidence in Gen Frémont's financial capacity, in Heaven's name send somebody here with funds to purchase necessary supplies in whom you have confidence. . . . It is cruel to put a man at the head of an army in the face of an enemy & then deny him supplies. I know you do not mean this, yet no man can go to St. Louis without feeling that this is just Gen. Frémonts condition."[57]

At the same time, Illinois's other senator, Orville Browning, reported to Lincoln that he had gone "twice to St. Louis to see and learn for myself all that I could." He acknowledged that Frémont "has made some mistakes, but in the main he seemed to be taking his measures wisely and well. Many of the charges against him appeared to me frivolous, and I did not know of any one who could take his position and do better amid the surrounding difficulties, and was confident his removal at the time and under the circumstances would be damaging both to the administration and the cause."[58]

Lincoln's personal emissaries would tell quite a different story.

Secretary of War Simon Cameron and Adjutant General Lorenzo Thomas arrived in St. Louis in the wee hours of October 11. They spent considerable time interviewing members of what Jessie Frémont called "the Blair clique." Now back in St. Louis, she was confident that once Cameron moved into the field and talked with her husband, "he will have his eyes wonderfully opened, & have some facts to carry back which will turn the tide."[59]

Before Cameron left Washington, Salmon Chase, who had been a supporter of Frémont's (although not for the western command), urged his cabinet mate, "For Heaven's sake bear in mind that we must have vigor, capacity & honesty. If F------ has these qualities sustain him. If not, let nothing prevent you from taking the bull by the horns. We have had enough of dilly dallying, temporizing and disgrace. Let us now have decision, action & honor."[60]

In addition to the discretionary removal letter for Frémont, Cameron carried a letter from Lincoln to General Samuel Curtis, which he delivered on October 11, asking the former Iowa congressman to weigh in. "I am greatly perplexed about Gen. Frémont," Lincoln wrote. Seeking the opinion of "an intelligent unprejudiced and judicious . . . professional military man on the spot," he asked, "Ought Gen. Frémont to be relieved from, or retained in his present command?" A "long and frank conversation" between Cameron and Curtis led the secretary to conclude that Curtis believed "the Army in Missouri could not be successful under [Frémont's] leadership—and that the safety of this great and important State could not be secured, unless he was superceded in his command." Cameron also reported, "This seems to be the general opinion here among all classes not interested in the profits of the expenditure of money for account of the Army."[61]

Curtis's report to Lincoln was just as direct. He blamed Frémont's staff, "adopted citizens, who do not know our language or laws," for much of the absence of military regularity in the department. As for Frémont himself, he "lacks the intelligence, the experience, the sagacity and regard for system and economy necessary to such a command as he now holds," a conclusion Curtis said he reached "reluctantly and gradually." Being a politician himself, Curtis acknowledged the need for Lincoln to take public opinion—that is, Frémont's popularity—into account. "Some acts of resentment may insue," he admitted, "but they will be temporary. . . . In my judgement Frémont must be superceded, but the time and manner should be well considered."[62]

That was also the judgment of Lincoln's earlier emissary, David Hunter, whom Cameron interviewed October 12 in Tipton. Hunter told Cameron that although he was second in command in the department, Frémont never shared his plans, and he "knew nothing of his intentions." His assessment was that Frémont was unfit to command, although Cameron explained that Hunter offered this opinion reluctantly since he knew he stood to inherit the department if Frémont were deposed. Hunter's opinion was not unknown to Frémont. He had told Jessie just before Cameron's arrival, "I think ---- is not friendly to me," meaning Hunter, but he did not seem to understand why he was there. "Therefore I have a right to demand that he be at once removed from my department," an indication that he still did not realize the precariousness of his position. He was about to find out. At this point, Cameron had decided to relieve Frémont. He told Lincoln, "Unless I shall have reasons for acting otherwise I shall in my interview with the General, hand him your letter directing him to surrender his command to the officer next below him."[63]

Cameron caught up with Frémont at Syracuse, forty miles west of Jefferson City. The commanding general pulled out the stops, putting on a "grand review of five or six thousand troops," where "one of our little white butterflies came flying around in front of my horse," John reported to Jessie, tenderly recalling the days at Las Mariposas. It was a nice show for the man who probably should have been Frémont's running mate in 1856 and now was his grand inquisitor. But no military spectacle could save him at this point. Cameron showed Frémont the order for his removal, leaving the general "very much mortified, pained, and, I thought, humiliated." Frémont made "an earnest appeal" for more time, telling Cameron that he had built a ragtag bunch of undersupplied men into a real army that should be given a chance to fight the enemy. And, as one politician to another, he told Cameron "that to recall him at this moment would not only destroy him, but render his whole expenditure useless." Cameron, who had supported Frémont's emancipation order, agreed to belay the removal order for the time being, giving Frémont a chance to fight the battle he believed was imminent. But Cameron assured him "that should he fail, he must give place to some other officer." Frémont promised that "should he fail, he would resign at once."[64]

Lincoln's friend Ward Hill Lamon, in Missouri to supervise the transfer of an Illinois regiment to the Potomac, caught up with Frémont in Warsaw and was as unimpressed with what he found as were the president's official envoys. "Things are in a terribly unorganized state here—and I find great complaints about the Commanding General—(and some jealousies)," he wrote. "He certainly knows but little of his command, i. e., about its organization and capacity—And there is about as much likelihood of his catching Price as there is of his being struck by lightning."[65]

Back in St. Louis, Jessie was trying to find out what was going on beyond dress reviews and butterfly sightings. She asked Gustave Koerner to come to the city to brief her, and he arrived on October 14. Koerner knew that Cameron had met with Frémont in camp at Tipton and, based on what he was hearing from his political sources in Springfield, Illinois, told her that "the removal of her husband seemed almost certain." He did not know that Cameron had given Frémont a temporary reprieve, but his report reversed the optimistic assessment she had given to Frederick Billings just a few days earlier. Then she got a letter from John detailing the meeting with Cameron. "I much doubt whether the Administration will permit me to make any progress," he told her, though "it is really now a matter of indifference whether I retire from this business or not. It has become almost too disgusting to endure."[66]

"Don't get agitated," John warned her. But, disheartened, Jessie told Isaac Sherman, "Mr. Frémont, unfortunately for himself & his work, is not a man to make terms." Even less was she. In the past, Jessie had used the good offices of her father to intervene on Frémont's behalf. While still a teenager, she had saved him from censure herself in 1843, delaying a message that came to her in St. Louis from his superiors in Washington. They wanted to recall him from his second expedition over the questionable requisitioning of a cannon for his ostensibly peaceful venture. She sent a messenger down the trail to urge him westward, and Frémont carried the howitzer into the mountains. Benton had served as buffer with the military authorities in Washington. Now, though, the elder Benton was dead, and Jessie Benton Frémont was powerless to protect her husband.[67]

Cameron's traveling companion, Adjutant General Lorenzo Thomas, prepared the report for Lincoln. It was highly critical of the expenditures on fortifications in and around St. Louis and ordered the work stopped, although Sherman was writing at about the same time that the city was at risk and losing it would be a greater defeat for the Union than the loss of Washington. Thomas also highlighted the department's slipshod contracting practices, without a hint of Meigs's earlier understanding that sometimes in war quick results are more important than meticulous record keeping. Thomas left no doubt about where he stood on Frémont's fate. "The opinion entertained by gentlemen who have approached and observed [Frémont] is that he is more fond of the pomp than of the stern realities of war; that his mind is incapable of fixed attention or strong concentration; that by his mismanagement of affairs since his arrival in Missouri the State has almost been lost, and that if he is continued in command, the worst results may be anticipated," Thomas wrote. "This is the concurrent testimony of a very large number of the most intelligent men in Missouri."[68]

Those "most intelligent men" were largely the friends and allies of Frank Blair, among whom Thomas himself, West Point Class of 1823, was counted. Thomas had some combat experience in Florida and served as a staff aide in Mexico but had been a desk soldier for most of his career. That did not stop him from proclaiming with certainty that Frémont had erred when he reinforced Cairo at the expense of Lyon. He was on stronger ground outlining how Frémont might have come to the rescue of Mulligan at Lexington, but the report nevertheless reads like a war game exercise that ignores the realities of weather, terrain, and recalcitrant division commanders. "General Thomas is my enemy," Frémont told Jessie even before his arrival. "He is one of those who opposed my appointment, and I am told indulged in some of the abusive and false language, which a certain class about Washington had habitually permitted to themselves in reference to me."[69]

Cameron and Thomas arrived back in Washington on October 21 and delivered the report to Lincoln in time for a cabinet meeting the next day, at which "the vexed question of the recall of Genl. Frémont" was the main event. Attorney General Edward Bates, a Missourian, argued that "beyond all question" Frémont must be removed "instantly," based on Thomas's report. "The president seemed to think so, and said it was now clear that Frémont was not fit for the command." (In his diary, Bates changed "fit to command" to "fit for the command," a significant softening of his criticism.)[70]

Seward urged delay, and Chase and Cameron—who had been swayed by Frémont's plea for more time—supported him. In response, Bates played his Missouri card:

> To leave him there now would be worse than prompt removal—for you have degraded him before the world and thereby unfitted him for the command, if otherwise capable—You have countermanded his orders, repudiated his contracts and denounced his contractors, suspended his officers and stopped the progress of his fortifications—If under these circumstances we still keep him in command, the public will attribute the fact to a motive no higher than our fears. For me—I think too well of the soldiers and the people, to be afraid of any Major General in the Army. I protested against having *my* State sacrificed on such motives and in such a cause.[71]

When Bates left the cabinet meeting, he still feared that Frémont "will be allowed to hang on until he drops in very rottenness. And if we persist in this sort of impotent indecision, we are very likely to share his fate—and, worse than all, *deserve it.*"[72]

At this point it still seemed barely possible, despite the Blairs and the investigations and the insubordination, that Frémont might survive long enough to have a chance at proving the doubters wrong. "Frémont was never fit for his post," Sherman argued to his senator brother, but he told his wife, "They should let Frémont fight his fight before destroying him." Bates thought that was going to happen. But Lincoln's mind was made up. Tucked into Thomas's report was a revelation that Frémont had ordered two hundred copies of his emancipation order printed and distributed to the army and "through the country" a week after it had been overruled by the president. Jessie's message to John to "have copies ready" after her meeting with Lincoln was coming back to haunt the couple.[73]

And then the report went public. The order of dismissal carried by Cameron was already grist for the newspapers, weakening Frémont's position. Thurlow Weed had weighed in with a hostile commentary on October 26. Now Thomas's report, intended only for Lincoln and the cabinet, was leaked to the newspapers. "We know not what the motive was which influenced the authorities at Washington to permit the publication of Adjutant-General Thomas's report of what he heard and saw in Missouri and Kentucky," the *New York Dispatch* reported, "but it is quite apparent to every thinking mind that it will do more to damage the cause of the Union than would the defeat of the army in half a dozen successive battles." That it was leaked with the clear intent of damaging Frémont and preparing the country for his dismissal is certain. Whether it came directly from Thomas, Montgomery Blair, or some other unhappy opponent of Frémont is not clear. Release of the report to the public did engender some hostile reaction on Frémont's behalf, but the substance of the charges—such as it was—got most of the attention.[74]

Jessie was not far off the mark when she called the report "gossip collected by Genl. Thomas." Chase wrote that the report "ought never to have seen the light. It was at best only evidence in a Grand Jury Room." The *New York Times*, no friend to Frémont, belittled it as the "diary of a travelling Adjutant." Journalist Henry Villard, who had observed Lincoln closely in Springfield, wrote that the president's reliance on ex parte information in deciding Frémont's fate was uncharacteristic. He typically preferred to act on "full and reliable information."[75]

But act Lincoln did. Two days after the cabinet meeting, he issued the order to relieve Frémont of his command. While losing the patronage of the Blairs was the crucial turning point in Frémont's downfall, it was Frémont's insubordination and, as Lincoln saw it, dishonesty related to the proclamation that was the last straw.

"WITHOUT PRECEDENT FOR GALLANTRY"
Meanwhile, the war continued.

If Frémont never shared his plans with Hunter or other subordinates, he kept Jessie informed back in St. Louis with a steady stream of letters from the field that would eventually make up the core of her first book, *The Story of the Guard*, her version of the events now unfolding in Missouri. He complained to her about the shortage of weapons and transportation while praising the high spirits of the troops. He warned her about the approach of Cameron and Thomas. He enlisted her to "do all that is humanly possible to get wagons, mules, harness[es], and drivers sent forward" and used her as his main conduit to send orders to Andrew Foote, in command of the navy's Mississippi gunboats. As so often before, he wrote, "I trust in you to do all that can be done." And he notified her, if not Hunter, of his "full plan," which he expected to carry out if not "interrupted" by Price's army.[76]

At the time of Frémont's worries about being interrupted, Price was "on the Osage, pretty high up." Marching southward, he arrived in Neosho in the far southwestern corner of the state on October 20, the same day a rump Missouri legislature convened there to pass an ordinance of secession. It meant little to the armies in the field but was confirmation that Missouri, like Kentucky, was going to be contested no matter how much the president believed that protecting slavery would aid border-state unionism. The next day, Oregon senator Edward D. Baker, Lincoln's close friend and Jessie's sometime salon mate at Black Point, was killed at the Battle of Ball's Bluff in Virginia. "I am so sorry for him," Frémont wrote to his wife. "The way, after long waiting, was just opening."[77]

Frémont plodded on but still could not "get the army nigh enough to the enemy to strike a blow, and so I lose a victory." From Syracuse to Warsaw his army crossed forty-five miles, the second half of which "is altogether one of the most execrable routes in existence," up hills, down valleys, and through mud holes. Frémont crossed the Osage River at Warsaw on October 22 and camped three miles south of town. That day, Owen Lovejoy noted, "It is growing cold and looks like winter." Despite Frémont's optimism, Lovejoy's outlook was as bleak as the weather. "Frémont says he will give us a victory before we return back. I am still doubtful about it."[78]

Frémont's army, "on the verge of starvation—i.e., living on beef and salt," moved on October 24 through Buffalo, thirty-five miles north of Springfield, where a local noted that "they made a splendid appearance" despite their deprivations and filled the town's unionists with jubilation. It might have filled Frémont's heart with joy to know that his army was so welcome. But on the same day back in Washington, Lincoln signed the order to relieve him of command.[79]

Also on that day, "nine contrabands came into camp," and Lovejoy advised Frémont to send them to Illinois. While fugitives didn't always make it across the river into a free state, Frémont would not allow contrabands to be returned to masters, loyal or not. Critics had lampooned his emancipation proclamation as freeing virtually no one, but his soldiers were, in historian Kristopher A. Teters's phrase, "practical liberators" as they moved across the state, even if they never engaged the enemy in a major battle.[80]

And they simply couldn't catch up to the enemy. Finally, on October 25, Charles Zagonyi, the Hungarian commander of Frémont's cavalry "Body Guard," took three hundred men against what he estimated to be about two thousand Missouri State Guard defending Springfield. Though Zagonyi's troops were vastly outnumbered, the State Guard were mostly recent local recruits with little training, and the sight of three hundred costumed cavalrymen charging at them with sabers swinging and sidearms blazing drove the rebels back. Zagonyi's charge was "without precedent for gallantry," according to some of the Texans who were on the receiving end of it. Frémont enthused, "The war will have nothing more splendid to record." Two and a half months after Wilson's Creek, the town was retaken, but it accomplished little militarily (supporting Frémont's original justification for reinforcing Cairo rather than Lyon). The main body of the army was still at least two days' march away, and Zagonyi could not hold the town with a few hundred men. He pulled back and waited for the army to come up.[81]

Frémont believed the attack "has given tone to the army." Jessie celebrated that Springfield's "long subjection to the rebels was over, and the Unionists were exultant."[82]

Her elation from that success quickly gave way to despondency. In a cry from the heart on October 26 to Ward Hill Lamon, she wished for someone to lay the reality of the war in Missouri before Lincoln but knew she was not the right messenger. "He is too prejudiced against me, I can't do it." While Zagonyi's charge was a cheering moment, it was too little, too late, and she knew it. "If the division under Genl.'s Hunter Pope & McKinstry had had transportation enough—they do not march light as Genl. Frémont does—there would have been a complete victory over Price & his whole force about the 20–22d."[83]

On October 28, "a beautiful, cool, bright morning," Frémont and his staff attended the funeral of the eighteen men killed in Zagonyi's attack on Springfield. Tears flowed from the rough soldiers who surrounded the grave. Lovejoy called it "a funeral unlike any one I ever attended," with the bodies loaded onto wagons and borne in procession from a makeshift hospital to a makeshift cemetery.[84]

October 29 was a "cold windy day." Price remained out of reach. "The enemy are said to be about 65 miles from here but I am still doubtful if they make a stand though they may," Lovejoy wrote. Price had withdrawn to Pineville, just north of the Arkansas state line. Without fighting a major battle, Frémont had effectively maneuvered the rebel army out of Missouri. As he later told a congressional committee, "The appearance of my advance at Sedalia was the signal for [Price's] precipitate retreat. . . . The state was, in reality, reclaimed, and in condition to leave the army free for the especial object of descending the Mississippi." That fact would do him no good.[85]

"I AM GETTING TIRED OF ALL THIS"

Francis Preston Blair Sr. would complain to anyone who would listen about Frémont, and in John Bigelow, now U.S. consul in Paris under William Dayton, he had a friendly ear. In a late October letter largely concerned with complaining about William Seward, Blair reiterated all his well-aired complaints about Frémont, highlighted by the ridiculous charge that the latter had "set himself up by a sort of Mexican *pronunciamento*—by Martial law superseding the Constitution, the law and the President—into a dictatorship." He also bemoaned the emancipation order and hinted that Seward was in league with Frémont in an effort to divide the North, allowing Seward—because of Frémont's "notorious incapacity"—to become "master of the field."[86]

Blair's blast was a fit of paranoia outdoing Frémont's own. But similar notes were coming to Lincoln from Frémont's own staff. Congressman John Gurley warned the president of "strong reasons for belief that Gen. Frémont does not mean to yield his command at your bidding." These hysterical admonitions were superfluous. Lincoln had already decided Frémont's fate, and it did not include his own private dictatorship in Missouri.[87]

Sometime in this period, Charles Sumner wrote to Lincoln recommending Sigel as a replacement for Frémont. The German had not exactly covered himself with glory at Wilson's Creek or on the retreat to Rolla, where he so annoyed both officers and men that he was forced to surrender command. But Sumner saw in him a kindred abolitionist spirit and so recommended him to the president as someone with "many of the conditions which you are seeking for the command West of the Mississippi. As a German he would be most acceptable in St Louis, where there are so many of that nation."[88]

Frémont was encumbered by division commanders who were not loyal to him and felt empowered to dawdle by the rumors of his impending dismissal. As Pope wrote to Hunter on October 26, "The prospect before us is appalling, and we seem to be led by madmen. . . . Should they be permitted to drag to destruction, or at least to great and unnecessary suffering, the 30,000 men of this army, for no other purpose than to save, if possible, their own official lives?"[89]

Pope and Hunter were West Pointers, but they had aspects of political generals, including the fact that both men had traveled with Lincoln on the train from Springfield to Washington. They were now engaged in the sort of military politics that would pain Lincoln and bedevil the Army of the Potomac for much of 1862, no little amount of it from Pope. Jessie had no use for him. "Pope is of that inferior nature of man which runs to the rising sun," she wrote at the time. Her later assessment encompassed others. "The great error committed by some of the ranking officers, was they supposed themselves in command of the entire army, and unless movements were made which fitted in with their preconceived ideas of what should be done, they were heartily discontented and took no pains to prevent their dissatisfaction from reaching their subordinates, and the troops under their command."[90]

"I am getting tired of all this," Frémont told his wife. But he still intended to fight. While urging his division commanders to move toward Springfield with greater speed, he was also taking steps he hoped would alleviate some of the burden of war on noncombatants. Both armies were guilty of attacks on civilians. Thurlow Weed had detailed some of those committed by northern troops in his October 26 anti-Frémont screed, quoting a witness: "The march was one continuous devastation, without the least regard for principles or antecedents."[91]

Frémont reached out to Price, and the two generals agreed on an exchange of prisoners; to take steps to suppress guerillas and confine the fighting to the organized armies; that neither side should arrest any citizen for merely voicing an opinion for or against secession; and that the state courts should continue to deal with legal disputes (as Frémont had ordered even in his martial law declaration). A savvy journalist traveling with the army called the Frémont-Price deal "probably a very good one, theoretically, but practically of no particular avail as the masses on neither side will respect it." Nor did the government. Frémont saw the arrangement as "preparatory to [Price] leaving the state." But the arrangement was voided shortly after Frémont was relieved of command.[92]

Thus, one of Frémont's last acts was to endorse an ineffective soft-war policy he had done so much to oppose with his August 30 declaration of martial law and emancipation order. It was a fittingly ironic end to his command.

Lincoln's order to Curtis was to "take safe, certain, and suitable measures" to ensure that the order was delivered to Frémont "with all reasonable dispatch." He was to withhold delivery if Frémont was about to fight a battle, or had just won one, or was "in the immediate presence of the enemy, in expectation of a battle." Once he had delivered the removal order to Frémont, he was to proceed on to give Hunter his orders to take over.[93]

Frémont had taken steps to slow any such message's arrival, but Curtis outwitted him by sending multiple copies, and one courier got through the lines. According to the man who delivered the order to headquarters on the evening of November 2, "Frémont was sitting at the end of quite a long table facing the door by which I entered . . . his piercing eye and his hair parted in the middle." The order had been sewn into the man's coat lining, and he had to rip the garment to retrieve it. Frémont took the paper and read the signatures but not the contents, slammed it on the table, and asked, "Sir, how did you get admission into my lines?"[94]

After receiving the order, Frémont still thought it possible that he could attack the enemy the next day if Hunter did not arrive. Scouts had spotted some cavalry and possibly skirmishers near the old Wilson's Creek battlefield, only a few miles southwest of Springfield. The idea, based on the notion that the bulk of Price's army was only a few miles farther away, was met with "no little enthusiasm" and "a tremendous cheer." "We expect to march soon," Lovejoy warned his family, "and I may not have time to write again soon." But the congressman's marching days were effectively over. While Frémont was briefing Pope and other officers on his plans, Hunter entered the headquarters and informed Frémont that he was there to take command immediately. Price had indeed intended to make a stand, but the rebels were fifty miles distant, not near enough in Hunter's estimation to invoke the "in the immediate presence of the enemy, in expectation of a battle" clause in Lincoln's order.[95]

When the order to relieve Frémont became known, there was some concern about what the army might do. A New Yorker had warned Lincoln earlier in the month about "an interview with a friend who has a son under [Frémont] as lieutenant, and he writes to his father that if Gen Frémont is superseded at this time, it will entirely or almost entirely disband the western army he fears; the men are all so much attached to him."[96]

Koerner remembered that the "excitement was tremendous. It amounted almost to a mutiny," the German troops being "particularly indignant." The newspapers reported "one or two companies throwing down their arms and declaring they would not serve." Some officers told Frémont that their men would fight only for him. Frémont quickly calmed the storm, putting the lie to the ridiculous fears that he planned to rise up against the government and establish an independent West under his dictatorship. He admonished the officers for suggesting the men would not fight, and one of his staff later told Congress that he was confident Frémont "would have put down by force, if necessary, any attempt at mutiny." Zagonyi told Congress, "He quieted them in the very best way." It was over, and Frémont accepted it. "Get quietly ready for immediate departure from St. Louis," he told Jessie. "I shall leave this place forthwith."[97]

Frémont's "perfectly simple and dignified" farewell to the troops was brief but heartfelt, a "short, manly, and feeling address," as one of his officers described it. "Although our Army has been of sudden growth, we have grown up together, and have become familiar with the brave and generous spirit which you bring to the defenses of your country, and which makes me anticipate for you a brilliant career," he wrote. He urged the grumbling Germans to "give to my successor the same cordial and enthusiastic support with which you have encouraged me. Emulate the splendid example which you have already before you, and let me remain, as I am, proud of the noble Army which I had thus far labored to bring together." He expressed his regret in leaving them and thanked them for the "regard and confidence" they had shown him. And he hinted at the aggravation he must have felt in being relieved with the enemy, as he mistakenly believed, in his front. "I deeply regret," he closed, "that I shall not have the honor to lead you to the victory which you are just about to win, but I shall claim to share with you in the joy of every triumph, and trust always to be fraternally remembered by my companions in arms."[98]

But before the message was even in the hands of Frémont's now former comrades, the new commander was plotting a retreat, though Frémont's staff remained in the dark about what was coming next.

"It is likely that I may turn homeward as it is probable the army may not go any farther," Lovejoy predicted on November 7. Early the next day he backtracked a bit: "This morning it looks a little as though we might advance." But after meeting with Hunter, he concluded, "I think it is at last settled that the army will not go forward and consequently I shall soon go home."[99]

Lincoln had decided more than a week before that the army should turn back. The first draft of his letter full of "suggestions" for Hunter began, "The command of the Department of the West, having, for a time, devolved upon you . . ." In the version he sent, Lincoln deleted "for a time," perhaps considering the effect such a feeling of impermanence might convey. He then went on to outline the movements he wanted Frémont's former army to take, which included retreating to Sedalia and Rolla and leaving Price to his own devices.[100]

St. Louis Germans were incredulous that Frémont was removed on what they believed was the eve of battle and the army ordered back to St. Louis. "It is as if a choir of a hundred clowns were singing," the *Anzeiger des Westens* commented. The paper had little doubt who was the chief clown. "The state has fallen victim to Frank Blair's despicable intrigues."[101]

Conducting the chorus, Blair and Schofield had scoffed at Frémont's plans, and Pope thought the idea of moving against Price and McCulloch folly. But, as one contemporary noted, "the same plan was adopted by the authorities in Washington" half a year later. The successful march on Pea Ridge was a rerun of Frémont's plan to pursue Price until the rebel stood and faced him. "The question is pertinent, how much more effective this move would have been if executed by General Frémont six months earlier," a St. Louis ally asked.[102]

John Hay, writing anonymously in the *Missouri Republican* immediately after Frémont was relieved, called him a "thief and an idiot" but urged him not to abandon the war.

> It is the earnest hope of Gen. Frémont's friends that he will allow nothing
> to goad him into resigning his position in the army. With youth, genius and
> friends (and nobody can deny his possession of the three), there is nothing that
> the future may not afford to a man like him. . . . Possibilities of vast utility

and honest fame are before him—not to be lightly cast aside, in a momentary revolt of sensibility against a seeming wrong. It will not take many months of service to remove the stains which reeking calumny has spread over his name. There is a blank page of our history waiting for Frémont's name. He should not disappoint Fate and baffle auspicious Destiny.[103]

Frémont marched out of camp the day after his dismissal to the tune of a band playing "The Red, White, and Blue," trailed by his Shawnee and Delaware scouts "in bright colors, yelling and dashing about in a manner more picturesque than alarming," according to Pope. A member of Frémont's staff thought "he seemed very much relieved; was much more pleasant and cheerful than he had been for weeks before." As Frémont passed through Jefferson City on November 8, one soldier thought he looked "careworn and appeared to be considerably depressed in spirits." Whatever Frémont's state of mind, his St. Louis reception "was a grand affair."[104]

Frémont's Hundred Days as commander of the Western Department provide "a study saturated with opinion, prejudice and (often less noted) fact," wrote retired U.S. Army special forces officer Dr. Robert L. Turkoly-Joczik, a scholar who was also a career military officer. "An analysis of his activities suggests that subsequent dismissive appraisals of his performance in this difficult and demanding leadership role resulted in unduly harsh judgments."[105]

Historians and biographers have generally been less kind in their analysis than was Turkoly-Joczik. Among contemporaries, the verdict was equally mixed. "I considered him in the midst of his misfortunes as being, with all his failings, head and shoulders above many of his enemies and traducers," wrote Benjamin Grierson, who served under Frémont at Cairo.[106]

Just before Frémont was relieved, Chase had told an Ohio antislavery ally, "You may be very sure that if Genl F. is recalled from his high command, his Proclamn. will not be the cause." By then, the secretary's views had evolved from a tepid endorsement that relied on Frémont not going beyond the Confiscation Act to a condemnation of the proclamation as "ineffectual" and "an act of insubordination."[107]

Chase had from the beginning "feared [Frémont's] recklessness in financial matters." He had also "opposed alone in the Cabinet his appt. as Maj-Gen., not because I doubted his efficiency or ability but because I feared he wd. be surrounded by unworthy men who wd. plunder the public." Owen Lovejoy might have summed it up best: the mistake, the abolitionist congressman and aide-de-camp concluded, was not in dismissing Frémont but in appointing him in the first place.[108]

The emancipation order had loosened the ground beneath Frémont's feet. His defiance of Lincoln shook the earth on which their relationship stood. His insubordination and dishonesty in printing and distributing the order after it had been rescinded sparked a landslide. His underlings' financial shenanigans, though relatively minor in the larger scheme of things, gave opponents something to complain about besides emancipation, lending a broader air of acceptability to their charges. The failure of the armies under Frémont's command to win victories in the field gave Lincoln the political cover to act. But, in the end, what doomed Frémont was the early loss of the Blairs' patronage, later inflamed by the arrest of Frank Blair. Thurlow Weed once described the Blairs as "smoothe but perfidious," and they would prove to be both in the matter of Frémont. From the moment the scion was taken into custody, the conservative forces in Washington led by his family united to oust the commanding general in Missouri. Emancipation, insubordination, inefficiency, and ineffectiveness were the justifications, with varying degrees of validity. But offending the Blairs, his onetime friends and patrons, was Frémont's capital offense.[109]

Frémont was gone. But the men who would follow him in command in Missouri over the next three-plus years would face many of the same problems and often vex Lincoln just as severely as Frémont had. The president's new problem was what to do next with Frémont.

CHAPTER SIX

"To strike some decided blow against the enemy"

"It is now certain that the rebels hope to profit by Frémont's removal, trusting that disaffection among our troops may insure them success," a *Chicago Tribune* correspondent wrote in a dispatch filed November 5, "but they will find in this calculation our troops took the news better than expected." Things calmed down in southwestern Missouri after Frémont left, and the army withdrew to Rolla in reasonably good order. While recruiting in the states of the Old Northwest briefly took a hit, it bounced back quickly.[1]

On the surface, so did Frémont. Loyalists in St. Louis greeted him with cheering and chants of "Frémont and the Union!" and escorted him through the darkened streets with a torchlight parade. His officers' mess was "about the jolliest, most sociable, most enjoyable spot of its kind that I have experienced," an aide recorded in his diary. The city's Germans led a subscription of ten cents a man to present a sword to Frémont "to be wielded for the reorganization of a great and free country," since "the administration had taken away or broken the sword of this warrior."[2]

Jessie was in a worse mood. Her chestnut hair had begun going gray almost overnight during the fall campaign. But amid the worry and bitterness, she remained sanguine that her husband would be vindicated. "Mr. Frémont can more than prove he has right on his side in all that is charged against him," she wrote to lawyer Frederick Billings. "There will be enough evidence to break down his accusers & leave them no escape." Frémont thought so, too, and spent a good portion of his two weeks in St. Louis collecting documents to help make his case.[3]

Allies were also rallying. A group of New England abolitionists formed the Emancipation League to coordinate an education campaign on the role slavery played in the rebellion. They cited Lincoln's revocation of Frémont's proclamation as one of their inspirations. They could have cited Lincoln, who in his debate with Stephen A. Douglas in Ottawa, Illinois, in 1858, said, "With public sentiment, nothing can fail; without it nothing can succeed." Schuyler Colfax of Indiana delivered a pro-Frémont speech in Hoboken, New Jersey, on November 26. The next night Colfax was on the stage when Charles Sumner spoke at Cooper Union, the same hall where Lincoln had won over an eastern audience in the early months of the 1860 campaign. He praised Frémont in a speech "received with tumultuous applause." After the speech, a resolution was adopted endorsing "the doctrine enunciated by Major-General Frémont with respect to the emancipation of the slaves of rebels" and asserting that the "eventual rooting out of slavery, as the cause of the rebellion" was "a moral, political, and military necessity; and, in the judgment of this meeting, the public sentiment of the North is now fully in sympathy with any practicable scheme which may be presented for the extirpation of this national evil, and will accept such result as the only consistent issue of this contest between civilization and barbarism."[4]

By the first week of December, the Frémonts had set up shop in New York's Astor House, where John had conferred with Lincoln in February before heading on to Europe. Frémont spent many days riding over the Hoboken Heights with Charles Zagonyi and other officers. The Arion Singing Society serenaded Frémont on the evening of Saturday, December 7, with a reception and more music following. The party didn't break up until after midnight, but, at the invitation of Reverend Henry Ward Beecher, the Frémonts were in attendance the next morning at Plymouth Church in Brooklyn. "I have something to say and I want you to be there," Beecher told Frémont. When the Frémonts entered, the entire congregation rose to its feet.[5]

"Calm as a judge summing up the evidence of a great crime," Jessie later wrote, "he brought to bear instances where men, forgetting the public welfare, had used for themselves their public position in efforts to ignore the consequences of intolerable injustice, and succeeding for the time, brought woe and annihilation to the innocent as well as the guilty, as in the French Revolution." But not just in France, Beecher averred. Abolitionist anger against Daniel Webster had blossomed in the wake of Black Dan's support of the Fugitive Slave Act; more than a decade later, Beecher still seethed. "In our country it had brought the political death of a great statesman; who turning from an honored record let personal aims place him among those maintaining injustice." Beecher's congregation nodded. They knew who he was talking about. "He died, and is dead," the reverend continued. Then, turning to Frémont, seated near the front, he said, "But your name will live and be remembered by a nation of freemen." After the service, the Frémonts made their way through the crowd outside in the cold sunshine, shaking hands as congregants assured the general, "God is with you."[6]

Wendell Phillips, sometimes compared to the voice of God, was certainly with Frémont. He had once suggested that the Kentucky-born Lincoln would never come around on emancipation because "no man gets over his birthplace," a position he did not hold on the Georgia-born Frémont. A reluctant John allowed Jessie to persuade him to attend the great abolitionist orator's speech at Cooper Union on December 19. Wanting to avoid a spectacle, they came in late and were careful not to draw any attention from the overflow crowd. Phillips made his usual case—that "slavery is the root of this war" and the administration in Washington wasn't doing enough to dig it out. When he invoked Frémont's name, "loud and long" cheers reverberated through the packed hall, justifying Jessie's insistence, which Frémont still doubted, that much of the North was with him on this issue.[7]

Jessie was doing more than toting her husband around from event to event to hear his name praised and cheered. In mid-December, she met with James T. Fields, co-owner of the Ticknor and Fields publishing house, to discuss the possibility of her writing a book—"the fire-side story of an incident of the war," she called it—about the Missouri army that served under Frémont. While claiming "I am incapable of writing a book," she was "drunk with a belief" that the story needed to be told. Jessie Frémont was, of course, perfectly capable of writing a book. She would write many, but she had already assisted in the writing of her husband's expedition reports and had handled correspondence for many years for both husband and father. She had the letters she and Frémont had written to each other during September and October for source material. She hoped to set the record straight for "those truly soldierly young men" of the Frémont Body Guard whose "knightly deeds had been misrepresented, slighted & finally insulted out of the service because of the name they bore." She planned to use any proceeds to support the widows and orphans of those soldierly young men. "My part is to give you the story of the Guard and yours is to make it profitable to them," she told Fields. She would spend the early part of 1862 writing *The Story of the Guard* and the rest of it waiting for circumstances to free her up to publish.[8]

In the interim, the vultures came out to gnaw on Frémont's carcass. Multiple investigations of the Western Department's procurement practices were underway. Personal attacks continued unabated. St. Louis lawyer Britton A. Hill insisted to Attorney General Edward Bates that "Frémont is an opium eater— that his behavior and manner, his starting and contortions prove it—moreover that he detected the odor upon his breath." An embittered Elizabeth Blair Lee also spread the rumor. Bates dismissed this story for the nonsense it was. "I never repeat as a fact what I hear from Mr. Hill," he wrote in his diary.[9]

Facts, as opposed to scandalmongering and grudge settling, were in short supply. Salmon Chase, at least privately, was among those leading the charge for an official inquiry. "I trust a speedy & impartial investigation will be had & that entire justice will be done," he wrote on November 11. Ten days later he was more specific, calling for the military or the president to act. "I thk. Fr. shd demand an investigation by a Court of Enquiry, or that the Prest. shd. order a Court Martial & let the real facts come to light whatever the result."[10]

There would be neither court-martial nor court of inquiry. Frémont's experience with official military justice hardly endeared the process to him, and he refused to ask for either. Instead, Congress moved on two tracks: committees investigating alleged malfeasance in the Department of the West and creation of a new panel, the Joint Committee on the Conduct of the War, that would serve as a radical balance to the White House and bedevil Lincoln for the remainder of the conflict. An executive branch War Claims Commission was also investigating.

"MANY OF THE CHARGES AGAINST HIM ARE GROUNDLESS"

The U.S. military grew from sixteen thousand troops at the beginning of the war to seven hundred thousand within a year. As one historian of the Civil War Contracts Committee put it, lawmakers critical of the procurement practices of Frémont and others were quickly faced with "the ironic revelation that victory sometimes depended on bureaucratic laxity." The quartermaster general, who understood the rules and tried to live by them, understood this principle instinctively. "The general is charged with saving the country," Montgomery Meigs had written of Frémont in late August. "The country will be very careful to approve his measures, and will judge his mistakes, if any, very tenderly if successful." Now that success was off the table, judging of the mistakes would begin in full.[11]

Maj. Gen. George McClellan, installed as general in chief the day before Frémont was officially relieved, ordered paymasters in the Western Department arrested and funds seized, and he told Gen. Samuel Curtis, "If you find it necessary to accomplish the object arrest Frémont."[12]

Curtis did not find it necessary to arrest Frémont. But Brig. Gen. Justus McKinstry was arrested on McClellan's order and held incommunicado in early November, along with his chief clerk and cashier, and his papers from the quartermaster's office were seized. He would be imprisoned in a single room in the St. Louis Arsenal for three months. When he was finally released on February 22, 1862, he was ordered not to leave the city.[13]

Ironically, it had been Frank Blair who saved McKinstry's job in the spring when the higher-ups in Washington wanted him removed for alleged malfeasance. "McKinstry is heartily disposed to do all that he can for the maintenance of the Government," Blair had written to Simon Cameron in May, "and there is no ground for the nonsense that has been put afloat by those who want his position here." It was precisely because he had been "heartily disposed to do all that he can for the maintenance of the Government," without regard to rules and regulations, that he was now in chains. But since McKinstry had now become a hammer with which to pound Frémont, Blair conveniently forgot his previous endorsement.[14]

The War Claims Commission appointed by Lincoln and Cameron had posted public notice in English- and German-language newspapers in St. Louis, Cairo, Jefferson City, and Keokuk inviting claims against the government. The panel—Joseph Holt, David Davis, and Hugh Campbell—convened in St. Louis on November 6, after Frémont's dismissal but while he was still in the city. McKinstry considered the commission the "secret workings of a Star chamber." While he was locked up in St. Louis, Frémont's former quartermaster was denied the opportunity to testify on his own behalf. Instead, he spent his time compiling an impressive defense, 102 pages of correspondence, affidavits, and narrative debunking both the executive branch and congressional investigating committees. He submitted it to Quartermaster General Meigs on June 2, 1862, two months after the commission filed its report. His court-martial wouldn't convene until September 1862.[15]

One focus of the commission was on "forced loans" Frémont had taken from local banks to fund his army in the absence of military appropriations coming from the federal government. "Naturally enough in a city under martial law, these advances have assumed the courteous designation of 'loans,' though the testimony makes it manifest that with the exceptions hereafter referred to, they were anything but voluntary," the panel decided. "The banks were generally given to understand, by unmistakable indications, that what the military authorities could not borrow, they would take." While the money kept the army in operation, the forced loans "exerted a most disastrous influence upon the credit of the

Union Bank. It was, in consequence, forced into insolvency; its notes ceased to circulate, except at ruinous rates, and its stock depreciated one-half below previous value." Some of the money was used to buy uniforms, a sufficiently worthy justification. But the biggest contractor was the son-in-law of Frémont's friend and assistant quartermaster, Edward M. Davis.[16]

The commission noted that, in addition to the hardship such loans placed on banks and bankers, the military authorities in Missouri were not keeping Washington apprised of their activities, nor were they getting approval for their actions. "The inference is very clear that, although within speaking distance through the telegraphic wires, the War Department was not consulted at all upon the subject," according to the commission report, which also asserted that "the treasury was understood to be meeting its liabilities," a dubious contention in some cases. In the end, though, no action was forthcoming. "Although this question naturally excites vigilance of inquiry as to the purpose for which the funds were obtained, and the objects to which they were in fact applied, still we do not feel called upon to pursue the investigation, since, in our judgment, the result could not affect the liability of the United States," the panel concluded.[17]

Still, the commission chastised Frémont's decision making. "Such transactions are wholly irregular, and, without some extreme emergency to justify them (which has not been alleged,) must receive the condemnation of the government." Apparently, in the eyes of Davis, Holt, and Campbell, civil war was not an extreme enough emergency to justify quick, decisive action regardless of cost or inconvenience.[18]

The commissioners decided it was the government that had put Frémont in charge, so it was the government that was finally responsible for paying the claims. "The government thought proper to place General Frémont in command in this department, and to arm him with a power which made resistance to his mandates on the part of the citizen absolutely impossible," the panel wrote. "He took what he chose, and disposed of private property on which he laid his hands as to him seemed good. His action was in the name, and claimed to be by the authority and in the interests of the United States; and as the citizen could not arraign or resist his course, if abuses occurred, either in the 'loans' or in the application of their proceeds, the consequences, according to the maxim that 'they who trust the most shall lose most,' should be borne by the government from which he had received his commission."[19]

Frémont was off the hook, financially at least, but somebody had to pay. McKinstry was the logical choice. Samuel T. Glover, a member of Frank Blair's St. Louis Safety Committee and counsel for the War Claims Commission—a fact that makes for a fair assessment of the panel's lack of impartiality—called McKinstry "a God damned scoundrel" who "ought to be shot" before the investigation even began. Once the panel began collecting evidence, things only got worse for McKinstry. "Our investigations from day to day have afforded strong and ever-multiplying proofs that the administration of the late Quartermaster McKinstry was marked by personal favoritism, by a complete indifference to the public interests, and by an unceasing anxiety to fill at the expense of the nation the pockets of a clique of men who surrounded him," read the report.[20]

When one of McKinstry's underlings dared to question the doings of his superiors, he was shunted off to some unhappy duty. One assistant quartermaster, after raising doubts about a steamboat project on which he was working, was removed to the clothing department. When he continued to raise questions about how money was being spent in his new department, he was sent to deal with horses and mules. Again he tried to report malfeasance, and again he was transferred—this time to Benton Barracks, where it was assumed he could do no more harm. His reports were, he assumed, all burned by his superiors. This all happened within two or three days.[21]

Joseph H. Pease, acting apparently on McKinstry's behalf, served as agent for buying field tents. He paid $22 for them and then resold them to the army for $30, collecting a healthy commission of 36 percent. On more expensive tents, such as those for hospitals, he sometimes lowered that number to a mere 8 percent. The use of middlemen—purchasing agents engaged by the quartermaster corps to speed procurement of essential material—"if not an original device with Quartermaster McKinstry, was certainly pushed by him to an extent which has no parallel in the history of official delinquencies as connected with the military service of the country."[22]

And on and on: the purchasing of horses, mules, boots, steamers, tugs, railroad transportation, telegraph equipment, and sundry other articles of military necessity, such as clothing, caps, canteens, and knapsacks, was "marked by looseness and improvidence." The building of river boats came in for special condemnation. Another middleman, Theodore Adams, was not a boat builder and was "understood to be without capital." The commission reasoned that "the mechanics of St. Louis, had they been allowed to compete for this heavy job, would have offered to construct the boats at a far lower price, and would have found it profitable to do so." Nevertheless, the boats got built and proved crucial in later operations on the Mississippi. Adams spent years trying to collect payment, with limited success.[23]

In a case that went all the way to the Supreme Court and wasn't settled until 1869, the government reneged on the deals Frémont had signed to quickly build mortar boats, tugboats, and pilot houses, at a cost of $347,900. Adams had been paid $160,155.24 and wanted the rest, about $187,000. But the government ended up paying the boat builder only another $75,959.24, as decided by the commission. The builder sued, and the federal Court of Claims overruled the board and ordered the government to pay the full amount. The government appealed, and the Supreme Court reversed that decision, a ruling a historian who closely examined the case called "from a legal point of view . . . not sound." There was no legal or financial liability for Frémont by that time, but his perfectly rational decision in the circumstances to speed the building of the boats and the cost be damned was not vindicated by a court that included Justice David Davis, who had been a member of the War Claims Commission, and Chief Justice Salmon P. Chase, who had been a key player in the contract controversy as secretary of the Treasury.[24]

McKinstry argued, with some justification, that middlemen were an essential component in the procurement process because of long delays in payment. Most suppliers could not afford to wait a year or more to get their money from the government, and such delays were not unusual. Middlemen paid the supplier and assumed the risk, for a profit. Without them, the army could not be provisioned.[25]

Frémont and McKinstry were far from the only players in this lucrative game. Frank Blair might have had reason to be genuinely upset about the riches lavished on Frémont's friends. But part of the motivation stirring him to action was that his friends weren't getting enough lavished on them.

"I shall be much obliged to you if you can give Mr. Aleck Peterson a contract for buying horses," Blair had written McKinstry on August 27. "He is a good friend of mine, a firm Union man, and I should be glad to serve him." Blair made similar requests on behalf of other friends, some of which McKinstry accommodated, many of which he did not. Even Lincoln was not above trying to get favors done for his friends. He appealed to McKinstry the very day Jessie Frémont met with him in the White House, pushing James L. Lamb of Springfield on the quartermaster as someone the president had known "for a great many years. His reputation for integrity and ability to carry out his engagements are both unquestioned, and I shall be pleased, if consistent with the public good, that you will make purchases of him of any army supplies needed in your Department." This missive went not through Frémont or Meigs or even Blair but directly to McKinstry, who must have viewed it less as a request than as an order, coming as it did from the commander in chief. Lincoln and Blair weren't trying to benefit financially from military contracts. They were simply using their positions to aid their friends, the same charge leveled against Frémont.[26]

"Frémont is surrounded by Scoundrels"
Created July 8, in the first flush of congressional action during the July–August special session, the Special House Committee on Government Contracts was headed by New Yorker Charles Van Wyck, who had survived an assassination attempt in February on the same night Lincoln traveled uneasily through Baltimore. Van Wyck shot and wounded one of his three attackers, all of whom escaped into the night. This was just the sort of bulldog mentality that made for successful congressional investigations. But Van Wyck was more interested in fighting the rebels in the field than dealing with alleged miscreants in his own army.[27]

Another committee member, Henry Dawes of Massachusetts, was at first unenthusiastic about serving on the panel but hoped "to reach some of the corruption with which every Department seems to be reeking here." He would become the committee's most ferocious defender against its many critics. Van Wyck was off raising a regiment and left Lincoln's friend Elihu Washburne to run the day-to-day affairs of the committee, along with Dawes. Washburne's presence did not insulate the panel from criticism by the administration.[28]

At first, the panel focused on senior officials, particularly Navy Secretary Gideon Welles and War Secretary Simon Cameron (whose reputation for shady dealings had nearly cost him the job in the first place). Writing anonymously, John Hay called the hearings "an absurd fiasco." Lincoln complained that Dawes did "more to break down the administration than any other man in the country." Some of the committee members' fellow lawmakers were no less critical. Thaddeus Stevens, no defender of Cameron, compared the panel to the Jacobins of the French Revolution and said the committee "committed more frauds than it had detected."[29]

When the committee questioned some of Welles's shipbuilding practices, Welles called its members a "cabal of lobby corruptionists and the weak tools whom they influenced." But the focus shifted to the field soon enough, with a particular emphasis on the Western Department. Iowa senator James Grimes was convinced that Lincoln was behind the Van Wyck committee's decision to "abandon Cameron and fall upon Frémont" in the hope that lawmakers would provide congressional sanction for Lincoln's removal of the popular general. At the same time, Grimes disavowed any devotion to the former western commander. "I was not and am not a partisan of Frémont," he told fellow senator William Fessenden of Maine. "I told you and others in July that I doubted his capacity for so extensive a military command as was assigned him." But Grimes was determined that justice be done, and he asserted that Frémont's failings paled before those of the commanders in the East, who seemed to him immune to official criticism.[30]

The committee ranged far and wide in search of corruption, traveling seven thousand miles, visiting eight cities, and interrogating 265 witnesses. Field hearings—including at Barnum's Hotel in St. Louis—helped gather evidence from people who couldn't get to Washington. Ulysses S. Grant testified on October 31 in Cairo about dissatisfaction among the troops with Austrian rifles Frémont had purchased in Europe. "I reported them several times to the commander of the western department as being useless," he told the panel. After hearing more than thirty witnesses over four days in Missouri, Washburne reported to Lincoln, "The disclosures of corruption extravagance and peculation are utterly astounding. . . . The history of the world affords no parallel to the state of things that has existed here since the advent of Frémont &Co." Appealing to his long friendship with Lincoln, Washburne continued. "You have known me long enough to know whether a judgment formed by me here is worth anything. I want to guard myself vigilantly against doing injustice to any man, but I should do you injustice did I not state to you that I believe Frémont is utterly incompetent in all respects and that under his administration there will be nothing but ruin and disaster." Washburne's assessment was based largely on the testimony of Blair allies and disgruntled would-be contractors. The St. Louis hearings were held in mid-October, while Frémont and McKinstry were in the field, affording them no opportunity to defend or explain themselves in person. The investigators were also running into some public relations problems. Newspapers noted the inherent irony of a committee focused on economy "roaming about the country, living like fighting cocks, spending largely of the public money, and having a good time generally."[31]

Frémont remained a popular figure inside and outside Congress. No matter what Washburne might say in private to Lincoln, the committee proceeded with care in public. Members knew they had to go at him obliquely, and in Justus McKinstry they had the perfect foil. His unsavory reputation in the army inspired little sympathy, and his methods—haphazard at best—were easy prey. He relied on brokers to speed purchases, but this dependence on middlemen inevitably drove up costs while creating the suspicion that McKinstry was taking a slice off the top. Commissions ranged as high as 5 percent on already inflated prices. McKinstry tried to play the victim. "Portions of the public press have assailed me, and the most foul and malicious slanders concerning me have been made public in two Congressional reports," he later complained. But his blustery manner made him ill suited to the role.[32]

Washburne had said he was "after McKinstry" even before the hearings got seriously underway. But the evidence against McKinstry, even accounting for the exigencies of the emergency and the bias of the investigators, was strong. Frémont was implicated in some of the shenanigans. He had appointed Edward Davis—his confidant in the emancipation order—as assistant quartermaster, even though he was a supplier of blankets to the army. He was directly involved in the procurement of the river boats. And he steered lucrative contracts to California friends.[33]

One particularly egregious case involved a contract for building the fortifications around St. Louis, for which E. L. Beard was paid $151,000 between August 29 and September 6. But this was three weeks before the contract was signed on September 25, and most of the fortifications had already been built by local labor under the supervision of army officers. In this instance, Frémont might plead ignorance but could not avoid responsibility. "All the amounts were paid upon the direct personal order of Major General Frémont," the committee concluded. In another instance, a contractor contributed $300 to pay for a horse and carriage for Jessie.[34]

Still, Frémont "was considered a vicarious martyr" to the graft around him rather than a direct participant in it. Henry Stevens had skin in the game. He had worked with his brother, Simon, as Frémont's agent for arms buying in Europe and defended their early actions in securing weapons that were sometimes overpriced and of dubious quality. "Our friend General Frémont has been treated shamefully," Stevens wrote to a navy friend. "I know that many of the charges against him are groundless, because of some of them I am part."[35]

At least one allegation related to Stevens was not entirely groundless. In what came to be known as the Hall Carbine Affair, the committee investigated Simon Stevens's sale to Frémont of five thousand rifles valued at $3.50 each for $22 a gun. The House adopted a resolution ordering the Treasury Department to cut the price to $12.50. The vote was seen by some as a slap at Frémont, though many of his supporters joined in voting for the resolution, which was adopted by a wide majority, 103–28. Frémont emerged relatively unscathed and insisted to Congress that the arms were worth every penny to his gun-starved troops and that "the purchase is not deserving of special censure."[36]

Van Wyck committee members Washburne and William S. Holman—neither particularly friendly to Frémont—told Orville Browning that "there are the most stupendous and astounding frauds in the Western Department and that Frémont is surrounded by Scoundrels." According to Browning, "They think him incompetent for command, but have no evidence of his dishonesty." During House floor debate on the committee's findings, Thaddeus Stevens came to the aid of Frémont, who thanked him for his "vigorous defense." At the end of 1861, the committee printed five thousand copies of its first preliminary report with all the evidence included and ten thousand of the report alone. It landed with a thud. Cameron crowed that the committee had accomplished nothing. Dawes complained of public indifference to the committee's findings. But worried citizens had other things on their mind, including McClellan's inactivity, which had taken some of the heat off Frémont and shifted it to the eastern theater of war. It also mattered that all the Western Department's contracts combined amounted to about $12 million, which the public was beginning to understand was a drop in the bucket compared with the cost of what was now looking like a long war. Frémont, hoping for another command, remained silent about what were, broadly speaking, the exculpatory (if unflattering) conclusions of both the congressional investigating committee and the commission appointed by Lincoln. He would have more to say to—and would get a friendlier reception from—the Joint Committee on the Conduct of the War.[37]

"LET THE COUNTRY KNOW WHAT ARE THE FACTS"

On November 1, 1861, Simon Cameron gave an anodyne speech to a regiment in New York. He was followed on the dais by Col. John Cochrane, a War Democrat and former member of Congress now commanding a regiment, who used the occasion of this speech to his troops to make a pitch for the enlistment of free blacks. Cameron sat passively by as Cochrane made an unassailable point about the objections raised from some quarters that arming the slaves was tantamount to emancipation: "The measure which restored the Government was not chargeable with an injury inflicted on its assailants," as he later described it. Two weeks later, Cochrane repeated his call, exhorting his troops "to take the slave and make him an implement of war in overcoming your enemy," again with Cameron in attendance. This time Cameron did not remain silent. He told a reporter that he approved of Cochrane's speech "as if it were uttered in my own words." On November 15, Cameron made those words his own at a cabinet meeting, where he pitched the president and his colleagues on the idea of putting former slaves into Federal uniforms. Soon after, Cameron delivered his department's contribution to the president's annual message. Cameron was not known as an abolitionist, but he had moved in that direction quickly. His interpretation of the Confiscation Act had lent teeth to the measure. Only the month before, he had had orders sent to a general in South Carolina that called for the organizing in "squads, companies or otherwise" of any liberated slaves that came into his lines. Although he included a caveat against any "general arming" of these men, the clear intent was to begin preparing them for military service. Charles Sumner averred that the secretary was out-Frémonting Frémont. When Cameron sent his department's portion of the president's annual message to Lincoln, it included a call for black troops. Just as he had with Frémont's emancipation proclamation, Lincoln rebuffed Cameron, ordering the passage excised. It was, but not before the original had been released to the press. A rearguard action by Montgomery Blair to have his postmasters intercept the report proved largely futile. One historian of Lincoln's cabinet called Cameron's provocative call "insolent insubordination." It might have been that. But it was also a sure sign that the war was changing in ways Lincoln couldn't control.[38]

In the special session of Congress in July and August, Congress had retroactively endorsed with barely a word of protest the steps Lincoln had taken since Fort Sumter. By December, things were different. The defeats at Manassas, Wilson's Creek, and Ball's Bluff had caused many to question the administration's military strategy. McClellan's inaction in Virginia was beginning to look to some Republicans like part of a broader unwillingness among Democratic generals to fight at all. The radicals believed an injustice had been done to Frémont because of his emancipation order and were further angered when Frémont's successor, Henry Halleck, barred fugitive slaves from coming into the army's lines. An increasingly vocal group, not just radicals, was beginning to question Lincoln's direction of the war and wanted Congress to assert a stronger hand.

The first days of the new congressional session in 1861 saw a flurry of activity related to emancipation, a sign that eight months of unsuccessful war had begun to change attitudes. Lyman Trumbull came forward with a tougher Confiscation Act. Owen Lovejoy proposed barring the army from participating in the capture of escaped slaves. Thaddeus Stevens asked the president to order the army to free every slave it encountered. Lincoln took no steps in that direction. But he did tell a visitor, historian George Bancroft, that "slavery has received a mortal wound. . . . [T]he harpoon [cast by the war itself] has struck the whale to the heart." And he told Orville Browning of a proposal in the works to pay the border states "$500 apiece for all the Negroes they had according to the census of

1860, provided they would adopt a system of gradual emancipation which would work the extinction of slavery in twenty years."[39]

The war was on the mind of Congress too. Several senators offered proposals for an investigating committee, starting with a plan to look into the defeats at Manassas and Ball's Bluff. James Lane of Kansas wanted to include Wilson's Creek. James Grimes of Iowa, who had suspected Lincoln of siccing the Contracts Committee on Frémont, wanted a broader investigation—a joint House-Senate panel empowered to "inquire into the causes of the disasters that have attended the public arms everywhere." As for the Kansan's proposal, which he insisted was not designed "to attach blame to any particular individual," Grimes advocated scrutiny even as Lane's amendment was defeated. Grimes and others suspected that the real target of Lane's proposal was Frémont. If, Grimes said, Frémont was at fault in the fall of Lexington, that "is a question which we ought to investigate, that the country may know whether they or those who condemn General Frémont are right." In the absence of an investigation by the army, it was Congress's duty to investigate the matter. "Let the country know what are the facts," he said. "If they condemn General Frémont, let him be condemned; if they justify him, then in God's name let him be justified."[40]

It was Ohio senator John Sherman, the brother of Gen. William T. Sherman, who proposed expanding the committee's brief beyond "military disasters" to include "inquiry into the general conduct of the war." That's what the Senate agreed to, on a vote of 33–3, on December 9. The House concurred the next day.[41]

Three senators and four House members were named to the committee, which had a radical, pro-Frémont tinge. Only one Democrat from each chamber was named. Republican senator Ben Wade of Ohio was appointed chairman, joined by Zachariah Chandler of Michigan and Democrat Andrew Johnson of Tennessee. The House members were Republicans Daniel Gooch of Massachusetts, John Covode of Pennsylvania, and George W. Julian of Indiana and Democrat Moses Odell of New York.[42]

They wasted little time getting started. On December 29, the Senate sergeant at arms showed up at the Astor House to deliver a subpoena for Frémont to appear before the Joint Committee on the Conduct of the War. Jessie poured some of her lingering bitterness out to Thomas Starr King that day. "This is the end of our silence & now will come justice & retribution," she wrote. As Jessie stewed indoors, John rode, reprising his habit from the 1856 campaign of spending his days ahorse while Jessie tended to official business and family matters. While Frémont rested, recuperated, and prepared his testimony in New York, his friends were busy in Washington.[43]

"Lecturing 'Honest Abe'"

Shortly after the attack on Fort Sumter, Joseph Henry, president of the Smithsonian since 1846, canceled the institution's scheduled 1861–1862 lecture series. A wartime capital was no place for such frivolity, he reasoned.

Henry had founded the Smithsonian lecture series in 1849. The talks were free to the public, but he considered them a small part of the institution's mission, more a publicity stunt than the type of real scholarship he wanted to focus on. The public, however, loved them. They were among the most popular such events in Washington during the 1850s. Occasionally, other groups, including the American Colonization Society, were allowed by the institution to schedule lectures, which typically took place in a two-thousand-seat room on the second floor of the Smithsonian castle. According to the Smithsonian's own guidelines, lectures were supposed to be free of politics—but they often weren't.[44]

A New Yorker by birth, Henry had many southern friends, including Jefferson Davis. He was, like a considerable portion of Washington society, a unionist with southern sympathies. Henry had supported Constitutional Unionist candidate John Bell for president in 1860 and was "bitterly opposed" to Lincoln, in the words of one of Henry's scientific colleagues. He refused to fly the U.S. flag during the war and refused to allow Federal troops to be housed at the Smithsonian—in contrast to most other public buildings in Washington. Henry was not disloyal, but he didn't do much to convince anyone otherwise.[45]

Abolitionists in and around the capital saw an opportunity. They formed the Washington Lecture Association (WLA) and appealed to Henry in summer 1861 to let them organize a series to replace the canceled lectures. Henry turned them down. They made another request in December when Congress reconvened, promising to avoid political topics. Henry didn't believe them, and he turned them down again. The abolitionists then turned to allies in government who were members of the Smithsonian's board of regents, including Vice President Hannibal Hamlin and Indiana congressman Schuyler Colfax. Frémont's former staff aide Owen Lovejoy also lobbied the board on behalf of the Washington Lecture Association. The two newest members added to the antislavery roster of the regents were Senators William Fessenden of Maine and Lyman Trumbull of Illinois, who replaced, as the *Christian Recorder* put it, "Stephen A. Douglas, deceased, and J. M. Mason, TRAITOR!" (a swipe at the former Virginia senator who was now a Confederate diplomat). Henry, at the mercy of the Republican-dominated board, had little choice but to give in.[46]

The Washington Lecture Association president was Unitarian minister John Pierpont, a member of the old Liberty Party who had been given a sinecure in the Treasury Department with the sponsorship of antislavery advocates in Congress. Pierpont invited several abolitionists (including Galusha Anderson, Henry Ward Beecher, Horace Greeley, and Wendell Phillips) to participate in the WLA's Smithsonian lecture series. But he also extended invitations to antislavery but nonabolitionist speakers, including Edward Everett and Ralph Waldo Emerson, among others. Emerson accepted, but Everett and several other nonabolitionist invitees didn't. Their spots on the schedule were given to abolitionists. In the end, twenty of the twenty-two speakers were part of the abolitionist movement.[47]

Unlike the free Smithsonian lectures, the WLA charged a quarter for admission, or $3 for a husband and wife to attend the entire series, which opened on December 13 with Orestes Brownson, editor of *Brownson's Quarterly Review* and a rare Catholic abolitionist. Ostensibly one of the "neutral" speakers, Brownson invited Charles Sumner to join him on the platform and proceeded to make light of Henry's demand that it be made clear that the Smithsonian was not a sponsor of the lecture series. "Ladies and Gentlemen: I am requested by Professor Henry to announce that the Smithsonian Institution is not in any way responsible for this course of lectures. I do so with pleasure, and desire to add that the Washington Lecture Association is in no way responsible for the Smithsonian Institution," drawing gales of laughter from the sell-out crowd. Brownson then proceeded to deliver a speech highly critical of the "slave interest" and blaming the war on slavery.[48]

When *New York Tribune* editor Horace Greeley's turn came on January 3, 1862, Lincoln was on the platform. He had never heard Greeley speak. "In print, every one of his words seems to weigh about a ton," Lincoln told John Hay and journalist William Croffut. "I want to see what he has to say about us." Lincoln was joined on stage by Treasury Secretary Chase and a host of Republican senators and congressmen. The room was "densely crowded" with more than three thousand in attendance, half again as many as the hall was designed to hold.[49]

"The election of 1860 was not the cause, but the opportunity of secession," Greeley declared, "and the Union is now to be restored either upon the basis of the new ideas of the South or upon the old ones of our fathers. . . . Compromise is impossible."[50]

Greeley extolled Frémont's emancipation order and, turning to Lincoln, asked the president why he had overturned it and why he had removed Frémont from command. Greeley's mention of Frémont brought a roar of approval from the crowd, which grew more raucous as Lincoln sat passively and jeered the president each time Greeley invoked Frémont's name.[51]

Lincoln told George W. Julian that Greeley's speech was "full of good thoughts, and I would like to take the manuscript home with me and carefully read it over some Sunday." The press was less availing than the president. "Greeley Lecturing 'Honest Abe Lincoln'" was the headline in Greeley's competitor, the *New York Herald*, two days later. "Looking full in the face of the President, he told him that 'the misfortunes of our country had been its reluctance to meet its antagonists [southern slaveholders] in the eye,'" the *Herald* reported. Greeley demonstrated for Lincoln, in person, the potency of Frémont as the symbol—virtually the military embodiment—of emancipation.[52]

Lincoln didn't attend any more of the lectures, but the criticism kept up. Even Emerson laid into the administration in his January 31 address. "Emancipation is the demand of civilization," he declared. "As long as we fight without any affirmative step taken by the government, any word intimating forfeiture in the rebel states of their old privileges under the law, they and we fight on the same side, for slavery."[53]

James A. Cravens, a Democratic congressman from Indiana, appealed to Lincoln as an ex officio member of the Smithsonian board to put a stop to the propaganda: "If we are to avoid the fatal consequences of division amongst our Selves, these Abolition lectures at the Institute, Should be immediately stopd," he wrote two days after Greeley's appearance.[54]

Kentucky senator Garrett Davis responded to the first few lectures from the floor of the Senate.

> These fanatics, these political and social demons, your Beechers, your Cheevers, your Phillipses, and your Garrisons, come here breathing pestilence from Pandemonium, trying to destroy this Union, so as to secure over its broken fragments the emancipation of slaves. They oppose Mr. Lincoln, as honest and pure a man as ever lived, because he stands by the Constitution, and is opposed to interfering with slavery. The utterances they have put forth in this city have desecrated the Smithsonian Institution. . . . What will you do with these monsters! I will tell you what I would do with them, and with that terrible monster Greeley, as they come sneaking around here, like hungry wolves, after the destruction of Slavery. If I had the power, I would take them and the worst Seceshers, and hang them in pairs.

Davis's senatorial colleagues offered a hearty round of laughter at the suggestion. Lincoln chose not to interfere with the lecture series, which continued through March, with one speaker after another criticizing the president's inaction on emancipation.[55]

"I SHOULD TAKE THE BEST MEASURES I COULD TO SUPPRESS THE REBELLION"

Frémont arrived in Washington on January 4, the day after Greeley's Smithsonian speech. Expecting to stay a while, he moved into a house on E Street rather than checking into a hotel. Frémont's critics noted his arrival and hoped to get in front of his testimony. "He is brought here simply to frame a plausible indictment against the Government," the pro-slavery *Washington Evening Star* asserted, "to be used to the end of forcing it to bow to their purposes of creating a red republican revolution throughout the loyal States." If so, he was hanging out with the right crowd. One evening, the Frémonts dined at the home of New York congressman Roscoe Conkling with a collection of radicals that included Joint Committee chairman Ben Wade, Senator Henry Wilson of Massachusetts, and Pennsylvania's Thaddeus Stevens, along with two antislavery generals, James Wadsworth and Abner Doubleday. As leavening, perhaps, New York Democratic representative Erastus Corning, who had been critical of Lincoln's alleged violations of civil liberties, was also in attendance.[56]

Frémont was originally asked to appear on January 6, but that was pushed to January 10 so that committee members could instead meet with Lincoln and the cabinet that day at the president's request. George W. Julian was dumbstruck to discover "that neither the President nor his advisers seemed to have any definite information respecting the management of the war, or the failure of our forces to make any forward movement. . . . Mr. Lincoln himself did not think he had any right to know, but that, as he was not a military man, it was his duty to defer to General McClellan." According to Julian, only Chase spoke up in support of "some early and decisive movement of our forces."[57]

Frémont's January 10 appearance amounted to nothing more than some pleasantries. Frémont told the panel that he had brought printed copies of "all the principal orders, communications, letters and dispatches concerning the most important events and acts" of his time in Missouri. After a brief discussion among the members, Chairman Wade asked Frémont to prepare a written statement to be presented in a week, giving the committee time to review the material. In the interim, Julian took to the House floor on January 14 to defend not just Frémont the general but also Frémontism. During the secession winter of 1860–1861, Julian wrote to President-elect Lincoln, "I expect to be a zealous supporter of your administration." It hadn't worked out that way. Fresh off the unsatisfactory meeting with the president and cabinet, he argued, "This is a war of ideas, not less than of armies, and no servant of the Republic should march with muffled drums against the foe."[58]

That foe, he insisted, was undergirded by slavery. When Frémont struck at the foe, he struck at an enemy that "burns our bridges; poisons our wells; destroys the lives of our people; fires our hospitals; murders our wounded soldiers; lays waste the country; turns pirate on the sea; confiscates our property of every description. . . . But when General Frémont declares that the slaves of rebels in arms against us within his military jurisdiction shall be free, the President—no doubt with the best motives, but as if determined to give all the aid in his power to the rebellion—countermands the proclamation." Julian highlighted the absurd dichotomy that said "the rebels may be shot, but while they keep up the fight against us their slaves shall supply them with provisions, without which their armies must perish, and the lives of loyal men might be spared." Julian had long labored in the moral vineyard of political antislavery. Now, like Frémont, he insisted on the "military necessity" of ending slavery. "A right to subdue the rebels carries with it a right to employ the means of doing it, and of doing it effectively, and with the least possible cost," he said.[59]

A war for the Union and a war to end slavery presented no dilemma. For Julian, they were one and the same, inseparable. "Do you say that the preservation of the Union must be kept in view as the grand purpose of the war on our part?" he asked rhetorically. "I admit it; but I say that nothing but slavery has brought the Union into peril. . . . I insist that our national life and liberty can only be saved by giving freedom to all, and that all loyal men, therefore, should favor emancipation."[60]

The Constitution was no impediment. "The Constitution itself recognizes the war power of the government, which the rebels have compelled us to employ against them," he continued, echoing Browning's argument in his September debate with Lincoln. "They have sown the wind, now let them reap the whirlwind." Julian considered himself bound to sustain the policy of the government "wherever I can honestly do so." He recognized the difficulties under which Lincoln operated. But he also had a duty "to point out its errors, whilst avoiding, if possible, the attitude of an antagonist."[61]

Whether Julian avoided the attitude of an antagonist was a matter of interpretation. When Frémont returned to Capitol Hill to present his prepared statement on January 17, his antagonism was barely concealed. He noted that he was given no plan of campaign and "no special object" to achieve. He was to raise an army that could descend the Mississippi and let the president know when he had done so. He then outlined the authority and responsibilities he believed the president had bestowed on him in July 1861. "Full discretionary powers of the amplest kind were conferred on me," he said. "Not a line of written instructions was given me." With the broad outline of a movement southward in mind, "the details of its accomplishment and the management of my department were left to my own judgment."[62]

Frémont recounted the military situation on his arrival: internal rebellion, a lack of arms for the loyal forces, and his appeals to Lincoln and others for weapons and money. He made a special point of defending his seizure of funds from disloyal banks in light of the Van Wyck committee's criticism of him on that score. He cited as evidence a telegram of July 26 from Montgomery Blair telling him, "You will have to do the best you can, and take all needful responsibility to defend and protect the people over whom you are specially set."[63]

He referred to his emancipation order only obliquely. "The turbulent condition of the State at the end of August rendered it, in my judgment, necessary to issue a proclamation, extending martial law to the State of Missouri, and enforcing some penalties for rebellion," he said before referring the committee to the early September exchange of letters with Lincoln for further explanation.[64]

Frémont also defended his use of private labor instead of troops in the construction of fortifications in St. Louis. Not only did this practice keep them out of the heat and humidity of the Mississippi Valley summer, but "the troops were so little acquainted with arms that all their time was needed to fit them for the field." It had the added benefit of creating employment for hundreds of men in a city whose economy had been pretty well wrecked by months of conflict. He otherwise defended his letting of contracts and purchase of arms against the charges of Frank Blair and the investigating committee.[65]

On military matters, Frémont explained his reasoning in sending reinforcements to Cairo and justified his relative lack of support for Nathaniel Lyon before Wilson's Creek. He would soon testify, "The whole point, in my mind, was whether General Lyon would choose to remain at Springfield or to retreat. General Prentiss could not retreat, and therefore I took the first relief to Cairo." He defended his response to the siege of Lexington, while insisting that "little advantage resulted to Price" in any case. "As a military position, its occupation had no value for him," as his "precipitate retreat" demonstrated. With all that, he concluded, "the state was in reality reclaimed, and in condition to leave the army free for the special object of descending the Mississippi." He reiterated his mistaken belief that he was in the presence of the enemy when he was relieved of duty. He was confident that he had always acted with the best intentions, he told the lawmakers. "Many acts which have been censured were, I think, for the public good. . . . I do not feel that in any case I overstepped the authority intended to be confided to me."[66]

When Frémont finished reading his statement, the committee members huddled. It was decided that Representative Gooch would review Frémont's statement and the other material he provided, work up questions based on those items, and bring the witness back to respond. When Frémont returned on January 30, Gooch began the hearing with a question about his power to act. Frémont cited his conversations with Lincoln, Cameron, and Montgomery Blair as the sources for his conception of the authority "to exercise any and whatever power was necessary to carry out the work I was sent to accomplish." Frémont did offer one caveat, learned from hard experience. "I would like to remark, in passing," he told the panel, "that I do not think it was clearly understood"—by the president, the cabinet officers, and perhaps even himself—"what was the nature of the power which a general commanding a department had."[67]

The questioning by Gooch served generally to allow Frémont to expand on what he had already told the committee in his opening statement. Julian also tossed in a few softballs. Only Representative Odell, the New York Democrat, asked any probing questions, for which he would secure the ire of Jessie Frémont, who threatened—without success—to "attend to his defeat" in the next election. Gooch's line of questioning on the St. Louis fortifications, though, did provide a moment of quintessential Frémontism.[68]

"Were you at any time ordered to discontinue the field-works around the city of St. Louis?" Gooch asked.

"I was," Frémont answered.

"And not to pay any more money on account of them?"

"I was."

"From whom did that order issue?"

"From the Secretary of War, through General Thomas."

"Was that order complied with?"

"By me, no sir," came Frémont's response. And then, "Perhaps I better state the circumstances under which I received that order." Frémont reasoned that work should continue while he protested the order. He believed the fortifications were essential and that stopping work would be "inexpedient, and possibly dangerous for the army in the field, and all my other positions; and having protested against it . . . I let the matter rest there." When Cameron didn't respond, Frémont took that as approval of his judgment. Cameron likely intended it as an indication that his cease-work order should stand.[69]

Odell made much of the instance when Lincoln's friend, Ward Hill Lamon, asked Frémont to detach a regiment of Illinois troops stationed in St. Louis for duty in Virginia. Frémont approved the transfer, assuming the order had Lincoln's approbation. It was a single regiment, not even in the field with Frémont at the time—it was mid-October—and cost Frémont nothing in readiness to release it. But Odell thought otherwise. He couldn't understand why Frémont had protested the transfer of five thousand troops in September but so easily released a few hundred in October. Wasn't there a military necessity to keep those troops in Missouri, Odell asked. "Not strictly, I think," Frémont responded. And then, for good measure, he added, "If there was not a military necessity for continuing the fortifications at St. Louis, there was not certainly a military necessity to keep one regiment, more or less, there." Having delivered that barb, he continued. "If you remember, there was a great deal done in the western department which was not consistent with strict military propriety; a great deal," he said, referring to his insubordinate division commanders and interference from Washington, oblivious that he was also indicting himself. With rumors flying that he was on his way out, "it was not a matter to me of very great importance whether that regiment was retained or not. . . . If it was agreeable to the president, and pleased him, that was all that concerned me." There is more than a hint of self-satisfied disingenuousness in Frémont's answer.[70]

Odell also tried to corner Frémont on the accusations that he was inaccessible to important visitors. Frémont denied this allegation. "I think that all officers having reason to see me, having business with me, could readily find access to me, taking their turn," he said. He admitted that sometimes visitors did have to wait as long as a week to get in to see him, but "there was a standing order that an officer coming to see me, no matter what his business was, should come up without any hindrance." Politicians and businessmen were a different story. "The business pertaining to the department I attended to first, and all other business as I could find time to dispose of it." Members of Frémont's staff backed him on this point when they testified the following month. One even offered that "he was not exclusive enough. . . . I considered that he was too anxious to accommodate those who called to see him."[71]

It was Gooch who finally brought up the emancipation order, simply asking Frémont to explain "the reasons which induced you to make the proclamation which has been so much talked of since."

"I judged it expedient to make the proclamation because I began to find myself pressed to meet what I considered serious dangers," Frémont responded. "I thought that the time had come when it was necessary to strike some decided blow against the enemy. . . . I judged that the condition of the country, the activity and the universality of the rebellion, and the strength of the force against us, rendered it necessary that I should take the best measures I could to suppress the rebellion there."

When Julian asked about the effect of Lincoln's revocation, Frémont called it "injurious." Frémont also told the panel that it was injurious to his command. "That was the first act which met the disapprobation of the Executive in any way," Frémont said, noting Lincoln's insistence that he meant no censure. "About that time, however . . . the confidence of the administration was withdrawn." Frémont went on to suggest that Frank Blair's dissatisfaction with him over contracting was at the core of the dispute between them and thus the Blairs' poisoning of the Lincoln-Frémont relationship. Blair was dissatisfied with Frémont's denial of some of his friends' bids for contracts. He was also concerned about his dwindling political capital. But that doesn't mean his concerns about Frémont's competency were not genuine or justified.[72]

That was a matter about which the committee could not fairly judge. No member had any serious military experience. Congress did not have expert staff in those days. Some members of Congress had objected to the creation of the committee on the grounds of the lack of expertise in the subject matter to be investigated. Supporters saw it differently. Defending the committee against charges of amateurism, Owen Lovejoy reminded objectors that the military is subordinate to the civil power, and he illustrated the value of nonexpert review. "You may tell me I do not know how to make a coat. Very true; but I know when it is made, and I know when it fits. And though I may not know how to conduct the details of military affairs, I know what results should be brought about."[73]

Gen. John Cochrane, the New York Democrat who had supported the arming of free blacks in late 1861, saw the committee's value—or lack thereof—with the politician's gaze. "Though the committee itself may be essentially ignorant of the science which they are judging, yet they are the efficient agents of publicity to facts, which lead to those conclusions upon which the public mind ultimately settles," he wrote. "Truth, thus evolved and accepted, is the education of a people in the art of war." While the panel's deliberations might prove "expensive to the reputation of individual commanders," they also provided "frequent valuable services." Cochrane, not always the most consistent of analysts, additionally referred to the "chronic malady" of the committee's activity.[74]

The committee's proceedings were secret, so there was no immediate official release of Frémont's testimony. But John and Jessie had prepped just that as part of their campaign to win him another command. Frémont prepared an abstract of the documentary evidence, which they had professionally printed, along with Frémont's prepared statement. In a clear indication they intended to leak the testimony, she told Frederick Billings that "the whole will occupy, quoted proofs & all, about four columns of a newspaper." In their eyes, Frémont had been slandered by the leaked report of Adjutant General Lorenzo Thomas. Publishing their defense would be sauce for the gander.[75]

"I BEHAVED PERFECTLY WELL BUT I DIDN'T LIKE IT"

On February 5, the Lincolns hosted a soirée to celebrate Mary Lincoln's refurbishment of the White House. The event was controversial not just because it appeared unseemly in war time but also because it broke with tradition in being by invitation only. Historically, such events had been open to the public, with state dinners being the rare exception. Lincoln disapproved—"I don't fancy this pass business," he said—but the first lady got her way.[76]

Among the seven hundred invitees were Senator and Mrs. Ben Wade, who were among the two hundred or so who decided not to attend. Half sent notes expressing their distaste. Wade, chairman of the Joint Committee on the Conduct of the War, indignantly asked, "Are the President and Mrs. Lincoln aware there is a Civil War? If they are not, Mr. and Mrs. Wade are and for that reason decline to participate in feasting and dancing." There was feasting. But deferring to the war and to the serious illness of his twelve-year-old son Willie, Lincoln barred dancing. The Lincolns' other son who still lived at home, nine-year-old Tad, was also ill but not in as dire straits as Willie.[77]

Guests began arriving in the White House courtyard just before nine in the evening. Among them were diplomats, members of Congress and the cabinet, and Supreme Court justices. A parade of generals showed up in dress uniforms: George McClellan with his wife and father-in-law/chief of staff, Randolph Marcy; James Shields and Louis Blenker, who would soon join Frémont in the Shenandoah Valley; and others including Winfield Scott Hancock, Joseph Hooker, Abner Doubleday, Erasmus Keyes, Irvin McDowell, Charles Stone, Samuel Heintzelman, and Silas Casey.[78]

In a "surprise and something of a shock" to Jessie, the Frémonts were also invited. Their first instinct was not to go. They were in mourning for friends—in Jessie's case, some on the Confederate side—who had died in battle. "I had no thought of going and we sent our regrets," she wrote. She also grasped that many would view the party as unseemly, calling it "a regular apple of discord." But Lincoln sent an emissary to New York "to say that he especially desired General Frémont to be present that night, and that it was his request that he should come." As Jessie noted, "That almost amounted to an order"; thus, they went.[79]

Unlike many of the other sharply dressed generals, Frémont showed up in a plain field uniform, bearing the Cross of Merit that the Prussian government had presented to him in 1860 for his achievements as an explorer. It was a "gentle hint that a prophet is not without honor save in his own country," Jessie told Billings. One attendee said he "seemed rather downcast." Parties were not his forte. McClellan, whom Frémont had never met, was standing with John Dahlgren, commander of the Washington Navy Yard and the only navy officer in attendance, who noticed the anomaly. "This is the first occasion I have heard of Frémont's appearance in such places," Dahlgren told Little Mac, who didn't much like Frémont's politics or his non–West Point credentials. But Jessie "more than made up for his moodiness by her animated and vivacious conversation."[80]

There was no dancing, but there was music, provided by the Marine Band, which greeted arriving guests at the foot of the steps and then moved into the corridor. The Lincolns received guests in the East Room, although each was frequently away checking on Willie upstairs. The Red, Green, and Blue Parlors were open for guests to mingle, but the dining hall remained locked as a safeguard against premature departures.[81]

When the Frémonts were presented to Lincoln in the East Room, Lincoln, instead of a routine greeting, "at once said that his son was ill and that he feared for the result." Jessie's anger over her September encounter began to melt a little. "A sadder face than that of the President I have rarely seen," remembered Jessie, who had lost her own baby daughter, Anne, less than a decade earlier. "On seeing his sad face and grieved appearance, the feeling with which we had gone gave way to pity." They offered their best wishes and hoped for the boy's recovery; then the couple moved on down the receiving line.[82]

Given the guest list and the location, war talk predominated. The new secretary of war, Edwin Stanton, made a point of being seen with the Frémonts. "The whole talk was on the necessary peremptory pursuit of the war to make the South realize that it could not maintain slavery under the protection of the North," according to Jessie. In her account, it was a dreary evening, and that is surely the way she remembered it. Others remembered the party as "a very large and brilliant one."[83]

In Jessie's telling, there was so much talk about the need for a harder war and emancipation "that it became embarrassing," and the Frémonts decided to leave after less than an hour. They were in the hallway, Jessie already with her shawl on, when Charles Sumner, having been sent by Lincoln, asked them to return with him. The president wanted to introduce Frémont to McClellan. Taking Jessie by the arm, Sumner escorted her and Frémont back to the East Room, where Lincoln met them. He took Frémont by the arm, and the four of them crossed the room to McClellan, where Lincoln introduced the two generals and their wives to each other. "We bowed, but as each seemed to wait for the other, neither of us spoke a single word," Jessie wrote. Lincoln finally broke the ice, and the generals and the president engaged in a few minutes of small talk. "I behaved perfectly well but I didn't like it," Jessie reported to Billings. The Frémonts then excused themselves and made for the door.[84]

Dinner wasn't served until midnight, but by then the Frémonts were long gone. Orville Hickman Browning reported not getting home until 2:00 a.m.[85]

Willie Lincoln died on February 20. Despite her sympathy for the bereaved president, Jessie remained unreconstructed as far as the administration was concerned. "In the absence of staff I am sole pen in waiting & have rather more writing than I can get on with," she told Billings, "but there's nothing like good hating for carrying on a war & being born on the rebel side of the line I think I have some advantages in the way of vindictiveness." She surmised that the success of Frémont's testimony and the committee's approbation cornered the White House, which now had "only two courses open. One, to give Mr. Frémont such a command as his position entitles him to & as the public will demand for him, or formally to recognize that he is so much identified with the principle of emancipation that they dare not endorse him & for that rule him out of the war." A few days after the party, Frémont met with Lincoln and Stanton to discuss the possibility of his returning to active service on the same day that the members of the Joint Committee on the Conduct of the War lobbied the president on Frémont's behalf. Stanton had, he assured Frémont, "only waited for their decision to give him" a new assignment. He told War Department investigator Charles Dana, "If General Frémont has any fight in him he shall (so far as I am concerned) have a chance to show it, and I have *told him so*. The times require the help of every man according to his gifts; and having neither partialities nor grudges to indulge, it will be my aim to practice on the maxim 'the tools to him that can handle them.'" The president, under pressure from Republican radicals to reinstate Frémont, would, as Jessie predicted, acknowledge "his recognition as the indispensable popular war cry." Frémont presented the secretary of war with a proposal for the creation of a far western department encompassing Louisiana, Texas, New Mexico, and California, with a plan for twenty thousand men to invade Texas and capture New Orleans. At around the same time, Lincoln met with Winfield Scott to discuss dismissing the slow-footed McClellan. Frémont was promoted in some quarters as a potential replacement, a possibility

McClellan and Halleck attributed to Germans in St. Louis conspiring with Franz Sigel. Lincoln had something else in mind.[86]

"The offspring of timidity"

The last thing Frank Blair wanted to see was John C. Frémont back on a battle-field. During debate in mid-December on a bill to appropriate money to pay the officers that Adjutant General Lorenzo Thomas had determined were appointed illegally by Frémont, Blair supported doing "justice to men who have done actual service to the Government." But he refused to be baited by Frémont's supporters in the House into a broader debate. "I do not care at this moment to meet this question," he said. "But, sir, I give gentlemen notice that whenever the appropriate occasion arises, and they desire to bring that matter up, I shall be ready to meet them."[87]

On March 7, 1862, he met them. Blair's speech on the House floor that day was an act of desperation, delivered against the advice of both his father and his brother. Montgomery had been embarrassed three days earlier by the publication of his August 1861 letter to Frémont critical of Lincoln. Montgomery apologized, and the president told his postmaster not to worry about it. But it was one more log on the fire for Frank. He felt he had to respond to the growing calls for Frémont's reinstatement. Frémont's leaked testimony (which included Montgomery's letter) had invigorated public support for him. A highly idealized version of events in Missouri written by William Dorsheimer, a Buffalo, New York, lawyer who had served as a private secretary to Frémont in St. Louis, had just been published to some acclaim in the *Atlantic Monthly*. Blair's hostile rebuttal of Frémont on February 7 (two days after a brief appearance by Montgomery) had made little impression on the Joint Committee's members. Chairman Wade suggested that after Frémont's testimony, no more witnesses were even needed. That same day they met with Lincoln to demand a new command for Frémont. Blair knew this, and he knew that Lincoln and Stanton's had met with Frémont on the same subject. The Contracts Committee had been critical of Frémont but placed most of the blame for corruption in the Western Department on McKinstry. Most significantly for Blair, radicals in Missouri were threatening his House seat. For all the worry from Lincoln about hard war driving southern unionists into the arms of secessionists, the opposite was just as often true in Missouri, where unregulated violence by guerrilla bands turned many a moderate conditional unionist into an emancipationist radical. The political sands were shifting beneath Blair's feet, and he hoped to firm them up by taking a bite out of the radicals' hero.[88]

Frank Blair's biographer noted that the scion, from his earliest days, exhibited a "tendency toward unrestrained vituperation against those with whom he disagreed." When Blair took to the House floor to slander John C. Frémont, that tendency was on full display. He started his speech with a lie, claiming that he never "desired to make any issue between General Frémont and myself." But he just couldn't help himself because Frémont's friends had had the audacity to defend him in public and demand his reinstatement. In reality, Blair had been stewing about Frémont for months, as his floor speech in December demonstrated.[89]

Blair then rehashed the Missouri campaign. He claimed Camp Jackson as a victory for the cause of union, although the consensus then and subsequently was that it achieved nothing except the deaths of twenty-eight civilians and the loss of many moderate unionists, including Sterling Price. Blair asserted that Frémont should have reinforced Lyon instead of Cairo and that Cairo could have been reinforced from many other points in the Northwest (echoing the Thomas report) but seemed not to be too sure of his own argument, as he then went on to insist that both could have been reinforced from St. Louis. That statement ignored the reality of the situation. Even Blair's sometime ally John Schofield, Lyon's senior aide, defended Frémont's decision and criticized Lyon for ignoring both his officers and his commander in choosing to fight at Wilson's Creek. "The fruitless sacrifice of Wilson's Creek was wholly unnecessary, and, under the circumstances, wholly unjustifiable. Our retreat to Rolla was open and perfectly safe, even if began as late as the night of [August] 9th," Schofield would write.[90]

The speech was snide and highly personal, almost like the wailing of a wronged lover in its vindictiveness. Blair referred to "the trivial and frivolous character of the man," in effect admitting that he had recommended for command a man who was trivial and frivolous. He also effectively called Frémont, who had braved more hazards than Frank Blair could conceive of, a coward— referring to him as "the commanding general, who never thought anybody to be in danger but himself." According to Blair, "The declaration of martial law by General Frémont was the offspring of timidity." And he accused Frémont of fomenting mutiny—a scurrilous charge that was the opposite of the truth. Mutiny was in the air in the first days of November 1861 in Missouri. It was Frémont who tamped it down.[91]

Blair considered the radical opponents who threatened his political viability "damned whelps" and accused Frémont of using his emancipation order to set himself up politically with abolitionists, a bizarre accusation to pair with one accusing Frémont of planning a presidential run in 1864. In 1861, abolitionism was a minority viewpoint in a minority party. There was no electoral advantage nationally to being an abolitionist, which is why Lincoln the moderate won the Republican nomination in the first place, supporting only the containment of slavery, not its extinction. There was as yet no majority, even in the North, even after eleven months of war, for immediate emancipation or abolition. Blair knew this but still argued in bad faith that the proclamation was "put out for a campaign in New England and elsewhere."[92]

If Blair proved an ineffective rhetorician, he was an equally bad prophet. "Humiliation, disaster, defeat, and disgrace, came with him, remained with him, and went away with him and his army of contractors," Blair declared of Frémont's Hundred Days in Missouri. But war more terrible than anything yet seen would ravage Missouri for three more years, long after Frémont and his contractors were gone. The February victories at Forts Henry and Donelson that Blair cited were Grant's, whom Frémont had launched on the road to command, armed with the river boats Frémont had commissioned and the building of which Blair had protested. On the very day Blair delivered his speech, the battle Frémont had sought with Sterling Price in southwest Missouri was fought and won by Samuel Curtis at Pea Ridge, Arkansas.[93]

One assessment of Blair's did ring true: "A man to be great must be able to do great things with small means." Frémont, undeniably left to fend with small means, failed to rise to the occasion. Blair had legitimate concerns that if Frémont were handed another command, he would again not be up to the task. Why, Blair blustered, if he were justified, did Frémont not demand a court-martial to clear his name? Blair knew why—Frémont's previous encounter with military justice was not, at least in Frémont's mind, a fair hearing. Nevertheless, Blair urged his friend the president not to return Frémont to action. "The President could not, with propriety, give an important command to an officer charged with the gravest offenses known to military law, and on account of such charges censured and deposed from his command, who yet quietly submits to this censure, and does not ask to have his character vindicated by a court-martial." Lincoln disregarded this advice: four days after Blair's speech, that's exactly what the president did.[94]

Frémont's allies rose to his defense. Immediately after Blair finished his tirade, Schuyler Colfax took the floor to respond. "I pass over many remarks of the gentleman from Missouri which I am sure, he will, himself, in his cooler moments, regret," Colfax said, which must have drawn a raised eyebrow or two from those who knew Blair. Disavowing any animosity toward his Missouri colleague, with whom he claimed "an attachment . . . almost since our boyhood,"

Colfax nevertheless suggested that Blair "has had his feelings and judgment perverted, or perhaps I should rather say influenced, by prejudice." He highlighted the hypocrisy of Blair's condemning Frémont's defenders as "idolators" when they were simply "the men who stand by him today, just as my friend did from the commencement of his acquaintance with him till the last of August 1861. . . . In August he was his friend, warm and true; in September he was not. All my crime is that I continue the same friendship." Blair, Colfax noted, now blamed Frémont for Lyon's death. But he had remained on friendly terms with the general for at least three weeks after Wilson's Creek, casting doubt on whether that was a genuine criticism on Blair's part or something he added to the pile after the fact.[95]

Frémont was not perfect, Colfax declared. He criticized the release of his testimony, while acknowledging that Frémont had for six months "been standing with closed lips, and listening to the allegations against him with a reticence which has commanded the approbation not only of his friends at home, but of thousands elsewhere in the civilized world, waiting patiently for the hour of his vindication." Colfax clearly believed that hour had come.[96]

Addressing Blair's suggestion of Frémont's cowardice, Colfax noted that Frémont was the only major general in the army who had taken the field with his troops. "No man will believe the intimations of the gentleman from Missouri that Frémont is a timid man," he said. "He may not have been fitted for the command of the military department of the West," the Hoosier almost conceded. "I think he was. But whether he was or not, he is a brave and fearless man." Blair rose to contest Colfax's characterization. "My friend does not state, I trust, that I called General Frémont a coward," Blair said. But he had. "The language that my friend used was 'timidity,' which is of course a qualified degree of cowardice."[97]

They continued to spar for more than an hour—about events in St. Louis, Lyon, the need to reinforce Cairo, the fall of Lexington, contracts, and the emancipation order. Blair had called it "bombastic." Colfax preferred "firm and decided." He defended Lincoln's reversal but refused to commit to whether Lincoln "erred or Frémont erred." In defense, he cited Andrew Johnson, a member of the Joint Committee on the Conduct of the War, who had suggested at around the same time as the proclamation order "that no rebel had a right to own anything." The only difference, as far as Colfax could see, was that "Frémont, as a commanding general, desiring thus to weaken the power and cripple the resources of the traitors, embodied it in a proclamation, as the Senator did in a sentence."[98]

"I should have been afraid to sleep with myself if I had not, with these convictions, stood forth in Frémont's vindication," Colfax told Sumner. For many in the abolitionist movement, Frémont had become the military embodiment of their cause, and that cause was gaining traction. "Slowly but surely as fate," Jessie wrote, "the northern sentiment is ruling the war." On March 11, Lincoln appointed Frémont as commanding general of the newly created Mountain Department encompassing western Virginia and East Tennessee.[99]

"THE THIN END OF THE WEDGE"
In mid-March, after John's appointment to the Mountain Department but before he reported for duty, the Frémonts had dinner with the man many considered the oratorical embodiment of abolitionism, Wendell Phillips. A group of antislavery leaders—Vice President Hannibal Hamlin, Mrs. Hamlin, and Charles Sumner, in addition to the Frémonts—gathered at the Washington, DC, home of Speaker of the House Galusha Grow of Pennsylvania. Phillips had only recently eschewed the anticonstitutionalism of the early abolitionist movement in favor of a more overtly political antislavery position. The man who had previously favored secession by the North now sat at the table of power during a civil war fought to preserve the Union he had once sought to leave.[100]

He was impressed with both Frémonts, whom he was meeting for the first time. "Frémont was all I fancied him, modest, able, Jessie was charming & very attentive to me," Phillips reported to his wife, Ann. "She told me many good things, especially all about her & Frémont coming incog. to hear me in NYC. He disbelieved somewhat his friends assertion that the *masses* loved him & she advised his going, guessing I shld allude to him & then he'd *see* the effect. He was totally overcome & convinced by the first uproar made when I alluded to him even without mentioning his name & wished instantly to escape, but Jessie made him stay to the end." Frémont expressed regret that he had not previously called on Phillips when both were in New York.[101]

When Phillips met with Lincoln for around an hour on the same trip, he commended the president for restoring Frémont to command but continued to chastise him for his shortcomings on emancipation. In response, Lincoln told Phillips a story of a Maine Irishman who, during that state's prohibition effort, asked for a glass of soda: "Couldn't ye put a drop of the crathur into it unbeknownst to myself." As Lincoln put it to Phillips, "I've put a good deal of Antislavery in it unbeknownst to themselves." In his letter to Ann, Phillips said that Lincoln "struck me as perfectly honest—trying to do what he thought his duty but a man of very slow mind," a trait others interpreted more generously as a methodical approach to problem solving. However slow the mind, Phillips complained, "I said what I could, not all I wished because he talked so fast and constantly it was hard to get a word in edgewise." Still, Phillips left the meeting feeling "rather encouraged" and favorably compared Lincoln to the congressional Republicans he had spent time with on his trip.[102]

When Phillips spoke at the Smithsonian as part of the Washington Lecture Association series that week, he praised Frémont as the North's best general. But he also said of Lincoln, "If the President has not entered Canaan, he has turned his face Zionward." Phillips's address marked the first time black Washingtonians were allowed to attend a lecture at the Smithsonian. Joseph Henry protested and then banned Frederick Douglass from closing the series, saying he "would not permit the lecture of a coloured man to be given in the room of the Institution." He also barred William Lloyd Garrison. But events in Washington were passing Henry by. Lincoln, who had halted the work of the first emancipator, was taking steps to satisfy his radical critics on his journey toward becoming the Great Emancipator. Tentatively, he was heeding the advice of Gerrit Smith, who in his Smithsonian lecture on March 1 urged the president to "stop taking counsel of Kentucky, and take counsel of the nation." The positive northern reaction to Frémont's proclamation empowered Lincoln to take his first steps toward putting slavery, as he had long hoped, on the road to ultimate extinction.[103]

He insisted, though, that those steps be taken by politicians—not generals. Benjamin Butler had cast the first stone by classifying escaped slaves as contraband of war. But when Lincoln sent him off to attempt to capture New Orleans in February, the president warned the general not to "interfere with the slavery question as Frémont has done at St. Louis." On March 6, Lincoln proposed that Congress subsidize gradual, compensated emancipation in the slave states, the plan he had outlined for Browning in December. He argued that such a move would shorten the war by demonstrating to the South that Missouri, Kentucky, Maryland, and Delaware were irreversibly attached to the Union. "The point is not that *all* the states tolerating slavery would very soon, if at all, initiate emancipation," he wrote. "But that, while the offer is equally made to all, the more Northern shall, by such initiation, make it certain to the more Southern, that in no event, will the former ever join the latter, in their proposed confederacy."[104]

The plan attracted some support. The *New York Times* called it "an epoch in the history of our country. It has no precedent; we trust it may have many consequences." That was the moral case. Practically speaking, John Dahlgren, commander of the Washington Navy Yard, called it "a dexterous hit just now, when the extreme party is contemplating a decisive blow at slavery. Being a mild measure, and optional with the Slave States, it will probably be adopted by moderate men as the best under the circumstances."[105]

Radicals considered it too meek. Abolitionist Moncure Conway called the plan "like shooting a gun a little at a time." Jessie was sarcastic. "At present the President who is fond of impossibility advises that if the South abolish slavery we will supply them with purchase money to be used at their discretion," she wrote Thomas Starr King. "We pay the money, and they takes their choice. I wish the Merrimac had steamed up the Potomac & shelled out the Congress that could tolerate such a concession." Democrats were largely opposed. And border-state congressman—the most important constituency—were nearly unanimous in their opposition. When Lincoln asked Frank Blair to bring some of his middle-border colleagues to the White House for a sit-down, Blair objected, arguing that Lincoln first needed some military victory to bolster his position. William Seward would later make the same argument, with more success, about the Emancipation Proclamation. To Blair, though, Lincoln was more insistent. "That is just the reason I do not wish to wait," he said. "If we should have successes, they may feel and say, the rebellion is crushed and it matters not whether we do anything about this matter." Blair organized the meeting, but it came to naught. Congress adopted the proposed resolution, but the states were unanimously opposed.[106]

Lincoln saw his gradual-emancipation proposal as a way to end the war. But his plea to Blair can also be read as Lincoln hoping to get the machinery of emancipation in gear before the war was over, as it appeared in spring 1862 it might soon be. Lincoln's inability to move even Delaware, where slavery was barely (if at all) economically viable, demonstrated that the slavery debate was about not just slavery itself but also the racism that undergirded the system. That issue reached far beyond Delaware and the other border states. Frank Blair was becoming a chief spokesman for the position that it was "the negro question and not the slavery question which made the rebellion," and he joined Lincoln in continuing to press for colonization. This act only confirmed the radicals in their belief that nothing short of an all-out war on slavery would ever conquer the South.[107]

Some abolitionists grew despondent at the lack of progress. Lydia Maria Child admitted that "courage flags a little, and hope grows faint." She had faith in the people but not in the president. "Thaddeus Stevens and Gen. Frémont almost despair of the ship of state." As for Lincoln, she wished "he were a man *strong* enough to *lead* popular opinion, instead of *following* it so conscientiously." But just a week after unveiling his compensated-emancipation proposal, Lincoln signed into law a bill by Frémont's former aide, Illinois congressman Owen Lovejoy, that barred military personnel from returning fugitive slaves to their former masters. The legislation was an outgrowth of the hash that Henry Halleck had made of contraband policy in Missouri following Frémont's dismissal. Halleck's General Orders No. 13, issued soon after Frémont's departure, had banned fugitives from Union lines, dubiously claiming they served as a source of intelligence for the Confederate Army. The opposite was more often true, and Halleck's order ran into opposition from several quarters, including men in his own army and Republicans in Congress. So lawmakers acted to create a safe haven for fugitives within the confines of the First Confiscation Act. "I am opposed to the Army of the United States being turned into slave catchers," Lovejoy said. "I am opposed to any general being allowed to give orders to throw back upon their masters those who desire to escape." Six months after Frémont's order was overruled, its purpose (if not its method) was vindicated by Congress and the president.[108]

A month later, the president somewhat reluctantly signed into law a measure to emancipate, with compensation for owners, the enslaved people of the District of Columbia. His friend Browning, with whom he had debated Frémont's proclamation, delivered the bill to the White House for his signature. Lincoln had proposed compensated, gradual emancipation for the District of Columbia, subject to a referendum, during his one term in Congress in the 1840s. His position had not changed over the ensuing fifteen years. "I have never doubted the constitutional authority of congress to abolish slavery in this district," he wrote in a message to Congress announcing his approval of the bill on April 16, "and I have ever desired to see the national capital freed from the institution in some satisfactory way." He would have preferred a gradual rather than immediate emancipation, that the voters of the district had the final say, and that one of the border states had acted on its own before emancipation in the nation's capital. He got none of those but signed the bill anyway. The *Liberator* observed, "A year ago, merely to propose the abolition of slavery in the District of Columbia was political heresy." Now it was law. The *National Anti-Slavery Standard* called the measure "the beginning of the end of slavery."[109]

Owen Lovejoy summed up the evolution, which included a ban on slavery in the territories, the issue that had been the founding principle of the Republican Party. "The Executive rail-splitter understands his business. He knows that the thin end of the wedge must first enter the wood. . . . The Executive has taken the Abolitionist wedge, and struck it into the log of Slavery." But the rail splitter was also a hair splitter. He never gave up on compensation, even after issuing the Emancipation Proclamation. It was not a backpedal, but it reflected Lincoln's lawyerly approach. He wanted the states to act on their own because he believed that was the surest way to guarantee a true end to slavery, short of a constitutional amendment. He continued to question the legal efficacy of military emancipation, especially once the shooting stopped, even after he invoked it.[110]

The fire-eaters of the South made no distinction between Frémont and Lincoln. "By their own recorded declarations, they would have seceded just as promptly if John C. Frémont had been elected four years previous," abolitionist leader William Lloyd Garrison wrote to the English abolitionist George Thompson in that busy March 1862. "When it is reproachfully said by the enemies of freedom, that, had it not been for the Abolition agitation, there would have been no secession, I accept the statement as a splendid tribute to the power of truth, the majesty of justice, and the advancement of the age."[111]

Garrison was right about what would have happened if Frémont had been elected in 1856. Wendell Phillips was mostly wrong in his declaration that "Abraham Lincoln simply rules; John C. Frémont governs." But he was not entirely wrong. Lincoln was coming around to Frémont's view of the war and emancipation's role in winning it.[112]

John C. Frémont

Jessie Benton Frémont

Abraham Lincoln
LIBRARY OF CONGRESS

Edward D. Baker
LIBRARY OF CONGRESS

Thomas Starr King

Montgomery Blair

Frank Blair

Elizabeth Blair Lee

Horace Greeley

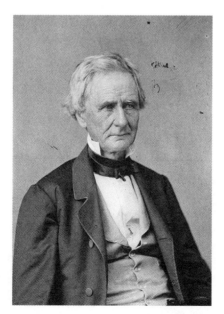

Simon Cameron

Nathaniel Lyon
WIKIMEDIA COMMONS [PUBLIC DOMAIN]

Edwin Stanton
LIBRARY OF CONGRESS

John Greenleaf Whittier

Owen Lovejoy

Zachariah Chandler

CHAPTER SEVEN

"A jackass you can't guide at all"

AGITATION BY FRÉMONT'S ALLIES HAD HELPED TO GET THE PATHFINDER A new command. Lincoln was still playing the political game with generalships, though opinion was divided on what that meant for the army. "There was a little too much sentiment and too little practical war in the construction of a department out of 500 miles of mountain ranges, and the appointment of the 'path-finder' to command it was consistent with the romantic character of the whole," one of Frémont's division commanders later wrote. Frank Blair took it badly, but Montgomery Blair had no objection. He believed that in shunting Frémont off to an out-of-the-way command, the president had "annihilated the abolition junto." That might have played a role. But Lincoln also believed that perhaps Frémont had "not had fair play" and so was determined to "give it to him." Or, as Jessie put it, "some atonement should be made for the unjust manner in which he had been treated."[1]

Frémont's March 11 appointment to command the Mountain Department was coupled with Lincoln's decision to relieve George McClellan of the post of general in chief, leaving no one in overall command in the East as Little Mac focused on moving his army to Virginia's York-James Peninsula for a movement against Richmond. In taking this step, Lincoln ignored his own advice to the radical senator Ben Wade, who had implored Lincoln to relieve McClellan as commander of the Army of the Potomac barely a month before. And replace him with whom, Lincoln wondered. Anybody, Wade responded. Wade's preference was Frémont or some other antislavery general. "Wade, *anybody* will do for you, but not for me. I must have *somebody*." In the case of the troika in western Virginia, the somebody turned out to be the tag team of Edwin Stanton and Lincoln. The western Virginia generals, as historian William J. Miller put it, "would take orders from the two lawyers in Washington."[2]

Lincoln reasonably concluded, as Montgomery Blair surmised, that putting Frémont in command in this thirty-five-thousand-square-mile backwater was low risk. If he succeeded, everyone would benefit. If he failed, it would not adversely affect the larger goals of the Virginia campaign. Nevertheless, this time the president did not give Frémont carte blanche. In a March 22 order, Adjutant General Lorenzo Thomas—whose leaked report had so damaged Frémont in Missouri—outlined the specific responsibilities "to which your attention is especially called." Foremost was protection of the Baltimore & Ohio (B&O) Railroad, a crucial east–west conduit of communication and supply at the northern end of Frémont's department. Next was the Virginia and Tennessee Railroad at the far southern end, "some one point of which within your command you will seize and hold with the troops under your command." This chimera would for a time be the organizing principle of Frémont's strategy. "Beyond these two cardinal points of duty," Thomas continued, "the Department refrains from giving specific instructions, leaving you the usual discretion of commanders in the field." He then went on for another two paragraphs delineating specific instructions related to what the administration clearly saw as Frémont's shortcomings in Missouri. "In consequence of embarrassments having been thrown upon the officers of the Government in the settlement of accounts growing out of contracts irregularly made," Thomas reminded Frémont, "no contract whatever will be made by your authority except in conformity with the Regulations of the Army and through the proper officers of the several departments of the Army." He was also ordered to "enter without delay upon your command" and to provide "frequent and full report[s] of your operations, in progress or contemplated."[3]

At the same time, Stanton ordered outgoing commanding Gen. William Rosecrans to provide an accounting of the more than thirty-four thousand infantry, cavalry, and artillery troops assigned to the Mountain Department. Stanton and the president wanted a detailed record of what they were providing the new commander in the way of men. This book count overstated the true number of men ready for duty by at least four thousand and took no account of how poorly armed and equipped they were. Shortly after Frémont assumed command, about nine thousand troops in eastern Kentucky and southwestern Virginia were removed from his command, leaving him with something like twenty thousand effectives. Both circumstances would contribute to the turmoil that was about to be unleashed on the ground in western Virginia and along the telegraph lines between the Mountain Department and Washington.[4]

No sooner had Frémont taken the job than Lincoln began looking to insert his eyes and ears into the general's camp. On the same day that Thomas forwarded his directions to the new commander, Lincoln wrote to "introduce my friend, Col. Thomas W. Sweeney, of Philadelphia, who has already done some service with volunteers, and is a gentleman of great intelligence and good principles. He would be glad to serve on your staff; but I do not know whether that is possible." Sweeney didn't get the job.[5]

Frémont wanted James Garfield, another political general and future president of the United States, but Stanton said no. Stanton also went out of his way to lambast Charles Zagonyi, head of Frémont's Body Guard in Missouri, whom the secretary considered "ignorant . . . of the military subordination due to the Government" and accused of recognizing "no authority but that of their military chief." In other words, he was too loyal to Frémont. Instead, Stanton would send Lt. Col. John Pilsen, another Hungarian officer. Zagonyi eventually joined the Shenandoah Valley campaign as head of Frémont's cavalry.[6]

Frémont arrived in Wheeling on March 28 and assumed command from Rosecrans the next day. As she had in St. Louis, Jessie joined John at his Mountain Department headquarters at the McLure Hotel, a couple of blocks from the Ohio River. They again had adjacent offices, with Jessie handling correspondence and greeting visitors. Daughter Lily, now twenty, and son Frank, almost seven, joined them. Their other son, Charley, nearly twelve, was away at school in Connecticut. It wasn't home, like St. Louis, but might prove more politically congenial. Wheeling, at the intersection of the Ohio River and the B&O Railroad, was sufficiently antislavery that it had been proposed by one overly optimistic Republican as the site for the 1860 party convention eventually held in Chicago.[7]

On his arrival, the orders began pouring in from the War Department: to occupy Moorefield, to bolster the lines at Cumberland and Romney, and to secure the B&O. Frémont dutifully replied at 11:00 p.m. that same night, reporting the dispositions he had ordered or inherited. The next day, he asked for reinforcements, which "are absolutely required for proposed operations." Those operations included protecting three hundred miles of railroad lines and two hundred miles of waterways, dealing with insurgents, securing supply depots, and making a three-hundred-mile march southward through the Allegheny Mountains, gathering up his dispersed commands as he went, severing the Virginia and Tennessee Railroad, capturing Knoxville, and securing Union-minded East Tennessee. Lincoln had outlined such an operation in a memorandum in October 1861, long before creation of the Mountain Department. Frémont believed he needed more troops to pull this operation off.[8]

The following day, Stanton informed Frémont, "Operations around Washington since your departure from this city will render it very difficult to furnish any additional troops immediately, but no effort will be spared to supply your wants." One solution was transferring a German division under Louis Blenker from the Army of the Potomac. The move made tactical sense for what Lincoln wanted Frémont to accomplish. McClellan was convinced it was a purely political move to satisfy Frémont's radical supporters in Congress. Lincoln all but admitted that this consideration had played a role—"If you could know the full pressure of the case, I am confident you would justify it," he confessed to McClellan. As a sop to Little Mac, Blenker was ordered to stay with Maj. Gen. Nathaniel Banks, closer to Washington, if Banks could find some use for him. Lincoln wanted to placate the Young Napoleon, ease the anxiety of Washingtonians worried that the Confederates might make a dash for the capital, and quiet critics who accused him of starving Frémont to the point that success was impossible. In the event, it took Blenker more than a month to connect with his new command.[9]

Jessie seemed optimistic. She told Frederick Billings, "All in regard to Mr. Frémont's Dept. is clearly known to the guiding heads & he has their constant & warm support. On his side patience & watchfulness—on theirs watchfulness and activity." As ever, suspicion remained: "I don't know what the Govt. meant by sending Mr. Frémont here, but the result will be to kill the *conditional* union sentiment & bring out the healthy feeling, which we find with pleasure does exist but has had no nourishment."[10]

Frémont's military focus for his first weeks on the job was dealing with guerrilla bands who were terrorizing unionists in western Virginia. This effort mostly involved infantry and cavalry skirmishes. His division commanders consistently reported two facts to headquarters: "The roads are still terrible and streams everywhere very high. The enemy are in small detachments." An expedition in the Cheat Mountain District about two hundred miles to the south was typical. "Five guerrillas killed; five houses burned. Much hindered by high water," Frémont reported to Stanton. These quick raids were about all that ever proved feasible in the Allegheny Mountains.[11]

It was ruthless warfare, reminiscent of the internecine battles that had pitted neighbor against neighbor in Missouri. And Frémont fought the lawless bands ruthlessly. "As a preventive measure certain of their class were, after full and fair trial by military commission, promptly executed by hanging," he wrote. "The effect was to correct a mistaken belief in immunity for their crimes, and to render more secure interior points and roads, as well as loyal inhabitants of the military districts."[12]

To Frémont's east, the conflict was more regular. At the northern end of the Shenandoah Valley was Frémont's old political ally Nathaniel Banks. Camped between Banks and McClellan was Irvin McDowell, who had lost at Manassas the previous June and now commanded forty thousand troops.

Banks, a mercurial Massachusetts politician of flexible ideology, had been a prime mover in Frémont's 1856 Republican presidential nomination. He was elected the first Republican Speaker of the House in early 1857 and was made a major general along with Frémont at the start of the war. His command was soon folded into McClellan's Army of the Potomac. As McClellan dawdled throughout the winter of 1861–1862, he held a tight rein on Banks, who made no moves against the enemy. But shortly after McClellan was relieved of his general-in-chief duties on March 11, 1862, Banks was back on his own (sort of) as commander of the Department of the Shenandoah.

Lincoln, annoyed that McClellan had misled him about the number of troops available to defend Washington while he was preparing to move against Richmond, assigned McDowell to the Department of the Rappahannock and ordered him to keep one eye looking eastward and the other westward. But it was James Shields who would play this army's key role in the coming campaign. Shields didn't even want to be there. Although he was a veteran of the Mexican War, Shields was a political general. He had appealed to his old Illinois friend in the White House to be sent to California so he could tend to personal business. The request was denied, though Lincoln had been inundated with warnings that Shields was disloyal. One critic, citing North Carolina unionist Edward Stanly as a source, issued the same warning to then secretary of war Simon Cameron.[13]

Lincoln had known Shields for a long time, although not always on the best terms. As Illinois politicians in 1842, Lincoln and Shields feuded over a series of articles Lincoln wrote anonymously that belittled Shields, the state auditor, calling into question both his honesty and his manliness. Shields twice demanded an apology. Both times Lincoln refused. So Shields challenged him to a duel, which Lincoln rather foolishly accepted, putting at risk both his career and his life. Lincoln, a much larger man than Shields, rather comically chose broadswords as the weapon with which to fight. Because dueling was illegal in Illinois, the men met on Bloody Island opposite St. Louis in the Mississippi, where twenty-five years earlier Jessie Benton Frémont's father had killed a man in a duel. In the event, neither laid a blade on the other, and the two men, though in different political parties, soon became friends. As bad as things got between Lincoln and Frémont, at least neither ever challenged the other to a duel.[14]

"Entire insufficiency of transportation has thus far crippled us"

The Shenandoah Valley mattered because it fed the Confederate armies and because it provided a pathway to both Richmond and Washington. Any invasion of the North contemplated by Jefferson Davis required a secure left flank in the Valley. Keeping the national capital safe required bottling up any rebel army in the Blue Ridge so it could not approach Washington. Posting a southern army in the Valley and threatening Washington, DC—even theoretically—would tie down a similar number of Federal troops that would then not be available to McClellan as he made his way up the York-James Peninsula toward Richmond.

The two armies thus arranged near the bottom (or northern) end of the Valley clashed for the first time on March 23 at Kernstown, on the southern outskirts of Winchester, seventy-five miles west-northwest of Washington. Shields was the ranking officer but was laid up with a broken arm and would play no active part in the fight, waged in the words of one participant "with all the fierceness of desperation." The initiative on the Union side was taken by Col. Nathan Kimball, who confronted Stonewall Jackson's army from a series of ridges and drove it back.[15]

Kernstown was a Pyrrhic victory for the Union. Jackson was pushed southward from Winchester but accomplished his strategic goal of keeping Banks from leaving the Valley to reinforce McClellan and forced McDowell to stand by immobilized to the east in case the Confederates made a move toward Washington. "Kernstown unhinged the entire Union offensive in Virginia that spring," a Jackson biographer wrote. Another chronicler of the campaign called Kernstown "among the most productive battles the South ever waged."[16]

Kernstown did not materially affect Frémont's immediate plans. Weeks would pass before he became the focus of the administration's attention. "The President desires to know when you intend to move toward Knoxville, and with what force and by what route," Stanton wired Frémont nearly a month after Kernstown.[17]

The move against Knoxville was a pipe dream of Lincoln's based on his understandable desire to see the liberation of the unionists of East Tennessee. William T. Sherman had tried and failed to launch an attack through Cumberland Gap in October 1861. Henry Halleck had warned Lincoln of the difficulties that largely mirrored the reasons that stymied Sherman: the impossibility of the terrain and the lack of usable roads. Lincoln had urged Don Carlos Buell, who had succeeded Sherman in command of the western army based in Louisville, Kentucky, to focus on Knoxville rather than Nashville, which was Buell's preference. "Of the two, I would rather have a point on the Railroad south of Cumberland Gap, than Nashville," Lincoln wrote in early January, "first, because it cuts a great artery of the enemies' communication, which Nashville does not, and secondly because it is in the midst of loyal people, who would rally around it, while Nashville is not." But Buell insisted on Nashville, and Lincoln gave way. Now he would push the same scheme on Frémont. Instead of explaining the almost insurmountable difficulties that such a movement across trackless mountains would entail, Frémont responded with a sketchy plan: He would leave behind enough troops to guard against guerilla depredations and protect the B&O Railroad and then move southward up the Shenandoah Valley by stages, unite his widely spread forces, and turn the Confederate position at Cumberland Gap. Then, having "perhaps seized some rolling stock," he would use the Virginia and Tennessee Railroad to move against Knoxville. Perhaps Frémont believed his experience in the Rockies would see him through. If so, it was hopelessly naive. But it was what the president wanted to hear.[18]

Stanton replied three days later with Lincoln's approval, with one amendment, advising, "After striking the railroad, as you propose, not to advance toward Knoxville without further instructions." The secretary also reminded Frémont that he was not in charge of Banks and not to count on being able to call on his command without prior approval. Despite Lincoln's desire to advance west, it appeared that the administration believed both Banks's and Frémont's forces might be needed to move south toward Richmond to support McClellan's attack from the east. That withdrawal would leave East Tennessee unliberated.[19]

In a portent of things to come weatherwise, a foot and a half of snow fell at Monterey, forty miles northwest of Staunton, Virginia, on April 24. On April 27, Frémont reported the disposition of his command to the War Department. Troops were spread across more than 250 miles of western Virginia, from the B&O Railroad in the north to Lewisburg in the southwestern corner. On May 3, Frémont took to the field as he had done in Missouri, the same day Shields and his nine thousand men were detached from Banks's command and sent to McDowell. Frémont, his wife, and his staff rode the train from Wheeling to the main supply depot at New Creek, about 175 miles to the east-southeast. There Jessie said her good-byes. "A happier (or handsomer) man never headed a column than the one I left at New Creek," she gushed to Billings. Two days later, with two regiments of infantry and one of cavalry, he struck south for Petersburg, arriving on May 7.[20]

Sixty miles to the south, Robert Milroy, an aggressive Hoosier, was about to lead Frémont's vanguard into its first major action of the campaign. In typical Frémont fashion, that contingent included a hodgepodge of Americans and Europeans, many bereft of shoes and some even of weapons. Milroy was reinforced by a brigade under a politician general, Robert Schenck, an Ohio congressman. They brought fewer than thirty-five hundred men against Jackson's nearly nine thousand. Outnumbered almost three to one, the "undaunted and impetuous" Milroy wanted to attack. Schenck overruled this plan, but he did allow Milroy to stage an assault on a Confederate position on Sitlington's Hill, sited above the village of McDowell, hoping that creating some disarray in rebel ranks would make it more difficult for Jackson to pursue them. It was already late in the day. After four hours of "severe and bloody" fighting, darkness called a halt. Early the next morning the Federals began pulling back toward Franklin, about twenty-five miles to the north. The same day, the ragged advance of Blenker's division, missing for more than a month, came straggling into the Union camp near Petersburg, thirty miles north of Franklin. Blenker's Germans would gain a reputation as "the most lawless men in the Federal Service" in the weeks ahead, refitting themselves at the expense of disloyal Virginians, one of whom derided the "Dutchmen" as "that famous brigade that fears not God, neither regards man." But Frémont was glad to have them. Schenck and Milroy joined them two days later.[21]

Moving south, Frémont reached Franklin, about fifty miles northwest of Harrisonburg, on May 14. He stayed for ten days, "getting into order and condition my troops" and firming up the details of his movement against the Virginia and Tennessee Railroad and thence to Knoxville. While at Franklin, Stanton again inquired about the status of that movement. Frémont stalled. His men were hungry, and he was awaiting the arrival of supplies from New Creek, seventy miles away over bad roads. The War Department had forbidden Frémont to buy horses on his own. Delays in going through channels left his wagons without engines and some of his cavalry without mounts. "Entire insufficiency of transportation has thus far crippled us," and there was no forage in the area for animals. Before getting to the railroad, he would have to deal with a part of Jackson's army that was only twenty miles away. But, he reassured Stanton, he would soon break the railroad and "execute with rapidity what you propose," which was now not an assault on Knoxville but a turn toward Richmond.[22]

The Federal armies were spread across a front of more than a hundred miles—from Franklin (in what is now central West Virginia) to Fredericksburg (between Richmond and Washington) to Lewisburg (in southwestern Virginia). The lack of concentration presented the rebels with an opportunity to attack if they could get their own forces together in time.

"YOU CAN NOT IF YOU WOULD, BE BLIND TO THE SIGNS OF THE TIMES"

While Frémont slogged through the mountains of western Virginia, Jessie continued working the political front, even in the face of her own complaint that "patience & silence are all the weapons I have." Criticism of Frémont from Henry Dawes of the Contracts Committee and Moses Odell of the Joint Committee on the Conduct of the War was getting under her skin. "It is not one man they are striking at but a representative of a clear policy against slavery," she complained to radical Hoosier congressman George W. Julian in early May. And it didn't stop with Congress. Even while he was pitching border states on gradual, compensated emancipation, Jessie's nemesis in the White House was about to strike again at yet another representative of a clear policy against slavery. In an ironic twist, that blow would fall on the man who had replaced her husband in Missouri.[23]

Maj. Gen. David Hunter's tenure in Missouri was temporary. He was shunted off to Kansas after handing the Department of the West to Henry Halleck. Hunter's brief assignment there proved to be unhappy. He referred to it as a "banishment" and pleaded with his friend Lincoln to either give him more responsibility or "place me in a different position." Like Frémont, he spent much of that winter working his contacts to that end, so much so that he began to annoy his erstwhile ally in the White House. "I am, as you intimate, losing much of the great confidence I placed in you, not from any act or omission of yours touching the public service up to the time you were sent to Leavenworth," Lincoln wrote at the end of 1861, "but from the flood of grumbling dispatches I have seen from you since." Still, like Frémont, Lincoln found a place for Hunter, who also used radical connections outside military channels to put pressure on the executive. Unlike Frémont, Hunter was overtly vocal about slavery being the inspiration for his desire to gain a new command.[24]

"Please let me have my own way on the subject of slavery," Hunter importuned the new secretary of war, Edwin Stanton, in late January 1862 while still in Kansas. "The administration will not be responsible. I alone will bear the blame;

you can censure me, arrest me, dismiss, me, hang me if you will, but permit me to make my mark in such a way as to be remembered by friend and foe."[25]

In mid-March, just as Lincoln had created the Mountain Department to employ Frémont and quiet the radicals, the War Department created the Department of the South, encompassing South Carolina, Georgia, and Florida. Hunter was named commander. He quite reasonably construed the appointment as Stanton, if not Lincoln, endorsing his position on slavery. Elizabeth Blair Lee reached that conclusion as well, calling Stanton "the promptor of Hunter's proclamation." Like Frémont's "carte blanche" from the president, Hunter would quickly be disabused of the notion that his appointment carried with it that kind of authority.[26]

Months before Hunter's arrival, Federal forces had seized coastal areas in South Carolina around Beaufort, including the Sea Islands, and points south all the way to Key West, Florida. Plantation owners fled, and thousands of blacks, now free, were left behind. These were some of the men Cameron had suggested arming in December. On March 27, one day before Frémont arrived in Wheeling, almost seven hundred miles to the north, Hunter arrived on Hilton Head Island, South Carolina. On April 11, Hunter's forces captured Fort Pulaski, fifteen miles downriver from Savannah. Two days later, Hunter's headquarters issued General Orders No. 7, declaring, "All persons of color lately held to involuntary service by enemies of the United States in Fort Pulaski and on Cockspur Island, Georgia, are hereby confiscated and declared free." Nobody noticed. Hunter occupied Cockspur, the island on which the fort sat, so his order was in conformity with the Confiscation Act. His desire to put the freed slaves to work in the "in the quartermaster's department at the rates heretofore established" raised nary an eyebrow in Washington or anywhere else. When he declared martial law in Georgia, Florida, and South Carolina on April 25, citing military necessity, no one objected. However, when Hunter issued General Orders No. 11, declaring, "Slavery and martial law in a free country are altogether incompatible; the persons in these three States, Georgia, Florida, and South Carolina, heretofore held as slaves, are therefore declared forever free," someone noticed.[27]

Hunter's order exceeded Frémont's in that it freed all slaves, not just those of rebels. It covered twice as much area and encompassed more than nine hundred thousand slaves, nearly nine times as many as in Missouri. He also wanted to enlist as many men as he could, drill them just as he did his white soldiers, and pay them the same. Word reached Washington and New York in the middle of the month, while Lincoln was entertaining Edward Stanly, the newly named military governor of North Carolina. Stanly told Lincoln he could not possibly assume the post if emancipation was going to be the policy he would be asked to enforce. Lincoln assured him he would not have to. As critics were quick to point out, Hunter's order covered land and slaves that the general's army couldn't reach. The *New York Herald* called Hunter's order "his silly, illogical proclamation, free- ing slaves who have never heard of him, and abolitionizing Georgia, Florida, and South Carolina, when he has not foothold enough in either of these three States to enforce his martial law or compel the execution of his orders."[28]

Treasury Secretary Salmon Chase, the most reliable abolitionist in Lincoln's cabinet, had originally supported Frémont's proclamation and then backed off. Now he invoked foreign opinion and military necessity in defending Hunter. "Of course I do not assume to judge of the Military necessity: but it seems to me of the highest importance, whether our relations at home or abroad be considered, that this order be not revoked," he told the president on May 16. "It has been made as a military measure to meet a military exigency, and should, in my judgment be suffered to stand upon the responsibility of the Commanding General who made it."[29]

Carl Schurz, a Wisconsin politician who had met with Lincoln only days before and would soon play a role in the Lincoln-Frémont debates, conceded that while Hunter's proclamation "is perhaps a little premature," he perceptively advised the president that "it must and will come to this all over the Cotton states during the summer, and a month or two hence a proclamation like Hunt- ers would be looked upon as the most rational thing in the world." Schurz had confidence in the North. "The people will readily acquiesce if you see fit to sus- tain Hunter in his act," he predicted. He likewise warned the president, "As our armies proceed farther South the force of circumstances will drive us into mea- sures which were not in the original programme, but which necessity will oblige you to adopt." For Schurz, these measures included "the arming of negroes." Most important, he stressed "that the government make no public declarations of policy which might be likely to embarrass it in the future. In fact you can hardly tell at the present moment how far you will have to go six weeks hence."[30]

"Six weeks hence" would prove to be perhaps the most accurate prediction of the war. But Lincoln ignored Schurz's advice about preserving Hunter's proc- lamation, the existence of which had not yet been confirmed by the administra- tion although it had been reported in the newspapers. On May 19, the president declared, "The supposed proclamation, now in question, whether genuine or false, is altogether void." But he acknowledged some of Schurz's prescience by including in the revocation a pitch for his compensated emancipation plan, and he issued a veiled warning to slave owners.

If it became necessary at any time for emancipation to be invoked as a military necessity, if indeed such a power existed, "I reserve to myself" the authority to do so, Lincoln wrote. It was too great an authority to leave "to the decision of commanders in the field." Then he hailed his compensated emancipation proposal of March 6 that the border states had thus far rejected. "To the people of those states I now earnestly appeal. I do not argue. I beseech you to make the arguments for yourselves," he wrote. Like someone standing under a teetering boulder, slave states needed to act before the boulder fell and crushed them. The president was begging them to get out of the boulder's way. "You can not if you would, be blind to the signs of the times." This stance was in keeping with Schurz's advice, although still couched in soft terms. His proposal for gradual freedom "would come gently as the dews of heaven, not rending or wrecking anything." Employing a biblical allusion, Lincoln said, "It acts not the pharisee," as presumably Frémont and Hunter had done by imposing their top-down emancipations. Lincoln's plan allowed the states to act on their own. He was telling the border states, whose feelings he had been so solicitous of, that their time was almost up. This was their last chance. "May the vast future not have to lament that you have neglected it."[31]

Lincoln complained to Gen. George Meade, who had congratulated him on revoking Hunter's order, "I am trying to do my duty, but no one can imagine what influences are brought to bear on me." The border states didn't take the hint, and the response otherwise was muted. That there was no great outcry from radicals, abolitionists, or antislavery northerners was a result of two factors. Lincoln had moved their way, and his wording of the revocation order hinted strongly that he was ready to move even further. This time, unlike with Frémont's proclamation, they were willing to hold their fire to see what happened next. The other factor was more personal. Hunter was no Frémont. He did not possess the charisma or the cachet Frémont had built up as a national hero predating the war or as the leader of the crusade-like campaign of 1856. The people of the North had an emotional attachment to Frémont that Hunter had not earned. Now they had some hope that Lincoln might also earn their devotion.[32]

"DO NOT LOSE A MINUTE"

On May 23, Col. George Crook bested Confederate Henry Heth in a minor engagement at Lewisburg, one hundred miles south of Frémont's camp at Franklin. Frémont congratulated the forces that fought the battle, looking optimistically to his own future. "The General Commanding is confident that the forces under his immediate command but lack the opportunity to emulate the gallantry and share the glory of their comrades of the army of the Kanawhas." That opportunity would soon present itself.[33]

That same day, Jackson bested Banks at Front Royal. Banks was a good politician and understood the political implications. At one point he shouted at a subordinate, "By God, sir, I will not retreat! We have more to fear, sir, from the opinions of our friends than the bayonets of our enemies." But his friends were seventy-five miles to the east, and Jackson's bayonets were right in front of him. Prudently, Banks ordered a withdrawal. His army slogged into Winchester after midnight and had to do battle again the next day, when Confederate forces again pushed his army back, "leaving their breakfasts cooking on the stoves, savory dishes that the hungry rebels enjoyed greatly," a diarist recorded. Banks retreated toward Maryland, and, as had occurred at McDowell, the exhausted Confederates could put up no serious pursuit. "At length we arrived at the brow of a hill opposite Williamsport," on the other side of the Potomac, an officer recorded in his diary. "Here were a hundred blazing campfires illuminating the wreck of Banks' army." This outcome worried Washingtonians, who envisioned Confederate hordes rushing down the Potomac and the Manassas Gap Railroad toward them. For the less panicky, though, it looked like something else. This was the opportunity of which Frémont had written. Lincoln, not prone to panic, saw it as an opportunity too. Jackson could be bagged.[34]

As one of Frémont's division commanders later wrote, "Banks's defeat deranged all plans." Stanton admitted that Washington was "left in an extraordinary state of uncertainty as to the real state of affairs," partly because one of McDowell's brigadiers, John W. Geary, had falsely reported Jackson east of the Blue Ridge. Rumor had Jackson invading Maryland. He wasn't, although he sorely wanted to. Unlike Stanton, Lincoln did not overreact. Confident that Banks, though defeated, was not destroyed, Lincoln ordered Frémont on May 24 to "move against Jackson at Harrisonburg and operate against the enemy in such a way as to relieve Banks." And the president stressed the need for speed in following his order. "Much—perhaps all—depends upon the celerity with which you can execute it. Put the utmost speed into it. Do not lose a minute." He also ordered half of McDowell's forty thousand men to move west from Fredericksburg, reversing Shields's transfer of three weeks earlier. That sent him back toward the Valley, where he would form the eastern tip of a triangle, with Frémont coming from the west and Banks securing the north, with—Lincoln hoped—Jackson trapped in the middle.[35]

The order disappointed both McClellan, who wanted McDowell's help on the Peninsula and had been assured of it only three days earlier by Lincoln, and

McDowell, who wanted to join the main theater of action, not be shunted to a sideshow in the Valley. Nevertheless, McDowell sent two divisions westward, with Shields in the lead.[36]

Jackson anticipated the squeeze, but there was nothing for him to do but run the gauntlet and hope for the best. "McDowell and Frémont are probably aiming to effect a junction at Strasburg, so as to head us off from the upper Valley," he wrote. Celerity was the key for Jackson as well. "'Press forward' was the constant order," an officer remembered. Jackson sent Maj. Gen. Richard Ewell westward from Strasburg to block Frémont, whom he expected to be making good time up the smooth valley turnpike from Harrisonburg. But despite Lincoln's order and Frémont's assurance that it would be followed promptly, Frémont wasn't on his way to Harrisonburg.[37]

Harrisonburg was forty miles southeast of Franklin on a road denuded by rain and sleet and strewn with obstructions by Confederates who had retreated from McDowell, with "culverts torn away, and trees felled across the whole," one of Frémont's officers reported. Frémont called the road "almost impassable." It looked simple from Washington, but Frémont knew there was no way to get his half-starved, ill-clad army down that road, another forty miles away from his supply base, in time to intercept Jackson. Instead, he headed north up a better road forty miles to Moorefield and that much closer to resupply from New Creek.[38]

In Frémont's mind, this decision was not defiance. It was common sense. He had other options, but they would have taken him away from Jackson's army. A roundabout southward route might have tended to relieve Banks, but it opened much of western Virginia to Jackson and put his supply base at risk. "Defying contact, Jackson would have escaped intact with his prisoners and plunder," Frémont later explained. "This was a contingency not desired by the President nor contemplated in his dispatch." So, Frémont decided to follow "the spirit rather than the letter of the order, or if the letter, the added expression to 'operate against the enemy in such way as to relieve Banks.'" He felt further justified by a note from Stanton on May 25 providing discretion to "direct your attention to falling upon the enemy at whatever place you can find him."[39]

As Frémont headed north on a muddy road, it rained and hailed, and the temperatures dropped. When he reached Petersburg, three-quarters of the way to Moorefield, he detached excess baggage and collected rations and ammunition. He also collected a telegram from the president: "I see that you are at Moorefield. You were expressly ordered to march to Harrisonburg. What does this mean?"[40]

Frémont's response, sent at 6:00 a.m. the next morning, comes as close as any single message exchanged between the two men—even more than the letters that passed back and forth during the Missouri emancipation controversy—to summing up their relationship. After explaining the poor condition of his troops and the necessity of taking a different route, Frémont wrote, "In executing any order received I take it for granted that I am to exercise discretion concerning its literal execution, according to circumstances. If I am to understand that literal obedience to orders is required, please say so. I have no desire to exercise any power which you do not think belongs of necessity to my position in the field." He followed that up the next morning with a more detailed description of the roads and the lack of food and fodder. And he assured the president, "We are now moving with the utmost celerity possible in whatever direction the enemy may be found."[41]

Lincoln was incensed. "There are three kinds of animals," he told a White House visitor. "There is a horse & a mule & a jackass. A horse when he is broken will obey the *reins* easily, a mule is hard to guide but still you can make him go rightly. But a *jackass* you can't guide *at all.*" However, that did not stop him from trying. Lincoln told Stanton to order Frémont to "halt at Moorefield and wait orders." By that time, Frémont was already half a day's march beyond Moorefield. Perhaps realizing he had stepped over the line in his last message to Lincoln, Frémont replied that he would retrace his steps in accordance with the president's wishes. But the action was in the other direction. In the middle of the Frémont-Lincoln-Stanton exchanges, word had come that Jackson had stopped between Winchester and Charles Town. With the chase back on, the hot tempers in Washington cooled a bit. Stanton wired back Lincoln's direction that Frémont "move upon [the enemy] by the best route you can," which is what Frémont had been doing all along. "The president's order will be obeyed accordingly," Frémont replied.[42]

Frémont sent out spies (named "Jessie Scouts" in honor of his wife) to try to discern Jackson's exact position. But Lincoln already knew Jackson's army was strung out from Harpers Ferry to Strasburg. He wanted Frémont to move to Strasburg to cut him off. "Where is your force?" he wanted to know. "It ought this minute"—it was 11:30 a.m. on May 30—"to be near Strasburg."[43]

It wasn't. Frémont had halted on the recommendation of his medical officer to give his weary army a day's rest at Fabius, five miles beyond Moorefield and forty miles west of Strasburg. But he promised the president he would be at Strasburg by 5:00 p.m. on May 31. Lincoln let him know that McDowell's force under Shields was coming from the other direction, confident that the trap was being set. But heavy rains slowed Frémont, and Shields was creeping forward even more tentatively.[44]

Frémont almost lived up to his promise. The advance guard of his army reached a point about five miles west of Strasburg on the evening of May 31, and the rest of the army was up by 10:00 a.m. on June 1. Lincoln's jackass in major general's stars was now confronting Jackson's advance under Richard Ewell. Combined with Banks, Shields, and other forces under McDowell, they outnumbered the Confederates three to one. But Frémont had heard nothing from Shields. That made him cautious. In the event, Shields would get no closer to Strasburg than Front Royal, where rebel resistance and fear of an imaginary attack from the rear caused him to hesitate. Frémont's army collided with Ewell at 7:00 a.m. on June 1, and an artillery duel ensued. By noon, Frémont had his troops in line of battle. "Before midday we will have Jackson bagged," a Federal officer sharing a meal with his Virginia hosts explained, "and the backbone of the Confederacy will be broken." But Frémont never ordered the bulk of his army to attack. McDowell never ordered Shields to move against Strasburg, and he stayed put. Frémont, "entirely ignorant of what had taken place in the valley beyond," feared Jackson's superior numbers in the absence of Shields or Banks. The Pathfinder, who had run risks few men could imagine, simply lacked the aggressive instinct and imagination to take the calculated gambles essential for a great field commander. The pincer never closed from either side, and Jackson slipped through to the south.[45]

The events of the last days of May and the beginning of June 1862 exposed Frémont's shortcomings. They also highlighted the problems with running the campaign from Washington, particularly but not limited to the lack of knowledge about conditions on the ground. The following year, when Lincoln was again dissatisfied with the performance of a general—George Gordon Meade following Gettysburg—he would exclaim to John Hay, "If I had gone up there I could have whipped them myself." He probably didn't believe it, and he apparently never considered leaving Washington for the Valley in 1862. But there was a clear disconnect between expectations and reality, and at least part of the responsibility for that issue lay in the War Department and the White House. Jackson had early on complained of the same problem. When Confederate secretary of war Judah P. Benjamin rearranged the forces under Jackson's command, Stonewall complained that Benjamin "ought to be made to understand at once that he cannot manage the details of a campaign sitting at his desk three hundred miles away." The secretary learned the lesson quickly. By the time Lincoln did, it was too late. "Lincoln's isolation from the realities of campaigning in the mountains had prompted him to direct Frémont to do the impossible," concluded historian William J. Miller.[46]

Attorney General Edward Bates was disheartened but looked elsewhere for blame. "It is shamefully true that the enemy's officers are vastly superior to ours in boldness, enterprise and skill," he wrote in his diary on June 4, "while our troops almost constantly beat theirs, with any thing like equal numbers and a fair field. If our Genls. now allow Jackson to escape, they ought to lose the public confidence, for obvious lack of enterprise and action."[47]

Shields blamed Frémont, or at least what he supposed was some conspiracy aimed at glorifying him. "We would have occupied Strasburg," he claimed, dubiously, "but dare not interfere with what was designed for Frémont. His failure has saved Jackson." It was a reasonable analysis except for the pronoun. The failure belonged to both political generals. Over the next several days, it would become obvious that Shields was going to be no help in any second attempt to bag Jackson.[48]

"DIFFICULTIES IN THE WAY WERE A MATTER OF FIRST INTEREST"

On June 2, the same day he whined to Stanton about Frémont, Shields noted that "roads in terrible condition" were preventing him from making progress. The next day a "terrible storm" slowed him further. "Large numbers left behind for want of shoes" made things worse. He asked Stanton to inform Frémont "that I will follow his rear" and promised to cross the Shenandoah "somehow." It was a promise the politician general and friend of Lincoln would fail to honor.[49]

After Jackson's escape from the triangle, Frémont moved south through Strasburg, chasing Jackson's tail, down a road strewn with the detritus of the rebel army's haste—"knapsacks, blankets and the like, with here or there a broken ambulance, or cast off extra artillery wheel," one of Frémont's officers noted. There were also occasional stragglers, with hundreds taken as prisoners. But he was traveling in the dark. "We hear nothing yet of General Shields," Frémont reported to Stanton on June 4.[50]

Frémont failed to match Jackson's haste, "moving ponderously" southward, in the words of one historian of the Valley campaign, fifty miles toward Harrisonburg, where Lincoln had wanted him in the first place. Through driving rain and hail, Frémont's troops kept in tenuous contact with Jackson's rear guard but were powerless to stop the rebels from burning bridges in front of them, slowing progress even more. The advance guard reached the outskirts of Harrisonburg on June 6 and clashed with Confederate cavalry under the storied Turner Ashby, who was killed in the fight, probably by his own men. Frémont brought up the rest of the army the next day. Another eight miles to the southeast stood the tiny village of Cross Keys, where the Confederates were camped. On the evening of June 7, Frémont and his officers decided this was the place to attack, and he dispatched a messenger in search of Shields to let him know. Early on the morning of June 8, Frémont sent his army down the Port Republic Road. Some six miles past Harrisonburg, where that road struck the Keezletown Road, Frémont turned his army southwestward at about 8:00 a.m. It was here that his forward units first encountered serious enemy fire.[51]

Frémont's goal was to turn the Confederate right, push the rebels back, and catch them between his force and Shields, who he hoped was coming in from the rear. But the topography favored the rebels sitting atop a ridge. Frémont, having not reconnoitered the ground himself or gathered much intelligence about it from anyone else, sent his force forward into an exposed position below that ridge. His better chance would have been on his own right, but there he delivered vague orders to a tentative Schenck, who stood mostly idle for much of the battle. By the time Schenck got his force ready to move forward—or so he claimed—Frémont ordered it to fall back, to stay in line with the retreating units to the left that had taken a beating. Schenck later complained, although he had not done much that day to warrant Frémont's confidence. There were grumblings in the ranks as well, perhaps with better foundation than Schenck's. Frémont seemed satisfied. "Generally I feel myself permitted to say that all our troops, by their endurance of this severe march and their splendid conduct in the battle, are entitled to the President's commendation," he wrote Stanton the day after. A grudging commendation would come, but Cross Keys was a battle Lincoln didn't want fought. Ignorant of the circumstances on the ground, the day after the Battle of Cross Keys, Lincoln telegraphed Frémont to halt his pursuit of Jackson, stand fast at Harrisonburg, and await fresh orders. It would be another two days before he had even semi-reliable information about what had happened. Frémont wasted a splendid opportunity at Cross Keys, the only battle during the Valley campaign in which he had a clear numerical superiority over the rebels—nearly twice as many as Ewell's five thousand Confederates. "The consequence of the Union's shadowboxing opposite the Confederate left was the loss of Frémont's brightest opportunity for winning a decisive victory," Valley campaign historian Robert Krick concluded. Lincoln, though, held Shields responsible. He told Zagonyi that if Shields "had moved in strength to Port Republic & held or destroyed the Bridge Frémont would have destroyed Jacksons entire army."[52]

But Shields hadn't burned the bridge across the South Fork of the Shenandoah. On June 9, he fared no better at Port Republic—"the most fierce and bloody battle I have ever been in," one of Shields's men wrote home—than Frémont had at Cross Keys. With Jackson safely across the river, Frémont could do little but stand pat five miles to the north. Frémont believed the hard marching—150 miles in less than two weeks, with soldiers on half rations—and the previous day's fight left them unfit for another battle. One officer remembered troops "marching in rather loose order . . . looked ragged, tired, and dejected. I heard a good deal of hard swearing in the ranks in various tongues, English, German, and Hungarian." At one point Frémont stooped to asking civilians whether they knew where Jackson was. If any did, none were telling the Yankees.[53]

The Valley campaign was over. The twin victories at Cross Keys and Port Republic helped seal Jackson's aura of invincibility and lifted the spirits of a South disheartened by a string of defeats. Southerners felt a special joy in the defeat of the two leading Republican politicians, Frémont and Banks, whose emancipation policies were especially galling to them. Jackson would soon head to the Peninsula, where some of his aura would be diminished. Frémont remained in the Valley to deal with recriminations for another failure.[54]

On June 10, the War Department ordered Frémont to detach cavalry, artillery, and infantry units on loan from McDowell back to that general. That day, Frémont at last heard from Shields, who was ordered to the Peninsula. With half the army leaving and his in tatters, he suggested that he fall back to join Banks and his Missouri colleague, Franz Sigel, who had joined Banks's army in May. On June 12, Lincoln reiterated his order to fall back to Harrisonburg and await further instructions, but by that time Frémont was already en route to Mount Jackson, another twenty-five miles north on the Valley turnpike, which he considered more defensible and "the key to the surrounding country." Lincoln approved that shift after the fact, but once again the lack of a commander on the spot had affected communications.[55]

Weary of the crossing messages, Frémont wrote a long dispatch detailing his army's status and sent Charles Zagonyi to Washington to deliver it to Lincoln and Stanton. He wanted Sigel to reinforce him toward Harrisonburg, where he believed the Confederates were gathering in force. But he wasn't even sure whether Sigel was under his command. He begged that "some position be immediately made strong" by uniting the scattered forces and sending reinforcements. Frémont was bracing for an attack from Jackson, but Lincoln had moved on. No longer worried about what Jackson was up to, the president had shifted his focus to McClellan's battles on the Peninsula. He wanted Frémont and Banks to hold the line in the Valley while Little Mac tended to business before Richmond.[56]

Stanton reminded Frémont that Sigel was under Banks and that Banks held an independent command, which Frémont knew all too well. The secretary ignored the implications of Frémont's plea. He and the president were happy, for the time being, to continue running the campaign from Washington because they believed it was over. "We have no indefinite power of sending re-enforcements," Lincoln told Frémont on June 15. The president mistakenly believed that Frémont had "alone beat Jackson" and so should need no more troops. But even had he been fully informed about the outcomes at Cross Keys and Port Republic, Lincoln wasn't sending any more troops to the Valley. He wanted Frémont and Banks to stay close enough that either could quickly support the other if the need arose. "This liberates McDowell to go to the assistance of McClellan," he explained. "I have arranged this, and am very unwilling to have it deranged."[57]

After Missouri and emancipation and Moorefield, Lincoln was predisposed to be annoyed with Frémont when he observed what he perceived as the same balky behavior again. He wanted a clearer picture. Carl Schurz, the Wisconsin politician who had urged Lincoln to uphold Hunter's emancipation order, would provide it. A Prussian émigré who had been commissioned a brigadier general in April 1862, Schurz was eager to join Frémont in the Valley. Lincoln happily obliged, with a request that Schurz send him "a confidential report about the condition of things" in the Mountain Department. Schurz, like Frémont, was a man of the world. He had served as minister to Spain in the first months of the war. He returned in January 1862 and began lobbying Lincoln for a commission. Like so many of Frémont's officers, Schurz was a veteran of the European revolutions of 1848 and wore a typically gaudy European-style uniform. He might be more welcome in Frémont's camp than David Hunter had been in Missouri. Schurz left Washington on June 2. Delayed by high water and bad weather, he arrived in Harrisonburg late on the evening of June 9, in the immediate aftermath of Port Republic and Cross Keys. He met with Frémont the next day and was impressed. "There was an air of refinement in his bearing," Schurz wrote later. "His manners seemed perfectly natural, easy, and unaffected, without any attempt at posing. His conversation, carried on in a low, gentle tone of voice, had a suggestion of reticence and reserve in it, but not enough to cause of a suspicion of insincerity." But, like so many others who encountered Frémont, Schurz wavered. "And yet, one did not feel quite sure."[58]

It took only a couple of days talking with Frémont and inspecting his own new troops to make him quite sure that Frémont had been assigned a task that was all but impossible to achieve with the resources he had been given. Schurz's biographer notes that corresponding with the president "was obviously subversive of discipline," just as it had been with Blair and Samuel Curtis in Missouri. But Schurz largely backed Frémont's version of events. "It is a fact, which admits of no doubt, that, when you ordered Gen. Frémont to march from Franklin to Harrisonburg, it was absolutely impossible to carry out the order," he reported back to the president after two days of observation. "The army was in a starving condition and literally unable to fight." Schurz, like Lincoln, mourned the missed opportunity and suggested that Frémont could have moved faster in pursuing the rear guard after failing to close the pincer. But he defended, point by point, Frémont's decision to fall back on Mount Jackson, to which Lincoln had quickly acquiesced in any case. And he stressed the need for shoes, clothes, horses, and a better supply system.[59]

Schurz also told Lincoln that even if Frémont had gotten in front of Jackson at Strasburg, he still "would have been in great danger of being beaten. Jackson would have used his whole force and fought with desperation. There is no doubt that he was numerically almost twice as strong as Frémont" with Shields nowhere to be found. Schurz would in time harden a bit toward Frémont. Writing years later, he added a classic "to be sure" to his assessment. "A very self-reliant and resolute commander would eagerly have taken the risk and strained every nerve to be on the decisive spot on time," he argued. "Frémont evidently was not of that class. To him, the difficulties in the way were a matter of first interest. It must be owned that they might well have discouraged a man of no more than ordinary inspiration."[60]

"READY TO COME TO A FAIR SETTLEMENT OF ACCOUNTS"

It's possible Schurz's corroboration of Frémont's assessment of things took some of the vinegar out of Lincoln's pique. He at least offered a grudging thanks for the efforts of Frémont's army at Cross Keys. If so, the new mood didn't last. On June 15, Frémont took the president to task for failing to live up to his end of the bargain that Frémont thought he had signed onto and for trying to manage a complicated strategic situation from behind a desk in Washington.[61]

"I respectfully remind the President that when assigned to this command I was informed that I should have a Corps of thirty five thousand men[.] I now ask from the President the fulfillment of this understanding and ask it only because under the conditions of the War here I should be able to render good and immediate service." A force of that size, he told Lincoln, would allow him to occupy Staunton and move south through the valley to capture the Virginia and Tennessee Railroad—the original plan the two men had contemplated in March. Frémont needed reinforcements, he insisted, because "the small corps scattered about the country not being within supporting distances of each other as the topography of the country will show, are exposed to sudden attack by greatly superior force of an Enemy to whom intimate knowledge of country and universal friendship of inhabitants give the advantages of rapidity and secrecy of movements." The Valley was still important as a granary and still a target for Confederate forces, whatever Lincoln might think of the focus now having shifted to Richmond. (On that very day, famed Confederate cavalryman Jeb Stuart had completed his ride around McClellan's army on the Peninsula.) Then came the gig. "I respectfully submit this representation to the President," Frémont concluded, "taking it for granted that it is the duty of his Generals to offer for his consideration such impressions as are made by knowledge obtained on operations on the ground."[62]

Lincoln, who had put up with a lot from recalcitrant generals, could not abide this jibe. He occasionally lost his cool and sometimes wrote letters while in that state. Often he then tucked those letters away without sending them. This time, he responded in kind to the "supposed understanding that I would furnish you a corps of thirty-five thousand men, and asking of me 'the fulfillment of this understanding.'" Now Lincoln scolded his general with more than a hint of finality: "I am ready to come to a fair settlement of accounts with you on the fulfillment of understandings."

Lincoln conceded that he had promised Frémont that he "would give you all the force I could, and that I hoped to make it reach thirty five thousand." He then reminded Frémont of his forlorn promise "that, within a reasonable time, you would seize the Railroad at, or East of, Knoxville, Tenn. if you could." At that point, Lincoln asserted, Frémont had at his disposal about twenty-five thousand men, which was true, although the number of men ready to fight was smaller by about five thousand. Adding Blenker's division brought the total number up close to the promised thirty-five thousand. Lincoln reminded Frémont that doing so came "at the expense of great dissatisfaction to Gen. McClellan. . . . My promise was literally fulfilled. I had given you all I could, and I had given you very nearly if not quite thirty-five thousand."

That was Lincoln's end of the account. As for Frémont's, "On the 23rd. of May, largely over two months afterwards, you were at Franklin Va, not within three hundred miles of Knoxville, nor within eighty miles of any part of the Railroad East of it—and not moving forward, but telegraphing here that you could not move for lack of everything. Now, do not misunderstand me. I do not say you have not done all you could. I presume you met unexpected difficulties; and I beg you to believe that as surely as you have done your best, so have I." There weren't enough men available to send thousands more to the Valley, which Lincoln had decided was not worth the effort, at least for the time being. "I am only asking of you to stand cautiously on the defensive, get your force in order, and give such protection as you can to the valley of the Shenandoah, and to Western Virginia. Have you received the orders? and will you act upon them?"[63]

The short answer was yes. Frémont, chastened for the moment, chose not to argue further with Lincoln. "Your dispatch of today is received," he answered. "In reply to that part of it which concerns the orders sent to me I have to say that they have been received, and that as a matter of course I will act upon them, as I am now doing."[64]

Lincoln also let it lie there. As unhappy as he was with Frémont, Lincoln still believed he had to tread carefully, telling Charles Sumner, "We can't do with Frémont as we should with another general. He has the people behind him." But he could do what he should have done three months earlier. Naming a commanding general to coordinate all the armies in Virginia was long overdue.[65]

On June 26, Lincoln ordered that the "forces under Major Generals Frémont, Banks and McDowell . . . shall be consolidated and form one army, to be called the Army of Virginia." Command of that army was assigned to Maj. Gen. John Pope. Frémont would command the new army's first corps, Banks the second, and McDowell the third. It mattered not a whit to Lincoln that all three of the officers being superseded outranked Pope. He would later tell William Rosecrans, the man Frémont replaced in Virginia, "Truth to speak, I do not appreciate this matter of rank on paper, as you officers do." Lincoln was searching for competence. He had proven a poor judge of generals up to this point in the war, and he still had some mistakes to make before finding the right combination.[66]

Putting someone in charge of Frémont, Banks, and McDowell was a good idea. However, Pope was the wrong man for the job, as would become apparent soon enough. Frémont suspected as much. His interactions with Pope in Missouri were enough proof. "Pope had developed into an insubordinate officer and an open enemy," Jessie would write. Pope didn't think much of Frémont either, telling one of Banks's officers that Frémont "is not a bad man nor dishonest. He is simply foolish. He has not the sense of a boy sixteen years old. In money matters and in responsible places he is the victim of sharpers."[67]

Frémont wasn't the only one in the army with a low opinion of the new commander. "Pope is a humbug and known to be by those who put him in his present place," wrote Charles Francis Adams Jr., who would travel to Washington near the end of August to take a place on Pope's staff. He was so repulsed by the general's behavior that he turned down the post.[68]

The day after Lincoln put Pope in command, Banks paid an afternoon visit to Frémont's headquarters, where Frémont informed his old ally that he had sent in his resignation. It was blunt and to the point. "I respectfully ask that the President will relieve me of my present command," he wired Stanton.

> I submit for his consideration that the position assigned me by his recent order is subordinate and inferior to those hitherto conceded me, and not fairly corresponding with the rank I hold in the army. I further desire to call his attention to the fact that to remain in the subordinate command to which I am now assigned would virtually and largely reduce my rank and consideration in the service of the country. For these reasons I earnestly request that the President will not require the order to take effect so far as I am concerned, but will consent immediately to relieve me.[69]

Immediate relief is what he got. When Frémont's wire, sent at 12:30 p.m., arrived on Stanton's desk, it took less than ten minutes for the relief order to be issued. Sigel was given command of Frémont's corps, much to Pope's chagrin. Pope's biographer suggests he might have preferred to stick with Frémont. Despite his intention to "march within days," Pope was soon complaining that the Valley armies were "much demoralized and broken down, and unfit for active service at the present." This description seemed to confirm Frémont's reports to Lincoln about the condition of his army. But Pope and Frémont would engage in a newspaper war in early 1863 in which Frémont, supported by Sigel and Banks, denied at least that his army was demoralized.[70]

Even if Frémont was justified in refusing to serve under an officer he outranked, especially one he considered bereft of both competence and character, his resignation still bore the whiff of putting self over country. Banks (a political general) and McDowell (West Point Class of 1838) both outranked Pope (Class of 1842) and yet stayed on to serve under him. Frémont remained popular in the ranks, but some officers were less than upset about his departure. One colonel characterized his leave-taking as "carrying with him everything but our regrets." Others, such as Capt. Robert Gould Shaw, an admirer of Frémont who served under Banks in the Valley before taking command of the famous 54th Massachusetts Regiment of black troops, wrote to his sister, "You can't realize how much the officers of the Regular Army hate him," and told his mother, "It seems such a pity that his chance of making his worth felt all over the country is gone." Jessie later gave her version of events to George W. Julian. Pope was only the trigger. "It was only a question of time, the resigning," she told the congressman. "It would have been so contrived that the General would have been forced to do so, but if he had stayed they would have prepared defeats & destroyed his reputation. He knew the men & would not trust them." She defended Frémont's giving "only a technical military reason for resigning." The alternative would have been for him to paint a vivid portrait of Pope. "This man you have put over me is my enemy, & will endeavor to make good his assertions against me," she spoke for John. "I cannot trust him with my honor or the lives of my command so I retire knowing it to be useless to ask justice where he is a court favorite & I am denied the ordinary rights of military usage."[71]

It sounded to some like sour grapes or, worse, placing concern about his rank above duty to his country. It was in keeping with Frémont's long history of intraservice battles going all the way back to Stephen Watts Kearny in California, at least as viewed through the eyes of his wife. Such an exit would have been unmanly and unmilitary, and Frémont was still a serving officer and would remain so for almost two years. He chose the path of bitter acquiescence for the moment, hoping for one more chance.

Frémont, still in the army but without a command, rode out on June 28, wearing a white slouch hat; "his manner was graceful, dignified, and prepossessed," an officer noted. He stopped by to see Banks for a quick visit on his way to catch the train north from Martinsburg. Some of Banks's underlings had urged him to follow Frémont in resigning, but Banks had less military pretense than Frémont and a better dynamic with Lincoln, who appreciated how Banks differed from Frémont. "I regard General Banks as one of the best men in the army," Lincoln told abolitionist editor Sydney Howard Gay. "He makes no trouble. . . . He always knows his duty and does it." Even the supportive Robert Gould Shaw was compelled to "confess that my faith in Frémont has been somewhat shaken since his resignation. I am afraid he will never recover himself entirely."[72]

Congressman James G. Blaine concluded that when Lincoln sent McDowell "to take part in the fruitless chase after Stonewall Jackson in the Shenandoah Valley, he was doing precisely what the President of the Confederate States would have ordered." It's a harsh assessment. Historians of the Valley campaign have been more forgiving, though differing on Lincoln's four months as de facto general in chief in 1862. Gary Gallagher praised his "sound grasp of Union and Confederate strategy, an understanding of his generals' personalities, and a resolute determination to prod—almost to will—his commanders to act in such a way as to forge victories outside Richmond and in the Shenandoah Valley." That they failed was, in Gallagher's estimation, due more to their own shortcomings than Lincoln's management. Peter Cozzens called Lincoln (and Stanton) "well-intentioned but too often ill-informed." While Lincoln did not panic, as some have suggested, "neither did he add positively" to the conduct of the campaign. That seems a reasonable assessment.[73]

The verdict on Frémont is similarly divided, although none credit him with anything like success. Most chroniclers of the Valley campaign view him as a failure. Emil Schalk, who wrote a quick history of the campaign in 1863, was highly critical of Frémont's decision making, although he made the same mistake Lincoln had in assuming simple distances between cities were a matter of taking a walk on a country road. Cozzens argues Frémont (and Banks) "performed reasonably well in view of the many factors working against them," especially the lack of an overall commander on the ground. Still, while he faced obstacles the commander in chief did not fully grasp, Frémont nevertheless failed to move quickly enough or to make the right moves at critical moments, let Jackson escape when he was all but caught, and lost the only major contest in which forces under his direct command fought, at Cross Keys. William Miller, while acknowledging their mistakes, argues that Banks and Frémont, if not Shields, both "[deserve] some credit for modest accomplishments in bad situations not of their making. . . . But if all the generals failed the test of greatness, so also did Lincoln and Stanton."[74]

In late May, the North had appeared poised to defeat the rebellion and restore the Union. McClellan was bearing down on Richmond. Jackson was trapped in the Valley. Victories in the West had sent Union armies into the heart of the South and disillusioned many southerners. The first ten days of June changed all that, shifting the military balance toward the South and emboldening political critics of the administration in the North.

"CONGRESS DONE WHAT FRÉMONT DONE"
Those critics were coming at Lincoln from both sides—those who wanted a harder war and a more direct attack on slavery and those who saw the war as wasteful and pointless and wanted a restoration of the Union as it was. That battle was being fought in Congress. Jessie Frémont had mentioned to Frederick Billings as far back as January the burgeoning congressional debate on a new Confiscation Act, which she believed would "test the govt. & Congress on the slavery question."[75]

Illinois senator Lyman Trumbull, instigator of the Confiscation Act that had become law in August, also took the lead on the sequel. When Congress reconvened in December, he immediately introduced a bill "for confiscating the property, and giving freedom to the slaves, of rebels." Where the First Confiscation Act was introduced and enacted over the course of a month, the more complicated and more comprehensive Second Confiscation Act would take seven. The significant difference, as far as abolitionists were concerned, was that the new measure would empower the government to free all slaves in rebel-held areas, not just those working directly on war-related duties. Much of the debate—and the president's main qualms—about the bill focused on the confiscation provisions, which would have seized the real property of rebels in perpetuity. The slavery debate centered on how much discretion the president should have: Should the bill empower him to issue an emancipation order? Or should it mandate such an order? Trumbull and others who would follow his lead in introducing their own versions would maintain the distinction between real property—land, homes, and things—and enslaved humans, who they had long argued were not property under the Constitution.[76]

Another aspect of the debate harkened back to the Lincoln-Frémont disagreement. Generally, Republicans supported the measure and Democrats opposed it. But Trumbull's Illinois colleague, Republican Orville Browning, who had argued with his friend Lincoln about the legality of Frémont's Missouri emancipation order, opposed the bill. Frémont's proclamation had cited military necessity and thus invoked the executive branch's war powers, which Browning endorsed. Browning saw Trumbull's bill as legislative overreach. Either the Confederates were to be treated as belligerents, and therefore subject to the laws of war (and thus the war powers that made Frémont's proclamation permissible), or they were not, in which case they were still subject to the Constitution. In Browning's view—and the view of most elected Republicans and every Democrat—that document barred any federal intervention with slavery in the states. Trumbull, however, saw a reliance on the executive branch and "military necessity" as akin to military dictatorship, telling his colleagues, "Necessity is the plea of tyrants." Trumbull also noted that the president himself rejected the notion and cited Frémont to prove it. "We all know that the President does not pretend to exercise any such power; that he, in fact, has rebuked a distinguished general for attempting to exercise it," Trumbull said during debate on his bill in April.[77]

Over several months, various versions of the measure emerged, receded, went through special committees, and finally landed in a conference committee after the House passed two separate bills, one addressing confiscation and the other emancipation, on June 17 and 18. The Senate stuck with one bill for both provisions and passed it, 28–13, with Browning one of only two Republicans opposed. Radical Zachariah Chandler of Michigan voted no because he believed the confiscation provisions had been weakened too much. The measure, he said, was not "worth one stiver. It is utterly useless as a bill to confiscate property." The House refused to go along and voted down the Senate bill. On July 11, a conference committee made up of members from both chambers sided with the Senate. The House finally agreed later that day, and the Senate adopted the conference version the next day, with Browning again voting no.[78]

The bill had been watered down from Trumbull's original draft, but he still took pride of authorship. "We have passed a good confiscation bill, much better & stronger than the synopsis in New York papers" would lead one to believe, he told his wife. "If the President does his duty, it will be very efficient, quite as much so as my bill."[79]

Whether the president would do his duty remained to be seen. Browning visited the White House to try to persuade Lincoln to veto the measure. Lincoln had doubts about the bill as well, although they differed somewhat from Browning's. While the senator focused on executive-legislative authority as related to emancipation, Lincoln was more worried about the legality of the confiscation provisions, which he saw as an unconstitutional forfeiture of property across generations and without judicial proceedings—"the divesting of title forever," as he put it. While there was "no formal attainder" in the bill (no one was convicted of a crime by legislative fiat), the effect was the same. "I am constrained to say I think this feature of the act is unconstitutional," he told lawmakers, while suggesting "it would not be difficult to modify it."[80]

Radicals were outraged by the possibility of a veto. Trumbull, who was not a radical, was "very much disturbed. . . . I cannot believe it possible." He tried to visit Lincoln on July 15 to argue his case but couldn't get an audience. "It is strange that Mr. Lincoln cannot appreciate the condition we are in," Trumbull told his wife. "I have felt more hopeful of late, because I thought the war was henceforth to be prosecuted on different principles."[81]

After considerable grumbling, Congress took Lincoln's suggestion to "modify" the bill. They adopted a joint resolution stating that the forfeiture of real estate ended with the life of the person in rebellion and could not be applied to his descendants, assuaging Lincoln's concerns about unconstitutional "corruption of blood." It also allowed for the return of property via pardon. Trumbull objected to the change, but senators had little choice. Without it, Lincoln would veto the bill, and they did not have the time or the votes to override. "It may be sometimes desirable to secure as much as we can," said New Hampshire Republican Daniel Clark, who had brought the change to the floor for consideration, "if we cannot get all we wish." The president signed the bill and the joint resolution the next day; then he made the "uncharacteristically tactless gesture," in the words of Lincoln's greatest biographer, of sending his already-prepared veto message to Congress anyway.[82]

Trumbull was satisfied. "The confiscation bill is in my opinion worth more to the Union cause than would be the taking of Richmond without it," he argued. Frémont likewise had to be satisfied that his view of the war was beginning to prevail. As a correspondent of Lincoln's put it, "Congress done what Frémont done."[83]

A Virginia-born officer in Banks's Valley army spoke for many when he wrote in his diary at the end of June, "Although a strong party had endeavored to make [slavery] the object of the war, I did not see that it had got the upper hand of the conservatism yet and I still had faith that it would not." Within a couple of weeks, he would be proved wrong. The Joint Committee on the Conduct of the War and the Second Confiscation Act were both outgrowths of Lincoln's countermanding of Frémont's emancipation order. Lincoln now had congressional sanction to do what Frémont had tried to do, what Browning argued both men already had the power to do. And, better, Lincoln was ready to use it.[84]

Finally, Lincoln had come to the same conclusion Frémont had reached almost a year earlier. Lincoln put up with more, and for longer, from McClellan than he ever did from Frémont. But it might have been Little Mac who finally pushed Lincoln around the bend on emancipation. On July 7, while the final machinations of the congressional debate on confiscation were grinding slowly toward a conclusion, McClellan offered Lincoln his opinion on the state of affairs.

"The time has come when the Government must determine upon a civil and military policy, covering the whole ground of our national trouble," the general wrote to the commander in chief, and then he proceeded to suggest what that policy ought to be. "It should not be a War looking to the subjugation of the people of any state, in any event: It should not be, at all, a War upon population; but against armed forces and political organizations: Neither confiscation of property, political executions of persons, territorial organization of States or forcible abolition of slavery should be contemplated for a moment." It was an argument Lincoln himself had made not so long ago. His military governor of North Carolina, Edward Stanly, called it "wise and patriotic advice." But Lincoln had moved past it. Now that he saw his chief military commander could not do the same, he made an argument that Frémont would have found familiar. Montgomery Blair later wrote that McClellan's letter was the turning point for Lincoln.[85]

On July 13, 1862, Lincoln told Navy Secretary Gideon Welles and Secretary of State William H. Seward that he "had about come to the conclusion that [emancipation] was a military necessity absolutely essential for the salvation of the union, that we must free the slaves or be ourselves subdued." Circumstances had changed. What had changed more was Lincoln's perception of them. Worrying too much about the feelings of "professed friends" in Missouri, Kentucky, and Maryland "has paralyzed me more in this struggle than any other one thing," he told a Maryland friend a couple weeks later. Warnings that moving troops through Maryland would "crush all union feeling" proved false. Steps toward emancipation, including Frémont's, had sparked the same kind of warnings from fretful Kentuckians. Lincoln heeded those, but they, too, proved false. Events had proven Lincoln wrong—about southern unionism, about the centrality of slavery to the southern case and cause—and he was now willing to acknowledge the fact. "Broken eggs cannot be mended," he told another correspondent a few days later. It had taken eleven months for the president to catch up with the Frémonts' view of the military necessity of emancipation. Lincoln's argument rested on the presidential war power, an authority that is delegated to officers and soldiers in the field for any number of tasks both routine and exceptional. Every rifleman who kills an enemy soldier in a war not declared by Congress does so under presidential war powers. If Lincoln had claimed the authority to emancipate under the presidential war power, he could have delegated that authority to Frémont and Hunter, much as Browning argued; he chose not to, for largely the same reason he appointed Frémont in the first place: politics.[86]

The combined efforts of John and Jessie Frémont had been unable to move Lincoln in September 1861, but time and events had finally persuaded him of the necessity of their cause, if not their methods. The president had, as he had long hoped, put slavery on the "course of ultimate extinction." He still had to fight a war to realize that hope. The Frémonts' war was over. Their battles with Abraham Lincoln were not.

CHAPTER EIGHT

"Frémont seems to be effectually laid upon the shelf"

ONCE AGAIN, THE FRÉMONTS RETREATED TO NEW YORK. JOHN TENDED TO long-neglected Las Mariposas business and waited for word from the War Department about another command. Massachusetts governor John Andrew suggested Frémont to lead a possible invasion of Texas, which Jessie reported as "under discussion." In the meantime, Frémont refused to let the bitterness of his departure from Virginia interfere with what he saw as his duty. He donated his military pay of $450 a month to charities benefiting the families of soldiers, largely the Western Sanitary Commission that he and Jessie had helped found. He rode with Lily and Charles Zagonyi in Central Park. And he spoke out in support of military recruiting and emancipation.[1]

In July, he spoke at an enlistment rally, still "in the field although not in the saddle," as Jessie wrote. A "vast sea of upturned faces" in Lower Manhattan was "anxious to see the countenance of the Pathfinder," the *New York Tribune* reported. After a raucous welcome and a prayer, Frémont sought (at first without much success) to make himself heard above the cheering crowd that refused to be stilled. "Go it, old Pathfinder, you are the General for us," came the shouts. But Frémont pressed on until the noise finally subsided.[2]

"It is hardly necessary to say that this great assemblage has been called to consider the situation of the country, with the object of adopting such measures as will enable you to respond most immediately and most effectively to the President's call for troops," he began. Having made the call for enlistment, he turned from the what to the why: "It is not in the ideas or possibilities of the day that you should consent to a dismemberment of our national territory," a sentiment met with deafening cheers and shouts of "Never!" He did not mention emancipation by name but closed with an oblique reference: "We intend to maintain our historic place in the family of nations at the head of the great Democratic idea, and . . . for the sake of Liberty we are resolved to maintain the Union."[3]

Despite his failures on the battlefield, Frémont still possessed a potent emotional hold on the devotees of the antislavery movement that Lincoln did not yet have. As Jessie had put it in a recent letter to Sydney Howard Gay, formerly an editor at the *National Anti-Slavery Standard* and now at the *New York Tribune*, "Hawthorne in comparing open fires & stoves says . . . 'what man would not die for his hearth? Who would die for his air tight stove.' The Govt. is the air tight stove but the dear old hearthstone of country is not to be abandoned." Ever devoted to her "chief," she saw Frémont as embodying the country and its finest ideals. Many still agreed with her.[4]

On August 28, as John Pope's Army of Virginia was about to be swept away by Robert E. Lee at Second Manassas, Frémont addressed another recruiting rally, this one at Boston's Tremont Temple, hallowed ground for the abolitionist movement. Here, with Jessie in attendance, he made a more overt pitch for the abolition of slavery as a war aim.

"The events of the war showed that there could be no lasting peace while slavery exists on this continent," the *New York Herald* reported Frémont as saying. "Abolition should be effected so as to deprive the enemy of his great means of resistance." He took on Lincoln's concerns about the border states and "injustice to the loyalists of the South." War required sacrifice: "The Unionists of the North had made sacrifices in giving their lives and those whom they held most dear to them. Such losses could never be repaid." If northern unionists could give up their lives to preserve the country, could not southern unionists give up their slaves? The North, which had made terrible sacrifices, would not stand for such an unequal burden. "While the people had given their choicest treasures, will they hesitate to strike with a vital force, which shall prove effectual, and will they be content that hereafter the bones of their dead shall be turned up where they be buried by ploughshares held by the hands of slaves?"[5]

Cheers and bouquets were flung at the stage. Later, the Frémonts were serenaded at the Revere House. Charles Sumner told Lincoln that Frémont's speech was "one of the most remarkable ever made on this continent; complete in statement & argument; elevated in sentiment; exquisite in language; constituting in itself an event & a victory. I understand that it was received by the immense audience, with indescribable assent & enthusiasm."[6]

The public calls for emancipation by Frémont and others made no visible impression on Lincoln. Out of view, however, the wheel was turning. He invited border-state congressmen to the White House for a last-ditch pitch of his compensated emancipation plan. "Can you, for your states, do better than to take the course I urge?" he asked them. It was in the form of a final warning, which they failed to heed, unanimously rejecting Lincoln's appeal. Despite his assurances to Gideon Welles and William Seward during debate on the Second Confiscation Act and a cabinet discussion on July 22 about the subject, the president remained publicly reticent. But the border-state members' rejection had sealed the deal. At the July 22 cabinet meeting, Lincoln did not invite debate but sought suggestions about the emancipation proclamation he had drawn up. Attorney General Edward Bates made a pitch for compulsory colonization. Welles questioned the efficacy of military emancipation, and Salmon Chase countered that point with an argument for proclamations by commanders in the field who had conquered territory and had the slaves within their lines. He also endorsed arming freed slaves, but Lincoln was not yet ready to take that step. Lincoln listened but, for the moment, made no changes to his two-paragraph proclamation that relied on the authority of the Second Confiscation Act to justify emancipation. Seward suggested—and the president concurred—that any proclamation of emancipation must await a military victory to avoid the appearance of being the last desperate act of a failed administration. When, after the defeat at Second Manassas in late August, he was pressed by a Massachusetts congressman about the role of emancipation in defeating the rebels, Lincoln employed Seward's reasoning: "You would not have it done now, would you? Must we not wait for something like a victory?"[7]

On August 14, Lincoln told a delegation of Washington-area black leaders that the physical differences between the two races compelled him to support colonization of free blacks. He seemed even to hold the slave responsible for the rebellion, telling the men, "Without the institution of Slavery and the colored race as a basis, the war could not have an existence." Lincoln had long been a supporter of colonization, and he would continue to back the idea up through congressional approval of the Thirteenth Amendment in 1865. It's possible that he was using the occasion of this meeting to soften the political blow of what he knew was coming, as the meeting had what historian James Oakes called a "strong element of political calculation."[8]

A week after the meeting came the blowback for Lincoln's public silence. In an open letter to Lincoln headlined "A Prayer for Twenty Millions," *New York Tribune* editor Horace Greeley spoke for "all who desire the unqualified suppression of the Rebellion" who "are sorely disappointed and deeply pained by the policy you seem to be pursuing with regard to the slaves of the Rebels." It was not more laws that were needed but the execution of the laws already on the books, especially the Second Confiscation Act, Greeley insisted. What was holding Lincoln back? In Greeley's view, it was the undue influence of "certain fossil politicians hailing from the Border Slave States." It was the same argument made against Lincoln's revocation of Frémont's emancipation order: less concern for Kentucky slave owners, more concern for the slave and the slave's role in supporting the Confederate war effort. "We complain that the Union cause has suffered, and is now suffering immensely, from mistaken deference to Rebel Slavery," Greeley continued. He pointed a finger at Lincoln's generals—with his longtime foe George McClellan likely in mind—who disregarded both Confiscation Acts. And he complained that while "Frémont's Proclamation and Hunter's Order favoring Emancipation were promptly annulled," Henry Halleck's order barring slaves from coming into Union lines "never provoked even your own remonstrance." Even if the rebellion were defeated, Greeley wrote, without emancipation, war "would be renewed within a year." The solution, he reiterated in his concluding paragraph, was a "frank, declared, unqualified, ungrudging execution of the laws of the land, more especially of the [Second] Confiscation Act."[9]

Lincoln was by this time inured to Greeley's "impatient and dictatorial tone," so in his reply he was happy to ignore it "in deference to an old friend, whose heart I have always supposed to be right." But he rejected the notion that there was or ever had been any lack of clarity in his policy. "I would save the Union," he stated simply, and he would do it the fastest way possible under the Constitution. "My paramount object in this struggle *is* to save the Union, and is *not* either to save or to destroy slavery," he wrote. "If I could save the union without freeing *any* slave I would do it, and if I could save it by freeing *all* the slaves I would do it; and if I could save it by freeing some and leaving others alone I would also do that."[10]

The sentiment was clear enough, but it still seemed to indicate that Lincoln had not accepted the idea that emancipation was the key to defeating the Confederacy. If he could save the Union by freeing all the slaves, he would do so. That was not the same as saying freedom was essential to saving the Union, a view espoused by such radicals as George W. Julian and Owen Lovejoy and promoted by Frémont in his Boston speech. The passage would grow famous over time. It garnered considerable support right away.

Sydney Howard Gay, who worked for Greeley, told Lincoln that his response "has infused new hope among us at the North who are anxiously awaiting that movement on your part which they believe will end the rebellion by removing its cause. I think the general impression is that as you are determined to save the Union tho' Slavery perish, you mean presently to announce that the destruction of Slavery is the price of our salvation."[11]

Thurlow Weed, no fan of Greeley, was happy to see a message that "rebukes the insolence of Journalists who seek to control the Government and to Command the Army." He likewise believed it "places the Government upon impregnable ground." But Weed also said that Lincoln's response "warmed the hearts, inspired the hopes, and stirred the patriotism of the People."[12]

Frederick Douglass had a different reaction. "The President of the United States seems to possess an ever increasing passion for making himself appear silly and ridiculous," Douglass wrote, "often saying that which nobody wanted to hear, and studiously leaving unsaid about the only things which the country and the times imperatively demand of him." Douglass called his response to the delegation of black leaders "the language and arguments of an itinerant Colonization lecturer." And he believed that Lincoln's insistence that there could be no war without the presence of blacks "explains the animus of his interference with the memorable proclamation of General Frémont." To slaves, Lincoln "is direct, undisguised, and unhesitating. He says to the colored people: I don't like you, you must clear out of the country. So too in dealing with anti-slavery Generals the president is direct and firm."[13]

The support from Gay and Weed, representing both ends of the Republican coalition, must have gratified Lincoln. He could take Douglass in stride because, unlike Douglass, he knew what was in store. In his responses to the black visitors and to Greeley, Lincoln was clearly playing for time. "For several weeks the subject has been suspended," Navy Secretary Gideon Welles wrote, "but the President says never lost sight of." He had already decided to go ahead with the proclamation and, as Seward had suggested, was simply waiting for a propitious moment. When George McClellan drove back Robert E. Lee's invasion of Maryland at the Battle of Antietam on Wednesday, September 17, the moment had come.[14]

Lincoln spent the rest of that week writing and sharpening his proclamation. He unveiled it at a cabinet meeting on Monday, September 22. Where he had cited the Second Confiscation Act in his first draft in July, he now relied solely on military necessity as justification for emancipation. It was done under the authority of "the executive government of the United States, including the military and naval authority thereof." This had been Frémont's justification as well. Lincoln opened with a pitch for his subsidized emancipation plan coupled with colonization and then got to the point. On January 1, 1863, "all persons held as slaves within any state, or designated part of a state, the people whereof shall then be in rebellion against the United States shall be then, thenceforward, and forever free." Seward offered a couple of suggestions that Lincoln accepted. Montgomery Blair expressed approval of the principle but questioned the timing, worried about the coming elections and the effect on the border states. His alarmist view was that emancipation would move those states "*en masse* to the Secessionists as soon as it was read." Lincoln said he had weighed those concerns and found them wanting, a wholesale reversal of his position during the Frémont controversy of the previous fall, when fear about the fate of Kentucky drove policy. But even Welles acknowledged that the "effect which the Proclamation will have on the public mind is a matter of some uncertainty."[15]

Lincoln worried about public opinion too, but he wrote with judges in mind. He was meticulous in constructing the proclamation, avoiding grandiose phrasing, appealing to legality rather than morality. He feared a legal challenge that would allow an unfriendly Supreme Court led by Chief Justice Roger B. Taney, author of the decision in *Dred Scott v. Sandford*, to block emancipation. And he maintained a faith that colonization would help ease the popular reception of emancipation.[16]

Any legal proceedings would take time, if they happened at all. Public response was swift. Letters and petitions of support poured into the White House. Longtime abolitionists praised the proclamation while tempering their endorsements by noting the relative reticence of its creator. "The President can do nothing for *freedom* in a direct manner, but only by circumlocution and delay. How prompt was his action against Frémont and Hunter!" complained William Lloyd Garrison. Wendell Phillips, who had been harshly critical of Lincoln, calling him a "first rate second rate man," on this occasion held his fire, believing "he has turned the corner and recognizes the fact not simply that the slaves of rebels, but that the *slaves* must be freed."[17]

Frederick Douglass, who only weeks before had castigated Lincoln as silly and ridiculous, now praised the president's "own peculiar, cautious, forbearing and hesitating way, slow, but we hope sure," and felt confident that "events greater than the President, events which have slowly wrung this proclamation from him may be relied on to carry him forward in the same direction." The proclamation was "the first chapter of a new history." New York abolitionist editor Theodore Tilton wired simply, "God bless you for a good deed."[18]

Democratic papers in the North and border states howled in protest. The stock market dipped. Edgy Republican politicians, especially in the Midwest, echoed some of Montgomery Blair's concerns about the impact of the proclamation on the fast-approaching elections. Democrats believed "there will be resistance throughout the Northwest." Irish Catholics in the East, a core Democratic Party constituency, were vocally opposed. New York archbishop John Hughes derided "in the name of all Catholics the 'Idea' of making this war subservient to the philanthropic nonsense of abolitionism." Lincoln, certain in his action, was less certain of the result. Vice President Hannibal Hamlin wrote Lincoln "to express my undissembled and sincere thanks for your Emancipation Proclamation. It will stand as the great act of the age—It will prove to be wise in Statesmanship, as it is Patriotic—It will be enthusiastically approved and sustained and future generations will, as I do, say God bless you for the great and noble act." In reply, Lincoln thanked Hamlin for the sentiment but admitted "my expectations are not as sanguine as are those of some friends."[19]

Preoccupied with his own doubts, how gratifying to Lincoln must have been a letter from Benjamin Sherwood Hedrick, a former professor at the University of North Carolina who had fled the South under threat of violence during Frémont's 1856 presidential campaign. "Permit me to thank you on behalf of myself, and such Southern men as have been for the Union first, last and all the time, for your proclamation of yesterday," he wrote when the proclamation hit the newspapers. "The measures there indicated will end the rebellion." Lincoln had at last overcome his long devotion to the idea of widespread southern unionism, at least enough to free the slaves and start the military on the road to a harder war. But hearing support from a southern unionist on this, the most important act of his life, surely removed some of the frustration that had accompanied that unrequited devotion.[20]

"OUT OF THE FRÉMONT SLOUGH"

The issue that first separated Lincoln and Frémont was now settled decisively—by Lincoln, using Frémont's reasoning. That fact might have given Frémont reason to believe that a new approach could work. He reached out to Chase seeking the supportive secretary's help in winning reinstatement to his old position in the western theater. Nothing came of it. Frémont had won the battle but was lost to the war.[21]

"Frémont seems to be effectually laid upon the shelf," William Lloyd Garrison told his wife in October 1862. "The friends of freedom should be clamorous for his restoration to his post." The closest of Frémont's friends would soon be making that case in a most unsubtle way. While those appeals fell on deaf ears, still the calls from ordinary citizens for his return continued, especially in the West. Citing Frémont's many military virtues, the citizens of Wyandot County in north-central Ohio urged Lincoln "to give Gen. Frémont command of the forces of the Mississippi Valley." The citizens of Preble County in the southwestern part of the state took an indirect route, asking the Senate to request Lincoln "to place the Federal troops in Eastern Virginia under the command of Genl. John C. Frémont."[22]

While he waited for the summons that wasn't coming, Frémont traveled to St. Louis to testify in the court-martial of his former quartermaster, Justus McKinstry. Arriving on October 20, he told a large group that called on him at his Chouteau Avenue home, "I could not have reconciled it with my conscience to be absent, believing as I do that the assaults upon him were made solely because he felt it an honorable duty to stand faithfully by the side of his chief." But the proceedings dragged on for more than two months, pushing Frémont's testimony back to the end of the year. In the meantime, he filled his days campaigning against Frank Blair, who was running for reelection to the House in the face of a growing threat from Missouri radicals to his congressional seat and his political future.[23]

The jaundiced view of Montgomery Blair was that a conspiracy of Frémont, St. Louis Germans, and secessionists was working to defeat his brother. Montgomery couldn't accept that Missouri politics, especially in St. Louis, were shifting away from the Blairs' conservatism toward a more radical approach to slavery and the war and that Frank was out of step. A few days before Frémont's arrival in St. Louis, Frank published an address to his constituents that accused the general of conducting a "conspiracy against the government." Fully five of the document's eight and a half pages are fulminations against Frémont and Blair's own German constituents. He endorsed emancipation while making a pitch for colonization. He argued that "compulsory deportation is unnecessary" but passed over the question of what would happen if enough freed slaves failed to take advantage of the voluntary variety. And he opposed the enlistment of blacks in the army because it would be "derogatory to the manhood of freemen to confess our inability to put down this rebellion without calling to our aid these semi barbarous hordes."[24]

Montgomery Blair had feared the political effects of emancipation from the beginning. He simultaneously argued that Frémont had promulgated his proclamation so he could be elected president and that Lincoln's proclamation would cost the Republicans victory in November. He never acknowledged the contradiction, much less tried to reconcile it. What he hadn't bargained for was that the fact of emancipation would create a class of voters, even in Missouri, ready to accept radical change. That's not to say that there was no consternation in the North over the preliminary proclamation. Plenty of voters were apprehensive, and plenty of politicians were demagogic. An unhinged Horatio Seymour, running for governor of New York, called the Emancipation Proclamation "a proposal for the butchery of women and children, for scenes of lust and rapine, of arson and murder unparalleled in the history of the world." No Democrat who claimed that slavery was a positive good or that slaves were content in their bondage ever explained why such happy, contented folk would turn so viciously on their captors. But they used the supposed certainty of such actions to stoke fear in the electorate.[25]

To a degree, it worked. Brig. Gen. John Cochrane, who had backed the arming of black troops in November 1861, wrote that a Democratic victory "would be the signal to rebels of their success at the North, and to loyal men everywhere, of the independence of the South." It did not come to that, but Democrats did gain twenty-eight seats in Congress, largely along the tier of states bordering the slave states—New Jersey, Pennsylvania, Ohio, Indiana, and Illinois—all except Ohio states that Frémont lost in 1856 but Lincoln won in 1860. Democrats also made significant gains in governorships and state legislatures. How much of that was due to emancipation and how much to the lack of progress on the battlefield is open to debate. Historian Mark Neely makes a strong case that it was a lack of effort on behalf of Lincoln and the party that left the rank and file uninspired and thus drove down turnout. Some Republicans, including Lyman Trumbull, Carl Schurz, and William Pitt Fessenden, suggested Lincoln's concern for mollifying Democrats and the border states also affected Republican turnout. "Fear of offending the Democracy has been at the bottom of all our disasters," Fessenden said. All these factors were likely at play. A New Yorker appalled by Seymour's election as governor wrote that the "elections demonstrate most clearly that *decisive* battles of this revolution are really to be fought on Northern soil." What was necessary to avert disaster was "our labors of educating aright public opinion by every available instrumentality, and to the fullest possible extent." Even with the losses, however, Republicans retained control of both chambers of Congress, although whether it was an emancipationist majority remained to be seen. Most important, Lincoln was still president and would be for at least two more years.[26]

"I am no prophet, though the daughter of one," Jessie wrote to her sister early in 1863, "but I foresee the fall of the House of Blair." On the election's eve in St. Louis, the citizens held a "great Frémont demonstration" and "immense torchlight procession" that ended with the general being presented a Tiffany sword in a rosewood case by the German community. Signs lining the path of the march proclaimed, "The country shall yet claim thy arm, Frémont" and "Emancipation—the first great step of the nation towards its manifest destiny." The procession ended at Frémont's one-time headquarters at the Brant Mansion, where he delivered some anodyne remarks praising the Germans' patriotism and dedication to liberty, which were loudly cheered. But Frémont wasn't on the ballot. Jessie was right about not being a prophet; she was wrong about the Blairs. Facing both a radical opponent and a Democrat, Blair won by 153 votes. Francis Preston Blair believed, incorrectly, that the victory "has got us out of the Frémont slough for all time." At the same time that he was running for Congress, Frank Blair was recruiting regiments he planned to lead into battle. He was having trouble recruiting from the German community and blamed Frémont for that population's animosity. Blair never paused to consider the possibility that perhaps it was his animosity toward Frémont that had turned the Germans against him. However much Blair and Lincoln had begun to drift in different directions on the questions of slavery and race, their partnership remained. It was to Blair that Lincoln turned for an analysis of the results of the Missouri election, which, in Blair's estimation, yielded a solid Republican majority in the state and an emancipationist state legislature "that secures two Senators to Support the administration."[27]

The results satisfied Blair because he was already beginning to pull away from his Republican-of-convenience status. Real Republicans were less sanguine. Carl Schurz called the election a "great political defeat" and blamed it on Lincoln's reliance on generals who did not share his emancipationist leanings. Lincoln blamed the fact that more Republicans had gone to war than Democrats, and so could not vote, and that dissenting Republicans, in "vilifying and disparaging the administration," had provided Democrats with ammunition to attack. The most immediate effect of the election was the dismissal on November 5 of George McClellan as commander of the Army of the Potomac. To Schurz, "the change of persons means little if it does not imply a change of system. Let us be commanded by generals whose heart is in the war, and only by such." Schurz named no names, but McClellan's firing once again started chatter about Frémont being named to replace him as commander. Massachusetts governor John Andrew was among the most prominent supporters of installing Frémont at the head of the Army of the Potomac. Those calls would grow louder a month later when McClellan's successor, Ambrose Burnside, led the army to slaughter at Fredericksburg. But nothing came of the talk. As Lincoln replied to Schurz,

"There are men who have 'heart in it,' that think you are performing your part as poorly, as you think I am performing mine." Many thought the same of Frémont, with at least as much justification as they thought it of Lincoln.[28]

"THE DEEDS OF THAT BRAVE YOUNG GUARD"

Jessie had finished the draft of her book on the Missouri campaign early in the year but withheld it from publication while John was still in active service and a chance remained that the Frémont Body Guard might be reconstituted for field duty. Once it became apparent that wasn't going to happen, even with John back in command in Virginia, she began to move ahead with the project. "I see no reason to keep it back any longer," she wrote her publisher, James Fields, on May 22, 1862, "and shall send it on to you as soon as it is fairly copied out."[29]

But she did nothing further while John led the Mountain Department. She returned to the manuscript only when they relocated to New York in July. In early October, she warned Fields, "I can't possibly send you the manuscript because you will have to talk it over with me." Once she did, though, she wondered whether he could announce its coming in the next issue of the *Atlantic Monthly*, which he owned. And she warned him that she would be a tough edit. "I may consent to leave out some things but I'll make a death struggle for each lost projectile & I will not alter facts," she told him. Still, she asked him to "shape it slenderly. Dumpy books are so unsuggestive of elegance of thought or deep feeling. It's cruel enough to have lost my own slenderness," she said self-deprecatingly, "without seeing that misfortune befall this child of my heart & memory." He must not "hesitate to draw your critical pen through anything that seems sentimental or stilted."[30]

Fields had the final draft in his hands by the third week of October, when Jessie asked, "Please let no one see what I have written." She wanted to make final changes before reviewers got their hands on it and to review proof sheets with both her husband and Zagonyi, who were in St. Louis for the McKinstry trial (and the Blair campaign).[31]

The Story of the Guard came out just before Christmas 1862. It cost a pricey $1.25 and was advertised alongside new titles by Henry Ward Beecher, Alexis de Tocqueville, and Wilkie Collins. Reviews were generally friendly. "Mrs. Frémont is a true woman and has written a true woman's book," wrote the *Atlantic Monthly* reviewer, who might have been Fields but, in any case, could hardly be anything other than friendly since Fields owned the magazine. "Her style is full, free, vivid, with plenty of dashes and postscripts,—the vehicle of much genius and many noble thoughts." The book contained little prose. "Zagonyi tells much of the story in his own words," the *Atlantic* noted, and "the letters of the General himself form one of the most interesting features of the book." Taking Frémont's side, the reviewer averred, "Certainly no worthier subject could be chosen than the deeds of that brave young Guard, which was at first the target for so many slanders, and at last the centre of heartiest love and pride to all the North."[32]

An equally friendly publication, the *New York Tribune*, said the book "possesses a charm from the open-hearted frankness of the narrative, and the delightful naivete of manner with which it comments on the scenes and events of intimate personal experience." The review filled more than two full columns and included nearly two thousand words of excerpts, giving potential buyers the full flavor of the story. The *Missouri Republican* stated simply, "She has produced an entertaining volume, which will be read with pleasure."[33]

The *Daily National Republican* reviewed *The Story of the Guard* in the same issue in which it reviewed a new edition of Victor Hugo's *Les Misérables* ("very neat, cleanly printed, and handsome"). *The Story of the Guard*'s typography and binding were also "exquisitely fine." The substance was "a reliable and interesting chapter in the history of the rebellion. It is admirably well prepared, the accomplished authoress having thrown around it the charm of romance."[34]

Most reviewers also mentioned that the author planned to donate the proceeds to the families of those members of the Guard who had died in battle. Within two weeks, Fields had already forwarded $500 in royalties for that purpose. "You're too good to be true," Jessie effused to Fields. "Is it possible that I have actually gotten tangible help for my people already?" Soon after, she suggested to Fields an "Army edition" that could be printed on cheaper paper and in a small size to send "among the soldiers as an encouragement." The "cheap knapsack edition" for soldiers in the field was duly announced in April 1863. She enlisted Thomas Starr King to promote sales in California. Appealing to the Frémonts' most loyal constituency, a German-language edition—*Die Liebgarde*—quickly followed.[35]

"THIS INTERFERENCE WAS EXERCISED BY FRANK BLAIR"

While Jessie was finalizing *The Story of the Guard*, the court-martial of Frémont's former quartermaster, Justus McKinstry, began in St. Louis. September preliminaries took up two weeks, including the unseating of Gen. William Harney from the court. Harney asked to be relieved because he had once been McKinstry's commanding officer. Testimony finally began toward the end of September. Frémont filled his days in the unsuccessful bid to unseat Frank Blair from Congress, waiting for his turn to testify. It was a long wait. The trial dragged on through December, resembling in length Frémont's own 1847–1848 trial. The local, pro-Frémont press covered the case extensively. The *Missouri Democrat* carried daily transcripts from September 30 through the end of the trial.[36]

McKinstry acted as his own attorney, displaying both his arrogance and, like Frémont, his lack of support among the West Point–educated officer class. Chester Harding, Nathaniel Lyon's adjutant, was called by the prosecution but sounded more like a defense witness. With no supplies coming from the East, Harding told the court, McKinstry had to decide whether and how to obtain them locally. "We thought he was unnecessarily careful, and adhered too much to the rules under the circumstances," Harding testified, likely to the chagrin of the judge advocate.[37]

Two days before Christmas, McKinstry called to the stand Harney, who told the court that McKinstry had performed his duties "entirely to my satisfaction." But when McKinstry sought to have the general talk about "interference" with his command in spring 1861, the judge advocate objected. This was a clear attempt on McKinstry's part to bring the actions of Frank Blair into the trial, both in the way it made McKinstry's job more difficult and in alleging profiteering by Blair and his allies. Blair's actions were relevant, McKinstry argued, because "if the Government created or sanctioned the impediments to a proper discharge of duty on my part, surely no court martial will permit the persecution to avail himself of his own acts to convict me of neglect of duty." The court adjourned so the judges could consider the objection and then ruled that Harney could answer the question. Harney responded as McKinstry expected: "Yes, this interference was exercised by Frank Blair to such an extent that it caused me to be removed from the command of the Department of the West, in consequence of the base falsehoods which he fabricated and communicated to the Administration through his brother, Montgomery Blair." This issue was about more than contracting, Harney assured the court. It went straight to the heart of good order and discipline. "His influence was such with General Lyon that I never communicated with General Lyon at all," Harney continued. "I communicated with Frank Blair! I know General Lyon was entirely under the influence of Frank Blair—entirely!"[38]

Frémont finally took the stand in defense of his "friend, that true soldier and loyal citizen," on December 29, the last day of testimony. He gave his version of the discombobulated state of affairs in St. Louis when he arrived in July 1861: a thousand troops a day arriving with no arms or supplies and no transportation available to get them into the field. McKinstry's response to Frémont's orders to do something about the situation was "diligent, attentive, and energetic," he said. McKinstry, whom Frémont had fired as quartermaster under pressure from Washington, "performed his duties in such a way as to command my unqualified respect and approbation."[39]

The *Missouri Democrat* said, "Frémont's statements decidedly exonerated the accused." In noting Frémont's appearance, the *Chicago Tribune* reported, "McKinstry has managed his case very adroitly, and his acquittal is confidently predicted."[40]

The judges were tougher graders than the pro-Frémont newspapers. On January 16, the court announced its verdict, finding McKinstry guilty of neglect and violation of duty to the prejudice of good order and military discipline. Of the sixty-one specifications in the indictment, he was convicted on twenty-seven. He was sentenced to dismissal from the service, although the sentence was suspended awaiting a review by the president. On January 28, Lincoln confirmed the sentence.[41]

"THE POLICY OF HIS PROCLAMATION HAS BEEN VINDICATED BY TIME"

The interval between the Preliminary Emancipation Proclamation and the release of the final document on January 1, 1863, was fraught with worry, particularly in the face of Democratic gains in the elections. Lincoln's annual message, in which he made yet another pitch for gradual, compensated emancipation by the states and for colonization, lent substance to those concerns. But Lincoln was not backing away. With the new year came the proclamation, as promised.[42]

Frémont made no immediate public comment on the Emancipation Proclamation. Still hoping for a new command, he chose silence over public spectacle, a stance that contrasted poorly with Benjamin Butler's enthusiastic approval. Garrison would come to criticize Frémont for failing to express "any satisfaction in regard to the President's emancipation proclamation." Privately, Jessie offered a qualified endorsement while noting that Lincoln was not first to the party. "Emancipation has proved a pivotal term after all," she wrote to her sister. "A few of us felt this in '61." For others outside the family, Frémont remained the military embodiment of emancipation, viewed in some quarters as "the only man who can put life into the proclamation." George W. Julian, in calling for a new command for Frémont, told Congress, "The policy of his proclamation has been vindicated by time, and more than vindicated by the administration itself." Any of the many commands his friends pushed him for would serve "as a guaranty of the Proclamation," the *New York Tribune* wrote in February. Giving Frémont a command "would be a Proclamation of Freedom which would be read in midnight darkness," the paper urged in March, "and by those who do not know one letter of the alphabet from another. No slave in the South would need further assurance that he would neither be abused nor betrayed by an army commanded by Frémont."[43]

Some abolitionists were uncomfortable with the reliance on military necessity to justify emancipation, feeling the absence of a moral element risked a reversal of the gains when the war ended. Parker Pillsbury called it "the most God-insulting doctrine ever proclaimed." Others credited Frémont with marking the path followed by Lincoln. "The country will not forget that it was John C. Frémont who first declared the doctrine of emancipation of slave property as a penalty for the treason of the master," noted a piece that *The Liberator* reprinted from the *Missouri Democrat*. "His Missouri proclamation was the first official recognition of slavery's accountability for the rebellion. It treated the institution as a rebel." Noting Lincoln's reversal and the censure that fell on Frémont from moderate and conservative Republicans, as well as Democrats, the paper suggested his proclamation likely was playing a role in Frémont's continued unemployment. "But at last in his case, as in every case in which a sound principle is enunciated, the vindication has come. Time proves an unfailing champion of the right."[44]

With vindication came a change in attitude. On January 21, Frémont turned fifty. His adoring wife described him as "gray, worn, and in poor health." Frémont, the vigorous nonpolitician, had prided himself during the 1856 presidential campaign on eschewing the niceties of politics, much to the chagrin of some of his advisors. Now he began to behave and sound more like an officeholder, pocketing the policy gain of emancipation and looking for more. Frémont was invited to join a parade of abolitionist speakers at a March 31 Cooper Union event but declined because he had already accepted an invitation from Henry Ward Beecher to join the minister at the Academy of Music in Brooklyn, where Beecher spoke and Frémont basked in the cheers from his chair on the platform, "evidently the star of the occasion," one reporter wrote.[45]

On April 12, the second anniversary of the attack on Fort Sumter, Frémont spoke at a huge rally in Union Square. Among the other speakers were Schuyler Colfax, George W. Julian, and Montgomery Blair. "We do not disparage the other distinguished gentlemen when we say that Gen. Frémont and Gen. Sigel were the lions of the day," the *New York Tribune* reported. Frémont "was greeted with a burst of enthusiasm which continued some minutes." When the crowd finally quieted, he began with a call for unity and support for the administration and "no wavering in your support of the Government." But that support meant something different now than it had on April 12, 1861. Once emancipation became a fact on the ground, support for it became a shorthand way to define loyalty, Frémont asserted, adding, "A feeling of unconditional loyalty is rapidly absorbing all varieties of opinion, and fusing all party distinctions into the single resolve to preserve our national unity, at every cost."[46]

Not known for displaying a sense of humor in public, Frémont then took an unusual turn. He told the crowd that he had thought, at first, that he would not speak at the event, being of the opinion that serving military officers should not engage in political debate in public forums. "I was informed, not very long since, that officers permitting themselves to take part in public affairs outside their professional duties had been characterized by high authority as 'political Generals,'" he said, drawing laughter from the crowd. "But in giving sway to this usage, I am not at all satisfied that it is the correct view of the scope of an officer's duty in this country, and amidst the disorders of a civil war."

The military, Frémont said, was not a "separate class" distinct from the people, as in some European despotisms. In America, it was a part of the people. "And it is absurd to say that in a war of ideas, a conflict of principles, in a revolution which is taking the shape of a reformation—a revolution which involves the civilization of the age, and to the results of which the friends of liberty are looking with the deepest anxiety and interest in every part of the world—in all this momentous struggle, that the men most actively concerned, taking the most active part and making the costliest sacrifices, should have no opinions."

Invoking Ben Butler's military and emancipationist successes in New Orleans—and, indirectly, his own actions—he asked, "Does it reflect on the soldierly qualities of that General that he had the ability to institute a policy which enabled him . . . to hold in subjection to the laws and to reduce into good order and healthy propriety, and to restore in its commercial relations to the Union, the great metropolis of the South?" Was Edward Baker, killed at Ball's Bluff, less of soldier because he spoke politically in the earliest days of the war on the same spot Frémont now occupied? No, came the answer. "You promise that you will never agree to a dismemberment of the country which he left you," to which his audience responded, "Never!" In a direct message to the Lincoln administration, he closed, "And that next to the crimes of the traitors who are striking in arms at the life of the nation, you will hold the guilt of those men who, placed in responsible positions, do not use every effort to direct, with most terrible energy, the power of this country to destroy the Rebellion." This peroration was met with "tremendous cheering, and three times three cheers for Gen. Frémont."[47]

The hostile *New York Herald* predictably disparaged the day's events as "riga-marole." But it praised Frémont, who "stands up like a man for free speech" and "has a right to complain that an attempt should be made to gag a loyal Unionist like him by a sneer at 'political generals.' This is not a fair mode of getting rid of a candidate for the next Presidential term, if, indeed, we shall have any republic to be presided over in the year 1865."[48]

When no immediate military benefits resulted from the proclamation, opponents questioned the value of emancipation. Supporters questioned Lincoln's commitment. A Boston newspaper suggested that Lincoln refused to put Frémont back into action precisely because he would be successful in rousing the slaves, creating a new problem that the president was not prepared to face. "He *could* send Frémont South, but then the negroes might take the edict in earnest, and then—what should we do with them?" the abolitionist *Boston Common-wealth* imagined Lincoln asking.[49]

Wendell Phillips praised the administration's advances but continued "to demand that Lincoln call Frémont to his right hand" while excoriating what he saw as the negative influence of the cabinet and West Point generals who were standing in the way of progress on emancipation. Generals were not the only problem. The army reflected the ambivalence of the people on emancipation. "While many soldiers came to sympathize and embrace emancipation on both moral and practical grounds," historian John Hennessey wrote, "others struggled mightily to reconcile their own opposition to abolition with a war effort newly intent on slavery's end." They wanted to fight for the Union, not become pawns in politicians' games.[50]

Southern unionists were caught in a similar trap. Attorney General Edward Bates echoed Frémont when he observed in May 1863 that support for emancipation was quickly becoming shorthand for loyalty. Historian William C. Harris argued that "Southern Unionists had no other choice but to accept emancipation" because they had "tied their fortunes and perhaps their lives to the Washington government." If this was true in Louisiana and East Tennessee, it was just as true in Missouri and Kentucky and had been all along.[51]

"THE PIONEER IN ANY MOVEMENT IS NOT GENERALLY THE BEST MAN TO CARRY THAT MOVEMENT TO A SUCCESSFUL ISSUE"

Though Jessie wrote that "Lincoln often promised that General Frémont should have certain commands," there's no record of any such promise. The newspapers were filled with rumors, including the old ones that he would be appointed secretary of war or lead an attack on Texas, but any "promise" was more implied than stated. Jessie was partly correct in her surmise, though, that "Lincoln's disinclination to give General Frémont any active duty, was probably based on other reasons than military ones," which is not to say there were no military reasons to deny him command. Senior military commanders, particularly Henry Halleck, were bitterly opposed to Frémont. Vice President Hannibal Hamlin lobbied on Frémont's behalf. Jessie at last interpreted the failure of repeated pleas as meaning Frémont "was to be given no position during the war again, in which he could become prominent." Hints of a coming command, from Edwin Stanton as well as Lincoln, were likely employed as a tactic to string Frémont along to keep him and his supporters quieter than they might otherwise have been. But when the opportunity finally came, it would be Frémont, not Lincoln, who balked.[52]

His military career remained up in the air, but with the new year came finality on other fronts. Frémont unloaded the albatross of Las Mariposas, selling his remaining stake in the property and turning his attention to railroad speculation, investing in several companies and joining the executive team of the Union Pacific's eastern division. He put out a bid for four thousand tons of railway iron for the proposed Atlantic and Pacific Railroad, intended to stretch from Springfield, Missouri, to the California state line. He settled his last legal bill with Montgomery Blair, paying the postmaster $3,000. Blair had sought $5,000, and even that he considered too little for all the work he had done. But he took the smaller amount, closing a professional relationship that went back a decade and a personal family relationship for Jessie that predated the Frémonts' 1841 marriage.[53]

Frémont's popularity with the public remained intact. During an early March visit to the White House to discuss the possibility of a new command—Frémont wanted to go to Texas—simply passing from the Green Room to the East Room, Frémont was met with "the most tumultuous greeting" from "Generals, Senators, and official dignitaries gathered in a great crowd around him." His "political friends lionized him," and the "irrepressible noise and enthusiasm testified to the respect and affection with which the great heart of the people yet envelopes the Pathfinder." On that occasion, Frémont slipped away from the mansion, but he would remain in contact with the administration about the possibility of future employment. Those talks would follow parallel tracks, one leading to the command of all black troops and the other to the position of military governor of North Carolina. Lincoln asked Stanton to intercede with Halleck, an inveterate Frémont foe and, according to journalist Noah Brooks, "the worst hated man in public life at the moment." After the March 7 meeting, Lincoln told Stanton that he had "promised to try to have [Frémont] told something definite by this evening. Please see Gen. Halleck to-day; and if you can get him half agreed, I agree." Halleck could not be brought to agree, and Lincoln was hesitant to move ahead without his approval.[54]

Lincoln had begun thinking about reconstruction almost as soon as the war began. His vision for reuniting the Union involved the appointment of military governors for seceded states or the parts of those states that came under the control of the Federal army. The governors would be tasked with establishing enough order to reestablish loyal state governments elected by the citizens. With the exception of East Tennessee, nowhere was his faith in the strength of southern unionism stronger than in North Carolina.

In February and March 1862, Ambrose Burnside led an expedition against the North Carolina coast from Roanoke Island to the Virginia state line. Capture of coastal forts in spring 1862 brought part of eastern North Carolina under Union control, although not far inland and hardly beyond the range of river gunboats. Encouraged by his belief that unionism remained strong in the state, and at the urging of Seward and Maryland senator Reverdy Johnson, Lincoln appointed former North Carolina congressman Edward Stanly as military governor in April. Stanly was a strong unionist, and much of his old congressional district lay within the territory that northern armies had already conquered. He was known to have a quick temper and had once fought a duel against a fellow lawmaker. Relocating to California in the early 1850s, he subsequently lost a race for governor as a Republican in 1857.[55]

As with Frémont's "carte blanche," Stanly's orders were vague, and Stanton told him he would be a virtual "dictator" who could "do what I pleased," according to Stanly. Like Frémont in Missouri, Stanly would learn otherwise. When he sailed for North Carolina in late May 1862, he took eighteen liberated Tar Heel POWs with him as a gesture of goodwill. Stanly arrived at his headquarters in New Bern on May 28. Within two weeks, the new governor was warning Stanton that any move toward emancipation would mean "no peace can be restored here for many years to come." At the same time, he was warning his fellow Carolinians that Federal troops would eventually make slavery untenable unless they speedily returned to the Union. They ignored his warning and were buttressed in their resistance by McClellan's defeat on the Peninsula.[56]

Stanly was accused of returning escaped slaves and closing a black school and inevitably clashed with abolitionist soldiers. Eventually, radicals in Congress got wind of Stanly's alleged activities. Charles Sumner introduced a resolution calling for his recall, and an investigation was planned. Neither effort went anywhere. Stanly denied the allegations, and what proof there was seemed to support him. Things calmed down, but that did not alleviate Stanly's underlying challenge. The Federal army was in control of a tiny portion of North Carolina. Union sentiment was much less prevalent than either Stanly or the administration believed even in that small area. And despite the overblown allegations against him, it was true that Stanly stood in opposition to Lincoln's evolving policy of emancipation. Still, after a dose of flattery from Lincoln and Stanton, he agreed to stay on even after the Preliminary Emancipation Proclamation was issued in September 1862.[57]

As with Frémont, it was a clash with the Blairs that effectively sealed Stanly's fate. In December 1862, he challenged a ban on trade instituted by navy admiral Samuel Phillips Lee, husband of Elizabeth Blair Lee, and the administration sided with the navy, which was trying to maintain a blockade. When Stanly threatened to resign, Washington ignored him. When Lincoln issued the Emancipation Proclamation on January 1, 1863, Stanly was convinced any chance of conciliation with North Carolina or anyone else in the South was gone. He also believed his usefulness had come to an end. Two weeks later, he submitted his resignation.[58]

On January 25, 1863, Moncure Conway, a Virginia-born abolitionist minister with brothers in the Confederate military, was part of an Emancipation League delegation—consisting of Wendell Phillips, Samuel Gridley Howe, Francis W. Bird, George L. Stearns, J. H. Stephenson, Elizur Wright, and Oakes Ames and escorted by Senator Henry Wilson—that met with Lincoln. As Conway recorded the meeting in his memoirs, Phillips was first to speak, expressing their happiness with the proclamation and asking how it was working. Lincoln replied that he did not expect instant results but hoped "something would come of it after a while." When Phillips questioned whether emancipation was being carried out effectively by officers and agents in the field and asserted that this issue was driving dissatisfaction in the North, Lincoln replied, "My own impression, Mr. Phillips, is that the masses of the country generally are only dissatisfied at our lack of military successes. Defeat and failure in the field make everything seem wrong." The conversation then shifted to the group's dissatisfaction with Edward Stanly. "Well gentlemen, whom would you put in Stanly's place?" the president asked. One of the men suggested nobody would be better than to have someone acting against the president's policies. Then another suggested Frémont, prompting Lincoln to avow "great respect for General Frémont and his abilities. But the fact is that the pioneer in any movement is not generally the best man to carry that movement to a successful issue. It was so in old times— wasn't it?" Lincoln said, smiling. "Moses began the emancipation of the Jews but didn't take Israel to the Promised Land after all. He had to make way for Joshua to complete the work. It looks as if the first reformer of a thing has to meet such a hard opposition and gets so battered and bespattered, that afterwards, when people find they have to accept his reform, they will accept it more easily from another man."[59]

During the David Hunter emancipation controversy, Lincoln had written that compensated, gradual emancipation "acts not the pharisee," in contrast to the executive edicts promulgated by Frémont and Hunter, who would remake southern society in an instant. In May 1862, Frémont was a Pharisee. Now, in January 1863, he was Moses, which could be considered progress. Soon he would be a Joshua.[60]

It got into the papers that Lincoln was being "strongly urged" to appoint Frémont military governor of North Carolina. "It is thought by those who press the change upon the Government that the name of Frémont would summon in a week almost an army of colored Unionists," the unfriendly *New York Herald* reported. The friendly *New York Tribune* asked, "Who doubts that the presence of Frémont in North Carolina, or any other insurrectionary state, would be welcomed by the negroes as a guaranty of the Proclamation? . . . Frémont's name has been a watchword in every cabin since 1856, and will be heard at once as a war-cry by the slaves waiting to rally under the Union flag. We know of no reason why he should not be summoned to such a task."[61]

Some Republicans in Congress urged Lincoln to replace Stanly with another North Carolinian, antislavery editor Daniel R. Goodloe. By this time, however, Lincoln was fairly well convinced that he had jumped the gun in North Carolina and chose not to appoint anyone. His view of the other track—Frémont as commander of black troops—seemed more promising.[62]

"YOU ARE THE JOSHUA TO LEAD US TO THE FIELD OF BATTLE"
Within ten days of the attack on Fort Sumter, John C. Frémont's name was being invoked in support of the formation of black regiments. Jacob Dodson, a free black man who had "been three times across the Rocky Mountains in the service of the country with Frémont," wrote in futility to Secretary of War Simon Cameron "of some 300 reliable colored free citizens of this city [Washington, DC] who desire to enter the service for the defense of the city." Cameron, who by the end of 1861 would put himself at odds with Lincoln over the question of black troops, told Dodson, "This department has no intention at present to call into the service of the Government any colored soldiers."[63]

Lincoln had objected when Cameron proposed including a call for black troops in his 1861 annual message. By summer 1862, he still had his doubts. He told Orville Hickman Browning in July that arming blacks "would produce dangerous and fatal dissatisfaction in our army and do more injury than good." To a delegation of Republican senators, he worried that the arms of southern unionists willing to fight would "be turned against us." It was the old Kentucky-first argument all over again. By the time he issued the Emancipation Proclamation, though, Lincoln had changed his mind. In early 1863, concurrent with the effort to promote Frémont as military governor of North Carolina, a concerted effort was begun by Frémont's allies to persuade Lincoln to appoint Frémont commander of all (or a large force of) black troops. "In the Gulf States, Frémont is the man," wrote one. Frémont endorsed the broad notion of a commander of all black troops, but he did not believe he was the right man for the job. That did not stop his supporters from lobbying on his behalf or the rank and file from making their voices heard. A private in the 54th Massachusetts invoked Frémont's name in a poem in praise of black troops.

Frémont told them, when it first began,
How to save the Union, and the way it should be done;
But Kentucky swore so hard, and old Abe had his fears
Till every hope was lost but the colored volunteers.[64]

More notable voices also weighed in. On February 22, in a speech at Cooper Union celebrating Washington's birthday, Wendell Phillips praised the Emancipation Proclamation while insisting that more was necessary to give it force. "The negro wants a symbol of freedom," he declared. "How can we give it to him? The quickest way we can give it to him is to put his own color into the United States uniform, with a Minié rifle to their right hand. Send a flesh and blood proclamation in the person of John Charles Frémont to Charleston." That proposal met with "great applause." Phillips had nothing but respect for generals like Hunter and Butler, who had done their part for emancipation. He believed in Joe Hooker. "But we are pressed for time. We cannot manufacture reputation. The name of Frémont has been a household word in the slave's hut ever since he believed, in 1856, that his election was to be the jubilee of his freedom. He has cherished it like the name of his Savior. He knows it; and if he heard he was there, he would not need the evidence of a written proclamation to believe that he bore freedom with his eagles." In another address, the mere mention of Frémont's name brought "loud and long-continued applause," *The*

Liberator reported. "Why won't you ever let me go on when I name Frémont?" Phillips jocularly asked the crowd. In yet another address, the spirit carried Phillips even further, when he likened Frémont to George Washington, "the bright consummate flower of our earlier civilization, and Frémont the ripe fruit of our noonday." This praise was too much for the Democratic *Washington Evening Star*, which observed, "Even Jessie must have laughed at that."[65]

In March 1863, Frémont met in Washington with allies from the Joint Committee on the Conduct of the War to discuss plans for his return, hoping for the long-discussed assignment to Texas. Committee member George Washington Julian visited Lincoln and urged the president to find a place for Frémont. Lincoln told Julian that Frémont's case "reminded him of the old man who advised his son to take a wife, to which the young man responded, 'Whose wife shall I take.'" Julian insisted that restoring Frémont to duty "would stir the country as no other appointment could." Lincoln replied, "It would stir the country on one side, and stir the other way on the other. It would please Frémont's friends, and displease the conservatives; and that is all I can see in the stirring argument. My proclamation was to stir the country; but it has done about as much harm as good." Lincoln told Illinois politician Isaac Arnold something similar. "In the early Spring, Gen. Frémont sought active service again; and, as it seemed to me, sought it in a very good, and reasonable spirit. But he holds the highest rank in the Army, except McClellan, so that I could not well offer him a subordinate command," he wrote in May. "Was I to displace Hooker, or Hunter, or Rosecrans, or Grant, or Banks? If not, what was I to do?" He would later observe to Schurz, "With a Major General once out, it is next to impossible for even the President to get him in again." Lincoln had already displaced William Rosecrans with Frémont once, in the Valley in March 1862, and not to good effect. Frémont had resigned that position for the very reason Lincoln now alluded to—his refusal to serve under a commander of lesser rank, although it's possible he might have made an exception for someone who was not John Pope. A delegation of Missouri radicals implored Lincoln to reemploy Frémont and Butler, whom they said Lincoln had "systematically kept out of command." Lincoln assured them this was not the case. He was "not only willing but anxious to place them again in command as soon as he could find spheres of action for them, without doing injustice to others." The problem, Lincoln said, was that "he had more pegs than holes to put them in."[66]

A black regiment recruited in Poughkeepsie, New York, dubbed the Frémont Legion, visited Frémont and Lincoln together in the White House in mid-March, bringing with them prepared statements they presented to each man. "We have been called cowards," they told the president. "We deny the charge. It is false." They asked Lincoln to accept the Frémont Legion into service. To Frémont they wrote, "We . . . feel to give you an expression of our gratitude; not forgetting the love you bear for suffering humanity, your generosity and sympathy for God's poor, will ever remain a lasting proof of that innate goodness, for which you have long and justly been celebrated." And then the appeal: "As a patriot and general, you have our confidence. We have offered the services of ten thousand men to his Excellency, the President, called the Frémont Legion, believing that you are the Joshua to lead us to the field of battle. We pray that you will accept."[67]

The Joint Committee on the Conduct of the War released its report on the Western Department, Bull Run, and Ball's Bluff on April 3. The Missouri section was characterized even in the Democratic press as "generally exculpatory of the conduct of Gen. Frémont." Daniel Gooch and Moses Odell refused to sign the report, legitimately arguing that the testimony was "incomplete." They had wanted to hear from more witnesses—a fair criticism of the committee's focus on clearing Frémont rather than getting to the bottom of the controversy. But the tone was positive, which was a welcome development for Frémont and those seeking to aid him. It emboldened Frémont to go public with a suggestion for using the thousands of freed slaves from the Mississippi Valley to help build and guard the line of the recently approved transcontinental railroad. This proposal lent further credence to the rumors of Frémont leading black troops.[68]

In the first week of May, the *New York Tribune* reported that a black minister in New York had received assurances from Lincoln that "if 10,000 colored troops were raised they would be accepted, and that General Frémont would be assigned to the command," as well as "that he had seen Gen. Frémont, and received from him a promise that he was willing to accept such a command." Thaddeus Stevens expressed his "hope Frémont may accept it, and beat all the white troops in action, and thereby acquire glory."[69]

On May 22, the War Department issued General Orders No. 143, creating a bureau to process recruits for the U.S. Colored Troops, adding more fuel to the rumors. Days later, a committee of New Yorkers that included two former members of Congress, *New York Tribune* editor Horace Greeley, and Peter Cooper (founder of the Cooper Institute) lobbied Lincoln to appoint Frémont and received assurances that Lincoln was amenable. When they returned to New York, they met with Frémont to inform him of the president's support for giving him authority to "organize and lead to the field an army of black men."[70]

The committee told Lincoln that free blacks in the North "are willing to volunteer for the Service upon the requisite assurance that they will be placed under leaders in Sympathy with the movement. Indeed, such is their intense enthusiasm and patriotism, that if the assurance can be given them, that upon their enlistment they will be in active Service under the command of Major General John C. Frémont, your memorialists are confident that a force of at least 10.000 could be placed under enlistment within Sixty days, forming a Grand Army of Liberation, Swelling in numbers as they pass along, thus giving effectiveness to the Proclamation of January, 1863." They asked Lincoln to appoint Frémont to a "suitable command" and empower him to accept the black volunteers into service. Lincoln told the New Yorkers he "would gladly receive into the service not ten thousand but ten times ten thousand colored troops" and "would with all his heart offer it to Gen. Frémont."[71]

Democratic papers were dismissive of both the troops and the would-be commander. "It is proposed that Gen. Frémont take command of all the nigger regiments raised," the *Washington Evening Star* reported. "But if we enroll niggers at all, why not give the poor devils half a chance?"[72]

In the face of such derision, Lincoln persevered despite his own concerns. "While it is very objectionable, as a general rule, to have troops raised on any special terms, such as to serve only under a particular commander, or only at a particular place or places, yet I would forego the objection in this case, upon a fair prospect that a large force of this sort could thereby be the more rapidly raised," he told Charles Sumner, who was acting as a go-between. And he laid out the conditions that would make such a scheme work. "I would very cheerfully send them to the field under Gen. Frémont, assigning him a Department, made or to be made, with such white force also as I might be able to put in." That might have to wait, though, because there were no such troops available at the moment and no "justifiable ground to relieve the present commander of any old one." Lincoln also noted that the same rules for recruitment would apply to any such force, requiring "the same consents of Governors . . . as in case of white troops." Frémont could take charge of organizing the force, or he could come in after it was assembled. Either option was fine with Lincoln.[73]

While Lincoln persevered, Frémont flagged. Presented with a genuine opportunity to get back in the fight, and in a way that aligned perfectly with his political beliefs, Frémont equivocated. When Sumner shared Lincoln's letter, he told the senator, "I beg you will say to the President that this movement does not, in the remotest way, originate with me. On the contrary when the Committee called upon me I declined positively to enter into it, or to consent to having my name mentioned to the President in connection with it." The committee had ignored that admonition, and now the ball was in Frémont's court. He argued that he "disapproved the project of raising and sending to the field, colored troops in scattered and weak detachments. That it would only result in disaster to the colored troops & would defeat effectually the expectations of the Govt. to mass them in a solid force against the rebellion." It wasn't clear whether this outcome was the intention of either the committee or Lincoln, but Frémont complained that "no short reaching or partial plans can possibly succeed."

He relayed to Sumner that he had told the New York committee that if he had been given the Texas command as he had discussed with Lincoln and "in which I should have had a suitable field for this organization and white troops to protect it—and ensure its success—I could have undertaken it & have undoubtedly organized a formidable force imminently dangerous to the Confederacy." But that was merely a hypothetical scenario to inform the committee of his thinking, he insisted. It was not a commitment to take any post. He asked Sumner to tell Lincoln "that I have no design to embarrass him with creating a Dept. for me."

And then he got to the heart of the matter: "This whole business is as dangerous and difficult as it is important. It demands ability and great discretion and a fixed belief in the necessity of the work and should only be undertaken upon some plan which would embrace the whole subject and then be entrusted only to some officer of ability and judgment to whom the President would be willing to give the necessary powers. He must have power and the President's confidence. Therefore I do not propose myself for this work."[74]

Frémont had reason to believe, based on his experience in Missouri and Virginia, that he did not hold (or could not keep) Lincoln's confidence. But after months of private lobbying and public pressure, the president had finally agreed to put Frémont back in the field, and Frémont had abjured. Lincoln and Frémont surely both feared the potential political implications of Frémont being named commanding general of black troops. Lincoln seemed willing to put his fears and his past problems with Frémont behind him. He knew that success for Frémont could create a wave of political support. Failure would raise questions about why the president, having already been twice burned, went back to the fire a third time. In the end, Frémont was less willing than the president to forget past slights. Perhaps he also considered what a third failure in the field could do to his reputation.

But there was another aspect that Frémont might not have wanted to make a public case about in summer 1863. On May 27, the *Pionier*, a German-language paper based in Boston, had endorsed Frémont for president, arguing that he had "saved the honor of the Republic" with his emancipation proclamation. Other German papers across the country quickly followed suit. German Americans in Washington, DC, were organizing a national convention to meet in Cleveland in October. Their agenda included waging hard war against the South, a constitutional amendment abolishing slavery, equal political rights for freed blacks, and confiscation of rebel property to be distributed to the freemen via a homestead policy. Among the movers and shakers was Missourian B. Gratz Brown, a former ally of Frank Blair, who had grown increasingly radical as the war ground on.[75]

Frémont knew of these efforts, though he had not yet taken any official steps to encourage them. But he was already thinking about challenging Lincoln for the 1864 Republican presidential nomination—or pondering a third-party candidacy if that plan failed. Being in contention for a military command was likely getting in the way of organizing that effort, and he would not have wanted to be tied down in the field if the opportunity arose. He also knew there was considerable opposition to the raising of black troops and fear among northern whites about what such service might mean for legal equality when the war was over.[76]

Elizabeth Blair Lee spoke for many when she commented on the subject in a letter to her husband. "Think how it must hurt Jessie—for no Southern woman could fail to feel some bitterness," she wrote in what might have been a keen observation about conservative Republican politics but revealed that she didn't really know her lifelong friend at all. Her references to "the abolition horde in the North" and "John Brownites" were telling, and her disdain for "Frémont proclivities" showed the very different worldviews of the Blairs and the Frémonts, who surely considered themselves part of the abolitionist horde. But the Blair philosophy remained a viable path to political success.[77]

Frémont's concerns about Lincoln's faith in him or about how black troops would be deployed were genuine. He also might have already chosen a political rather than a military path. Jessie wrote to one of his former staff aides in July regarding the "irresponsible" Lincoln administration, "Thank Heaven & the Constitution that limits them to four years, & more than two are over now." Perhaps Frémont saw an intimate association with black troops as a political dead end, knowing, as Lincoln had told Julian in March, that "it would stir the country on one side, and stir the other way on the other." Whatever the reasons, the famous Pathfinder, who had entered military service in 1861 with such great promise and hope attached to his name, passed up what might have been his best opportunity to make a difference on the battlefield in the Civil War.[78]

"I'M AFRAID OF 'TOMORROW'"

With two senior major generals—Frémont and McClellan—out of action, Benjamin Butler had applied in late May to be named ranking officer in the army. His claim included superseding Nathaniel Banks and John Dix, who also outranked him. Frémont protested in a letter to Stanton, citing his earlier date of rank, and the letter quickly found its way into the papers. The War Department invited Frémont to submit a defense of his position, to which Frémont responded that he did not "think the question open to discussion." His date of rank was May 14, 1861, the same as McClellan's, and Butler's was May 16, and that settled it. But several generals had had their date of ranks retroactively adjusted, including Frémont, who was officially appointed on July 1 but had his date of rank backdated to May 14, the day his nomination was sent to the Senate. Aside from the fact that Frémont and McClellan were idle and Butler was in the field, there was precedent for making such a change.[79]

Stanton appointed a five-man board whose members included Montgomery Meigs and Joseph Holt—no fans of Frémont—to reach a determination. They didn't take long to decide. On July 1, they announced that the date of rank, as determined by the order in which their names were included on the list of nominations sent to the Senate, would stand for each of the five generals. Frémont remained second, Butler remained fifth.[80]

This decision did nothing to change the employment status of Frémont, Butler, or any of the more than a dozen major generals in the army without a command. But as Robert E. Lee's Army of Northern Virginia moved toward another invasion of the North, residents of New York and Pennsylvania pleaded with Lincoln to send them Frémont. "In the present Emergency will you allow Genls Frémont & Sigel to issue a call for volunteers to march at once to the defence of Pennsylvania & the Nation?" three German Americans active in Republican politics telegraphed the president. A worried Pittsburgher told Lincoln, "We need John C. Frémont who will create an enthusiasm by which we can raise twenty-thousand men in forty-eight hours." A Philadelphian wanted "Frémont and Sigel who can whip the devil." On June 30, the day before the beginning of the Battle of Gettysburg, a group of western Pennsylvanians forwarded a petition to Lincoln arguing that the "safety or devastation" of their region depended on the appointment of Frémont.[81]

Lincoln ignored the pleas from the Pennsylvanians. He responded disingenuously to the New Yorkers, advising them that Governor Horatio Seymour—a virulently anti-Frémont Democrat—"promises to send us troops; and if he wishes the assistance of Gen. Frémont & Gen. Sigel, one or both, he can have it." Lincoln knew Seymour would not want Frémont or Franz Sigel. Maj. Gen. George Gordon Meade, who had replaced Joseph Hooker as commander of the Army of the Potomac just days before the battle, managed to fend off Lee without the assistance of either. Jessie jibed both the president and the general a week after the battle, when Lincoln was annoyed with Meade for not making a stronger pursuit of his vanquished foe. "The admin changes Generals nearly as often as a bad housekeeper changes servants, but not quite in the first week," she wrote to John's former topographical engineer, John Fiala. "So Genl. Meade will be allowed to 'stay his month' & if he defeats & utterly routs Lee he may be President & if he fails or gets roughly handled himself we will have a new Napoleon for the dog-days."[82]

A week and a half after Gettysburg, antidraft riots terrorized New York City and threatened the safety of Frémont's home and family. Black New Yorkers were special targets, "as if by preconcerted action," the *New York Tribune* reported. As supporters of emancipation and the enlistment of black troops, the Frémonts were too. Amid the arson, murder, and mayhem, their home at 21 West 19th Street was "seriously endangered," according to newspaper reports. The home was "one of those marked in chalk, to be destroyed," young Frank Frémont remembered. Some of Frémont's idle staff aides helped out, building troughs on the roof to repel incendiary devices hurled at the house. Plenty of arms and ammunition were on hand in case of a full-fledged attack, which was rumored around town but never came. No major damage was sustained by the Frémont home, and everyone inside remained safe. Elsewhere in the city, more than one hundred people were killed before army regiments began arriving in force on the fourth day of violence and the city started to calm down.[83]

That summer the Frémonts bought a house in Nahant, Massachusetts, northeast of Boston, where they entertained abolitionist guests and courted their support. Henry Wadsworth Longfellow lived next door. In September, Jessie, Lily, and Charles Zagonyi visited John Greenleaf Whittier in Amesbury, thirty-five miles up the Gulf of Maine from their cottage in Nahant, while John was in New York. The poet was not home, but a niece asked the visitors to wait, and he returned shortly. It was their first meeting. Jessie told him how he had influenced her as a young adult and that his lines "the throbs of wounded pride to still, and make our own our Father's will" had had a special impact on her. She playfully refused to identify herself immediately, instead describing the scene at which her husband had read Whittier's poem, "To John C. Frémont," beside the firelight of a Missouri army camp. At that point, he insisted, "What is thy name." When she answered "Frémont," he brought his sister into the room and introduced the two women. "Elizabeth, this is Jessie Frémont—under our roof. Our mother would have been glad to see this day."[84]

They stayed until near dark and then took the return train to Nahant. Whittier followed up with a letter a month later, thanking Jessie for coming. "We have in some sort known and loved thee and thine for a long time, and seeing thee has confirmed our impressions," he wrote. And, he told her, "I am very happy to know that my word of encouragement was not wholly in vain, during your trials in Missouri." He told her that he had sent the poem to them in St. Louis, before publication, but that they must have already left the city. And, certainly gratifying to Jessie, he said the residents of Amesbury "have complained sadly because I did not let them know that Jessie Frémont was in the place. . . . When thee comes again we will have the bells rung and satisfy them." He also asked to be remembered to "the general. Would that he were at Washington, commander-in-chief."[85]

A month later, Jessie sent another letter, recounting her and John's first reading of his poem "To John C. Frémont" (see chapter 5) and growing wistful at the uncertainty of the coming year. "We have had so much to make us thankful & happy this summer and this little sea-side place is so unmarked with any care or grief, that I wish we could have had you with us this year," she wrote, evoking the days of her literary salon at Black Point. "I'm afraid of 'tomorrow.' . . . I am nervous about what must follow this lull in our stormy lives."[86]

Jessie was joking when she suggested George Meade might be in line for the presidency, but more than a year before Election Day the jostling for position was already well underway. Lincoln worried that without the support of radicals like Salmon Chase and Ben Wade, he could not be renominated, and he saw Chase as the main threat. "I have all along clearly seen his plan of strengthening himself," Lincoln told John Hay. Lincoln believed Chase acted in bad faith in instances when difficult presidential decisions had to be made. "He always ranges himself in opposition to me and persuades the victim that he has been hardly dealt by and that he would have arranged it very differently," including in the cases of Frémont's and Hunter's emancipation orders. At the same time, the New York Herald warned the friends of Chase, thought by many besides Lincoln to be the logical radical challenger to the president's renomination, that they had better get to work on their campaign "or he will be ousted by the powerful movement afoot in behalf of General Frémont. They have not, by a long shot, killed him off at Washington."[87]

In that city, Lincoln was expressing his desire to see Frank Blair store his army uniform and return to Congress, where he could lend aid to the moderate and conservative forces against the radicals. Writing to Montgomery Blair, he took a familiar tone—"What I would say, if Frank Blair were my brother instead of yours." He urged that Frank should "come here, put his military commission in my hands, take his seat, go into caucus with our friends, abide the nominations, help elect the nominees, and thus aid to organize a House of Representatives which will really support the government in the war." Lincoln's plan was to see Blair elected Speaker of the House; if that plan failed, he could return to the army. He warned the hot-tempered Blair to ignore "provocations," without mentioning Frémont or the Missouri radicals by name. Lincoln's letter was a warning to Blair that he was getting on the wrong side of Republican politics, "in danger of being permanently separated from those with whom only he can ever have a real sympathy—the sincere opponents of slavery." Blair took Lincoln's advice, for the moment. He returned to Washington when Congress convened. He was nominated for Speaker by one of reconstructed Louisiana's House members, but he got only two votes. The job went to Frémont's friend Schuyler Colfax of Indiana. Still, Blair would do Lincoln one more good service in early 1864 before resuming his military career.[88]

Another Lincoln friend was busy on a different political front. Orville Browning, who had supported Frémont's Missouri emancipation proclamation based on military necessity and the executive branch's war powers, was no radical. He had been turned out of the Senate in January after Democrats captured the Illinois state legislature, and he blamed Lincoln's Emancipation Proclamation for costing him his seat. He now believed radicals in both parties posed the greatest threat to the Union. Sounding a lot like Frank Blair, in mid-June 1863, Browning broached the possibility of a third party "between these extremes, composed of the true patriots of all parties, which would have before it, as its sole purpose, the suppression of the rebellion, the restoration of the union, and the re-establishment of the authority of the constitution and laws?" He appealed to Ohio senator Thomas Ewing (father-in-law of Maj. Gen. William Tecumseh Sherman) to work with Senator John Sherman (the general's brother—and Ewing's foster son), Ira Harris of New York, and others to "save us from foes more dangerous than the rebels." He also tried to enlist Attorney General Edward Bates, who warned him against "the extreme folly," pointing out the nature of politicians "who will not fail to see, in such a course, their own defeat and downfall."[89]

Browning's idea went nowhere, largely because the middle position he was describing was already occupied by Lincoln. Those dangerous foes who so worried Browning now included John C. Frémont, the man he had once defended against his friend the president. As the election year of 1864 dawned, they were having more success than Browning in getting organized for the struggle ahead.

CHAPTER NINE

"The whole future of our Republic depends on the result"

THE ELECTIONS OF 1863 REVERSED MANY OF THE STATE-LEVEL LOSSES THE Republicans had suffered the previous year. They regained several governorships and boosted their statewide vote in such battlegrounds as Pennsylvania and Ohio by tens of thousands of votes. That result lent credence to the belief held by some Republican politicians that it was a lack of effort on the part of the administration, more than emancipation or a paucity of progress in the war, that had hurt Republican turnout in 1862. Lincoln could not afford to let that happen again. This time, he would be on the ballot, and challengers were already lining up for what would be the most important election in American history. "This is not an ordinary election," Frémont said. "It is a contest for the right to even have candidates, and not merely, as usual, for the choice among them."[1]

Wendell Phillips enumerated the stakes in a speech to the Massachusetts Anti-Slavery Society on January 28, 1864. "The Southern leader says—'Let me hold on a few months longer, no matter at what cost—let me keep the stars and bars flying six months longer, and in the turmoil of that fight, in the selfish ambition of that struggle, I may find, if not a confederate, at least so much sympathy that I shall go out of this contest with very good terms, if not victorious.'" The military strategy of the Confederacy in 1864 would be to instill a sense of defeatism in the North that would serve to defeat Lincoln and give the rebels someone else with whom to negotiate. Indiana's Republican governor, Oliver Morton, observed, "Considerations of the most vital character demand that the war shall be substantially ended within the present year."[2]

Phillips and Morton understood this situation, and so did almost everyone else. John C. Frémont lived in the hearts of abolitionists as the military embodiment of the movement, not just because he had been there first on emancipation but also because they believed he would be harsher in victory than would Lincoln. He and Jessie had assiduously cultivated antislavery leaders over the past several months while in Nahant; Phillips was one of his most vociferous backers. But Frémont did not enjoy universal support. When Wendell Phillips attempted to get the Massachusetts Anti-Slavery Society to condemn Lincoln and support Frémont, William Lloyd Garrison cited the latter's silence on the Emancipation Proclamation for opposing Phillips's resolution, which was adopted. "I believe it will be the game of the rebels on the one hand, and of the Copperheads on the other, to urge rival Republican candidates to take the field, and thus to 'divide and conquer,'" William Lloyd Garrison predicted in February 1864. Garrison typically eschewed electoral politics. But he admired Lincoln's progress on emancipation and feared splitting the antislavery vote would result in a Democratic victory. "A thousand incidental errors and blunders are easily to be borne with on the part of him who, at one blow, severed the chains of three millions three hundred thousand slaves," Garrison wrote. For perhaps the only time in their lives, Garrison and Confederate vice president Alexander Stephens were in agreement. Stephens despised the Georgia-born Frémont as a traitor and believed that Lincoln's reelection would be better than a Frémont victory for the South.[3]

Frémont spoke at Cooper Union on February 29, introducing famed British abolitionist George Thompson. "It may not seem to you entirely appropriate that I should preside over this meeting," Frémont said. "It might seem more fitting that some one of the older date in the Anti-Slavery struggle—some one of those who also had incurred the censorious criticisms and social martyrdom to which his life has been much exposed, should stand at his side tonight to receive and to share in your generous recognition." But this was a new day, Frémont told the audience, much different from the last time Thompson had visited the United States in 1850. "In giving him this welcome back to the country, we desire to bring distinctly before him the new phase through which it is passing," he explained. "Slavery, now held to be incompatible with Union; liberty, then denied speech, now holding the sword; the nation in arms for the principle he advocated, hostile to compromises, impatient of delays; its old tolerance changed into settled hatred against the cause of this war, and deeply resolved so to deal with it that the places which knew it shall know it no more." For the abolitionist movement, Frémont was the perfect person to deliver that message. He was "cheered throughout," but the *New York Herald* derided his remarks as "in accordance with Talleyrand's definition of diplomacy. His words were used to conceal his ideas. . . . We wanted that other speech, which we have no doubt he talks over among his confidential friends—that speech which embraces his platform and programme for the Presidential campaign; his ideas and purposes concerning President Lincoln."[4]

It was not what Frémont said about Thompson or about how America had changed but what Thompson said about Frémont that was far more noteworthy. After introductory remarks recounting his life in the movement, Thompson turned to Frémont to tell him of "the satisfaction it gives me to see you presiding over this assembly, and to be by you introduced. . . . Your name is a household word among all the friends of liberty and humanity in England." Cheers and applause followed Thompson's praise, and he continued to heap it on, extolling Frémont's virtues as a presidential candidate in 1856. Had he defeated James Buchanan, "there would have been no subserviency to the slave power. I believe you would have worked a miracle as great as that of St. Patrick in Ireland," Thompson said, drawing laughs from the crowd. "You would have banished all kinds of snakes from the country, whether they be rattlesnakes or copperheads." But it was as the "daring Pathfinder" that most Englishmen knew of Frémont, blazing a trail through the Rocky Mountains. "And then, amid the rockier mountains of Rebellion, in Missouri, you found a path there," he said, drawing even louder cheers. "It was the right path. It was the necessary path. It was the plain path. It was the path of justice, humanity, right, duty, and would have been the path of glory. I shall not say why you did not pursue it," Thompson said mischievously. "But you have your reward. The Chief Executive of this mighty Republic has followed the Pathfinder," he said, amid even louder cheering. He praised Lincoln for taking the step and freeing millions. "The path commenced in Missouri culminated there. Honor to him who pursued it so far and so well; honor to the man who discovered it for himself." It was not exactly an endorsement of a presidential candidacy, but, coming from Thompson, it lent gravitas to the idea.[5]

The president of the Central Bank of New York claimed to know no one who was voting for Frémont. That might have been more a reflection of the circles in which the banker moved than the level of support for Frémont in New York. Two weeks after the Thompson speech, the Frémont Campaign Club of New York met at Cooper Union, peopled by supporters of Frémont and probably an equal number of people opposed to Lincoln but uncommitted to any other candidate. Attendees adopted a platform: "We, the members of the Frémont Campaign Club, being impressed with the increasing dangers of the country, and foreseeing the necessity of placing the Government in the hands of men of firm nature, of fixed principles, and uncompromising patriotism: and being opposed, moreover, to a continuance of the present irresolute and feeble National policy (both foreign and domestic) do hereby nominate Maj.-Gen. John C. Frémont as our candidate for the next President of the United States."[6]

Frémont launched a short-lived newspaper, the *New Nation*, and installed as editor one of his former military aides, the Frenchman Gustave Cluseret. The paper ran the usual array of pieces praising Frémont and criticizing Lincoln. In April, as part of a broader effort to postpone the Republican convention scheduled for June to see what the Democrats did at their convention, scheduled for the end of August, the paper called for a national committee to push the Republicans to write an acceptably radical platform—and nominate an acceptably radical candidate. One critic derided the paper as "got up for the election only" and said it "cannot stand after that, (if Frémont be defeated), having no merit of its own."[7]

That prediction would prove correct. By far the most effective advocates on Frémont's behalf were German Americans, who "constitute the heart and nucl[e]us—the body and strength of the Radicals," Attorney General Edward Bates correctly surmised. With population centers in St. Louis and Cincinnati and across the upper Midwest, as well as in New York City, they proved a potent organizing tool for Frémont.[8]

Lincoln was able to make some inroads. He had recognized the power of the Germans from the restart of his political life in the mid-1850s and had secretly bought a German-language newspaper in Illinois, the *Staats Anzeiger*, to support his campaigns. He also had opposed the anti-immigrant stance of the Know Nothings from the moment they entered the political arena. Franz Sigel, hoping for a return to active duty, sided with Lincoln over his former commander. Gustave Koerner assured Lincoln that the Germans he knew in Missouri, Wisconsin, and Illinois were "men of no political sense, nor were they able to manage a campaign." Koerner was confident most would eventually come Lincoln's way.[9]

Some were tougher sells, including the paper he had once owned, which did not endorse Frémont but did declare its opposition to Lincoln. Other German-language papers in Illinois followed suit. "There is a hard feeling amongst most of the Germans in the West against your nomination & re-election, and I am afraid that a great many will not vote for you if nominated unless they are set aright," William H. Haase, president of a Frémont Club in Chicago, wrote to Lincoln, while promising to rejoin the Republicans for much the same reason as Sigel. He wanted to "be remembered by you when re-elected." The power of incumbency was, at this point, Lincoln's greatest asset. Frémont's strength was in his symbolic value as the military embodiment of emancipation, although he hadn't been on a battlefield in almost two years. Other contenders brought various strengths and weaknesses to the table.[10]

Whomever the Democrats nominated, the general election would be about the fate of the Union and the resilience of emancipation. But first came the contest for the Republican nomination. In early January the Democratic *New York World* assessed the chances of Republican candidates, ranking Lincoln at the top, followed by Salmon Chase, Frémont, and Nathaniel Banks, with Benjamin Butler bringing up the rear. In snobbishly comparing Lincoln to Frémont, the paper found the president wanting. "In general character Frémont contrasts favorably with Lincoln in two respects: Fearless promptitude of decision against Lincoln's timid vacillation, and social cultivation against Lincoln's uncouthness."[11]

The "vacillation" charge, anchored in Lincoln's pandering to the border slave states, reflected his relationship with the Blairs. The previous October, Montgomery Blair had delivered a blistering antiradical speech in Rockville, Maryland. The Blairs were running out of political space and were sounding more like War Democrats than Republicans, a fact Lincoln acknowledged in a late-night conversation with John Hay, John Usher, and Norman Judd in December 1863. Frémont's popularity and the radicalization of the state party had left Frank "ashore" electorally, forcing him to "seek for votes outside the Republican organization."

The same dynamic was now happening in Congress. Samuel Knox, who had lost the 1862 House race to Frank, was challenging the result, and members of Congress were questioning Frank's legal right to serve simultaneously as a major general and a congressman. Speaker Schuyler Colfax refused to give Frank a committee assignment pending the outcome of the challenge. Fifty members signed and sent to Lincoln a petition demanding Montgomery Blair's dismissal. Ostensibly designed to shore up support for Lincoln, Montgomery's speech in Rockville conceded that in no case could any former slave be returned to bondage. But he attacked the "ultra-Abolitionists" whose despotism was the mirror image of the "Slavocrats of the South" they claimed to detest. "The Abolition party whilst pronouncing philippics against slavery, seek to make a caste of another color by amalgamating the black element with the free white labor of our land." Blair also issued a call for an easy reconstruction, "practically restoring the constitutional relation between the United States and each of the States." Lincoln defended Frank and uttered no objection to Montgomery's speech, and the *New York Herald* pronounced, "This is President Lincoln's plan." One of Lincoln's strongest supporters, Pennsylvanian John Forney, suggested to

Montgomery that it might be better if he "leave the cabinet, and not load down with your individual and peculiar sentiments the administration to which you belong." The Rockville speech fired up the radicals and would eventually come back to haunt the postmaster general. Ohio congressman James A. Garfield complained that Lincoln was "bound hand and foot by the Blairs and they are dragging him and the country down the chasm." This divide made clear that, with emancipation a settled issue in the party, the Republican contest was going to be not about slavery but about reconstruction.[12]

Besides Frémont, two other generals looked to as potential saviors of the Republican Party were Benjamin Butler and Ulysses S. Grant. Grant had left no footprint in the political sands and evinced no interest in running for president. That didn't stop people from putting his name forward. *New York Herald* editor James Gordon Bennett was a prominent supporter, going so far as to suggest that the radicals switch from the battlefield failure of Frémont to a successful general, Grant, who could then make Frémont his vice presidential candidate. Democrats also considered courting Grant, but he shut them down as well. He considered the possibility of Lincoln's defeat a "great national calamity" and expressed astonishment at the Democrats' overtures. "I do not know of anything I have ever done or said which would indicate that I could be a candidate for any office whatever within the gift of the people," he told party leaders. Lincoln believed him. "The disaffected are trying to get him to run," he told one of Grant's aides, "but I don't think they can do it." Lincoln believed Grant was a great general, and great generals want to finish the jobs they start. Butler was another of those candidates whose partisan flexibility recommended him to more than one party. He had been a Democrat before the war and was viewed as a potential candidate by both anti-Lincoln Republicans and some War Democrats. Butler's contraband order in the first summer of the war was the first official step taken toward emancipation, setting the stage for the Confiscation Act and Frémont's emancipation order, and it quickly endeared him to abolitionists. But he always seemed to be an afterthought—less appealing to radical antislavery men than Frémont or Chase, less of a general than Grant, less of a true Republican than Lincoln.[13]

Treasury Secretary Salmon P. Chase's long career in the antislavery movement—longer by decades than that of Lincoln, Frémont, or Butler—made him, in the words of New York politician and general John Cochrane, "a central point, to which converged the multifarious strands of the radical web." Journalist Noah Brooks called him "an eminently fit candidate for what is known as the radical wing of the loyal party of the North. . . . Chase keeps ahead of public sentiment. Lincoln prefers to be led by it." During his deliberations on building a cabinet in early 1861, Lincoln had called Chase "the foremost man in the party." Had Chase been able to solidify radical support behind his candidacy, Frémont most likely would have had no path to victory. But he couldn't. Chase was admired but unloved. He had drifted from the Democrats to the Liberty Party to the Free Soilers to the Republicans and felt at home in none of them. Critics said he lacked loyalty to anything but his own ambition, a characteristic he sanctimoniously refused to admit he possessed. Fellow Ohioan Rutherford B. Hayes described him as "cold, selfish, and unscrupulous." On the verge of Frémont's removal from command in Missouri in 1861, Chase had snidely commented that "it is [difficult] to resist the inference" that Frémont's friends suggesting Lincoln was motivated by electoral concerns somehow reflected badly on Frémont, "that they are animated by politl. aspirations wh., at the present crisis, no Patriot can indulge. He who is thinkg. abt. the Prescy. in 1864, cannot properly perform the duties of 1861." Coming from Chase, who had started running for president in 1840 and wouldn't stop even after he joined the Supreme Court in 1864, it was an especially ironic criticism.[14]

Mariposa Land and Mining Company partner George W. Wright, who had accompanied Frémont to Europe in early 1861, backed Chase and solicited him as early as summer 1863 for a position in any future administration in return for his support. Chase had assured him that "nothing could be more uncertain than the currents of popular sentiment; that I was by no means anxious that they should turn towards me, and that if they did, and the result should be such as he predicted, it must be without any pledges from me in relation to appointments." By early 1864, the currents seemed to be flowing in Chase's direction. Progress in the war was stalled, the party was riven by divisions, and both leaders and the rank and file seemed to be looking for someone more radical and more competent than the incumbent. Chase fit the bill.[15]

The first Chase boom would not survive the winter—or the machinations of his friends. Kansas senator Samuel Pomeroy effectively drove Chase from active candidacy by producing the so-called Pomeroy Circular, published under his name although drafted by *New York Times* Washington correspondent James M. Winchell. The circular argued that Chase would have remained quiescent had not Lincoln's men brought the "party machinery, and official influences" onto the canvas. Now Chase had no choice but to respond. Lincoln could not be reelected "against the union of influences which will oppose him," the circular claimed. But if he were somehow reelected, things would only go "from bad to worse in his hands, and the war will languish till our public debt will overwhelm us." Chase was "the right man for the succession," and his "claims rest upon a solid popularity, and that he can be elected."[16]

Reaction from Republicans to the Pomeroy Circular was swift and devastating. "Are these men mad?" the *New York Times* wondered. "Do they seriously think that they are advancing Mr. Chase's interests by this public notification that they intend to rend the party unless the majority of the party will agree to nominate him?" Chase apologized to Lincoln, offered to resign, and announced that he would not be a candidate for president. In response, Lincoln had "very little to say." He would not hold Chase responsible for what others did in his name, and politics would play no part in who ran the Treasury Department. "I do not perceive occasion for a change," he concluded. By the first week of March, the *New York Herald* was espousing the opinion that Frémont had supplanted Chase: "General Frémont, with the radical black republican and red republican German legion devoted to his advancement is really a more dangerous rival to President Lincoln than Mr. Chase."[17]

Frank Blair didn't want to do Frémont any favors, but he did want to drive a stake through the heart of Chase's candidacy. Blair had lost the race for House Speaker and would soon be off to William Tecumseh Sherman's army, but he had one last service to perform for Lincoln. In February, he had taken to the House floor to defend Lincoln's reconstruction plans; excoriate the radicals of his home state, the "Jacobins of Missouri"; and criticize Chase, whom he accused of using Treasury Department patronage to aid his presidential campaign and of illegally selling trade permits to benefit both himself and his supporters. Blair also took aim at the Pomeroy Circular. "It is a matter of surprise," he said, "that a man having the instincts of a gentleman would remain in the Cabinet after the disclosure of such an intrigue against the one to whom he owes his portfolio." Blair was back again in April to accuse Chase of using Treasury Department funds to pay for his behind-the-scenes presidential campaign and "to carry on his war against the Administration." He was so violent in his assault that the Speaker repeatedly ruled him out of order and Blair had to win the assent of the House to continue. Along with castigating Chase, he got in a few digs at the "whitewashing report" of the Joint Committee on the Conduct of the War that had effectively exonerated Frémont. He called Frémont a stalking horse for the Treasury secretary: "The work is now being done in Frémont's name and that poor creature is unconscious of being made a cat's paw to accomplish the objects of his intriguing rival." Blair compared Chase's machinations vis-à-vis Frémont to how "Calhoun used poor John Tyler to hold a side convention in 1844 to force the Democrats to drop Van Buren." That was bad history on Blair's part and a distortion of what had happened in 1844. But since he had not been able to per-suade anyone not already convinced that the Joint Committee on the Conduct of the War's report on Frémont's time in Missouri had been a "whitewash," he had to try something. In the course of trying to belittle Chase and smear Frémont, he accomplished neither. But he had enraged the radicals enough that they voted to unseat him in favor of Samuel Knox, who had challenged Blair's 1862 election victory. Blair then returned to Sherman's army.[18]

Chase was incensed at the attack from Blair, believed Lincoln had inspired it in response to the Pomeroy Circular, and again threatened to resign. There was little else he could do, and Lincoln again brushed it aside. Frémont was not a stalking horse for Chase, except perhaps in the minds of some Chase supporters. But Chase's withdrawal did not unite Lincoln's Republican foes behind Frémont, despite the fact that Frémont had a devoted following of many years standing, had bested Chase for the nomination in 1856, and possessed a popularity and charisma the Ohioan did not. He also had a considerably baser justification for his candidacy than simply running interference for another candidate. "After he had given his private means, turned away from his native State, and friends, as well as from the management of his property, and devoted even his pay as Major General to the care of the wounded," Jessie reflected years later, it was ill treatment by the Lincoln administration that "paved the way for" his candidacy. Frémont was drawn into the race by his power as a symbol of emancipation. He, more than most, had legitimate reasons to doubt Lincoln's devotion to the cause of abolition. But striking back at the man he believed had done him wrong was what propelled Frémont forward.[19]

"I feel very indifferent about the White House"

George McClellan was in some ways the mirror image of Frémont. Where the radicals viewed Frémont as the military embodiment of abolition, Democrats saw McClellan as the military embodiment of the peace movement. Party lead-ers had begun courting him within days of his being relieved of command in fall 1862. With half the party having seceded in 1860–1861, Democrats were denuded of national leadership. The rump minority in Congress and in state-houses, although somewhat increased in the elections of 1862, had again been diminished in 1863. The loudest voices to be heard were among the Peace Dem-ocrats—such as Ohio's Clement Vallandigham, whom Ambrose Burnside had arrested and Lincoln had sent South before his return to run unsuccessfully for governor in 1863 (after McClellan refused the nomination). But the peace wing had no serious challenger to McClellan for president, so it focused on driving the party platform toward the idea of an immediate peace, whatever the eventual candidate might think.[20]

McClellan maintained a public stance of disinterestedness, but he had begun intriguing for the nomination almost as soon as he was dismissed from command of the Army of the Potomac in November 1862 and relocated first to New Jersey and then to New York City. Democratic movers and shakers wooed him with the gift of a free home on West 31st Street. In February and March 1863, he testified before the Joint Committee on the Conduct of the War, an unhappy occasion for the former commanding general. The members of what he called "that confounded committee" were largely unfriendly to him. McClellan filed his final campaign report in August and felt free enough from military discipline to publicly endorse the Democratic candidate for governor of Pennsylvania, George Woodward, who lost to Republican Andrew Curtin. McClellan would write a letter intending to resign his commission in November, but he never sent it and would not finally leave the army until Election Day 1864. The presidency came up in a letter from his mother that month; in reply, McClellan told her, "I feel very indifferent about the White House—for many reasons I do not wish it—I shall do nothing to get it & trust that Providence will decide the matter as is best for the country."[21]

The Blairs had earlier lobbied Lincoln to reinstate McClellan to command, partly because they were in sympathy with his view of soft war and partly because they thought he would be less of a threat inside the tent than outside. They would continue to work on McClellan through the middle of 1864. But Republicans assumed they would be facing the Young Napoleon, and the press acted the same.[22]

Like the Blairs, although with different motivations, Frémont seemed open to joining forces with McClellan and the Democrats. Edward H. Wright, a former aide-de-camp to McClellan and the son of New Jersey senator William Wright, was approached by a Frémont supporter in mid-March 1864 about the possibility of Frémont and McClellan joining forces, with one becoming the Democratic nominee and the other being appointed general in chief. Wright wrote to McClellan about this arrangement; McClellan said the encounter "confirms many little hints that had reached my ears" and called the idea "a strange one." Nothing came of it directly, but rumors of a potential deal persisted to the extent that McClellan had to throw out of his office a man who came to see him about "the meeting that had been arranged with F." More contacts between the two campaigns would follow, and many of Frémont's supporters believed his end goal was uniting with the Democrats. But the Frémont forces were not the only parties interested in trying to make a deal with McClellan.[23]

In early May 1864, Montgomery Blair took another run at keeping McClellan onside, suggesting that if he bowed out and endorsed Lincoln, he would be reinstated to a senior army command. Blair didn't understand where either man was headed politically, and McClellan rejected the idea instantly. Francis Preston Blair tried one last time in July, meeting with McClellan at the Astor House in New York, where Frémont and Lincoln had met more than three years earlier. Lincoln did not know of the meeting beforehand, though Blair caught him up after the fact. McClellan remained unmoved. He would not ask Lincoln for anything and, bizarrely, insisted that he was not even a candidate for the Democratic nomination. "I think that the original object of the war, as declared by the Govt., viz: the preservation of the Union, its Constitution & its laws, has been lost sight of . . . & that other issues have been brought into the foreground which either should be entirely secondary, or are wrong or impossible of attainment," McClellan told Blair in a clear reference to emancipation and abolition. "I think the war has been permitted to take a course which unnecessarily embitters the inimical feeling between the two sections & much increases the difficulty of attaining the true objects for which we ought to fight." News of the meeting was leaked to the press, probably by Blair, and an account ran in the *New York Herald* on August 4.[24]

"A diversion in favor of Lincoln"

Back in 1861, before meeting with Frémont at the Astor House, Lincoln had attended a reception on February 20 at New York's City Hall at which he was asked about the possibility of reelection. "I think when the clouds look as dark as they do now," he responded, "one term might satisfy any man." As the clouds got darker, Lincoln only grew more determined to see his task through to the end. The taste of defeat in the 1862 elections informed Lincoln's approach to 1864. He started early in getting organized for the campaign while still expressing some reluctance. At a February 1864 meeting of the Union League in Philadelphia, one of the earliest endorsers of his reelection, he said that while he wished to be the Republican candidate, "I shall not shrink from another man's nomination for the Presidency with any greater hesitation than I would from my own. If it shall be made to appear in any way that the elements upon which the salvation of the country is to depend can be better combined by dismissing me, the country can have no difficulty in getting rid of me." Conscious of how this position might sound to voters, he and the organizer of the meeting—John

Forney, secretary of the Senate and president of the Union League—decided not to release the text or any news of the speech.[25]

Lincoln did want to be reelected, and his operatives and patronage benefactors were at least as busy as the Frémont, Chase, and McClellan forces. Friendly state legislatures and state conventions from New England through the Midwest endorsed his candidacy. Even the Maryland legislature took this step. Lincoln also beat back attempts to delay the scheduled early June convention until after the Democrats met in late August. He did not want to give his opponents more time to organize against him. The strong show of support for the incumbent largely put an end to talk of Frémont challenging Lincoln for the party nomination. The focus shifted to a third-party challenge.[26]

Even as the campaign began to take shape, the war killed California for the Frémonts. Any hope of returning to the idyllic days at Black Point died in October 1863 when the government seized the property for use as a military post, leveling their home and gardens to make way for earthworks and an artillery battery. Adding insult to injury, they renamed the site Fort Mason, in honor of Richard Mason, a toadying aide to Gen. Stephen Watts Kearny who succeeded Kearny as military governor of California during the Mexican War. Mason had so insulted Frémont that the Pathfinder challenged him to a duel, which Kearny halted. Then, on March 4, 1864, Jessie's great friend Thomas Starr King died. Grief stricken, she told her husband, "I've a certain conviction that when I have a garden again, I'll meet Mr. King walking there." To John Greenleaf Whittier, she wrote of "a loss and loneliness that cannot be repaired." With Whittier, Bret Harte, and others, she helped prepare a memorial volume that she sold along with *The Story of the Guard* at a U.S. Sanitary Commission fund-raiser. In one of her last letters to King, Jessie reported how she and Ellen McClellan, the wife of George B. McClellan, "work together on a committee for 'Arms & Trophies'" for the Sanitary Commission. "After that let your lambs & lions go to work together too."[27]

In the campaign, the lambs themselves were having enough trouble working together. Wendell Phillips was one of Frémont's most visible supporters. But he was having little success bringing along even some of his closest friends and family: His son-in-law, lawyer and journalist George Smalley, wrote Phillips, "You ask why not publicly join the Frémonters. For two classes of reasons—the first against Frémont generally—the second specially against your appearing as his advocate." Smalley, who had been instrumental in persuading Phillips to be less ethereal and more politically practical, went on in great detail to hector Phillips about the role he believed abolitionists should be playing.

"I think you sacrifice your position the moment you pronounce decisively for any man as President," he warned Phillips. "One strong hold you have on the people is your absolute independence of politics, & being beyond suspicion of *personal* motives. If you speak as the partisan of Frémont can you retain it? Losing it, do you gain, or can you accomplish, anything to compensate for it?" Would anyone take his criticisms of Lincoln seriously again, or would they simply assume he was trying to gain an advantage for his candidate?

Aside from that, Smalley, who as a journalist had covered Frémont's Shenandoah Valley campaign, simply didn't "believe in Frémont for Pres. I do believe him able & personally as honest as most public men. I grant all you can say about his executive capacity &c. But he is the worst judge of men in America, and is surrounded by swindlers." He also considered Frémont "vain & selfish— his natural simplicity of character corrupted by the men who have long been his personal followers, devoted to making their own fortunes under pretence of advancing his. . . . He is a *weak* man, sure to be a tool in others' hands." Smalley was also concerned that Frémont

> is said to be resolved to run against Lincoln—or perhaps any Baltimore nominee—anyhow; preferring to give the election to the Copperheads rather than not gratify his revenge. Don't say that I judge him harshly when I say that I think him capable of this. I know what scores he has to pay off—I know his Virginia quarrel with L. & how shamefully he was treated—but I remember also that even at that moment he sank into bitterness against the Gov't & asked to be relieved not because Pope's appointment over his head would destroy his usefulness, but because it "largely reduced his rank and consideration in the service." That is not the language of a man of generous impulses & unselfish purpose.

Smalley feared a divided Republican Party would hand the election to the Democrats and thought a better option than a third-party led by Frémont would be to take the argument to the Republican convention. He believed "there is a better chance to unite against Lincoln—& to carry the Baltimore convention—with Butler or with some candidate not yet prominent, & I regard the F. movement as a diversion in favor of Lincoln."[28]

This was perhaps the major challenge facing those who sought an antislavery alternative to Lincoln. "Some will now only vote for Frémont, others only for Butler, almost all would like a change, but they have no one to change for," an Illinois radical wrote to Lyman Trumbull. There were plenty of potential contenders—Chase, Frémont, Butler, even Grant—but no consensus alternative.

Each of the contenders had major strikes against him. And anyone "not yet prominent" by March 1864 was unlikely to capture the imagination of voters by the time of the Republican convention in June.[29]

At this crucial moment, the world lost one of the few men with a foot in both camps: Owen Lovejoy died on March 25. He had served briefly on Frémont's staff in Missouri but was a congressional ally of Lincoln—perhaps the most reliable among the radicals. The president felt his death keenly, both personally and politically. "He was one of the best men in Congress," Lincoln told fellow Illinois lawyer and pol Shelby Cullom. Lovejoy could always be counted on to "do about as I wanted." To another acquaintance of both men, Lincoln wrote, "Throughout my heavy and perplexing responsibilities here to the day of his death, it would scarcely wrong any other to say, he was my most generous friend."[30]

Another link between the Lincolnites and the radicals was Massachusetts senator Charles Sumner. He had begun the war as a critic of the president but came around somewhat in the early months of the administration. Sumner had served as go-between for Frémont and Lincoln as they negotiated Frémont's military future in 1863. The differences between Lincoln and Sumner were vast, though, and were illustrated by a pair of stories, one told by each man.

English abolitionist George Thompson, who had been so effusive in his praise of Frémont just a few weeks earlier, brought a group of abolitionists to the White House in April 1864, hoping to push Lincoln to move faster on abolition. Lincoln responded with a story. "It is my conviction that, had the Proclamation been issued even six months earlier than it was, public sentiment would not have sustained it," he told the group.

> Just so, as to the subsequent action in reference to enlisting blacks in the Border States. The step, taken sooner, could not in my judgment, have been carried out. A man watches his pear-tree day after day, impatient to force the process, and he may spoil both fruit and tree. But let him patiently wait, and the ripe pear at length falls into his lap! We have seen this great revolution in public sentiment slowly but surely progressing, so that, when final action came, the opposition was not strong enough to defeat the purpose. I can now solemnly assert that I have a clear conscience in regard to my action on this momentous question.[31]

Sumner had heard this reasoning many times because, from the very early days of the war, he had also been pushing Lincoln to move faster on emancipation. After Lincoln reversed Frémont's proclamation in September 1861,

Sumner told a story to Lincoln "of a neighbor of ours in Connecticut, to whom, one fall, we gave some apples, with directions how to preserve them. They were to be laid down in a barrel of dry sand, headed up, and not opened till the 4th of July, the next year. On that morning he paid us a visit, and announced that he had opened his apples. 'Well, did they keep?' 'Yes,' said he, 'they *kept*: but they were all *rotten!*'"[32]

The parables of the apples and the pears defined the Lincoln-Sumner relationship. But the two men grew closer as Lincoln edged ever nearer to Sumner's abolitionist agenda. Sumner was spending more time at the White House and even getting chummy with Mary Lincoln. One of Sumner's friends, though, suspected politics was at work. "I suppose all this civility to you in the White H. is to help getting L. right with the N. Engl. antislavery people," wrote Francis Lieber, an attorney who penned the military's code of conduct being employed by northern soldiers in the field. Even if this cynical interpretation was on point, it mattered little. Both parties got what they wanted. Sumner enjoyed the attention and got to play in the big sandbox, and Lincoln got to appear friendly with a leader of the group he needed to hold on to the nomination.[33]

Like Sumner, Clara Barton, who had many friends in the abolition movement, was sticking with Lincoln. "Who am I going to vote for?" she asked jokingly of a friend. "Why I thought for president Lincoln, to be sure. I *have* been voting for him for the last three years." Without a vote to cast, she would support in whatever way she could whomever the Republicans nominated, but her preference was for the incumbent. Her devotion to Lincoln came despite her admiration for Frémont, who "did see more clearly than Mr. Lincoln the great drift of this war, and to what it tended and did proclaim it, and did suffer for it."[34]

For Garrison, Phillips, Sumner, Barton, and every other abolitionist, the presidential campaign became intwined with the congressional debate on a proposed Thirteenth Amendment to the Constitution outlawing slavery. Discussion began in the House on March 19, with James Wilson of Iowa offering a joint resolution and noting "the incompatibility of slavery with a free Government." The issue came up in the Senate nine days later, with Lyman Trumbull, author of both Confiscation Acts, leading the way. The debate would continue off and on for three months, ensuring that the proposed amendment would be a key issue as the presidential nominating contests played out.[35]

A key supporter in the Senate was Reverdy Johnson of Maryland, who had come a long way on the issue since 1856, when he represented John Sanford in his case against Dred Scott before the Supreme Court, in which the opposing counsel was Montgomery Blair. The Senate approved the amendment 38–6 on

April 8, easily clearing the necessary two-thirds threshold. The House vote was expected to be a tougher challenge for supporters. Lincoln uttered no public opinion on the vote. He had recently reiterated to a Kentucky newspaper editor his feeling that "if slavery is not wrong, nothing is wrong. . . . And yet I have never understood that the Presidency conferred upon me an unrestricted right to act officially upon this judgment and feeling." Lincoln's public silence gave Frémont's Radical Democrats a way to clearly distinguish themselves from the president, if not from the congressional Republicans who were pushing ahead on abolition. Lincoln also told Kentucky newspaperman Albert G. Hodges, "I claim not to have controlled events, but confess plainly that events have controlled me." That wasn't strictly true. But on the question of abolition, events were converging in a way that might give the president a chance to guide (if not control) them.[36]

"THE MOST MAGNIFICENT FIZZLE I EVER LOOKED IN UPON"

In early May, the papers were still reporting on talk about Frémont, as well as McClellan, going into the field under his onetime subordinate, Grant. "Frémont could not make to Grant," now a lieutenant general, "the objection that he naturally made to Pope," whom he had outranked. But that time was past for both Frémont and McClellan. They had left the battlefield for the campaign trail.[37]

Conventions of Frémont supporters around the country began in late winter, planning for a third-party nominating convention. Organizers firmed up those plans in early May, sending out the call for a national convention at the end of the month. The call for the Cleveland convention of the Radical Democracy Party declared "that we do not recognize in the Baltimore Convention the essential conditions of a truly National Convention." But the "National Union" convention in Baltimore that would follow the Cleveland gathering would represent the leaders of the party. None showed up in Cleveland, although a few sent letters of support. Those conspicuous by their absence were several men in open opposition to Lincoln who chose not to associate themselves with Frémont, including Horace Greeley, Salmon Chase, Thaddeus Stevens, and Lyman Trumbull.[38]

Frederick Douglass endorsed the effort. Writing in support of the proposed abolition constitutional amendment, he wanted to leave no room for doubt about how he defined the term in light of the army forcing freed slaves to continue working on southern plantations under onerous wage-labor contracts. "I mean the complete abolition of every vestige, form and modification of Slavery in every part of the United States, perfect equality for the black man in every State before the law, in the jury box, at the ballot-box and on the battle-field.

. . . Supposing that the convention which is to meet at Cleveland means the same thing, I cheerfully give my name as one of the signers of the call." Other black leaders, including some who admired Frémont, stuck with Lincoln. "Much of the failure of Mr. Lincoln to do [his] duty is owing to the failure of the people of the land whose agent he is," explained William Howard Day, a New York–born editor and educator who had decamped to Canada. "Do we complain that Mr. Lincoln and the government do not recognize the manhood of the negro? Let us find the cause of that in the people at home."[39]

Twenty-seven radical German delegates met in Cleveland on May 29, a day before the opening of the convention proper, joined by John Cochrane and others from the Frémont campaign. They endorsed the creation of a new party and the principles outlined at their October meeting. The next day, the Germans stepped aside as the convention opened at 11:00 a.m. at Chapin Hall in Public Square in downtown Cleveland. "Nearly every one of Frémont's Missouri Staff is here engineering the convention," *The Liberator* reported, and non-German politicians were chosen as chairman and secretaries.[40]

The convention lacked a national sanction. About four hundred delegates from sixteen states attended, none of whom were leading figures in either the Republican or the Democratic parties. None were credentialed. People could just wander into the convention from the street. New York lawyer George Templeton Strong mockingly referred to the convention as a "conventicle," a secret or unlawful religious meeting, typically of people with nonconformist views. One reporter described the attendees as "the radical men of the Northwest, the German republicans, the war democracy and a squad of administration office holders, contractors, wire pullers and right bowers of President Lincoln." The radicals and Germans were ascendant and for Frémont. The War Democrats were for Grant but were present in much smaller numbers. The Lincoln men were there to watch and report back to Washington. The delegates were "a heterogenous mixture of weak and wicked men," according to Navy Secretary Gideon Welles.[41]

Speeches focused on criticizing Lincoln more than praising Frémont. A letter was read from Lucius Robinson, the New York State comptroller and a leading Grant supporter, wondering, "How can we hope to live as a nation through the crisis before us with a weak executive and a cabinet in a state of discord and anarchy?" Another speaker dwelled on the "failure of the administration to go in for a Constitutional amendment to forever abolish slavery" and "interference with the liberty of the press."[42]

After several more speeches, a recess was called until late afternoon. When delegates returned, the work of the platform committee was read. The first two planks called simply for the preservation of the Union and the Constitution. Only slightly less controversial was the insistence that "the rebellion must be suppressed by force of arms, and without compromise." Plank four resolved "that the rights of free speech, free press, and the *habeas corpus* be held inviolate, save in districts where martial law has been proclaimed." This was a Democratic plank aimed at Lincoln's suspension of habeas corpus and his underlings' shuttering of newspapers. Insisting "that the rebellion has destroyed slavery," the fifth plank called for a constitutional amendment "to prohibit its reestablishment, and to secure to all men absolute equality before the law." The platform also endorsed a one-term presidency and elimination of the Electoral College in favor of a direct popular vote for president. Most controversially, the platform supported congressional reconstruction and "the confiscation of the lands of the rebels, and their distribution among the soldiers and actual settlers." The confiscation plank was backed by legislation introduced in March by George W. Julian that would provide homesteads to northern veterans of the war on land confiscated from rebels. Anything less, Lydia Maria Child wrote Julian in endorsing his plan, would be just "another form of slavery."[43]

Before voting on the platform took place, a letter from Wendell Phillips was read to the delegates. Phillips had ignored the advice from George Smalley and jumped into the Frémont campaign with at least one foot. He lambasted Lincoln, charging him with thinking "more of conciliating rebels than of subduing them." The administration had abjured use of emancipation as a weapon of war "until it was thought indispensable, and even then has used it in a half-hearted, halting way, wishing to save the feelings of rebels. . . . If I turn to Gen. Frémont, I see a man whose first act was to use the freedom of the negro as his weapon." Frémont was his first choice, but he would endorse the ticket as long as Frémont or Butler was at its head. If the Republican convention in Baltimore should cast Lincoln aside in favor of a candidate acceptable to the radicals, "I hope we shall be able to arrange some plan which will unite all on a common basis, and carry our principles into the Government."[44]

Following the reading of Phillips's letter, a long debate followed that "thinned the hall very materially," a reporter noted, as delegates considered each plank separately. The delegates who remained then serially endorsed the platform and moved on to the nomination of candidates. It was late and dark. Grant supporters moved to adjourn, not because it was late but because they wanted another day to make their case. But the Frémont men, led by the Missouri

Germans, had the numbers and pushed for a vote, which Frémont won "unanimously, with great applause."[45]

John Cochrane, the New York Democratic general who had endorsed black troops in late 1861, was chosen as the vice presidential candidate. It was a constitutional error. Perhaps to put an exclamation point on the platform's call for a direct popular vote for president, the convention had nominated two candidates residing in the same state. Under Article II, Section 1, because both Frémont and Cochrane lived in New York, that state's presidential electors could not give their votes to the Radical Democratic ticket in the unlikely event that they won the state.

That wasn't the only problem presented by Cochrane. "The choice of a cypher like John Cochrane . . . is a confession of weakness," wrote his fellow New Yorker, George Templeton Strong. Gideon Welles concurred about Cochrane, who had been at various times "a Democrat, a Barnburner, a conservative, an Abolitionist, an Anti-abolitionist, a Democratic Republican, and now a radical Republican." There was not a "coincidence of views between him and Frémont," Welles noted. John Hay noted in his diary that Cochrane had recently told Lincoln "that he was going up to Cleveland to try to forestall and break up that bolting institution." Now he was its nominee for vice president.[46]

Four days after the convention, Frémont resigned his army commission, "a sacrifice it gave me pain to make," and accepted the nomination. In doing so, he recognized that he was now "exposed to the reproach of creating a schism in the party with which I have been identified." But, Frémont insisted, he was a symptom of the schism, not the cause. "Had Mr. Lincoln remained faithful to the principles he was elected to defend, no schism could have been created, and no contest could have been possible." Frémont grasped the significance of the 1864 election. "This is not an ordinary election," he declared. "It is a contest for the right even to have candidates, and not merely, as usual, for the choice among them." The principles enunciated in the party platform "have my unqualified and cordial approbation," he wrote, but one specific item he could not endorse. "I do not believe that confiscation extended to the property of all rebels, is practicable, and if it were so, I do not think it a measure of sound policy." As a temporary war measure, it made sense. As a peacetime practice, Frémont objected. "In the adjustments which are to follow peace no considerations of vengeance can consistently be admitted."[47]

Echoing Wendell Phillips, Frémont agreed to withdraw from the race if the Republicans rejected Lincoln and nominated a candidate acceptable to the mass of his supporters. "But if Mr. Lincoln should be nominated—as I believe it would be fatal to the country to endorse a policy and renew a power which has cost us the lives of thousands of men, and needlessly put the country on the road to bankruptcy—there will remain no other alternative but to organize against him every element of conscious opposition with the view to prevent the misfortune of his re-election."[48]

Frémont was the candidate, but Lincoln was the target. Opining on Frémont's acceptance letter, one journalist concluded, "The animus which governed the writer . . . was personal animosity to Abraham Lincoln."[49]

"Their object is not the election of Frémont but the defeat of Lincoln," the *New York Herald* complained. The paper might have been correct in this analysis, although it weakened its case by citing the canard that the Liberty Party candidacy of James G. Birney had cost Henry Clay the electoral votes of New York and thus the presidency in 1844. Lincoln shared the concern that Frémont might siphon enough German and radical votes away to cost him New York and perhaps Missouri, Wisconsin, and Illinois. Clay had managed to lose New York and the election on his own. But Frémont's actions over the next three and a half months lent credence to the belief that he was in it not to win it but to ensure that Lincoln lost it.[50]

To that end, he was willing to continue his unsavory dalliance with Democrats. George Templeton Strong wondered whether the Democrats might "try to overbid their opponents by nominating some ultra anti-slavery and war-to-the-knife man?" If so, "they may endorse Frémont. That would be a revolution, indeed," although he believed "Frémont is not nearly as strong as he was in 1856, and will run badly."[51]

Frémont's toying with the idea of running as a Democrat or making a deal with McClellan lent substance to the accusations of Copperheadism leveled at the Cleveland convention—accusations based on the convention's criticism of Lincoln's actions against civil liberties, particularly the suspension of habeas corpus and the shuttering of newspapers. Many actual Copperheads had cited these points as examples of Lincoln's authoritarianism. That they made their arguments in bad faith did not mean that the criticisms were without merit. Genuine civil libertarians like some of those gathered in Cleveland had legitimate complaints about the contrast between the soft hand laid on the enemy in the field during the first year of the war and the tough-as-nails approach to administration critics behind the lines. Phillips joined in criticizing Lincoln's record. "He crushes habeas corpus," Phillips said. "He imprisons individuals." That Frémont and even Phillips now seemed ready to make common cause with Democrats of every stripe was another instance of supposed nonpoliticians playing politics as usual. There would be more to come in his campaign to woo, or even usurp, the Democrats.[52]

Expanding the base is essential to any candidate. But Frémont's moves were a concern to potential allies, including some black Americans who couldn't vote but possessed moral authority in the abolitionist movement. "I am for Mr. Lincoln against Copperheadism, as threatened in a coalition with Mr. Frémont," wrote Reverend J. Sella Martin. "As a negro, I am for the man whose party and policy have given us a free capital, a confiscation law, and a proclamation of freedom, as against the man who, with honest enough intentions, expects to drive out devils by Beelzebub."[53]

As they prepared for their own convention, the men whom Lincoln had engaged to keep an eye on things in Cleveland didn't seem too worried. "Convention tremendous fizzle, less than two hundred from abroad Consisting of disappointed contractors sore-heads Garrisonians and Copperheads," the postmaster of Cleveland alerted Montgomery Blair, understating the number of attendees but getting the gist about right. Another administration partisan in attendance called it "the most magnificent fizzle I ever looked in upon claiming to be a convention."[54]

Henry Halleck called it a "ragtail convention." Invoking Frémont's contracting travails in St. Louis, he wrote to Francis Lieber, "I don't believe there are bladders enough in this country, if every one should be inflated to its utmost capacity, to float such a mass of corruption and humbugs." Lieber did not share Halleck's disdain for Frémont, but even he believed it was "bitter hatred against Lincoln," not a devotion to abolitionism, that was the "chief motive" of his supporters—and maybe of Frémont himself.[55]

Frémont ignored the naysayers and got to work. He invited Wendell Phillips and German newspaper editor Karl Heinzen to meet with him and Jessie in Nahant to discuss strategy. The New York Frémont Club organized a mass meeting at Cooper Union, although Democratic papers questioned the commitment of those attending. "The cheers for Frémont were feeble and infrequent," one reporter wrote, while "hosannas . . . were sent up when the names of McClellan and Vallandigham were mentioned."[56]

The Radical Democrats' strange bedfellow coalition was willing to step aside if the Republicans—now calling themselves the National Union Party—abandoned Lincoln. Whatever the party was called, it had no intention of doing so. Outsiders seemed to understand that Lincoln's nomination was a foregone conclusion. Lincoln remained guarded. "I don't quite forget that I was nominated for president in a convention that was two-thirds for the other fellow," he told

Pennsylvania politician Alexander McClure. Holding little suspense, the convention was having a hard time getting much attention.[57]

"The Convention which seems to us of absorbing interest is that which Gen. Grant is now holding on the banks of the Chickahominy," Greeley wrote on the eve of the Republican convention in Baltimore. Grant's Overland Campaign was pushing Robert E. Lee's army southward toward Richmond. Casualties were high, but so were hopes. "Next to this, we place that which Gen. Sherman is reassembling around the ramparts of Atlanta." Grant was in the middle of his movement against Cold Harbor, ten miles east of Richmond, which would end a week later with an inconclusive slaughter. Sherman's tentative steps around Atlanta would take longer but bear more immediate fruit for Lincoln. Greeley could be flighty, but his message in this case was spot on. The war, not the political campaign, was what mattered. Success on the battlefield would likely determine who enjoyed success in politics.[58]

Lincoln was nominated 484–22, with Missouri's radical delegation—seated at the insistence of Lincoln—casting its votes for Grant and then relenting and making Lincoln's nomination unanimous. With the president having endorsed the Thirteenth Amendment, even the platform lacked much suspense. Once again, as with the military necessity of emancipation, Lincoln followed where Frémont led. Politically, the abolition plank usurped the Radical Democrats' greatest organizing principle and main policy reason for being. There was some drama about the selection of a vice presidential nominee. The convention, likely with the connivance of Lincoln, chose Tennessee War Democrat Andrew Johnson, a former senator now serving as military governor of his home state. Lincoln considered him "the Andrew Jackson of the war."[59]

A few days after the convention, William Lloyd Garrison met with Lincoln in the White House. "Mr. Lincoln, I want to tell you frankly that for every word that I have ever spoken in your favor, I have spoken ten in favor of General Frémont," he told the president. "But, Mr. President, from the hour that you issued the Emancipation Proclamation, and showed your purpose to stand by it, I have given you my hearty support and confidence." Five days later, the House failed to approve the proposed Thirteenth Amendment. It gained a majority, 93–65, with twenty-three absences and one abstention, but that was thirteen votes short of the two-thirds needed to win adoption. If Lincoln could fend off his intraparty opponents on questions of reconstruction and keep the nomination, he would still have to debate the question of slavery's abolition in the general election. The House would not approve the Thirteenth Amendment until January 31, 1865.[60]

That was months in the future. For Lincoln, though, the first fight was not over. Disgruntled Republicans would spend much of the next three months questioning whether he was the right man to bear their standard. The debate about the Republican nomination would continue to be about what was to happen when the war was over, with freedom and Union secured. Lincoln's reliance on local unionists, however recently converted, to carry out reconstruction was a continuation of his misplaced faith in southern unionism. As far back as April 1862, Frank Blair had worried not about winning the war (which he said he always had full confidence the North could do) but about whether the North could subjugate the rebels "without maintaining a vast army and without changing the very form of our Government." Maintaining the freedmen in the face of southern opposition would require "an immense force equal to that which is required to set them free." Was the North ready to assume that responsibility? That question was being put to the test in a presidential campaign.[61]

"THE FEELING AGAINST MR. LINCOLN WAXED STRONGER AND STRONGER"

First, the North had to win the war. Whether it would depended to a great extent on the progress of the spring and summer offensives in Virginia and Georgia, neither of which was making much progress. After some initial success in May, Grant's push toward Richmond was grinding his army down. He was inflicting terrible casualties on Lee's Army of Northern Virginia while failing to move him out of the way. Sherman was taking a different tack in Georgia, avoiding head-on collisions like the disastrous Federal charges at Cold Harbor, but he was nonetheless making slow progress maneuvering toward the great prize of Atlanta. Southerners believed that if they could hold off the northern armies until November, discontent in the Union electorate would send them a new president and a chance for peace and independence.

In July, fifteen thousand Confederates under Gen. Jubal Early launched an attack toward Washington from north of the city. Union forces, with the president on hand for part of the battle, drove the attackers away, but not before they occupied the Blair family home at Silver Spring and destroyed some outbuildings on the estate.

Maj. Gen. John C. Breckenridge, vice president under James Buchanan, had once enjoyed Francis Preston Blair's hospitality at Silver Spring and acted as a defender of the property now that it was in his hands. One disgruntled neighbor wondered why her home was trashed while the Blairs' remained safe. "Nobody knew which side them Blairs were onto, anyhow," she told journalist

Noah Brooks, who called the complaint "a statement which will find popular approval."[62]

The Battle of Monocacy meant nothing militarily. Washington was never in any serious danger, and Early quickly retreated to the Shenandoah Valley. But rebel cannon fire within earshot of the White House sent a bad signal. At the same time, Frémont's old Missouri nemesis, Sterling Price, was gearing up for a last-ditch invasion of his politically divided state, with politics foremost in mind. Not only would a successful attack in Missouri depress northern morale (and perhaps the vote for Lincoln), but any ground gained and held would also be a bargaining chip in the hoped-for negotiated peace should Democrats win the White House.[63]

Off the battlefield, Lincoln faced other worries. On June 29, Treasury Secretary Chase resigned, citing a dispute over a departmental appointment in New York. Chase had frequently threatened to quit and had submitted his resignation as recently as February in the wake of the Pomeroy Circular. Lincoln had always demurred accepting Chase's resignations. Chase was an effective manager of the nation's finances and, Lincoln reasoned, less of a political wild card inside the cabinet than outside. Now, though, he had seen enough. "I thought I could not stand it any longer," he told John Hay. In accepting Chase's resignation, Lincoln told his former Treasury secretary, "You and I have reached a point of mutual embarrassment in our official relation which it seems can not be overcome, or longer sustained, consistently with the public service."[64]

Lincoln chose Ohio governor David Tod to replace Chase. Members of the Senate Finance Committee, led by Maine senator William Fessenden, protested, and then Tod telegraphed Lincoln that he didn't want the job. So Lincoln nominated Fessenden, whom he called "a radical—without the petulant and vicious fretfulness of many radicals." Fessenden didn't much want the job either, but he took it, giving Lincoln another radical arrow—however unpetulant or nonfretful—in his quiver.[65]

Having lost Lovejoy in March, Lincoln needed all the radical allies he could get. On July 2, Congress sent the president its plan for reconstruction, the Wade-Davis Act, named for its sponsors, Senator Ben Wade of Ohio (Frémont's great defender on the Joint Committee on the Conduct of the War) and Maryland congressman Henry Winter Davis. The president insisted, "There is no essential contest between loyal men on this subject," but that wasn't any more the truth than was his belief in March 1861 that the extension of slavery was "the only substantial dispute" separating North from South. His "ten percent plan" left room for other ideas but would have allowed states to return their members to Congress when only 10 percent of those who had voted in the 1860 election swore a loyalty oath and endorsed—or at least acquiesced to—emancipation. Until then, those states would be run by military governors appointed by the president without congressional approval. Once enough voters had sworn loyalty, all but a handful of senior Confederate officials would have all their political and civil rights restored, and elections would be held. He left the protection of blacks' civil rights up to these new state governments.[66]

The Wade-Davis bill, cleared by Congress on July 2, was much tougher on the South. It would have the states temporarily run by civilian governors, and it required a majority of voters to take a more stringent oath—that they had never fought against the Union—rather than Lincoln's requirement that they would henceforth be loyal. Only once that majority was met could states hold elections for constitutional conventions. Those conventions would then bar senior Confederate officials from civic life as well as abolish slavery and guarantee civil rights to blacks—but not the right to vote. The bill also would have freed all slaves in any state still in rebellion when the bill became law.[67]

The measure was sent to the president two days before the end of the extended legislative session, which typically ended in March but had now run into the early days of July. Rumors quickly spread that Lincoln was considering a veto. Objecting to the Wade-Davis provision freeing all slaves in states in rebellion, Lincoln told Senator Zachariah Chandler, "I conceive that I may in an emergency do things on military grounds which cannot be done constitutionally by Congress." Chandler worried that it would cost Lincoln votes in the Northwest, but Lincoln wasn't too worried about how radicals would react. "They have never been friendly to me, and I don't know that this will make any special difference as to that."[68]

It probably didn't. Radicals had their own objections, especially the lack of a guarantee of voting rights. Lincoln pocket vetoed the bill. In lieu of a veto message, on July 8, he issued a "Proclamation Concerning Reconstruction" that listed his policy and constitutional objections to the Wade-Davis bill while leaving the door open to some of the provisions, if individual states chose to implement them.[69]

Lincoln's rejection of congressional reconstruction probably did not create any new opponents, but it confirmed many existing ones. Radicals still opposed Lincoln as much as they supported Frémont, but his pocket veto of Wade-Davis confirmed for some that Frémont was the safer choice for the postwar world. "The feeling against Mr. Lincoln waxed stronger and stronger among his opposers," George W. Julian wrote, and "further exasperated a formidable body of earnest and impatient Republicans."[70]

Wade and Davis followed up with a "manifesto" excoriating Lincoln without overtly endorsing any alternative. Abolitionist editor Orestes Brownson, who had been the leadoff speaker at the pro-emancipation Smithsonian lecture series in winter 1861–1862, did endorse an alternative. In a long piece in his own magazine, Brownson noted that he had evinced no great enthusiasm for Lincoln in 1860 but supported him anyway "as a choice of evils." Now, four years later, "the whole future of our Republic depends on the result of the coming elections." The antislavery policy included in the Republican platform was a "rebuke to the slavery policy of the President." Neither the Cleveland nor the Baltimore convention truly represented the Republican Party in its entirety, Brownson argued, and worries about splitting the vote were immaterial. "We do not think the Republic could possibly lose by exchanging the Baltimore Convention for the Chicago Convention. . . . No worse thing can befall this nation than the re-election of Abraham Lincoln." Citing Frémont's "strong individuality of character," Brownson told readers that Frémont "is in 1864 the same man he was in 1856, only older, wiser, more experienced." Sounding as if Jessie were the author, the piece claimed that, ever since the Missouri emancipation fight, the administration "has feared him as the great man of his country, and done its best to disgrace him, to crush him, to annihilate him, both as a military man and as a political man." Despite all that, the administration had failed to drive Frémont from the arena. Frémont's political and military sagacity were extolled, as was his fearless manliness. As for accusations that Frémont was a bad judge of men, "we have not seen evidence of this," the author averred, praising Frémont's "independent mind. . . . [H]e is firm, not obstinate . . . a man who always preserves his own individuality." Frémont had several campaign biographies published in 1856, but the press of time prevented any such endeavor in 1864. The *Brownson's* article, a bit over the top even for a campaign bio, served the same purpose.[71]

Frémont also had a campaign song, "When Abe Comes Marching Home Again," written by Andrew Dickson White, a New York politician and educator and a founder of Cornell University. The song was more anti-Lincoln and anti-McClellan than pro-Frémont.

When "Abe" comes marching home again, Huzza! Huzza!
The people all will cry "Amen! Huzza! Huzza!"
The boys will cheer, the ladies shout,
To see Old Abra'm going out,

And we'll all be free when
"Abe" comes marching home.

Also:

Now "Mac" for "peace" has got to go, Huzza! Huzza!
For President he's got no show, "Huzza! Huzza!"

Only at the end did the lyricist get around to praising Frémont:

Stand by your colors! Every man, Huzza! Huzza!
Frémont and Cochrane in the Van, Huzza! Huzza!
For men they are both good and true,
If you stand by them, they'll stand by you,
And we'll all be free when
"Abe" comes marching home.[72]

Despite such praise, leading Republicans began publicly calling for both Lincoln and Frémont to step aside in favor of a new convention, to meet in Buffalo, New York, in September, to nominate a new ticket. This move was intended as a vehicle to get Chase or Butler the nomination they could not win on their own. Another Cincinnati-based group led by abolitionists had the same goal. Frémont's admission that he would retire from the race if another acceptable candidate put himself forward helped hold open the door to such scheming.

Ohio businessman Edgar Conkling complained to Ben Butler, who was still on active duty in Virginia, about the "Lincoln men from pure necessity" who were "anxiously looking for some chance to secure with a certainty a competent, loyal President, in place of our present imbecile incumbent." Conkling assured Butler that if he ran and got "the support of the *War Democrats* and *Frémont Party*" of Cincinnati, "Lincoln would be greatly defeated as he ought to be." He urged Butler to employ his "friends that might induce Frémont to favor and recommend this policy." Conkling made his own appeal to Frémont, pitching the idea of his and other Republicans supporting Butler as the candidate of War Democrats. Butler was interested, but Frémont was not just yet. And there was no indication from the Democrats, Peace or War, that they were ready to shift their support from McClellan to anyone else, particularly someone as identified with emancipation as Butler.[73]

As any serious possibility of Frémont being elected began to fade—if one ever existed—Jessie seemed consumed with anti-Lincoln venom. She suggested to John Greenleaf Whittier that a Lincoln victory would bring the twin disasters of European recognition of the Confederacy and secession by the Northwest, which would then make a separate peace with the South. Rebels were counting on Lincoln's reelection "as their most speedy & easy means of independence." Neither Frémont would yet trust Lincoln on slavery. If someone firmer on the issue stepped forward, "the General will thankfully retire & give his most active support to such a man."[74]

The process was sketchy. The Buffalo convention idea seemed to be the only workable solution. The *New York Herald*, no fan of either man, asserted, "In view of the Frémont abortion and the demoralized condition of the forlorn democracy, we regard the next Presidency as clearly within the grasp of this proposed independent Union Convention at Buffalo." Lincoln wasn't having it. Despite Jessie's insistence to the contrary, neither was Frémont just yet.[75]

Lincoln unburdened himself to Carl Schurz in late July during a visit to the Soldiers Home, where Lincoln spent many a summer day trying to escape the heat of swampy lowland Washington. The president expressed exasperation at the postconvention attacks and the insistence of his Republican opponents that he surrender the nomination "to make room for a better man. I wish I could," he told Schurz, who had given up his army commission to become a full-time campaigner for Lincoln. "Perhaps some other man might do this business better than I," Schurz remembered Lincoln saying. "That is possible. I do not deny it. But I am here, and that better man is not here." Not only was that hypothetical man not there, but there was no guarantee that, even if one showed up, he would actually be a better man or have any better luck in uniting the fractious party than Lincoln himself. Lincoln named no names, but he certainly did not believe that Frémont, Chase, or Butler was that better man.[76]

Republicans unhappy with Lincoln met in New York City on August 18 to ponder their options. Chase was invited to a follow-up meeting the next day and deputed New York attorney William Noyes to attend on his behalf. In typically coy fashion, Chase told former New York mayor George Opdyke, who had invited him, "My views are, by no means, as clear as I could wish, and I should be very glad to have the advantage of the clearer & better knowledge of other better informed gentlemen."[77]

On August 20, the disaffected Republicans hoping to get rid of both Lincoln and Frémont and replace them with a man of their own choosing wrote to Frémont in Nahant seeking his assent "to unite the thorough and earnest friends of a vigorous prosecution of the war in a new Convention. . . . It is emphatically advisable that the candidates nominated at Cleveland and Baltimore should withdraw," they wrote, "and leave the field entirely free for such a united effort." Frémont did not reject the idea out of hand, suggesting a "really popular convention, upon a broad and liberal basis, so that it could be regarded as a convocation in behalf of the people, and not the work of politicians, would command public confidence." But he insisted that "peace" meant reunion without slavery, and he included pitches for both "practical liberty and constitutional rights."[78]

All the talk of replacing him on the ticket, combined with the dismal state of the war, left Lincoln bereft. At a cabinet meeting on August 23, he presented the officials with an envelope that had no writing on it but a paper inside. He asked them to sign it, sight unseen, which each man did. The paper inside read, "This morning, as for some days past, it seems exceedingly probable that this Administration will not be re-elected. Then it will be my duty to so co-operate with the President elect, as to save the Union between the election and the inauguration; as he will have secured his election on such ground that he can not possibly save it afterwards."[79]

Just when things seemed as though they couldn't get any worse for Lincoln, the Democrats came to his rescue at their Chicago convention, which began six days after Lincoln presented his "blind memorandum" to the cabinet. Despite a late boomlet for New York governor Horatio Seymour, George McClellan's nomination was as foregone a conclusion as Lincoln's had been in Baltimore. The drama was over the platform, where McClellan's inexperience as a candidate sowed the seeds of his defeat.

The platform committee was dominated by Clement Vallandigham and his allies. They might be willing to go along with McClellan because they had no viable alternative. But the platform they produced included planks that made a mockery of McClellan's insistence that he was not a peace candidate. The first resolve swore allegiance to the Union, but the second called the war to preserve that Union a failure and insisted that "immediate efforts be made for a cessation of hostilities." McClellan's biographer called the peace plank "a political disaster for the party second only to its fatal split at the Charleston convention in 1860." Grant's assessment also invoked Charleston in an even harsher manner. "Treason was talked as boldly in Chicago at that convention as ever it had been in Charleston," he wrote in his memoirs.[80]

After approving the peace plank by a voice vote, the party then nominated a war candidate on the first ballot, with McClellan easily besting Seymour. The delegates next nominated Ohioan George H. Pendleton, a vehement antiwar congressman and close ally of Vallandigham, for vice president. Unfortunately for the Democrats, peace on their terms was unacceptable to a majority of northerners, including their nominee. McClellan couldn't rid himself of Pendleton, but he repudiated the peace plank while making clear that he was ready to accept slavery. "The preservation of our Union was the sole avowed object for which the war was commenced," he wrote in accepting the nomination. "It should have been conducted for that object only, and in accordance with those principles which I took occasion to declare when in active service," a reference to his "Harrison's Landing" letter of July 1862 in which he instructed Lincoln on his view of the proper course of the war. He was prepared to make a "frank, earnest, and persistent effort" to reach an accord with the rebels but would not endorse peace at any price. "The Union must be preserved at all hazards."[81]

There was some dissatisfaction, especially among border-state men, that the ticket was composed of two northerners. It presented the oddity that the "sectional" Republicans had a border-state-born nominee and a southerner leading their ticket; the Radical Democrats had Frémont, born in Georgia and raised in South Carolina, leading their ticket; and the peace-seeking Democrats were running two Yankees against them. They did have Edward Stanly, the former military governor of North Carolina, who jumped on the McClellan bandwagon, stating, "The same reasons which induced me, voluntarily, to resign that place, now compel me to vote for McClellan." That reason was emancipation, which Stanly argued would prolong the war "for fifty years." He had never been a Democrat, he said, but he was now because he was for peace, and "peace on the President's terms is an impossibility." Lincoln was unimpressed by McClellan's halving of the loaf. "Of all the men I have had to do with in my life," he said, "indecision is most strongly marked in General McClellan."[82]

The details of Frémont's involvement in the Chicago convention are somewhat murky. In 1856, he had been in contention for both the Democratic and the Republican nominations. Again in 1864, for a brief moment, it seemed history might be repeating itself. In early July, Elizabeth Blair Lee repeated a rumor that Democratic representative Samuel Cox of Ohio and Senator William Richardson of Illinois, a onetime confidant of Stephen A. Douglas, met with Jessie to discuss John becoming the Democratic nominee. As the Democrats gathered in Chicago, Justus McKinstry rolled into town. Frémont was supposedly ready to endorse a cease-fire in exchange for the Democratic nomination.[83]

McKinstry would not have been acting on his own. But the logic of Frémont endorsing such an idea is hard to fathom. It could be explained only by a growing enmity toward Lincoln. The noble cause had given way, as the *New York Herald* put it, to "his personal disappointments, his offended vanity, or some family quarrel." In no circumstance could it be possible for a Democratic Party that had endorsed the peace plank and nominated George Pendleton for vice president to entertain the candidacy of or cooperation with John C. Frémont. But the effort kept on, with another representative of Frémont meeting with McClellan's father-in-law and adviser, Randolph Marcy, after the convention to discuss swinging a deal for Frémont's support in exchange for "a good office." McKinstry followed up with Marcy claiming he had Frémont's go-ahead for "any arrangement which the Democrats determined to be best in regard to running or withdrawing from the Presidential contest." The idea made no sense. McClellan despised Frémont personally. He had once threatened to have Frémont arrested for malfeasance. He had no respect for Frémont as a general. And he hated Frémont's support of abolition. In addition, Frémont had considered and rejected the idea of running as a Democrat in 1856 because he could not endorse the Kansas-Nebraska Act, which allowed settlers to determine whether slavery would be allowed in new territories. How he thought he could fit into the Democratic Party of 1864 is an unsolvable mystery.[84]

If peace on Vallandigham's or McClellan's terms was unacceptable to voters, peace on Sherman's terms seemed to be an increasing possibility. In Virginia, Grant remained stalled at Petersburg. But on September 1, the day after McClellan's nomination, Atlanta fell to Sherman's army. Maj. Gen. Phil Sheridan was simultaneously routing Confederates in Virginia's Shenandoah Valley, where Frémont had failed to bag Stonewall Jackson two years earlier. Admiral David Farragut's capture of Mobile a few weeks earlier had seemed relatively minor at the time. Now it seemed like the beginning of a pattern of northern success. Sterling Price's politically motivated invasion of Missouri spread death and destruction across the middle of the state but failed to alter Missourians' devotion to the Union. Price eventually fled to Kansas.

War is never popular for long, but victory holds political value. McClellan and Frémont, the military failures of 1862, were now the political challengers of 1864. However, the improved military outlook and the Democratic peace plank flipped the equation. "The fall of Atlanta puts an entirely new aspect upon the face of affairs," wrote a correspondent of Gideon Welles. Lincoln was now the favorite. The only threat to his reelection seemed to come from the Republican schism represented by Frémont, who still might be able to steal enough votes from the incumbent to cost him crucial states such as New York, Pennsylvania, Massachusetts, Ohio, and Indiana.[85]

With the war going well and the Republicans/National Union Party endorsing the Thirteenth Amendment, the logic of Frémont's candidacy was waning. Wendell Phillips continued to urge Frémont to stay the course, but other abolitionists were pushing in the opposite direction. William Lloyd Garrison met John Cochrane at Gerrit Smith's home in Peterboro, New York, on September 5, where Smith told Cochrane "that he and Frémont, as good patriots, must let the Cleveland nomination slide, and give their hearty support to the nomination of 'honest Abe.' Cochrane smiles, but is reticent. . . . It must be apparent, I think, to all but the blindest of the blind, that the Frémont movement has proved an abortion; and the best thing that its nominees and its partisans can do, for themselves and for their country, is to accept what is inevitable, and join the general mass of loyal men in sustaining Mr. Lincoln."[86]

An even more influential voice as far as the Frémonts were concerned came from Amesbury, Massachusetts. Jessie had made another trip to John Greenleaf Whittier's home seeking counsel. Whittier, a notorious recluse, promised to journey to Nahant to talk with her husband. True to his word, he made the trip in September. Frémont told Whittier, "Although I am not gratified at contemplating myself as an opponent of Mr. Lincoln, I feel wholly committed to the course which I have begun." But he invited Whittier to speak his mind. The poet told Frémont that he would best serve his country by doing what was necessary to ensure that Lincoln defeated McClellan. "There is a time to do, and a time to stand—aside," the gentle poet told the general. Coming from Whittier, this "deciding word" pulled Jessie along with it. She called it a "wise and necessary view of what the time demanded of Mr. Frémont."[87]

Phillips at first even refused to believe that the famously reclusive Whittier had made the visit. "You are imaginative and saw a vision," he joked to Jessie. "Whittier goes *nowhere*." Even after being assured that Whittier had come, the great orator still objected to Frémont withdrawing. But Whittier's advice would prove decisive. Frémont had made his decision. All that was left was to announce it. He would refuse "all offers of political positions or any *personal* considerations," Jessie wrote. "The safety of the Republican Party was his one and only reason for . . . withdrawing from the nomination." It certainly wasn't to help Abraham Lincoln.[88]

Michigan senator Zachariah Chandler, an enthusiastic Frémont supporter as a member of the Joint Committee on the Conduct of the War, did want to help Lincoln. He also hated McClellan. But he was one of the few who maintained good relations with all Republican camps—he was a leader among congressional radicals, he had long been friendly with Frémont, and he had a good working relationship with Lincoln. He was a logical choice to mediate among the factions.[89]

Chandler traveled to Ohio to enlist Ben Wade, who insisted that Montgomery Blair must go as part of any deal to get Frémont out of the race. He next got Simon Cameron to go along. "I am more and more of the opinion that the election of Mr. Lincoln & the salvation of the country depend on my mission," Chandler grandiosely told his wife. He wasn't the first politician to believe that he held the fate of the country in his hands—but, in this case, he might have been right. On September 3, Chandler led a delegation that included Iowa senator James Harlan and Lincoln's friend and Illinois congressman Elihu Washburne to meet with Lincoln at the White House. They offered a bargain— dump Blair in exchange for Frémont's withdrawal and the support of radicals, including Wade. Lincoln had repeatedly resisted radical demands for Blair's head. This time it took Lincoln a day, but he agreed to proceed, possibly because he had already decided to cut Blair loose after the election anyway. In that case, Frémont's withdrawal would be like getting something for nothing.[90]

Chandler then hurried to New York to meet with Frémont. He had hoped to have Wade at his side, but the Ohioan was a no-show. With Frémont supporters David Dudley Field and George Wilkes in tow, Chandler laid out his case. Lincoln was not going to withdraw under any circumstances. With three men in the race, McClellan would be elected. If Frémont withdrew, he would get a high command and Blair would be booted out of the cabinet. Field assured Frémont that though the war had not been fought satisfactorily up to now, he was confident the administration had finally seen the light. Frémont was not interested in another command at this late date, as he was determined to avoid any connection with the administration. Playing coy, he made no commitment on withdrawal but said he would consider it. Chandler must have talked to the press as if Frémont's response were more concrete: the *New York Herald* reported the next day, "General Frémont will withdraw his name from the Presidential contest within ten days." The wish was not father to the fact. Frémont returned to Nahant, and Chandler followed him, hoping to get a firmer agreement.[91]

The Frémonts' bitterness toward Lincoln was unabated, but Whittier had carried the day—and they could read the writing on the wall. The war, which had looked so hopeless only a few months earlier, was turning in the North's favor. The Democratic peace plank made a McClellan victory untenable for both Frémonts. But John wanted no part of any bargain, even one that struck a blow at Montgomery Blair. On September 17, he notified a close circle of advisers and friends that he had decided to withdraw, without conditions. A few days later he met Chandler in New York and told him the same thing. Chandler was aghast. He wanted to use Frémont to get rid of Blair. Now here was Frémont telling him that he would make no deal and wanted nothing in return. He had already delivered his announcement to the newspapers. Nothing would change his mind. McKinstry, through Marcy, informed McClellan of Frémont's decision.[92]

In his withdrawal letter, Frémont said he was exiting the campaign "not to aid in the triumph of Mr. Lincoln, but to do my part towards preventing the election of the Democratic candidate." As for Lincoln, "I consider that his administration has been politically, militarily, and financially a failure, and that its necessary continuance is a cause of regret for the country." Lincoln had wasted the unanimity of purpose the nation had possessed in the wake of Fort Sumter. He "divided the North, when he declared to the South that slavery should be protected." But Frémont could not run the risk that McClellan might win. "United the Republican party is reasonably sure of success," he concluded. "Divided the result of the Presidential election is at least doubtful."[93]

Chandler raced back to Washington to meet with Lincoln. He told the president that Frémont had agreed to withdraw, withholding the Pathfinder's refusal to countenance a deal. Chandler simply told Lincoln that it was now his turn to do his part. Lincoln said he would—in his own good time. Lincoln had read Frémont's graceless withdrawal statement, and it nearly scuttled the deal. He had expected an endorsement. Frémont, refusing to observe the niceties of politics, instead offered more criticism. Chandler reminded the annoyed president that it was the substance, not the form, of the withdrawal that mattered— and that he had agreed to. Lincoln acknowledged that fact, and the "deal," as Chandler still viewed it, was done.[94]

Frémont's second presidential campaign lasted only a couple weeks longer than his Hundred Days in Missouri. He once again came out on the short end of the stick to Lincoln. But this time, at least, he beat the Blairs, to whom Lincoln immediately turned his attention. "You have generously said to me more than once, that whenever your resignation could be a relief to me, it was at my disposal," he wrote to Montgomery on September 23. "The time has come. You very well know that this proceeds from no dissatisfaction of mine with you personally or officially. Your uniform kindness has been unsurpassed by that of any friend." Blair resigned the same day.[95]

Lincoln had every confidence that the newly former postmaster general would land on his feet. He told Hay that if Blair "will devote himself to the success of the national cause without exhibiting bad temper towards his opponents, he can see the Blair family up again." Montgomery took the advice. He began making speeches in support of the administration and supporting the pro-emancipation side in Maryland's state elections. Frank reacted differently.

"It is somewhat mortifying to reflect that this triumph has been given to those who are equally the enemies of the President & 'the Blairs,'" he wrote to his father at the end of the month. He commended his brother for acting in the best interests of the country but let go of none of his hostility to "Chase, Frémont & all the rest of the enemies & persecutors of the 'Blairs.'"[96]

The speed with which Blair's resignation followed Frémont's withdrawal indicates Lincoln didn't mind voters drawing the conclusion that the two events were related. However Frémont and Lincoln perceived the goings-on, the public and most politicians saw Frémont's withdrawal and Montgomery's resignation as a quid pro quo. The Blairs did too. In August, Lincoln had told Francis Preston Blair that "he did not think it a good policy to sacrifice a good friend to a false one or an avowed enemy" and that "nobody but enemies wanted Montgomery out of the Cabinet." In the end, though, that's what happened. Montgomery acknowledged that he was a "peace offering to Frémont and his friends." The offering did little to placate Frémont, but many of his friends saw it for what it was.[97]

The *New York Herald* claimed, "The leading men of the republican party, who were secretly pledged to support the Cleveland nomination, have all eaten humble pie, and are now making speeches for Lincoln." The truth, though, was that very few of the party's actual leading men had ever endorsed Frémont. Most of the lesser lights had now crossed over. German Frémont clubs did a quick about-face and became Lincoln clubs. Frederick Douglass, who was a leading light but not in the party, endorsed Lincoln. "While there was, or seemed to be, the slightest possibility of securing the nomination and election of a man to the Presidency of more decided anti-slavery convictions and a firmer faith in the immediate necessity and practicability of justice and equality for all men, than have been exhibited in the policy of the present administration," Douglass was for Frémont. Now that it was "plain that this country is to be governed or misgoverned" by either Lincoln or McClellan, "all hesitation ought to cease," and every antislavery man should vote for Lincoln.[98]

Lincoln was relieved to be rid of Frémont, satisfied to have the controversy surrounding Blair behind him, and now more hopeful that victory—in the election and the war—lay ahead. Still, he worried. "I am just enough of a politician to know that there was not much doubt about the result of the Baltimore convention," he told Noah Brooks, "but about this thing I am far from being certain." By his own reckoning, he had almost no margin for error, predicting a mere six-vote advantage in the Electoral College, with New York, Pennsylvania, New Jersey, Delaware, Maryland, Missouri, Kentucky, and Illinois scored in

McClellan's column. In that scenario, he could not afford to lose Indiana's thirteen electoral votes. That state's Republican governor, Oliver Morton, had asked the president to delay the upcoming draft, which he feared would cost Republicans the state. Lincoln refused. The governor also asked the president to intercede with his commanders to allow soldiers to come home to vote. Most states allowed soldiers to vote from the field, a lesson Republicans learned in 1862 and applied for 1864. But Indiana's Democratic legislature had stubbornly refused. Lincoln asked Sherman to allow Hoosier soldiers in his army to be granted leave to go home to vote in the October state elections on October 11 if it could be done safely. "They need not remain for the Presidential election," Lincoln assured Sherman. The general declined to allow mass furloughs as he marched through Georgia but did permit most of his sick and wounded Hoosiers to go home. Safely reelected, Morton then upped the ante, asking for the returnees to be allowed to stay and vote for president in November. Lincoln, having made the request of Sherman only for the state elections, refused to press the general further on the point. But the soldier vote would prove crucial to Lincoln across the nation.[99]

"'FATHER ABRAHAM' HAS GOT NO REVENGE IN HIS NATURE"

Lincoln was easily reelected, winning 2,213,665 votes to McClellan's 1,802,237, and an even larger, 212–21 majority in the Electoral College. McClellan won only one free state, New Jersey, and only two border slave states, Delaware and Kentucky (despite all the attention lavished on it by the president). Lincoln also dominated in the soldier vote, 116,887 to 33,748. Any residual loyalty to McClellan felt by men in the ranks had been killed by the party's planks calling the war a failure and insisting on peace at any price. Lincoln's state-by-state majorities were such that Frémont's continued presence in the race might have cost him Connecticut, New Hampshire, and possibly New York, which Lincoln won by less than 7,000 votes out of more than 730,000 cast. With or without Frémont in the race, however, Lincoln would have been reelected.[100]

"Lincoln elected: all right. More war—tedious but necessary," Virginia novelist and poet John Esten Cooke, a cavalry staff officer, wrote in his diary.[101]

"The rebellion continues," Lincoln told a gathering of serenaders a few days after the election, and he also believed it necessary, if not tedious. With the election over, he urged those who had opposed his reelection to "re-unite in a common effort, to save our common country." He had, he said, "striven, and shall strive to avoid placing any obstacle in the way. So long as I have been here I have not willingly planted a thorn in any man's bosom." And he pleaded with "those who have not differed with me, to join with me, in this same spirit towards those who have."[102]

Chicago Tribune publisher Joseph Medill took Lincoln at his word. In January 1865, he recommended Frémont for minister to France in the new administration—coming full circle from Frémont being considered for the same job in 1860–1861. "The French mission is not yet filled I suppose," Medill wrote to the president.

> Could you do better on the whole, than to appoint Frémont? Would it not be heaping coals of fire on his head and that of his particular friends? Would it not be a good selection in itself for the French Court? Would he not be as good & useful and influential a man as you can find to send there? . . . I know it is a rather imprudent thing to propose his name to you after his course towards you. But some few have got it into their heads that "Father Abraham" has got no revenge in his nature and that his magnanimity is boundless. Your appointment of Chase [as] Chief Justice was one of the most popular acts of your life. So I suspect would be the sending of Frémont to the Court of Versailles.[103]

Chief Justice Roger B. Taney had died on October 12, and Lincoln decided not to nominate a successor until after the election. When Lincoln nominated Chase on December 6, he told a Massachusetts congressman that he had no concerns regarding how Chase had talked about him. "I do not mind that," the president said. "Chase is, on the whole, a pretty good fellow and a very able man." Lincoln had, in the past, said similarly praiseworthy things of Frémont, but the former general's graceless withdrawal from the presidential race in September likely removed him from the president's list of good fellows and able men. There is no evidence that Lincoln seriously considered Medill's proposal. He had bypassed Frémont for the same job at the start of his administration and then given him two nearly impossible tasks during the war. When Frémont failed at both, turned down a third, and then gratuitously insulted Lincoln on his way out of the election contest, the president felt justified in casting him aside. After nearly four years of controversy, hostility, and mistrust, John C. Frémont would play no role in the three months of life Lincoln had left.[104]

Epilogue

"History dwells on results"

There was still a thorn in Jessie Benton Frémont's bosom, what her best biographer called "a brooding anger." Just as she had ignored the pleas of a dying Stephen Watts Kearny for a deathbed forgiveness of his vendetta against her husband during the Mexican War, Jessie never forgave Abraham Lincoln for what she considered the president's disgraceful treatment of her husband during the Civil War. Even a dozen years after the war, when the subject of emancipation came up, she would say, "I have a tale to tell, but the manner of Mr. Lincoln's death bars the truth at present." Another sixteen years on, she asserted, "Mr. Lincoln's cruel death silenced much truth, and since then he has been shaped and exalted into such 'a faultless monster as the world ne'er saw,'" quoting the Duke of Buckingham.[1]

Lincoln was not the only target of her wrath. "In the evening called on General Frémont, who had retired," Indiana radical congressman George W. Julian wrote in his diary on April 7, 1865. "But had a long talk with Jessie, and Lilly, the daughter, a charming girl. Jessie rages at all sorts of people, especially at Greeley, Beecher, and Garrison. According to her, the General was shamefully betrayed by pretended radical and anti-Lincoln men who deserted him in time of greatest need, after encouraging him to stand in the breach."[2]

A week later Lincoln was dead, and Julian's assessment of his fellow radicals' view was unsparing. "Their hostility towards Lincoln's policy of conciliation and contempt for his weakness were undisguised; and the universal feeling among radical men here is that his death is a god send." Most northern people saw it differently. Lincoln was now a martyr. Frémont was just a failed general.[3]

William Webb, a slave who had conducted secret pro-Frémont meetings in Mississippi during the presidential campaign of 1856, believed that God had sent John C. Frémont to deliver "the idea of freedom to the colored people."

Despite Frémont's failure to capture the presidency, Webb told his fellow enslaved Americans after the election, he still embodied that idea. "Frémont was a small light," Webb told them, "and it would keep burning till it was spread over the whole world."[4]

Frémont's Missouri emancipation proclamation helped keep that light burning during the early days of the Civil War, when the step-by-step progression toward freedom that would begin in spring 1862 was by no means certain. Abraham Lincoln eventually turned Frémont's small light into the bonfire of emancipation. "History dwells on results rather than the means employed," Charles Sumner wrote of emancipation in the months after Lincoln's assassination. Lincoln got results. Frémont did not.[5]

Lincoln's cautious approach to emancipation and his similar approach to the border states worked. These efforts kept the border states in the Union and, eventually, freed the slaves. The fact that these approaches worked, however, does not mean they were the only ones that might have. In any case, Kentucky and Missouri had to be fought for and won to the northern cause over three bloody years following their supposed securing to the Union by the end of 1861. Ample evidence exists to support alternative conclusions that history never had a chance to test. As William Gienapp concluded, "In broad terms, Lincoln's policies were fairly successful in Maryland, produced a mixed record in Kentucky, and were largely a failure in Missouri."[6]

We'll never know whether launching a more aggressive war sooner, including an earlier deployment of military emancipation, would have worked as well or better. Many contemporaries believed it would. There are legitimate arguments on both sides. In Frémont's case, military failure tainted other accomplishments. New heroes—Ulysses S. Grant, William T. Sherman, and the martyred Lincoln—replaced those of the prewar generation. Frémont's heroic days were two decades in the past; by the end of the war, they were overshadowed by his dismal record in battle and two electoral defeats. No general starved of men, arms, and supplies as Frémont was could have accomplished the goals Lincoln set out for him in Missouri or Virginia. But Frémont's incompetence made an untenable situation worse.

His successes are lost in the cloud of defeat. His innovations with the Western Sanitary Commission saved hundreds or thousands of lives. He gave Grant his first field command, relaunching the military career of the general most responsible for Union victory. He commissioned the gunboats that helped conquer Forts Henry and Donelson. Eventually, Frémont's vision of a movement down the Mississippi was accomplished by his appointee, Grant. Frémont finally filed his official report on the 1862 Virginia campaign on December 30, 1865. Comparing his closing word on the war to the best-selling expedition reports cowritten by Jessie, it's clear that her guiding editorial hand was missing from the Virginia report. Instead of highlighting his successes, the report was littered with excuses and dry with the details of defeat.[7]

Long after the war, Confederate-turned-Republican James Longstreet derided "such men as Shields, Banks, and Frémont" while calling Lincoln "without doubt, the greatest man of rebellion times, the one matchless among forty millions for the peculiar difficulties of the period." Lincoln's successes and failures as commander in chief were debated during the war and have been debated endlessly by historians since. Students of the Civil War can choose which side they're on and find a historian who agrees with them. But neither Frémont nor Lincoln demonstrated much inherent aptitude for military strategy or administrative organization. One recent study, by Elizabeth Brown Pryor, offers a devastating critique of Lincoln's performance, largely using the words of his contemporaries. "Had Lincoln shown true military capacity," she wrote, "the great majority would have cheered. As it was, their confidence was destroyed by bureaucratic chaos, miscasting, and derelict discipline from the Executive Mansion." Of all the miscasting, Frémont's was perhaps the most egregious example.[8]

"A WIDE AND HONORABLE FAME"
Justice would have dictated that Jessie Benton Frémont deliver the keynote address at the unveiling of a statue honoring her father in Lafayette Park in St. Louis on May 27, 1868. The statue itself was cast in bronze by Harriet Hosmer, an American woman living in Rome. But politics and patriarchy trumped justice. Instead, Frank Blair was invited to give the speech, with Jessie and John Frémont sitting by on a platform specially constructed for the event, as forty thousand people looked on. With the Frémonts in attendance, Blair had to be careful. He saw the speech as an opportunity to polish his credentials as a national candidate for the Democrats. He was a possible presidential or vice presidential candidate that year. He enlisted Montgomery and his father to help write his speech, calling on Francis Preston Blair's decades of friendship with Thomas Hart Benton.

Before the speech came the unveiling, in which Jessie played the lead part. In a "simple but impressive" ceremony, Jessie climbed the three steps up to the granite pedestal on which was inscribed Benton's famous quote in praise of westward expansion: "There is the East—there is India." She pulled a tassel breaking the fastenings holding in place a muslin robe veiling the bronze statue of Benton, in the form of a Roman orator. An honor guard sent by Edwin Stanton fired a thirty-gun salute, one for each year Benton served in the Senate.

Blair's pedestrian speech went off without a hitch. He praised Benton as "Jackson's right hand in the great contest that liberated the Government and the people from the thraldom of the banks," for his support of the soon-to-be-completed transcontinental railroad, and for his vision in promoting westward expansion. He magnanimously nodded to Frémont's central role in the latter, acknowledging the young lieutenant to whom "belongs the merit of the early and most important explorations" and praising "the additions which he made to science and geographical knowledge," which "gave him a wide and honorable fame." All was political and pleasant. But other than a short notice in *Harper's Weekly* nearly a month after the event, the speech did Blair little good but no harm. Two months later, he accepted the vice presidential nomination on the Democratic ticket.[9]

The election of 1868 was a vindication for the Frémonts. Republican Ulysses S. Grant, the man Frémont had raised to his first field command, was elected president of the United States. His running mate was Schuyler Colfax, who had vehemently defended Frémont's emancipation proclamation and urged Lincoln to put him back in the field. On the losing side as Democrat Horatio Seymour's running mate was Blair, always a Republican of convenience. In the late days of the war, Blair had helped form a regiment of black troops among Georgia refugees. But he never came to see blacks as entitled to the same civil and political rights as whites, never gave up on colonization, and, when the war was over, had—perhaps inevitably—defected from the cause and signed up with many of his former enemies in the Democratic Party.[10]

Blair's political misfortunes might have been satisfying, but they did the Frémonts no practical good. Despite repeated appeals, both legal and political, the Frémonts were never compensated for government seizure of Black Point, a loss worth tens of thousands of dollars to the family at a time when they could have used the money.[11]

They purchased a mansion, Pocaho, about twenty-five miles up the Hudson River from New York City. Their lifestyle included lavish entertaining and travel to Europe. But it couldn't last. Frémont had no head for business, and he frittered their fortune away on speculative investments, principally in railroads. In the late 1860s, he got involved with another set of unscrupulous men happy to use his fame to help make their fortunes. When a French bond deal intended to prop up one of his railroad investments went sour, criminal charges followed. Frémont pleaded ignorance of any wrongdoing but was convicted by a French court and sentenced to five years in prison in absentia. The Panic of 1873 did away with what little of Frémont's fortune wasn't already gone, largely due to the failure of nearly a hundred railroads. Over the next few years, the Frémonts sold land in California, personal treasures, and, eventually, their Hudson River estate. Jessie turned to writing to support the family.[12]

In 1878, President Rutherford B. Hayes—who had served under Frémont during the Civil War and was instrumental in renaming the town of Frémont, Ohio—appointed John governor of the Arizona Territory, at a salary of $2,000 a year. It was a booming time in the desert, reviving Frémont's interest in mining, but no new fortune was made. He served three undistinguished years and then moved back to New York.[13]

"ALWAYS YOUR OLD FRIEND"

Elizabeth Blair Lee's anger toward Jessie had turned to pity as early as October 1861. "Jessies part in this matter has disappointed me sorely—Things which I had learnt to believe about her husband made me think him unreliable—but only added to my pity & affection for her—I am now convinced that in countenancing & covering his sins she has shared & been degraded by them—& yet I can see in her efforts to elevate him & excite his ambition a struggle to win him from his grovelling nature."[14]

Two years later, she again claimed, privately to her husband, that "in matters of feeling I am unhappily tenacious for I do not cease to love those who ever maltreat me—Even Jessie & Minna [Montgomery's wife] retain warm places in my heart a fact I'll confess to none but you." But she had no interest in reviving the friendship. "I have no bitterness or ill will towards them . . . & yet I hope never to encounter" either of the Frémonts again. After the war, Lizzie had been more forgiving of and sympathetic toward Varina Davis than she had toward Jessie. She wrote warmly about Confederate generals Joseph Johnston and Stonewall Jackson but not of John.[15]

Lizzie's husband stayed in contact with Jessie, who confided to him in fall 1865 that "the color was taken out of my life in that hard first year of the war." In her occasional letters to him, she always included family details, assuming Lee showed the letters to Lizzie. Later, Lee helped Charley Frémont gain admission to the Naval Academy. But it would be nearly two decades after the war before the two old friends would reconcile.[16]

In July 1883, the Frémonts were living in an apartment on West 59th Street, overlooking Central Park. Word had gotten to Elizabeth Blair Lee of their straitened circumstances, and she at last decided to visit her friend. They avoided old feuds and new travails and talked mostly of their families, their children and grandchildren, and their health. Jessie followed up the visit with a letter. "It was so good of you to come and see me—every way," she wrote. She recalled the Blairs' tender care of her at the time of her infant daughter's death in 1853. And she touched on the divisions that had separated them, without resorting to bitterness or regret, and of the vicissitudes of her own life without self-pity. "Life narrows and grows chill when one is as transplanted as I have been time after time—it was more to me than you who have 'lived among your own people' can realize, to have the earlier time of unbroken home and friends brought livingly to me." She signed the letter, "always your old friend."[17]

"ALL THE QUALITIES OF GENIUS EXCEPT ABILITY"

In the aftermath of Lincoln's revocation of Frémont's emancipation order in September 1861, an old acquaintance of Frémont's wrote to Lincoln in support of the general, his praise leavened considerably by experience. Charles Homer had invested in Mariposa and lost his shirt, and he had other business dealings with Frémont. "J. C. Frémont, is courteous—humane—cautious—energetic—truthful—brave! Resembling Joan of Arc—an enthusiast in all things:—like her, Genl. Frémont, should be made servicable to his country." But, Homer warned Lincoln, "history, has overrated his abilities. . . . I would not trust Gen. Frémont with money:—but, I would follow his fortunes in the field and there: and for the field: aid him with money, or with blood."[18]

In the preface to her unpublished memoir, Jessie Benton Frémont wrote, "To no one fact in his eventful life, was General Frémont more profoundly indifferent than to that of the systematic misrepresentation of which he was made the object." He was made the object of many representations, mis- or otherwise, during his life, and more would follow. An early biographer's assessment was that Frémont's "entire career was built largely on a series of circumstances over which he exercised little or no control." As a constant protégé of powerful men, as a tool in the hands of more savvy politicians, as a lamb in the wolf-driven world of business, and as the weaker vessel in a marriage to a more intelligent and more ambitious woman, Frémont never lived up to his promise.[19]

Despite failing to live up to that promise on the battlefields of the Civil War, Frémont was able to maintain his hold on the public imagination as a symbol of the radicals' desire for Lincoln to move with greater purpose against slavery. "Thousands of young men in Illinois, Missouri and the Western States generally would never have volunteered but for him," Gustave Koerner believed. And not just in the West. Among those eager to join Frémont was Robert Gould Shaw, scion of an affluent abolitionist family in Massachusetts who would miss his chance to serve under Frémont but would win glory as the colonel of the famed 54th Massachusetts Regiment of black troops.[20]

Benjamin Grierson, an officer serving at Cairo, Illinois, in 1861, believed that if Frémont had been more successful in battle, his political ideas would have gained currency even sooner with the powers that be and might well have brought emancipation sooner and shortened the war.

> Had he been as capable of equipping, commanding, and maneuvering an army in the field, as he was in grasping the keynote of the problem, which was finally solved by striking off the shackles of nearly 4,000,000 slaves . . . the end of the terrible conflict might have been hastened. . . . Although premature and inoperative, his bold attempt to confiscate the property and free the slaves of those found in arms against the government of the United States was correct in theory, as subsequently fully demonstrated, and possibly might have been successfully inaugurated at an earlier date than that established by the Emancipation Proclamation.[21]

That was what if. What actually was, using Sumner's standard, was that Lincoln succeeded where Frémont came up short. Lincoln was a great leader. Frémont was a flawed subordinate. In the great cause to which both men were dedicated, they were far from the only actors. "The slaves who defected to Union army lines initiated the process of emancipation," wrote the historian of abolition Manisha Sinah. Ben Butler gave their action military sanction. Congress, led by Lyman Trumbull, gave it legislative voice. Frémont then failed as an emancipator but succeeded in becoming a potent symbol of military emancipation at a moment when the North needed such a figure. Abolitionists drove public opinion toward supporting military emancipation—and, finally, Lincoln. "Viewed from the genuine abolition ground, Mr. Lincoln seemed tardy, cold, dull, and indifferent," Frederick Douglass said long after the war. "But measuring him by the sentiment of his country, a sentiment he was bound as a statesman to consult, he was swift, zealous, radical, and determined."[22]

Late in life, Frémont published his memoirs—mostly a compilation of the reports he and Jessie had produced of his first three expeditions. Philosopher Josiah Royce called the book "disappointingly unenlightening as to what we most wished to know." But Frémont included a closing note that looked back on his happier days as an explorer. "No treachery lurked behind the majesty of the mountain or lay hidden in the hot glare of the inhospitable plain," he wrote.

"And though sometimes the struggle was hard, it was an honest one and simple; and I had my own free will how to combat it." Better, he seemed to be saying, to just leave it there. "I close the page because my path of life led out from among the grand and lovely features of nature, and its pure and wholesome air, into the poisoned atmosphere and jarring circumstances of conflict among men, made subtle and malignant by clashing interests," a world Frémont spent half his life in but was never fully of.[23]

John C. Frémont died on July 13, 1890. His most perceptive obituary was written by Royce, twice that rarest of things in the nineteenth century, an American-born philosopher and a native Californian. "This personal effectiveness of his manner was itself a quality such as ought to have graced, a political genius, a born leader of men," Royce wrote. "In fact, one may say that General Frémont possessed all the qualities of genius except ability."[24]

When Jessie Benton Frémont died in Los Angeles eleven years later, on December 27, 1902, newspapers published lengthy tributes. The *St. Louis Republic* and *Lexington Intelligencer* in Missouri ran front-page features. Galusha Grow, who had defeated Frank Blair for Speaker of the House in 1861, remembered, "When she took up the foils it was a worthy conversational opponent on whom she did not score." Abraham Lincoln could attest to that ability personally. She had led, the *San Francisco Call* wrote with great understatement, "an eventful life." The *Washington Times* went one better, asserting, "Possibly no woman in this country has passed a more eventful life than Jessie Benton Frémont."[25]

During that eventful life, the vast expanse of the American continent often separated the Frémonts. In death it would again, with John buried in Rockland Cemetery in Orangeburg, New York, overlooking the Hudson, and Jessie's ashes interred at Rosedale Cemetery, twenty-eight hundred miles away in Los Angeles. Nearly equidistant between husband and wife, in John C. Frémont City Park in Frémont, Nebraska, stands a statue, erected in 1921—of Abraham Lincoln.

ACKNOWLEDGMENTS

I BEGIN BY ACKNOWLEDGING MY DEBT TO THE COUNTLESS SCHOLARS AND authors who have studied and written about Abraham Lincoln, John C. Frémont, and Jessie Benton Frémont. They proved invaluable pathfinders for my project.

I extend my thanks to the librarians and archivists who help make historical research a joy. In particular, I'd like to thank Lauren Menzies of the Society of California Pioneers; Dean Smith at the Bancroft Library, University of California; Karen Needles, director of the Lincoln Archives Digital Project; Sara Quashnie of the William L. Clements Library at the University of Michigan; Dennis Northcott of the Missouri Historical Society; and Alaa Aldeen Kayali of the Houghton Library at Harvard.

A special thank-you goes to Teri Barnett, Matthew Deihl, Meghan Harmon, Michelle Miller, and Steven Ward of the Abraham Lincoln Presidential Library and to Fran Lower of the Moweaqua Public Library. Like Santa Claus, every time I asked for something, they delivered.

A shout-out to Jon Lauck for indulging my varied and continuing interest in John C. Frémont.

Thanks to Glenn LaFantasie, for sharing the Frémont chapter of his upcoming book on Lincoln and Grant and publishing an excerpt from this book in the *Journal of the Abraham Lincoln Association*, and to Michael Conlin, for reading a portion of the manuscript.

This book would not have been possible without the good folks at Stackpole. Thanks especially to Dave Reisch, Stephanie Otto, Patricia Stevenson, and Jennifer Kelland.

I've written millions of words in my life and still haven't come up with the right ones to fully thank Arwen Bicknell—faultless friend, loving wife, ruthless editor.

This book is dedicated to our son Thomas, who, unlike John C. Frémont, possesses all the qualities of genius, *including* ability.

NOTES

INTRODUCTION
1. Foote, *The Civil War*, 1:156.
2. Conway, *Autobiography, Memories and Experiences*, 380.

PROLOGUE
1. Blair and Tarshis, *Lincoln's Constant Ally*, 200. The full text of Baker's speech is included in an appendix.

2. Blair and Tarshis, *Lincoln's Constant Ally*, 77; Herr, *Jessie Benton Frémont*, 316; *Daily Alta California*, October 27, 1860.

3. Blair and Tarshis, *Lincoln's Constant Ally*, 110, 207; E. R. Kennedy, *Contest for California in 1861*, 150; *San Francisco Bulletin*, October 27, 1860; Elizabeth Benton Frémont, *Recollections of Elizabeth Benton Frémont*, 119; Rather, *Jessie Frémont at Black Point*, 62–64.

4. Villard, *Lincoln on the Eve of '61*, 44.

5. Blair and Tarshis, *Lincoln's Constant Ally*, 207.

6. *Chicago Tribune*, November 17, 1860.

7. JBF, *Far West Sketches*, 92; C. C. Phillips, *Jessie Benton Frémont*, 228; Winks, *Frederick Billings*, 124.

8. Starr, *Americans and the California Dream*, 369.

9. For Baker's spending habits, see Matheny, "A Modern Knight Errant," 30.

10. Etulain, "Abraham Lincoln, Political Founding Father of the American West," 8.

11. JBF, "Great Events," a typescript memoir with manuscript revisions written by JBF and son Frank Frémont, in the Frémont Family Papers, BL, 216.

12. Greeley, *An Overland Journey from New York to San Francisco in the Summer of 1859*, 268; *Daily National Democrat*, December 28, 1860. Frémont had failed to carry California in 1856, winning only 19 percent of the vote. Lincoln won 32.2 percent, a half-percentage-point margin over Stephen Douglas.

13. JBF, "Great Events," Frémont Family Papers, BL, 257; Denton, *Passion and Principle*, 268; JBF, *Far West Sketches*, 28, 42; *Nevada Democrat*, December 13, 1860; *Daily National Democrat*, November 22 and December 12 and 15, 1860; Chaffin, *Pathfinder*, 455.

14. C. C. Phillips, *Jessie Benton Frémont*, 233.

15. Bicknell, "A Stream of Clear, Swift-Running Water," 166.

16. Walpole, *Four Years in the Pacific*, 215.

17. Polk, *Diary of a President, 1845–1849*, 244.

18. JBF to James K. Polk, September 21, 1847, JBF, *Letters of Jessie Benton Frémont*, 35–36; Polk, *Diary of a President, 1845–1849*, 240–241, 271–272, 300–303. For JBF's version of the conflict with Kearny and the court-martial, see JBF, "Great Events," Frémont Family Papers, BL, 36–75.

19. For the cannibalism charge, see Roberts, *A Newer World*, 228–230.

20. Denton, *Passion and Principle*, 270; Stephen A. Douglas to James Washington Sheahan, October 6, 1856, Douglas, *The Letters of Stephen A. Douglas*, 68.

21. Herr, *Jessie Benton Frémont*, 277.

22. JBF, "Great Events," Frémont Family Papers, BL, 214.

23. *Daily Alta California*, November 1, 1859, quoted in Herbon, "Public Wife," 195; Horner, *Lincoln and Greeley*, 167; Rowan and Primm, *Germans for a Free Missouri*, 101, 106, 110; Bates, *Diary of Edward Bates*, 126.

24. *San Francisco Bulletin*, September 10, 1860.

CHAPTER ONE

1. Nicolay and Hay, *Abraham Lincoln*, 3:347.

2. Charles Billinghurst to Lincoln, November 14, 1860, Abraham Lincoln Papers, LOC.

3. See D. K. Goodwin, *Team of Rivals*.

4. Leonard Swett to Lincoln, November 30, 1860, Abraham Lincoln Papers, LOC; Hannibal Hamlin to Lincoln, November 27, 1860, *CW*, 4:145.

5. Alexander McClure to Lincoln, December 29, 1860, Abraham Lincoln Papers, LOC.

6. Miers, *Lincoln Day by Day*, 297; Lincoln to Nathaniel P. Paschall, November 16, 1861, *CW*, 4:140.

7. *New York Herald*, November 22, 1860; Lincoln to Lyman Trumbull, December 10, 1860, *CW*, 4:150.

8. Nicolay and Hay, *Abraham Lincoln*, 3:246.

9. Parrish, *Frank Blair*, 69, 88–89; Stevens, "Lincoln and Missouri," 74; Lyman Trumbull to Lincoln, December 18, 1861, Abraham Lincoln Papers, LOC; Covington, "The Camp Jackson Affair," 198. Regarding Frémont and the Blairs, see Bicknell, *Lincoln's Pathfinder*, 26–35; regarding Banks, see Holzer, *Lincoln President-Elect*, 143; also see Hannibal Hamlin to Lincoln, December 8, 1861; Lincoln to Hannibal Hamlin, December 24, 1861, *CW*, 4:147, 161.

10. Welles, *Diary of Gideon Welles*, 1:82.

11. Nicolay and Hay, *Abraham Lincoln*, 3:246; Leonard Swett to Thurlow Weed, December 10, 1860, Barnes, *Life of Thurlow Weed*, 2:301–302.

12. Lincoln to Hannibal Hamlin, December 8, 1860, *CW*, 4:147; Hamlin, *Life and Times of Hannibal Hamlin*, 372–373.

13. For recent interpretations of Lincoln's preinaugural activities, see Holzer, *Lincoln President-Elect*; Widmer, *Lincoln on the Verge*.

14. *New York Herald*, December 9, 1860; Henry Adams to Charles Francis Adams Jr., December 18, 1860, H. Adams, *Letters of Henry Adams*, 66.

15. Lincoln to William Kellogg, December 11, 1860, *CW*, 4:150.

16. Lyman Trumbull to Lincoln, December 4, 1860, Nicolay and Hay, *Abraham Lincoln*, 3:254, 257.

17. John Bigelow to Preston King, January 14, 1861, Bigelow, *Retrospections of an Active Life*, 1:324.

18. Bates, *Diary of Edward Bates*, 157.

19. William Fessenden to undetermined, December 1860, Fessenden, *Life and Public Services of William Pitt Fessenden*, 1:116.

20. Richard Corwine to Lincoln, December 14, 1860, Abraham Lincoln Papers, LOC.

21. Villard, *Lincoln on the Eve of '61*, 24; William Cullen Bryant to Lincoln, December 25, 1860, *CW*, 4:164 (annotation).

22. Lincoln to Thurlow Weed, December 17, 1860, *CW*, 4:150.

23. Barnes, *Life of Thurlow Weed*, 2:292–295; *New York Herald*, December 25, 1860; Procter, *Lincoln and the Convention of 1860*, 6–7.

24. Lincoln to William H. Seward, December 29, 1860, *CW*, 4:164.

25. Pratt, "Simon Cameron's Fight for a Place in Lincoln's Cabinet," 6; Villard, *Lincoln on the Eve of '61*, 45; Lincoln to Hannibal Hamlin, November 26, 1860, *CW*, 4:145; Miers, *Lincoln Day by Day*, 299; Kahan, *Amiable Scoundrel*, 153–155; Pratt, "Simon Cameron's Fight for a Place in Lincoln's Cabinet," 1, 9–10.

26. Kahan, *Amiable Scoundrel*, 151; Bates, *Diary of Edward Bates*, 170.

27. *New York Herald*, January 1, 1861; *Frank Leslie's Weekly*, January 19, 1861.

28. George Eckert to Lincoln, November 5, 1860, Abraham Lincoln Papers, LOC; Thaddeus Stevens to Salmon Chase, February 3, 1861, Nicklason, "The Civil War Contracts Committee," 234; Lincoln to Simon Cameron, January 3, 1861, *CW*, 4:169–170.

29. Edward Bates to Schuyler Colfax, December 24, 1860, Edward Bates Papers, ALPL.

30. Elizabeth Blair Lee to Samuel Phillips Lee, January 12 and 21, 1861, E. B. Lee, *Wartime Washington*, 23, 27; Foote, *The Civil War*, 1:4.

31. Francis Preston Blair to Lincoln, January 14, 1861, Abraham Lincoln Papers, LOC.

32. Lincoln to Simon Cameron (unsent), January 21, 1861, *CW*, 4:177.

33. *New York Herald*, January 19, 1861; "Remarks to a Pennsylvania Delegation," *CW*, 4:179–180; Fehrenbacher and Fehrenbacher, *Recollected Words of Abraham Lincoln*, 333.

34. Villard, *Lincoln on the Eve of '61*, 62; Horace Greeley to Lincoln, February 6, 1861, Abraham Lincoln Papers, LOC; Elizabeth Blair Lee to Samuel Phillips Lee, February 6, 1861, E. B. Lee, *Wartime Washington*, 32; Fehrenbacher and Fehrenbacher, *Recollected Words of Abraham Lincoln*, 329.

35. Lincoln to Andrew Curtin, February 4, 1861, *CW*, 4:181; Pratt, "Simon Cameron's Fight for a Place in Lincoln's Cabinet," 10; Kahan, *Amiable Scoundrel*, 155.

36. Burlingame, *Abraham Lincoln*, 2:56–57; Lincoln to William H. Seward, March 4, 1861, *CW*, 4:273.

37. Lincoln to William H. Seward, March 11 and 18, 1861, *CW*, 4:281, 292; William H. Seward to Lincoln, March 11, 1861, Abraham Lincoln Papers, LOC; *Daily Alta California*, January 10, 1861; *New York Herald*, February 28, 1861; Denton, *Passion and Principle*, 282; Hannibal Hamlin to Lincoln, December 24, 1860, Hamlin, *Life and Times of Hannibal Hamlin*, 373; Villard, *Lincoln on the Eve of '61*, 34.

38. Nicolay and Hay, *Abraham Lincoln*, 3:373; DuBois and Mathews, *Galusha A. Grow*, 264.

39. *Daily National Democrat*, December 23, 1860.

40. JBF to Thomas Starr King, early 1861, JBF, *Letters of Jessie Benton Frémont*, 233; *National Republican*, January 21, 1861; Bell, "Trenor Park," 166; Winks, *Frederick Billings*, 123.

41. Chaffin, *Pathfinder*, 453–454; Denton, *Passion and Principle*, 287; Rolle, *John Charles Frémont*, 187–188; Winks, *Frederick Billings*, 123, 139; *New York Times*, February 27, 1861, lists Frémont, Corbett, "and child" on the passenger list of the steamship *Africa* bound from New York to Liverpool.

42. JBF, "Great Events," Frémont Family Papers, BL, 219; *New York Herald*, February 21, 1861; C. C. Phillips, *Jessie Benton Frémont*, 234; Denton, *Passion and Principle*, 288; *National Republican*, March 1, 1861.

43. Moran, *Journal of Benjamin Moran*, 1:788, 792, 812.

44. Rolle, *John Charles Frémont*, 188; Winks, *Frederick Billings*, 134, 137.

45. Dallas, *Diary of George Mifflin Dallas*, 442–443; Tuffnell, "Expatriate Foreign Relations," 637.

46. Charles Francis Adams Civil War Diary, May 15, 1861, MassHS; Moran, *Journal of Benjamin Moran*, 1:811, 2:850; Procter, *Lincoln and the Convention of 1860*, 5.

47. Parker, *Henry Stevens of Vermont*, 233, 239; for the Humboldt library, see also JCF to Henry W. Stevens, September 7, 1874, Henry W. Stevens Papers, WLC.

48. Parker, *Henry Stevens of Vermont*, 239–243; Winks, *Frederick Billings*, 136.

49. William Dayton to William Seward, May 22, 1861, Message of the President of the United States to the Two Houses of Congress, at the Commencement of the Second Session of the Thirty-Seventh Congress, Office of the Historian, U.S. Department of State.

50. *New York Herald*, June 14, 1861.

51. *National Republican*, June 17, 1861; *New York Tribune*, June 14, 1861; C. Goodwin, *John Charles Frémont*, 214; *Christian Recorder*, June 22, 1861.

52. Charles Francis Adams Civil War Diary, May 25, 1861, MassHS; JCF to Francis P. Blair, May 24, 1861, C. Goodwin, *John Charles Frémont*, 215.

53. Charles Francis Adams to Charles Francis Adams Jr., June 14, 1861, Ford, *A Cycle of Adams Letters*, 11; Charles Francis Adams Civil War Diary, June 4, 1861, MassHS.

54. Charles Francis Adams Civil War Diary, June 7, 1861, MassHS; Henry Shelton Sanford to William H. Seward, June 4, 1861, *O.R.*, 3:1:247; Shannon, *Organization and Administration of the Union Army*, 1:114; Tuffnell, "Expatriate Foreign Relations," 645.

55. Charles Francis Adams to William H. Seward, June 7, 1861, *O.R.*, 3:1:293; Huse, *The Supplies for the Confederate Army*, 23.

56. William Dayton to William H. Seward, June (no date), 1861, Office of the Historian, U.S. Department of State, https://history.state.gov/historicaldocuments/frus1861/d127; JCF to Francis P. Blair, May 25, 1861, C. Goodwin, *John Charles Frémont*, 215; Bulloch, *The Secret Service of the Confederate States in Europe*, 48–53; Huse, *The Supplies for the Confederate Army*, 25.

57. Huse, *The Supplies for the Confederate Army*, 15.

58. Huse, *The Supplies for the Confederate Army*, 22, 28–29, 38.

59. Simon Cameron to George Schuyler, July 29, 1861, *O.R.*, 3:1:363.
60. *Christian Recorder*, June 8, 1861.
61. C. L. Davis, *Arming the Union*, v, 63.
62. *New York Tribune*, May 23, 1861; *Washington Evening Star*, June 27, 1861.
63. JBF, "Great Events," Frémont Family Papers, BL, 217.
64. C. C. Phillips, *Jessie Benton Frémont*, 231–232.
65. Thomas Starr King to Randolph Ryer, March 10, 1861, Matthews, *The Golden State in the Civil War*, 88–89; Wendte, *Thomas Starr King*, 162. For the deer hunting trip, see Thomas Starr King to Thomas B. Fox, May 11, 1861, Wendte, *Thomas Starr King*, 90.
66. JBF to Thomas Starr King, early 1861, JBF, *Letters of Jessie Benton Frémont*, 233.
67. JBF to Thomas Starr King, January 16, 1861, JBF, *Letters of Jessie Benton Frémont*, 234.
68. JBF to Elizabeth Blair Lee, March 10, 1861, JBF, *Letters of Jessie Benton Frémont*, 238.
69. *Daily Alta California*, February 26, 1861; Herbon, "Public Wife," 187.
70. *Daily Alta California*, February 26 and 27, 1861.
71. *Daily Alta California*, February 27, 1861; JBF to Elizabeth Blair Lee, March 10, 1861, JBF, *Letters of Jessie Benton Frémont*, 238.
72. Herr, *Jessie Benton Frémont*, 318; Herbon, "Public Wife," 202.
73. *Daily Alta California*, March 2, 1861.
74. JBF to Elizabeth Blair Lee, March 10, 1861, JBF, *Letters of Jessie Benton Frémont*, 238.
75. Herr, *Jessie Benton Frémont*, 319.
76. C. C. Phillips, *Jessie Benton Frémont*, 232; JBF to Edward F. Beale, May 21, 1861, JBF, *Letters of Jessie Benton Frémont*, 239; JBF, "Great Events," Frémont Family Papers, BL, 218.
77. Matthews, *The Golden State in the Civil War*, 75. 135; JBF to Elizabeth Blair Lee, June 14, 1860, JBF, *Letters of Jessie Benton Frémont*, 230; *New York Herald*, July 4, 1861.
78. JBF, "Great Events," Frémont Family Papers, BL, 218.
79. JBF, "Great Events," Frémont Family Papers, BL, 218; *Washington Evening Star*, July 17, 1861.
80. JCF, "In Command in Missouri," 1:278.
81. *Christian Recorder*, June 8, 1861.
82. *Frank Leslie's Weekly*, June 8, 1861.
83. *New York Herald*, May 8, June 3, and June 4, 1861.
84. Burlingame, *Lincoln's Journalist*, 84.
85. Koerner, *Memoirs of Gustave Koerner*, 2:162, 169.

Chapter Two

1. Parrish, *Frank Blair*, 64.
2. Elizabeth Blair Lee to Samuel Phillips Lee, January 12, 1861, E. B. Lee, *Wartime Washington*, 23.
3. Rollins, "Some Impressions of Frank P. Blair," 352; Brooks, *Mr. Lincoln's Washington*, 309; Parrish, *Frank Blair*, 23–24, 40–41, 45.

4. Rollins, "Some Impressions of Frank P. Blair," 353; Sherman, *Memoirs of General W. T. Sherman*, 558–559; William T. Sherman to John Sherman, April 18, 1861, Sherman, *Sherman's Civil War*, 73.

5. Bull and Bull, *Missouri Brothers in Gray*, 90–91.

6. C. Phillips, *Missouri's Confederate*, 235.

7. Parrish, *Frank Blair*, 90–93; *JCCW: Missouri*, 154; C. Phillips, *Damned Yankee*, 127.

8. C. Phillips, *Damned Yankee*, 145.

9. Kirkpatrick, "Missouri on the Eve of the Civil War," 103.

10. Claiborne Jackson to Simon Cameron, April 17, 1861, *O.R.*, 3:1:82–83; Gerteis, *Civil War St. Louis*, 141.

11. C. Phillips, *Damned Yankee*, 160; G. R. Adams, *General William S. Harney*, 227; *History of Clay and Platte Counties*, 197.

12. William T. Sherman to John Sherman, January 16 and February 1, 1861, Sherman, *Sherman's Civil War*, 40–41, 51; William T. Sherman to John Sherman, March 22 and April 8, 1861, Sherman, *Sherman's Civil War*, 64, 68; William T. Sherman to John Sherman, April 18, 1861, Sherman, *Sherman's Civil War*, 70.

13. Simon Cameron to Nathaniel Lyon, April 30, 1861, *O.R.*, 1:1:675; C. Phillips, *Damned Yankee*, 82–83; Parrish, "General Nathaniel Lyon," 1–2.

14. Kelso, *Bloody Engagements*, 9–10.

15. William T. Sherman to Thomas Ewing Jr., April 26, 1861, Sherman, *Sherman's Civil War*, 76; Covington, "The Camp Jackson Affair," 197.

16. William T. Sherman to John Sherman, January 16, 1861, Sherman, *Sherman's Civil War*, 40; William T. Sherman to Ellen Sherman, January 20, 1861, Sherman, *Sherman's Civil War*, 45; Bull and Bull, *Missouri Brothers in Gray*, 6–7; Covington, "The Camp Jackson Affair," 203.

17. C. Phillips, *Missouri's Confederate*, 238; William T. Sherman to John Sherman, April 22 and 25, 1861, Sherman, *Sherman's Civil War*, 73–74.

18. Covington, "The Camp Jackson Affair," 204; Parrish, *Frank Blair*, 100–101; C. Phillips, *Damned Yankee*, 182–183.

19. U. S. Grant to Jesse Root Grant, May 6, 1861, Simon, *Papers of Ulysses S. Grant*, 2:21; Grant to Julia Dent Gant, May 6 and 10, 1861, Simon, *Papers of Ulysses S. Grant*, 2:24, 2:28; Peckham, *Lyon and Missouri*, 145–146; "Report of Captain Nathaniel Lyon," *O.R.*, 1:3:5.

20. Covington, "The Camp Jackson Affair," 209; Bull and Bull, *Missouri Brothers in Gray*, 12; Sherman, *Memoirs of General W. T. Sherman*, 190–192.

21. C. Phillips, *Damned Yankee*, 196.

22. Kirkpatrick, "Missouri in the Early Months of the Civil War," 241; C. Phillips, *Missouri's Confederate*, 252; William T. Sherman to Thomas Ewing Jr., May 11, 1861, Sherman, *Sherman's Civil War*, 80; Parrish, *Frank Blair*, 24; Parrish, "General Nathaniel Lyon," 12.

23. Lincoln to Frank Blair, May 18, 1861, *CW*, 4:372–373; G. R. Adams, *General William S. Harney*, 254.

24. William T. Sherman to John Sherman, May 20 and 24, 1861, Sherman, *Sherman's Civil War*, 87, 93; Lorenzo Thomas to William S. Harney (possibly drafted by Lincoln), May 27, 1861, *CW*, 4:387.

25. Snead, "First Year of the War in Missouri," 1:267; Parrish, *Frank Blair*, 11; Castel, *General Sterling Price*, 24.

26. Wilkie, *Missouri in 1861*, 83; Rorvig, "The Significant Skirmish," 141–145; Nathaniel Lyon to George McClellan, *O.R.*, 1:3:12.

27. *New York Times*, June 20, 1861; Rorvig, "The Significant Skirmish," 146–147; Snead, "First Year of the War in Missouri," 1:268.

28. C. Phillips, *Damned Yankee*, 228; Nevins, *Frémont*, 475.

29. Rowan and Primm, *Germans for a Free Missouri*, 270–271.

30. *Washington Evening Star*, June 29, 1861; *New York Herald*, June 29, 1861; Riddle, *Recollections of War Times*, 273.

31. W. C. Davis, *Battle at Bull Run*, 74; Elizabeth Blair Lee to Samuel Phillips Lee, June 30, 1861, E. B. Lee, *Wartime Washington*, 54; *New York Herald*, June 30, 1861; JBF to Thomas Starr King, July 20, 1861, JBF, *Letters of Jessie Benton Frémont*, 253; Schurz, *Reminiscences of Carl Schurz*, 2:341–342.

32. *National Republican*, July 2, 1861.

33. JCF, "In Command in Missouri," 1:278.

34. *New York Herald*, June 3, 1861; JCF, "In Command in Missouri," 1:278–279.

35. Lincoln to William Seward, July 3, 1861, *CW*, 4:420; Simpson, "Lincoln and His Political Generals," 64–65 and 76–77.

36. Elizabeth Blair Lee to Samuel Phillips Lee, July 11, 1861, E. B. Lee, *Wartime Washington*, 60.

37. Hollandsworth, *Pretense of Glory*, 51–52; William T. Sherman to Thomas Ewing Jr., June 3, 1861; Sherman to Thomas Ewing Sr., May 27, 1861, Sherman, *Sherman's Civil War*, 96–97; Thomas J. Jackson to Alexander Boteler, May 6, 1862, quoted in Robertson, *Stonewall Jackson*, 371.

38. *New York Herald*, July 6 and July 7, 1861.

39. Tuffnell, "Expatriate Foreign Relations," 645; Parker, *Henry Stevens of Vermont*, 241–242.

40. JCF, "In Command in Missouri," 1:279.

41. Browning, *Diary of Orville Hickman Browning*, 1:479; *New York Herald*, July 11, 1861.

42. Burlingame, *Abraham Lincoln*, 2:179.

43. Vasvary, *Lincoln's Hungarian Heroes*, 46; *New York Tribune*, July 13, 1861.

44. JBF, "Great Events," Frémont Family Papers, BL, 218; JBF to Thomas Starr King, July 20, 1861, JBF, *Letters of Jessie Benton Frémont*, 253.

45. *New York Herald*, July 17, 1861; Phisterer, *New York in the War of the Rebellion*, 3:2319.

46. F. Blair, *Frémont's Hundred Days in Missouri*, 8; E. D. Townsend to JCF, *O.R.*, 1:3:399; JCF to William Dennison, July 20, 1861, John C. Frémont Papers, ALPL; JCF to Owen Lovejoy, July 21, 1861, John C. Frémont Papers, ALPL.

47. *New York Herald,* July 24, 1861; JCF, "In Command in Missouri," 1:279; Elizabeth Benton Frémont, *Recollections of Elizabeth Benton Frémont,* 126; JBF to Elizabeth Blair Lee, July 27, 1861, JBF, *Letters of Jessie Benton Frémont,* 255.

48. John A. Palmer to Lyman Trumbull, July 24, 1861, Abraham Lincoln Papers, LOC; JCF, "In Command in Missouri," 1:279; JCF to Lincoln, August 5, 1861, Abraham Lincoln Papers, LOC.

49. Rowan and Primm, *Germans for a Free Missouri,* 274; *Missouri Democrat,* July 26, 1861; Rombauer, *The Union Cause in St. Louis,* 297. Paradoxically, the *Missouri Republican* was the Democratic Party organ in St. Louis; the *Missouri Democrat* was, after 1857, the Republican paper.

50. JBF, *Souvenirs of My Time,* 100; Elizabeth Blair Lee to Samuel Phillips Lee, July 11, 1861, E. B. Lee, *Wartime Washington,* 60; Joyaux, "The Tour of Prince Napoleon," 1957; JBF, *Far West Sketches,* 92.

51. Parrish, "Western Sanitary Commission," 21; Elizabeth Benton Frémont, *Recollections of Elizabeth Benton Frémont,* 126; Piston and Hatcher, *Wilson's Creek,* 41.

52. Parrish, *Frank Blair,* 57; Blum, "The Political and Military Activities of the German Element in St. Louis," 106; Bull and Bull, *Missouri Brothers in Gray,* 3n.

53. Blum, "The Political and Military Activities of the German Element in St. Louis," 103–104.

54. Blum, "The Political and Military Activities of the German Element in St. Louis," 106; Rowan and Primm, *Germans for a Free Missouri,* 103–104; William T. Sherman to Thomas Ewing Jr., May 17, 1861, Sherman, *Sherman's Civil War,* 85; Wilkie, *Missouri in 1861,* 72.

55. JBF, *Souvenirs of My Time,* 101; Sears, *George B. McClellan,* 100; George McClellan to Ellen McClellan, August 13, 1861, McClellan, *Civil War Papers of George B. McClellan,* 84; *JCCW: Missouri,* 71.

56. JBF, "Great Events," Frémont Family Papers, BL, 257.

57. JBF to Elizabeth Blair Lee, July 27, 1861, JBF, *Letters of Jessie Benton Frémont,* 255.

58. *Chicago Daily Democrat,* July 1, 1861.

59. Montgomery Blair to JCF, July 26, 1861, U.S. Congress, *Congressional Globe,* 37th Congress, 2nd Session, 1126.

60. "Memorandum of Military Policy Suggested by the Bull Run Defeat," *CW,* 457–458; Rombauer, *The Union Cause in St. Louis,* 300–302; Nevins, *Frémont,* 484.

61. Grierson, *A Just and Righteous Cause,* 44–45; Bellows, "Notes of a Preliminary Sanitary Survey," 1:5–6.

62. JCF to Lincoln, July 30, 1861, *O.R.,* 1:3:416; Nathaniel Lyon to Lorenzo Thomas, June 5, 1861, *O.R.,* 1:3:382; Johannsen, *Stephen A. Douglas,* 859. For analyses of Frémont's decision to defend Cairo, see Rombauer, *The Union Cause in St. Louis,* 303; Turkoly-Joczik, "Frémont and the Western Department," 373–374; J. C. Kelton to JCF, August 2, 1861, *O.R.,* 1:3:419.

63. Keyes, *Fifty Years' Observation,* 440.

64. Vasvary, *Lincoln's Hungarian Heroes,* 16, 18; "Resolutions of Sympathy with the Cause of Hungarian Freedom," *CW,* 2:62; N. Harris, *A Most Unsettled State,* 4.

65. John T. Fiala Papers, MHS; Vasvary, *Lincoln's Hungarian Heroes,* 43–46, 52, 85.

66. R. E. Miller, "Zagonyi," 177–178.

67. Koerner, *Memoirs of Gustave Koerner*, 2:172.

68. Montgomery Blair to JCF, July 15, 1861, *O.R.*, 1:3:395.

69. C. L. Davis, *Arming the Union*, 45, 47.

70. McKinstry, *Vindication of Brig. Gen. J. McKinstry*, 8, 15.

71. JCF to Lincoln, July 30, 1861, *O.R.*, 1:3–416–417; McKinstry, *Vindication of Brig. Gen. J. McKinstry*, 9.

72. McKinstry, *Vindication of Brig. Gen. J. McKinstry*, 10–12, 15; Koerner, *Memoirs of Gustave Koerner*, 2:170.

73. Salmon Chase to JCF, August 4, 1861, Chase, *The Salmon P. Chase Papers*, 3:85–86; *Chicago Tribune*, June 22, 1861.

74. Frederick Billings to JCF, August 1, 1861, Abraham Lincoln Papers, LOC; R. E. Miller, "Zagonyi," 175.

75. Rowan and Primm, *Germans for a Free Missouri*, 257; Bellows, "Notes of a Preliminary Sanitary Survey," 1:10, 15. Jefferson Barracks is now home to the Missouri Civil War Museum.

76. Elizabeth Blair Lee to Samuel Phillips Lee, August 20, 1861, E. B. Lee, *Wartime Washington*, 74.

77. Nevins, *Frémont*, 489–490; Burlingame, *Lincoln's Journalist*, 100; J. M. Cowell to JCF, September 23, 1861, LADP, http://www.lincolnarchives.us/cgi-bin/lincoln?a=d&d=&sf=&d=Drg94-164-c-8&page=1.

78. Nevins, *Frémont*, 489; Simon Cameron and Lincoln to Hamilton Gamble, August 3, 1861, *CW*, 4:470–471.

CHAPTER THREE

1. Salmon Chase to William P. Mellen, July 23, 1861; Salmon Chase to JCF, August 4, 1861, Chase, *The Salmon P. Chase Papers*, 3:79 and 3:85–86. Elizabeth Blair Lee noted Patterson's shortcomings before the battle, writing in a July 18 letter to her husband, "Johnston is too quick for old Patterson." Elizabeth Blair Lee to Samuel Phillips Lee, July 18, 1861, E. B. Lee, *Wartime Washington*, 64.

2. Piston and Hatcher, *Wilson's Creek*, 45, 74, 134.

3. Chase Diary, Charles M. Chase Papers, SHSM; Driscoll, *Rogue*, 48, 68; Wilkie, *Missouri in 1861*, 211.

4. George McClellan to Nathaniel Lyon, July 6, 1861; George McClellan to E. D. Townsend, July 6, 1861, McClellan, *Civil War Papers of George B. McClellan*, 48, 49; Nathaniel Lyon to E. D. Townsend, July 17, 1861, *O.R.*, 1:3:398.

5. "Report of Major General John M. Schofield," August 20, 1861, *O.R.*, 1:3:57–58; Driscoll, *Rogue*, 122, 128.

6. Nathaniel Lyon to Chester Harding, July 13 and 17, 1861, *O.R.*, 1:3:394, 397.

7. C. Phillips, *Damned Yankee*, 237–238; Piston and Hatcher, *Wilson's Creek*, 165; Bearss, *The Battle of Wilson's Creek*, 7–8, 44; Lincoln to Simon Cameron, August 7, 1861, *CW*, 4:475; "Memorandum by Colonel Phelps, from General Lyon, to General Frémont," July 27, 1861, *O.R.*, 1:3:408.

8. Samuel R. Curtis to Belinda Curtis, August 5 and 6, 1861, Colton, "With Frémont in Missouri," 24:117, 119; Grierson, *A Just and Righteous Cause*, 46.

9. Kelso, *Bloody Engagements*, 19; Wilkie, *Missouri in 1861*, 131; Jacob Bitner to Emeline Bitner July 17, 1861, Larimer, *Love and Valor*, 46; Chase Diary, Charles M. Chase Papers, SHSM.

10. Nathaniel Lyon to Adjutant General, U.S. Army, July 13, 1861, *O.R.*, 1:3:394.

11. C. Phillips, *Damned Yankee*, 87.

12. Snead, *Fight for Missouri*, 253; Koerner, *Memoirs of Gustave Koerner*, 2:169.

13. Frederick Steele et al. to Henry Halleck, February 17, 1862, *O.R.*, 1:3:96.

14. Piston and Hatcher, *Wilson's Creek*, 31, 175; Schofield, *Forty-Six Years in the Army*, 29–30; Nathaniel Lyon to JCF, August 9, 1861, *O.R.*, 1:3:57; Bearss, *The Battle of Wilson's Creek*, 46; Kelso, *Bloody Engagements*, 19.

15. Piston and Hatcher, *Wilson's Creek*, 9–10, 19–23, 57, 62.

16. Castel, *General Sterling Price*, 5; Ben McCulloch to L. P. Walker, July 18, 1861, *O.R.*, 1:3:611; Piston and Hatcher, *Wilson's Creek*, 19–20, 108, 161.

17. Piston and Hatcher, *Wilson's Creek*, 287; Sterling Price to Claiborne Jackson, August 12, 1861, *O.R.*, 1:3:100. As the best chroniclers of the Battle of Wilson's Creek concluded, "Compared to Cairo and the Mississippi and Ohio River valleys, southwestern Missouri held little strategic importance for the Union war effort." Piston and Hatcher, *Wilson's Creek*, 166.

18. JCF to E. D. Townsend, August 13, 1861, *O.R.*, 1:3:54, and August 30, 1861, *O.R.*, 1:3:55–57; Chase Diary, Charles M. Chase Papers, SHSM.

19. JCF to E. D. Townsend, August 13, 1861, *O.R.*, 1:3:54; Engle, *Yankee Dutchman*, 81; Forman, *Western Sanitary Commission*, 5–6.

20. Forman, *Western Sanitary Commission*, 6.

21. William Buckingham to Hamilton Gamble, August 14, 1861, Hamilton Gamble Papers, MHS; C. Phillips, *Damned Yankee*, 260; General Orders No. 4, *O.R.*, 1:3:92.

22. Elizabeth Blair Lee to Samuel Phillips Lee, August 14, 1861, E. B. Lee, *Wartime Washington*, 71.

23. Francis Preston Blair to JBF, August 13, 1861, Abraham Lincoln Papers, LOC; JCF to Hamilton Gamble, August 18, 1861, Hamilton Gamble Papers, MHS; Lincoln to Frank Blair, August 21, 1861, *CW*, 4:495.

24. Edward Bates to Hamilton Gamble, August 12, 1861, Hamilton Gamble Papers, MHS; "Proclamation," *O.R.*, 1:3:442.

25. Parrish, *Frank Blair*, 98; Rombauer, *The Union Cause in St. Louis*, 336; Lincoln to JCF, August 15, 1861, *CW*, 4:484; JCF to Henry Stevens and Frederick Billings, August 17, 1861, Henry W. Stevens Papers, WLC; JCF to U. S. Grant, August 20, 1861, National Archives Record Group 393.

26. "Proclamation," *O.R.*, 1:3:109.

27. Forman, *Western Sanitary Commission*, 5; Kelso, *Bloody Engagements*, 24; Lincoln to JCF, August 2, 1861, *CW*, 4:469.

28. Parrish, "Western Sanitary Commission," 18–19; General Orders No. 159, William Greenleaf Eliot Papers, MHS.

29. Parrish, "Western Sanitary Commission," 19; Forman, *Western Sanitary Commission*, 8–9.

30. Forman, *Western Sanitary Commission*, 10; Parrish, "Western Sanitary Commission," 19–20.

31. C. C. Phillips, *Jessie Benton Frémont*, 235; Herr, *Jessie Benton Frémont*, 328.

32. Parrish, "Western Sanitary Commission," 21.

33. Engle, *Yankee Dutchman*, 86; Rowan and Primm, *Germans for a Free Missouri*, 280–281.

34. Pope, *Military Memoirs of General John Pope*, 23.

35. U. S. Grant to Jesse Root Grant, August 27, 1861, Simon, *Papers of Ulysses S. Grant*, 2:146; Samuel Curtis to Belinda Curtis, August 5, 1861, Colton, "With Frémont in Missouri," 24:118.

36. Frank Blair to Montgomery Blair, August 24 and 29, 1861, Blair Family Papers, LOC; Montgomery Blair to JCF, August 24, 1861, *New York Tribune*, March 4, 1862; Samuel Curtis to Belinda Curtis, August 14, 1861, Colton, "With Frémont in Missouri," 24:122.

37. Lincoln to JCF, August 26, 1861, *CW*, 4:499. Rousseau would go on to return runaway Kentucky slaves to their masters during the war, making him an odd choice for Frémont. After the war, Rousseau gained a measure of infamy while serving one term in the House of Representatives for attacking a colleague from Iowa, Representative Josiah Grinnell, who had allegedly made disparaging remarks about the Kentuckian.

Chapter Four

1. "Message to Congress in Special Session," *CW*, 4:426, 431; Taylor, "Blair Family in the Civil War," 57.

2. Owen Lovejoy to Lucy Storrs Denham, July 14, 1861, Owen Lovejoy Papers, WLC; Lyman Trumbull to Julia Trumbull, July 16, 1861, Lyman Trumbull Family Papers, ALPL.

3. U.S. Congress, *Congressional Globe*, 37th Congress, 1st Session, 209.

4. *Chicago Tribune*, July 1, 1861; Julian, *Political Recollections*, 198.

5. Rego, *Lyman Trumbull and the Second Founding of the United States*, 247n.

6. Butler, *Butler's Book*, 258.

7. Benjamin Butler to Winfield Scott, May 27, 1861, *O.R.*, 2:1:754; Simon Cameron to Benjamin Butler, May 30, 1861, *O.R.*, 2:1:754–755; William Herndon to Wendell Phillips, February 1, 1861, Crawford Blagden Papers, HL; *New York Times*, May 31, 1861.

8. U.S. Congress, *Congressional Globe*, 37th Congress, 2nd Session, 508.

9. U.S. Congress, *Congressional Globe*, 37th Congress, 1st Session, 216, 427; Oakes, "Reluctant to Emancipate?" 460; C. Phillips, *The Rivers Ran Backward*, 213; Blaine, *Twenty Years of Congress*, 1:342.

10. Burlingame, *Abraham Lincoln*, 2:174.

11. Simon Cameron to Benjamin Butler, August 8, 1861, *O.R.*, 2:1:761–762.

12. "Message to Congress in Special Session," *CW*, 4:437; Varon, *Armies of Deliverance*, 18.

13. William Seward to Thurlow Weed, December 2, 1860, Barnes, *Life of Thurlow Weed*, 2:308; Lincoln to Edward Bates, December 18, 1860, *CW*, 4:154.

14. Grimsley, *Hard Hand of War*, 3, 21.

15. Bicknell, *Lincoln's Pathfinder*, 166–167; *New York Tribune*, June 14, 1861; Grimsley, *Hard Hand of War*, 35–36, 48; C. Phillips, "Lincoln's Grasp of War," 185–187; Lyman Trumbull to James R. Doolittle, August 31, 1861, Trumbull, "A Statesman's Letters," 48–49.

16. Ulysses Grant to John Kelton, August 30, 1861, *O.R.*, 2:1:766.

17. Montgomery Blair to JCF, August 30, 1861, Frank and Montgomery Blair Papers, MHS. The message was originally addressed to "Col. Blair," which Montgomery crossed out and replaced with "Gen. Frémont"; for implications of Frank Blair's election to Congress, see *National Era*, August 14, 1856; Brooks, *Mr. Lincoln's Washington*, 309.

18. JCF to Lincoln, September 8, 1861, *O.R.*, 2:1:767; Parrish, *Turbulent Partnership*, 60; Andrew Brownlow to Hamilton Gamble, August 1, 1861; Charles Gibson to Hamilton Gamble, August 2, 1861, Hamilton Gamble Papers, MHS; *New York Times*, August 9, 1861; Herr, *Jessie Benton Frémont*, 332–333; J. McPherson, *Struggle for Equality*, 72.

19. Stevens, "Lincoln and Missouri," 75; "Proclamation," *O.R.*, 1:3:466–467. For an examination of Missouri being under federal occupation, see C. Phillips, *The Rivers Ran Backward*, 169.

20. "Proclamation," *O.R.*, 1:3:467.

21. Rowan and Primm, *Germans for a Free Missouri*, 283; Strong, *Diary of the Civil War*, 177; "Proclamation," *O.R.*, 1:3:467; Samuel Curtis to Belinda Curtis, September 2, 1861, Colton, "With Frémont in Missouri," 24:129.

22. Samuel Curtis to Belinda Curtis, September 2, 1861; Samuel Curtis to Lincoln, October 11, 1861, Colton, "With Frémont in Missouri," 24:129, 141; *New York Times*, September 3, 1861; JBF, "Great Events," Frémont Family Papers, BL, 6.

23. William Lloyd Garrison to Gerrit Smith, September 5, 1861, Garrison, *Let the Oppressed Go Free*, 5:33.

24. James Bowen to John Bigelow, September 4, 1861, Bigelow, *Retrospections of an Active Life*, 1:363.

25. Salmon Chase to Green Adams, September 5, 1861, Chase, *The Salmon P. Chase Papers*, 3:95–96.

26. Frank Blair to Montgomery Blair, September 1, 1861, Abraham Lincoln Papers, LOC.

27. *Statutes at Large*, 37th Congress, 1st Session, 319; JBF, "Great Events," Frémont Family Papers, BL, 251–252.

28. JBF to JCF, September 23, 1857, JBF, *Letters of Jessie Benton Frémont*, 172.

29. Joseph Holt to Lincoln, September 2 and 12, 1861, Abraham Lincoln Papers, LOC.

30. Robert Anderson to Lincoln, September 13, 1861, Abraham Lincoln Papers, LOC.

31. Joshua Speed to Lincoln, September 1 and 3, 1861, Abraham Lincoln Papers, LOC.

32. Lincoln to Joshua Speed, August 24, 1855, *CW*, 2:320.

33. Robert Gould Shaw to Sarah Shaw, September 5, 1861; Robert Gould Shaw to Susannah Shaw, September 17, 1861, Duncan, *Blue-Eyed Child of Fortune*, 136, 142.

34. John L. Scripps to Lincoln, Monday, September 23, 1861, Abraham Lincoln Papers, LOC.

35. Gerrit Smith to Lincoln, August 31, 1861, *National Anti-Slavery Standard*, September 14, 1861.

36. Fehrenbacher and Fehrenbacher, *Recollected Words of Abraham Lincoln*, 295; J. McPherson, "Lincoln as Commander in Chief," 5.

37. Lincoln to JCF, September 2, 1861, Abraham Lincoln Papers, LOC; "Proclamation," *O.R.*, 2:1:181.

38. Lincoln to JCF, September 2, 1861, Abraham Lincoln Papers, LOC.

39. Oakes, "Reluctant to Emancipate?" 462.

40. Winfield Scott to Lincoln, September 5, 1861, Abraham Lincoln Papers, LOC; George McClellan to Lincoln, September 6, 1861, Abraham Lincoln Papers, LOC.

41. Lincoln to David Hunter, September 9, 1861, Abraham Lincoln Papers, LOC.

42. JCF to Lincoln, September 8, 1861, Abraham Lincoln Papers, LOC; Browning, *Diary of Orville Hickman Browning*, 1:499.

43. Rowan and Primm, *Germans for a Free Missouri*, 279.

44. JBF, "Great Events," Frémont Family Papers, BL, 268–269; Joyaux, "The Tour of Prince Napoleon," 83.

45. JBF, "Great Events," Frémont Family Papers, BL, 269.

46. Frank Blair to Montgomery Blair, September 1, 1861, Abraham Lincoln Papers, LOC.

47. Frank Blair to Montgomery Blair, September 1, 1861, Abraham Lincoln Papers, LOC.

48. Parrish, *Frank Blair*, 20.

49. U.S. Congress, *Congressional Globe*, 35th Congress, 1st Session, 296.

50. Jessie Benton Frémont's account of the meeting with Lincoln is in JBF, "Great Events," Frémont Family Papers, BL, 269–272.

51. Herr, *Jessie Benton Frémont*, 337; Lincoln to JBF, September 10, 1861, *CW*, 4:515.

52. Lincoln's version of the meeting is from Hay's diary entry of December 9, 1863, Hay, *Inside Lincoln's White House*, 123–124.

53. Grinnell, *Men and Events of Forty Years*, 174.

54. Elizabeth Blair Lee to Samuel Phillips Lee, September 12, 1861; October 16, 1861, E. B. Lee, *Wartime Washington*, 77, 86; JBF, "Great Events," Frémont Family Papers, BL, 272; Herr and Spence, "I Really Had Something like the Blues," 18.

55. Elizabeth Blair Lee to Samuel Phillips Lee, September 17, 1861, E. B. Lee, *Wartime Washington*, 78–79; JBF, "Great Events," Frémont Family Papers, BL, 272.

56. Elizabeth Blair Lee to Samuel Phillips Lee, September 17, 1861, E. B. Lee, *Wartime Washington*, 79; JBF, "Great Events," Frémont Family Papers, BL, 272.

57. JBF to JCF, September 11, 1861, JBF, *Letters of Jessie Benton Frémont*, 269.

58. JBF to Lincoln, September 12, 1861, JBF, *Letters of Jessie Benton Frémont*, 270–271; JBF, "Great Events," Frémont Family Papers, BL, 272.

59. Lincoln to JBF, September 12, 1861, *CW*, 4:519.

60. Lincoln to John C. Frémont, September 11, 1861, Abraham Lincoln Papers, LOC.

61. Julian and Child, *Speeches on Political Questions*, 172; Douglass, *The Civil War*, 3:160.

62. John Greenleaf Whittier to Major George L. Stearns, September 19, 1861, Pickard, *Life and Letters of John Greenleaf Whittier*, 467.

63. Whittier, *In War Time and Other Poems*, 19.

64. Lydia Maria Child to John Greenleaf Whittier, January 21, 1862, Child, *Letters of Lydia Maria Child*, 160.

65. William Lloyd Garrison to James Miller McKim, October 13, 1861, Garrison, *Let the Oppressed Go Free*, 5:39; William Lloyd Garrison to Oliver Johnson, October 7, 1861, Garrison, *Let the Oppressed Go Free*, 5:37.

66. Ben Wade to JCF, October 24, 1861, JBF, "Great Events," Frémont Family Papers, BL, 291.

67. Charles Sumner to Francis Lieber, September 17, 1861, Donald, *Charles Sumner and the Rights of Man*, 26.

68. J. McPherson, *Negro's Civil War*, 41–42.

69. Mrs. L. C. Howard to Lincoln, September 17, 1861; Abner Williams to Lincoln, October 11, 1861, Abraham Lincoln Papers, LOC.

70. Thomas H. Little to Lincoln, September 17, 1861, Abraham Lincoln Papers, LOC.

71. John L. Scripps to Lincoln, September 23, 1861, Abraham Lincoln Papers, LOC.

72. Baxter, "Orville H. Browning," 449; Orville Browning to Lincoln, April 30, 1861, Abraham Lincoln Papers, LOC.

73. Orville Browning to Lincoln, September 11, 1861, Abraham Lincoln Papers, LOC.

74. Orville Browning to Lincoln, September 17, 1861, Abraham Lincoln Papers, LOC.

75. Lincoln to Orville Browning, September 22, 1861, Abraham Lincoln Papers, LOC.

76. Lincoln to Orville Browning, September 22, 1861, Abraham Lincoln Papers, LOC.

77. Browning, *Diary of Orville Hickman Browning*, 1:502.

78. Orville Browning to Lincoln, September 30, 1861, Orville Hickman Browning Papers, ALPL.

79. Fehrenbacher and Fehrenbacher, *Recollected Words of Abraham Lincoln*, 506.

80. Henry Adams to Charles Francis Adams Jr., October 15, 1861, Ford, *A Cycle of Adams Letters*, 58.

81. William T. Sherman to Thomas Ewing Sr., September 15, 1861, Sherman, *Sherman's Civil War*, 137–138.

82. *New York Herald*, September 21, 1861.

83. Bicknell, *Lincoln's Pathfinder*, 264–267; *New York Dispatch*, July 20, 1861.

84. Douglass, *The Civil War*, 3:161.

85. C. Phillips, *Missouri's Confederate*, 283.

86. Grierson, *A Just and Righteous Cause*, 55–56, 60.

Chapter Five

1. Parrish, *Frank Blair*, 122–123; Brooks, *Mr. Lincoln's Washington*, 248.

2. Weigley, *Quartermaster General of the Union Army*, 186–191; John Schofield to Frank Blair, August 28, 1861, *O.R.*, 1:3:464.

3. Weigley, *Quartermaster General of the Union Army*, 193–195; Robert Allen to Simon Cameron, October 11, 1861, *O.R.*, 1:3:549.

4. Montgomery Blair to Lincoln, September 14, 1861, Abraham Lincoln Papers, LOC; Weigley, *Quartermaster General of the Union Army*, 193.

5. Montgomery Blair to Lincoln, September 14, 1861, Abraham Lincoln Papers, LOC; JBF, "Great Events," Frémont Family Papers, BL, 276; Parrish, *Frank Blair*, 124.

6. Samuel Curtis to Belinda Curtis, August 12, 1861, Colton, "With Frémont in Missouri," 24:120. See U. S. Grant to Frémont, September 9, 10, 15, and 20, 1861, Simon, *Papers of Ulysses S. Grant*, 2:216, 225, 262, 287; U. S. Grant to Colonel John T. Fiala, September 29, 1861, Simon, *Papers of Ulysses S. Grant*, 2:320.

7. Montgomery Blair to Lincoln, September 14, 1861, Abraham Lincoln Papers, LOC; Parrish, *Turbulent Partnership*, 54, 57–58.

8. George McClellan to Simon Cameron, September 13, 1861, McClellan, *Civil War Papers of George B. McClellan*, 100; JCF to Simon Cameron, September 15, 1861, *O.R.*, 1:3:493; JBF, "Great Events," Frémont Family Papers, BL, 276; U.S. Congress, *Congressional Globe*, 37th Congress, 2nd Session, 1128.

9. Hamilton Gamble to Edward Bates, September 17, 1861, Abraham Lincoln Papers, LOC; Lincoln to Simon Cameron, September 20, 1861, *CW*, 4:529–530.

10. J. T. K. Hayward to Hamilton Gamble, August 17, 1861, Parrish, *Turbulent Partnership*, 54.

11. Engle, *Gathering to Save a Nation*, 107; Pope, *Military Memoirs of General John Pope*, 19–20, 25; Grimsley, *Hard Hand of War*, 39.

12. U. S. Grant to Julia Dent Grant, August 31, 1861; U. S. Grant to JCF, September 6, 1861, Simon, *Papers of Ulysses S. Grant*, 2:160, 196; Grant, *Annotated Memoirs of Ulysses S. Grant*, 249–250.

13. Gerteis, *Civil War in Missouri*, 102–108; "Appeal from the Citizens of Lafayette County," Robert White Papers, MHS; E. E., Miller, *Lincoln's Abolitionist General*, 74; Parrish, *Turbulent Partnership*, 67.

14. Pope, *Military Memoirs of General John Pope*, 17; John Schofield to Edwin Stanton, May 16, 1862, *O.R.*, 1:13:386; C. Phillips, *The Rivers Ran Backward*, 246–247; Unsigned in Lexington to Hamilton Gamble, August 13, 1861, Hamilton Gamble Papers, MHS.

15. Grierson, *A Just and Righteous Cause*, 44; Browning, *Diary of Orville Hickman Browning*, 1:497, 499; L. W. Hall to Simon Cameron, September 18, 1861, Abraham Lincoln Papers, LOC.

16. John Howe to Montgomery Blair, August 4, 1861, Abraham Lincoln Papers, LOC.

17. Charles Zagonyi to Alexander Asboth, August 24, 1861, LADP, http://www.lincolnarchives.us/cgi-bin/lincoln?a=d&d=&sf=&d=Drg94-164-d-13&page=1; Frank Blair to Henry Halleck, January 5, 1862, LADP, http://www.lincolnarchives.us/cgi-bin/lincoln?a=d&d=&sf=&d=Drg94-164-d-8&page=1.

18. Hamilton Gamble to Charles Gibson, September 19 and 20, 1861, Hamilton Gamble Papers, MHS; Parrish, *Turbulent Partnership*, 64–65.

19. William T. Sherman to Ellen Sherman, September 18, 1861, Sherman, *Sherman's Civil War*, 138–139.

20. Parrish, *Frank Blair*, 120; Frank Blair to Montgomery Blair, September 1, 1861, Abraham Lincoln Papers, LOC.

21. Schofield, *Forty-Six Years in the Army*, 36.

22. Royce, "Frémont," 548; U. S. Grant to Captain John Kelton, August 25, 1861, Simon, *Papers of Ulysses S. Grant*, 2:133–134.

23. Denslow, *Frémont and McClellan*, 17.

24. Fehrenbacher and Fehrenbacher, *Recollected Words of Abraham Lincoln*, 194; Brooks, *Mr. Lincoln's Washington*, 256; *New York Times*, September 9, 1861.

25. Stevens, "Lincoln and Missouri," 65–67; Carl Sandburg wrote of Frank Blair, "No other man of the time, probably, spoke more urgently for deportation and colonization of Negroes as a solution of the slavery problem," including compulsory deportation. Sandburg, *Abraham Lincoln, the War Years*, 1:153.

26. Frank Blair to Montgomery Blair, September 1, 1861, Abraham Lincoln Papers, LOC; Edward Bates to Schuyler Colfax, May 25, 1860, Edward Bates Papers, ALPL; Elizabeth Blair Lee to Samuel Phillips Lee, July 6 and August 10, 1861, E. B. Lee, *Wartime Washington*, 58–59.

27. Elizabeth Blair Lee to Samuel Phillips Lee, September 5, 1861, E. B. Lee, *Wartime Washington*, 76.

28. Elizabeth Blair Lee to Samuel Phillips Lee, October 15, 1863, E. B. Lee, *Wartime Washington*, 313.

29. Nevins, *Frémont*, 520; Elizabeth Blair Lee to Samuel Phillips Lee, September 17, 1861, E. B. Lee, *Wartime Washington*, 78.

30. JCF to E. D. Townsend, September 16, 1861, Abraham Lincoln Papers, LOC; Parrish, *Frank Blair*, 126; JBF to JCF, September 12, 1861, JBF, *Letters of Jessie Benton Frémont*, 271.

31. Tasher, "The Missouri Democrat," 407; Frank Blair to William Denison, September 19, 1861, W. E. Smith, *Francis Preston Blair Family*, 2:80.

32. "Frank Blair, Charges Against Frémont," October 2, 1861, Abraham Lincoln Papers, LOC; *New York Herald*, October 7, 1861.

33. Winfield Scott to JCF, September 19, 1861, Abraham Lincoln Papers, LOC; Burlingame, *Abraham Lincoln*, 2:209.

34. Edward Bates to Hamilton Gamble, September 27, 1861, Hamilton Gamble Papers, MHS.

35. Elizabeth Blair Lee to Samuel Phillips Lee, October 1 and 8, 1861, E. B. Lee, *Wartime Washington*, 81, 84; Montgomery Blair to W. O. Bartlett, September 26, 1861, W. E. Smith, *Francis Preston Blair Family*, 2:81–82.

36. JCF to Lincoln, August 5, 1861, Abraham Lincoln Papers, LOC; Lincoln to JCF and JCF to Lincoln, September 22, 1861, *O.R.*, 1:4:265.

37. Frank Blair to Montgomery Blair, October 1, 1861, Abraham Lincoln Papers, LOC.

38. JCF to E. D. Townsend, September 23, 1861, Abraham Lincoln Papers, LOC.

39. Rowan and Primm, *Germans for a Free Missouri*, 285; *New York Times*, October 1, 1861, clipping in Abraham Lincoln Papers, LOC.

40. Edward Bates to Hamilton Gamble, October 3, 1861, Hamilton Gamble Papers, MHS.

41. Thomas Gantt to Hamilton Gamble, October 6, 1861, Hamilton Gamble Papers, MHS.

42. Koerner, *Memoirs of Gustave Koerner*, 2:174; Strong, *Diary of the Civil War*, 183.

43. Castel, *General Sterling Price*, 57.

44. Koerner, *Memoirs of Gustave Koerner*, 2:175–176.

45. Koerner, *Memoirs of Gustave Koerner*, 2:176–177.

46. Koerner, *Memoirs of Gustave Koerner*, 2:180; Wilkie, *Missouri in 1861*, 199.

47. Rowan and Primm, *Germans for a Free Missouri*, 286–287; Koerner, *Memoirs of Gustave Koerner*, 2:175.

48. Eaton, *Grant, Lincoln, and the Freedmen*, lxxii.

49. Owen Lovejoy to Mary B. Denham, October 1, 1861, Owen Lovejoy Papers, WLC; Koerner, *Memoirs of Gustave Koerner*, 2:173, 181. In 1863, Gurley was appointed first governor of the Arizona Territory but died before taking office. Frémont would be appointed to the same post fifteen years later.

50. Magdol, *Owen Lovejoy*, 290.

51. Carpenter, *Six Months at the White House with Abraham Lincoln*, 18; JBF, *Story of the Guard*, 81.

52. Owen Lovejoy to Elijah Parish Lovejoy II and Charles P. Lovejoy, October 6, 1861, Owen Lovejoy Papers, WLC.

53. Wilkie, *Missouri in 1861*, 194, 201.

54. Pickard, *Life and Letters of John Greenleaf Whittier*, 2:462–463; JBF to John Greenleaf Whittier, October 17, 1863, JBF, *Letters of Jessie Benton Frémont*, 357.

55. "Lorenzo Thomas Report," *O.R.*, 1:3:544; James Love to Molly Wilson, October 13, 1861, Love, *My Dear Molly*, 84; Wilkie, *Missouri in 1861*, 205.

56. Owen Lovejoy to Sarah Moody Lovejoy, October 20, 1861, Owen Lovejoy Papers, WLC; Isidor Bush to Lincoln, October 1, 1861, Abraham Lincoln Papers, LOC; Nevins, *Frémont*, 532.

57. Lyman Trumbull to Lincoln, October 1, 1861, Abraham Lincoln Papers, LOC.

58. Orville Browning to Lincoln, September 30, 1861, Orville Hickman Browning Papers, ALPL.

59. JBF to Frederick Billings, October 12, 1861, JBF, *Letters of Jessie Benton Frémont*, 273–274.

60. Salmon Chase to Simon Cameron, October 7, 1861, Chase, *The Salmon P. Chase Papers*, 3:100.

61. Lincoln to Samuel Curtis, October 7, 1861, *CW*, 4:549; Simon Cameron to Lincoln, October 12, 1861, Abraham Lincoln Papers, LOC.

62. Samuel R. Curtis to Lincoln, October 11, 1861, Colton, "With Frémont in Missouri," 24:140–142.

63. "Lorenzo Thomas Report," *O.R.*, 1:3:545, 547; JCF to JBF, October 10, 1861, JBF, *Story of the Guard*, 77; Simon Cameron to Lincoln, October 12, 1861, Abraham Lincoln Papers, LOC.

64. Wilkie, *Missouri in 1861*, 207; JCF to JBF, October 15, 1861, JBF, *Story of the Guard*, 88; Simon Cameron to Lincoln, October 14, 1861, Abraham Lincoln Papers, LOC.

65. Ward Hill Lamon to Lincoln, October 21, 1861, Abraham Lincoln Papers, LOC.

66. Koerner, *Memoirs of Gustave Koerner*, 2:186; JCF to JBF, October 14, 1861, JBF, *Letters of Jessie Benton Frémont*, 279n.

67. JCF to JBF, October 15, 1861, JBF, *Story of the Guard*, 88; JBF to Isaac Sherman, October 15, 1861, JBF, *Letters of Jessie Benton Frémont*, 276; Bicknell, *America 1844*, 114–115.

68. "Lorenzo Thomas Report," *O.R.*, 1:3:547; William T. Sherman to John Sherman, October 5, 1861, Sherman, *Sherman's Civil War*, 144.

69. Chaffin, *Pathfinder*, 471; Nevins, *Frémont*, 537; "Lorenzo Thomas Report," *O.R.*, 1:3:542–547; JCF to JBF, October 12, 1861, JBF, *Story of the Guard*, 96–97.

70. Bates, *Diary of Edward Bates*, 198.

71. Bates, *Diary of Edward Bates*, 198–199.

72. Bates, *Diary of Edward Bates*, 199.

73. William T. Sherman to John Sherman, October 5, 1861; William T. Sherman to Ellen Sherman, October 6, 1861, Sherman, *Sherman's Civil War*, 144–145; "Lorenzo Thomas Report," *O.R.*, 1:3:543; JBF to JCF, September 11, 1861, JBF, *Letters of Jessie Benton Frémont*, 269.

74. *New York Herald*, October 19, 1861; *New York Tribune*, October 30, 1861; *New York Dispatch*, November 2, 1861.

75. JBF to Ward Hill Lamon, October 30–31, 1861, JBF, *Letters of Jessie Benton Frémont*, 287; Salmon Chase to Cornelius S. Hamilton, November 21, 1861, Chase, *The Salmon P. Chase Papers*, 3:111; *New York Times*, October 31, 1861; Villard, *Lincoln on the Eve of '61*, 37.

76. JCF to JBF, October 9, 10, 18, 23, and November 1, 1861, JBF, *Story of the Guard*, 72–75, 91, 115, 194.

77. Castel, *General Sterling Price*, 58; JCF to JBF, October 24, 1861, JBF, *Story of the Guard*, 117–118.

78. JCF to JBF, October 19, 1861, JBF, *Story of the Guard*, 93; Owen Lovejoy to Lucy Storrs Denham, October 22, 1861, Owen Lovejoy Papers, WLC.

79. JCF to JBF, October 22, 1861, JBF, *Story of the Guard*, 111; Kelso, *Bloody Engagements*, 46.

80. Owen Lovejoy to Sarah Moody Lovejoy, October 24, 1861, Owen Lovejoy Papers, WLC; C. Phillips, *The Rivers Ran Backward*, 217; Teters, *Practical Liberators*, 10–11.

81. Wilkie, *Missouri in 1861*, 252; JCF to JBF, October 28, 1861, JBF, *Story of the Guard*, 162; Gerteis, *Civil War in Missouri*, 118–119.

82. JCF to JBF, October 30, 1861, JBF, *Story of the Guard*, 177; JBF, *Story of the Guard*, 185–186.

83. JBF to Ward Hill Lamon, October 26, 1861, JBF, *Letters of Jessie Benton Frémont*, 283.

84. JCF to JBF, October 28 and 29, 1861, JBF, *Story of the Guard*, 161, 164.

85. Owen Lovejoy to Eunice Storrs Denham Lovejoy, October 29, 1861, Owen Lovejoy Papers, WLC; Castel, *General Sterling Price*, 59; *JCCW: Missouri*, 42.

86. Francis P. Blair Sr. to John Bigelow, October 26, 1861, Bigelow, *Retrospections of an Active Life*, 1:376.

87. John A. Gurley to Lincoln, October 27, 1861, Abraham Lincoln Papers, LOC.

88. Charles Sumner to Lincoln, undated (probably September/October 1861), Abraham Lincoln Papers, LOC.

89. John Pope to David Hunter, October 26, 1861, quoted in Nevins, *Frémont*, 536.

90. JBF to Ward Hill Lamon, October 31, 1861, JBF, *Letters of Jessie Benton Frémont*, 290; JBF, "Great Events," Frémont Family Papers, BL, 286.

91. JCF to JBF, October 30, 1861, JBF, *Story of the Guard*, 176; J. H. Eaton to David Hunter, October 31, 1861; J. H. Eaton to John Pope, November 1, 1861, *O.R.*, 1:3:558, 559; *New York Herald*, October 30, 1861.

92. JCF, "In Command in Missouri," 1:287; JBF, "Great Events," Frémont Family Papers, BL, 303–304, 312; Wilkie, *Missouri in 1861*, 230; *JCCW: Missouri*, 75.

93. Lincoln to Samuel R. Curtis, October 24, 1861, *CW*, 4:562.

94. Nevins, *Frémont*, 540.

95. Wilkie, *Missouri in 1861*, 233; Owen Lovejoy to Elijah Parish Lovejoy II and Charles P. Lovejoy, November 2, 1861, Owen Lovejoy Papers, WLC; Nevins, *Frémont*, 535–536, 542; Pope, *Military Memoirs of General John Pope*, 35.

96. Rowland Johnson to Lincoln, October 4, 1861, Abraham Lincoln Papers, LOC.

97. Koerner, *Memoirs of Gustave Koerner*, 2:189; Wilkie, *Missouri in 1861*, 232; *JCCW: Missouri*, 192, 196; JCF to JBF, November 2, 1861, JBF, *Story of the Guard*, 198.

98. Robert Gould Shaw to Sarah Shaw, November 11, 1861, Duncan, *Blue-Eyed Child of Fortune*, 159; Grierson, *A Just and Righteous Cause*, 60; "Farewell Address," John C. Frémont Collection, MHS.

99. Owen Lovejoy to Elizabeth S. Denham, November 7; Lovejoy to Eunice Storrs Denham Lovejoy and to Lucy Storrs Denham, November 8, 1861, Owen Lovejoy Papers, WLC.

100. Lincoln to David Hunter, October 25, 1861, *CW*, 5:1.

101. Rowan and Primm, *Germans for a Free Missouri*, 288–289.

102. Rombauer, *The Union Cause in St. Louis*, 334.

103. Burlingame, *Lincoln's Journalist*, 130.

104. *JCCW: Missouri*, 207; Pope, *Military Memoirs of General John Pope*, 35; Grierson, *A Just and Righteous Cause*, 60.

105. Turkoly-Joczik, "Frémont and the Western Department," 363.

106. Grierson, *A Just and Righteous Cause*, 60.

107. Salmon Chase to Jesse Stubbs, November 1, 1861, Chase, *The Salmon P. Chase Papers*, 3:105.

108. Salmon Chase to Richard Smith, November 11, 1861, Chase, *The Salmon P. Chase Papers*, 3:108; Chase to Cornelius S. Hamilton, November 21, 1861, Chase, *The Salmon P. Chase Papers*, 3:111; Lovejoy, *His Brother's Blood*, 272.

109. Thurlow Weed to William Seward, May 20, 1860, Van Deusen, "Thurlow Weed's Analysis of William H. Seward's Defeat in the Republican Convention of 1860," 103.

CHAPTER SIX

1. *Chicago Tribune*, November 6, 1861.

2. Herr, *Jessie Benton Frémont*, 346; Nevins, *Frémont*, 55; *New York Herald*, November 28, 1861; Rowan and Primm, *Germans for a Free Missouri*, 291.

3. JBF to Frederick Billings, November 23, 1861, JBF, *Letters of Jessie Benton Frémont*, 297.

4. J. McPherson, *Struggle for Equality*, 76; "First Debate with Stephen A. Douglas at Ottawa, Illinois," *CW*, 3:27; W. H. Smith, *Schuyler Colfax*, 162; JBF, "Great Events," Frémont Family Papers, BL, 324; *New York Herald*, November 28, 1861.

5. JBF, "Great Events," Frémont Family Papers, BL, 325; JBF to Thomas Starr King, December 29, 1861, JBF, *Letters of Jessie Benton Frémont*, 305.

6. JBF, "Great Events," Frémont Family Papers, BL, 325–326.

7. Herr, *Jessie Benton Frémont*, 351–352; *New York Tribune*, December 20, 1861; Wendell Phillips to Ann Phillips, March 31, 1862, Crawford Blagden Papers, HL; *The Liberator*, August 30, 1861.

8. JBF to James T. Fields, December 14, 1861, JBF, *Letters of Jessie Benton Frémont*, 298–301.

9. Elizabeth Blair Lee to Samuel Phillips Lee, October 19, 1861, E. B. Lee, *Wartime Washington*, 88; Bates, *Diary of Edward Bates*, 217.

10. Salmon Chase to Richard Smith, November 11, 1861, Chase, *The Salmon P. Chase Papers*, 3:109; Chase to Cornelius S. Hamilton, November 21, 1861, Chase, *The Salmon P. Chase Papers*, 3:111.

11. Lippman and McMahon, "Professionalism and Politics in the Procurement Process," 65; Nicklason, "The Civil War Contracts Committee," 232; Montgomery Meigs to Frank Blair, August 28, 1861, *O.R.*, 1:3:464.

12. McClellan to Samuel R. Curtis, November 7, 1861, McClellan, *Civil War Papers of George B. McClellan*, 126.

13. Driscoll, *Rogue*, 164–165.

14. Frank Blair to Simon Cameron, May 4, 1861, *O.R.*, 1:1:680.

15. McKinstry, *Vindication of Brig. Gen. J. McKinstry*, 5.

16. U.S. Congress, *War Claims*, 3; Driscoll, *Rogue*, 155.

17. U.S. Congress, *War Claims*, 4.

18. U.S. Congress, *War Claims*, 4.

19. U.S. Congress, *War Claims*, 4–5.

20. McKinstry, *Vindication of Brig. Gen. J. McKinstry*, 4; U.S. Congress, *War Claims*, 5.

21. U.S. Congress, *War Claims*, 5.

22. U.S. Congress, *War Claims*, 5–6.

23. U.S. Congress, *War Claims*, 11, 17; Murray, "Frémont-Adams Contracts," 519–524.

24. Murray, "Frémont-Adams Contracts," 518–519, 521, 524.

25. Lippman and McMahon, "Professionalism and Politics in the Procurement Process," 74.

26. Frank Blair Jr. to Justus McKinstry, McKinstry, *Vindication of Brig. Gen. J. McKinstry*, 61; Abraham Lincoln to Justus McKinstry, September 10, 1861, *CW*, 4:515–516.

27. U.S. Congress, *Congressional Globe*, 37th Congress, 1st Session, 23; Freeman, *Field of Blood*, 269.

28. Henry Dawes to Electa Dawes, July 12, 1861, Nicklason, "The Civil War Contracts Committee," 232; Nicklason, "The Civil War Contracts Committee," 232–233.

29. Burlingame, *Lincoln's Journalist*, 188; Burlingame, *Abraham Lincoln*, 2:175; Kahan, *Amiable Scoundrel*, 189; U.S. Congress, *Congressional Globe*, 37th Congress, 2nd Session, 1753.

30. Gideon Welles to George D. Morgan, December 31, 1861, Nicklason, "The Civil War Contracts Committee," 235–237; James Grimes to Mrs. Grimes and James Grimes to William P. Fessenden, November 13, 1861, Salter, *Life of James W. Grimes*, 154–155.

31. Nicklason, "The Civil War Contracts Committee," 233; Simon, *Papers of Ulysses S. Grant*, 3:90; Driscoll, *Rogue*, 159–160; Elihu Washburne to Lincoln, October 21, 1861, Abraham Lincoln Papers, LOC; *New York Herald*, December 19, 1861.

32. Lippman and McMahon, "Professionalism and Politics in the Procurement Process," 72; McKinstry, *Vindication of Brig. Gen. J. McKinstry*, 3–5.

33. McKinstry, *Vindication of Brig. Gen. J. McKinstry*, 5; Driscoll, *Rogue*, 142–143.

34. Shannon, *Organization and Administration of the Union Army*, 1:62–635.

35. Shannon, *Organization and Administration of the Union Army*, 1:57; Parker, *Henry Stevens of Vermont*, 248.

36. U.S. Congress, *Congressional Globe*, 37th Congress, 2nd Session, 1743; U.S. Congress, *U.S. House Journal*, 37th Congress, 2nd Session, 83; Tap, "Reconstructing Emancipation's Martyr," 51; *JCCW: Missouri*, 40.

37. Browning, *Diary of Orville Hickman Browning*, 1:507; U.S. Congress, *Congressional Globe*, 37th Congress, 2nd Session, 116, 1753; JCF to Thaddeus Stevens, April 28, 1862, Nicklason, "The Civil War Contracts Committee," 243n; Nicklason, "The Civil War Contracts Committee," 239; Nevins, *Frémont*, 538.

38. Cochrane, *American Civil War*, 15–16; Cochrane, *Arming the Slaves*, 9; Trefousse, *Radical Republicans*, 208; Kahan, *Amiable Scoundrel*, 200–205; Thomas A. Scott to Thomas W. Sherman, October 14, 1861, *O.R.*, 1:6:176–177; Hendrick, *Lincoln's War Cabinet*, 230.

39. Guelzo, *Lincoln's Emancipation Proclamation*, 70; Fehrenbacher and Fehrenbacher, *Recollected Words of Abraham Lincoln*, 21; Browning, *Diary of Orville Hickman Browning*, 1:512.

40. U.S. Congress, *Congressional Globe*, 37th Congress, 2nd Session, 16, 29–30.

41. U.S. Congress, *Congressional Globe*, 37th Congress, 2nd Session, 31–32, 40.

42. U.S. Congress, *Congressional Globe*, 37th Congress, 2nd Session, 110, 153.

43. JBF to Thomas Starr King, December 29, 1861, Jessie Benton Frémont Papers, SCP.

44. Conlin, "The Smithsonian Abolition Lecture Controversy," 303, 306.

45. Conlin, "The Smithsonian Abolition Lecture Controversy," 307.

46. Conlin, "The Smithsonian Abolition Lecture Controversy," 308–309; *Christian Recorder*, December 28, 1861.

47. Conlin, "The Smithsonian Abolition Lecture Controversy," 310.

48. Croffut, "Lincoln's Washington," 58; Julian, *Political Recollections*, 369–370; Conlin, "The Smithsonian Abolition Lecture Controversy," 311–312.

49. Croffut, "Lincoln's Washington," 58; *Washington Evening Star*, January 4, 1862.

50. *Washington Evening Star*, January 4, 1862.

51. Conlin, "The Smithsonian Abolition Lecture Controversy," 312; Magdol, *Owen Lovejoy*, 317.

52. Fehrenbacher and Fehrenbacher, *Recollected Words of Abraham Lincoln*, 272; *New York Herald*, January 5, 1862.

53. Emerson, *Complete Works*, 11:304–305.

54. James A. Cravens to Abraham Lincoln, January 5, 1862, Abraham Lincoln Papers, LOC.

55. *The Liberator*, January 31, 1862.

56. *National Republican*, January 6, 1862; *Washington Evening Star*, January 8, 1862; *New York Tribune*, January 11, 1862.

57. Julian, *Political Recollections*, 201.

58. *JCCW: Missouri*, 32; George W. Julian to Lincoln, December 26, 1860, Abraham Lincoln Papers, LOC; Julian and Child, *Speeches on Political Questions*, 154.

59. Julian and Child, *Speeches on Political Questions*, 172–173.

60. Julian and Child, *Speeches on Political Questions*, 163.

61. Julian and Child, *Speeches on Political Questions*, 165, 169.

62. *JCCW: Missouri*, 33.

63. *JCCW: Missouri*, 35.

64. *JCCW: Missouri*, 40.

65. *JCCW: Missouri*, 38–40.

66. *JCCW: Missouri*, 42–43, 64.

67. *JCCW: Missouri*, 43–44.

68. JBF to George W. Julian, May 1, 1862, JBF, *Letters of Jessie Benton Frémont*, 320.

69. *JCCW: Missouri*, 53–54.

70. *JCCW: Missouri*, 59–60. Historian Bruce Tap makes much of this Frémont-Odell exchange in his criticism of Frémont, accusing him of being willing to "weaken himself militarily for political leverage," but the charge does not hold water. The departure of a few hundred raw troops stationed hundreds of miles from the front meant nothing militarily. Rather than playing for leverage, it's more likely Frémont was playing with Odell, the most hostile member of the committee. See Tap, *Over Lincoln's Shoulder*, 89–90.

71. *JCCW: Missouri*, 69, 195, 205.

72. *JCCW: Missouri*, 70–71, 75–77.

73. Lovejoy, *His Brother's Blood*, 284.

74. Cochrane, *American Civil War*, 40–41, 55–57.

75. JBF to Frederick Billings, January 21, 1862, JBF, *Letters of Jessie Benton Frémont*, 309.

76. Burlingame, *An American Marriage*, 209.

77. Trefousse, *Benjamin Franklin Wade*, 167.

78. Poore, *Perley's Reminiscences*, 115, 118.

79. JBF, "Great Events," Frémont Family Papers, BL, 327; JBF to Frederick Billings, February 7, 1862, JBF, *Letters of Jessie Benton Frémont*, 312.

80. JBF to Frederick Billings, February 7, 1862, JBF, *Letters of Jessie Benton Frémont*, 312; Poore, *Perley's Reminiscences*, 2:118–119; Dahlgren, *Memoir of John A. Dahlgren*, 356.

81. JBF, "Great Events," Frémont Family Papers, BL, 328; Poore, *Perley's Reminiscences*, 2:116.

82. JBF, "Great Events," Frémont Family Papers, BL, 328.

83. JBF, "Great Events," Frémont Family Papers, BL, 328; Browning, *Diary of Orville Hickman Browning*, 1:529. Stanton replaced Cameron on January 20. Cameron was dismissed for lack of competence in managing the department, although John Cochrane and others suggested his support of arming former slaves contributed to his dismissal and subsequent appointment as minister to Russia (see Cochrane, *American Civil War*, 17).

84. JBF, "Great Events," Frémont Family Papers, BL, 328–329; JBF to Frederick Billings, February 7, 1862, JBF, *Letters of Jessie Benton Frémont*, 312.

85. Browning, *Diary of Orville Hickman Browning*, 1:529.

86. JBF to Frederick Billings, January 21 and February 7, 1862, JBF, *Letters of Jessie Benton Frémont*, 309–311; Tracy, "Frémont's Pursuit of Jackson," 168; Edwin Stanton to Charles Dana, February 1, 1861, quoted in Flower, *Edwin McMasters Stanton*, 129; Henry Halleck to George McClellan, February 2, 1862, *O.R.*, 1:8:828–829; Henry Halleck to Lincoln, January 6, 1862, Abraham Lincoln Papers, LOC; George McClellan to Henry Halleck, February 6, 1862, McClellan, *Civil War Papers of George B. McClellan*, 171–172; Marvel, *Lincoln's Autocrat*, 158.

87. U.S. Congress, *Congressional Globe*, 37th Congress, 2nd Session, 118.

88. Elizabeth Blair Lee to Samuel Phillips Lee, March 6, 1862, E. B. Lee, *Wartime Washington*, 106–107; Parrish, *Frank Blair*, 134–135; Dorsheimer, "Frémont's Hundred Days in Missouri," 115–125, 247–258, 372–384; Tap, *Over Lincoln's Shoulder*, 91; Montgomery Blair and Frank Blair's testimony is in *JCCW: Missouri*, 154–186; C. Phillips, *The Rivers Ran Backward*, 262.

89. Parrish, *Frank Blair*, 14; U.S. Congress, *Congressional Globe*, 37th Congress, 2nd Session, 1118.

90. F. Blair, *Frémont's Hundred Days in Missouri*, 6–7; Schofield, *Forty-Six Years in the Army*, 31.

91. F. Blair, *Frémont's Hundred Days in Missouri*, 11–13, 16.

92. Rollins, "Some Impressions of Frank P. Blair," 353; F. Blair, *Frémont's Hundred Days in Missouri*, 15.

93. F. Blair, *Frémont's Hundred Days in Missouri*, 15.

94. F. Blair, *Frémont's Hundred Days in Missouri*, 3, 15.

95. U.S. Congress, *Congressional Globe*, 37th Congress, 2nd Session, 1124–1126.

96. U.S. Congress, *Congressional Globe*, 37th Congress, 2nd Session, 1125.

97. U.S. Congress, *Congressional Globe*, 37th Congress, 2nd Session, 1125.

98. U.S. Congress, *Congressional Globe*, 37th Congress, 2nd Session, 1127; Hollister, *Life of Schuyler Colfax*, 183n.

99. Schuyler Colfax to Charles Sumner, March 26, 1862, quoted in W. H. Smith, *Schuyler Colfax*, 165; JBF to Frederick Billings, April 8, 1862, JBF, *Letters of Jessie Benton Frémont*, 317; "President's War Order No. 3," *O.R.*, 1:5:54.

100. Stewart, *Wendell Phillips*, 234; Wendell Phillips to Ann Phillips, March 31, 1862, Crawford Blagden Papers, HL.

101. Wendell Phillips to Ann Phillips, March 31, 1862, Crawford Blagden Papers, HL.

102. Wendell Phillips to Ann Phillips, March 31, 1862, Crawford Blagden Papers, HL.

103. *The Liberator*, March 14 and 21, 1862; Conlin, "The Smithsonian Abolition Lecture Controversy," 314, 320.

104. Fehrenbacher and Fehrenbacher, *Recollected Words of Abraham Lincoln*, 72; "Message to Congress," *CW*, 5:144–145.

105. *New York Times*, March 7, 1862; Dahlgren, *Memoir of John A. Dahlgren*, 356–357.

106. Conway, *Autobiography, Memories and Experiences*, 1:346; JBF to Thomas Starr King, March 10, 1862, Jessie Benton Frémont Papers, SCP; Burlingame, *Abraham Lincoln*, 2:341.

107. U.S. Congress, *Congressional Globe*, 37th Congress, 2nd Session, 1632; Guelzo, *Lincoln's Emancipation Proclamation*, 65.

108. Lydia Maria Child to John Greenleaf Whittier, January 21, 1862, quoted in J. McPherson, *Struggle for Equality*, 95; Child to Charles Sumner, June 22, 1862, quoted in Karcher, *The First Woman in the Republic*, 458; Oakes, *Freedom National*, 189; Anders, *Henry Halleck's War*, 59; "General Orders No. 13," *O.R.*, 1:8:405–407; U.S. Congress, *Congressional Globe*, 37th Congress, 2nd Session, 76.

109. Guelzo, *Lincoln's Emancipation Proclamation*, 97; "Message to Congress," *CW*, 5:192; Lincoln to Horace Greeley, March 24, 1862, *CW*, 5:169; *The Liberator*, May 16, 1862; *National Anti-Slavery Standard*, April 26, 1862.

110. *New York Times*, June 13, 1862.

111. William Lloyd Garrison to George Thompson, March 7, 1862, Garrison, *Let the Oppressed Go Free*, 5:81–82.

112. *The Liberator*, May 16, 1862.

Chapter Seven

1. Cox, "West Virginia Operations under Frémont," 2:278; Elizabeth Blair Lee to Samuel Phillips Lee, March 13, 1862, E. B. Lee, *Wartime Washington*, 109; *New York Post*, March 13, 1862, quoted in Burlingame, *Abraham Lincoln*, 2:303; JBF, "Great Events," Frémont Family Papers, BL, 330.

2. Burlingame, *Abraham Lincoln*, 2:294; W. J. Miller, "Such Men as Shields, Banks, and Frémont," 52.

3. W. J. Miller, "Such Men as Shields, Banks, and Frémont," 49; Lorenzo Thomas to JCF, March 22, 1862, *O.R.*, 1:12/3:8.

4. William S. Rosecrans to Lorenzo Thomas, March 22, 1862; William S. Rosecrans to JCF, March 28, 1862, *O.R.*, 1:12/3:9–12, 24–25; Cozzens, *Shenandoah 1862*, 229; JBF, "Great Events," Frémont Family Papers, BL, 331.

5. Lincoln to JCF, March 22, 1862, *CW*, 5:167.

6. Edwin M. Stanton to JCF, March 23, 1862, *O.R.*, 1:12/3:14.

7. "Frémont's Report," *O.R.*, 1:12/1:4; Chaffin, *Pathfinder*, 474; JBF, "Great Events," Frémont Family Papers, BL, 330; Achorn, *The Lincoln Miracle*, 71–72.

8. "Memorandum for a Plan of Campaign," *CW*, 4:544; W. J. Miller, "Such Men as Shields, Banks, and Frémont," 58.

9. Edwin M. Stanton to JCF, March 28, 1862, *O.R.*, 1:12/3:23–24; JCF to Edwin M. Stanton, March 28, *O.R.*, 1:12/3:24; JCF to Edwin M. Stanton, March 29, *O.R.*, 1:12/3:29; Edwin M. Stanton to JCF, March 30, *O.R.*, 1:12/3:31; Trefousse, *Radical Republicans*, 192; Lincoln to George B. McClellan, March 31, 1862, *CW*, 5:175–176.

10. JBF to Frederick Billings, April 8, 1862, JBF, *Letters of Jessie Benton Frémont*, 317–318.

11. Jacob Cox to JCF, April 26, 1862, *O.R.*, 1:12/3:108; JCF to Edwin Stanton, April 21, 1862, *O.R.*, 1:12/3:96.

12. "Frémont's Report," *O.R.*, 1:12/3:5.

13. James Shields to John Hay, undated February/March 1862, Abraham Lincoln Papers, LOC. Regarding Shields's supposed disloyalty, see Alexander J. Spencer to Abraham Lincoln, December 4, 1861; Alfred Barstow to Lincoln, December 9, 1861; F. B. Murdock to Lincoln, December 10, 1861; Ira P. Rankin to Simon Cameron, December 10, 1861, Abraham Lincoln Papers, LOC.

14. Burlingame, *Abraham Lincoln*, 1:190–193; "Memorandum of Duel Instructions to Elias H. Merryman," *CW*, 1:300–302.

15. Ransom Bedell to Theoda S. Fulton, March 31, 1862, Ransom Bedell Letters, ALPL.

16. Robertson, *Stonewall Jackson*, 347; Tanner, *Stonewall in the Valley*, 141.

17. Edwin Stanton to JCF, April 21, 1862, *O.R.*, 1:12/3:96.

18. "Memorandum for a Plan of Campaign," *CW*, 4:544–545; Henry Halleck to Lincoln, January 6, 1862, Abraham Lincoln Papers, LOC; Lincoln to Simon Cameron, July 10, 1862, *CW*, 5:95; Lincoln to Don Carlos Buell, January 6, 1862, *CW*, 5:91; "Frémont's Report," *O.R.*, 1:12/3:7.

19. Edwin Stanton to JCF, April 24, 1862, *O.R.*, 1:12/3:104.

20. JCF to Edwin Stanton, April 26 and 27, 1862, *O.R.*, 1:12/3:108, 110; JBF to Frederick Billings, May 7, 1862, JBF, *Letters of Jessie Benton Frémont*, 323; "Frémont's Report," *O.R.*, 1:12/3:7–8.

21. Armstrong, *Battle of McDowell*, 43–44, 52; Imboden, "Stonewall Jackson in the Shenandoah," 2:286–287; Schenck, "Notes on the Battle of McDowell," 2:298; "Frémont's Report," *O.R.*, 1:12/3:8; Townsend, *Rustics in Rebellion*, 202; McDonald and Gwin, *A Woman's Civil War*, 56.

22. "Frémont's Report," *O.R.*, 1:12/3:10; JCF to Edwin Stanton, May 16, 1862, *O.R.*, 1:12/3:197.

23. JBF to Annie Adams Fields, May 29, 1862; JBF to George W. Julian, May 1, 1862, JBF, *Letters of Jessie Benton Frémont*, 325, 320.

24. David Hunter to Lincoln, December 23, 1861, Abraham Lincoln Papers, LOC; Lincoln to Hunter, December 31, 1861, *CW*, 5:84–85.

25. David Hunter to Edwin Stanton, January 29, 1862, quoted in Williams, *Lincoln and the Radicals*, 136.

26. Elizabeth Blair Lee to Samuel Phillips Lee, May 26, 1862, E. B. Lee, *Wartime Washington*, 152.

27. "General Orders No. 7," *O.R.*, 1:14:333; "General Orders No. 11," *O.R.*, 1:14:341.

28. J. C. G. Kennedy, *Population of the United States in 1860*, xiii; E. E., Miller, *Lincoln's Abolitionist General*, 100; Brown, *Edward Stanly*, 203–204; *New York Herald*, May 20, 1862.

29. Salmon Chase to Lincoln, May 16, 1862, Abraham Lincoln Papers, LOC.

30. Carl Schurz to Lincoln, May 16, 1862, Abraham Lincoln Papers, LOC.

31. "Proclamation Revoking General Hunter's Order of Military Emancipation of May 8, 1862," *CW*, 5:222–223.

32. Fehrenbacher and Fehrenbacher, *Recollected Words of Abraham Lincoln*, 324.

33. "Congratulating the Army," May 24, 1862, LADP, http://www.lincolnarchives.us/cgi-bin/lincoln?a=d&d=&sf=&d=Drg94-164-c-11&page=1.

34. Gordon, *Brook Farm to Cedar Mountain*, 192–193; McDonald and Gwin, *A Woman's Civil War*, 51; Strother, *A Virginia Yankee in the Civil War*, 45.

35. Edwin Stanton to D. S. Miles, May 24, 1862, *O.R.*, 1:12/3:226; Ashby, *The Valley Campaigns*, 126; Cox, "West Virginia Operations under Frémont," 2:280; "Frémont's Report," *O.R.*, 1:12/3:10; Lincoln to JCF, May 24, 1862, *CW*, 5:230–231; Lincoln to Irvin McDowell, May 24, 1862, *CW*, 5:232–233.

36. Lincoln to George B. McClellan, May 21, 1862, *CW*, 5:226.

37. Hale, *Four Valiant Years in Lower Shenandoah Valley*, 164; Robertson, *Stonewall Jackson*, 416; JCF to Lincoln, May 24, 1862, Abraham Lincoln Papers, LOC.

38. Tracy, "Frémont's Pursuit of Jackson," 174–175; "Frémont's Report," *O.R.*, 1:12/1:11; Cozzens, *Shenandoah 1862*, 385.

39. "Frémont's Report," *O.R.*, 1:12/1:12; Edwin Stanton to JCF, May 25, 1862, *O.R.*, 1:12/1:644.

40. Cozzens, *Shenandoah 1862*, 386; Lincoln to JCF, May 27, 1862, *O.R.*, 1:12/1:644.

41. JCF to Lincoln, May 27 and 28, 1862, *O.R.*, 1:12/1:644–645.

42. Burlingame, *Abraham Lincoln*, 2:318; Edwin Stanton to JCF and JCF to Stanton, May 28, 1862, *O.R.*, 1:12/1:645–646.

43. Cozzens, *Shenandoah 1862*, 389; Lincoln to JCF, May 30, 1862, *O.R.*, 1:12/1:648.

44. JCF to Lincoln, May 29 and 31, 1862, *O.R.*, 1:12/1:647, 649; Lincoln to JCF, May 30, 1862, *O.R.*, 1:12/1:648.

45. Cozzens, *Shenandoah 1862*, 408–409; Ashby, *The Valley Campaigns*, 133; "Frémont's Report," O.R., 1:12/1:14.

46. Lincoln to JCF, May 24, 1862, *CW*, 5:230; Hay, *Inside Lincoln's White House*, 63; Jackson quoted in Cozzens, *Shenandoah 1862*, 102; W. J. Miller, "Such Men as Shields, Banks, and Frémont," 66.

47. Bates, *Diary of Edward Bates*, 261.

48. James Shields to Edwin Stanton, June 2, 1862, *O.R.*, 1:12/3:322.

49. "Calendar of Events," James Shields Papers, ALPL; James Shields to Irvin McDowell, June 3, 1862, *O.R.*, 1:12/3:326.

50. Tracy, "Frémont's Pursuit of Jackson," 185; JCF to Edwin Stanton, June 4, 1862, *O.R.*, 1:12/1:652.

51. Krick, *Conquering the Valley*, 137; W. J. Miller, "Such Men as Shields, Banks, and Frémont," 70–71; Tracy, "Frémont's Pursuit of Jackson," 332–333; "Calendar of Events," James Shields Papers, ALPL.

52. Strother, *A Virginia Yankee in the Civil War*, 64; JCF to Edwin Stanton and Lincoln to JCF, June 9, 1862, *O.R.*, 1:12/1:655; Krick, *Conquering the Valley*, 154, 239; Burlingame, *Abraham Lincoln*, 2:318.

53. Ransom Bedell to Theoda S. Fulton, June 12, 1862, Ransom Bedell Letters, ALPL; Krick, *Conquering the Valley*, 481; W. J. Miller, "Such Men as Shields, Banks, and Frémont," 71; Schurz, *Reminiscences of Carl Schurz*, 2:343.

54. Tanner, *Stonewall in the Valley*, 312.

55. Lorenzo Thomas to JCF, June 10, 1862, *O.R.*, 1:12/1:655; JCF to Edwin Stanton, June 10, 1862, *O.R.*, 1:12/1:656; Lincoln to JCF, June 12, 1862, *CW*, 5:267; JCF to Lincoln, June 11, 1862, *O.R.*, 1:12/1:656; Edwin Stanton to JCF, June 12, 1862, *O.R.*, 1:12/1:657.

56. JCF to Edwin Stanton, June 12, 1862, *O.R.*, 1:12/1:657–658; Lincoln to JCF, June 13, 1862, *O.R.*, 1:12/1:658; JCF to Edwin Stanton, June 14, 1862, *O.R.*, 1:12/1:660.

57. Edwin Stanton to JCF, June 14, 1862, *O.R.*, 1:12/1:660; Lincoln to JCF, June 15, 1862, *O.R.*, 1:12/1: 661.

58. Carl Schurz to Abraham Lincoln, May 22 and June 12, 1862, Abraham Lincoln Papers, LOC; Ruess, *Carl Schurz*, 94, 96; Schurz, *Reminiscences of Carl Schurz*, 2:341–344.

59. Carl Schurz to Lincoln, June 12, 1862, Abraham Lincoln Papers, LOC; Ruess, *Carl Schurz*, 95.

60. Carl Schurz to Lincoln, June 16, 1862, Abraham Lincoln Papers, LOC; Schurz, *Reminiscences of Carl Schurz*, 2:346.

61. Lincoln to JCF, June 12, 1862, *CW*, 5:268.

62. JCF to Lincoln, June 15, 1862, Abraham Lincoln Papers, LOC.

63. Lincoln to JCF, June 16, 1862, *CW*, 5:273–274.

64. JCF to Lincoln, June 16, 1862, *O.R.*, 1:12/1:663.

65. Fehrenbacher and Fehrenbacher, *Recollected Words of Abraham Lincoln*, 434.

66. "Order Constituting the Army of Virginia," *CW*, 5:287; Lincoln to William S. Rosecrans, March 17, 1863, *CW*, 6:139.

67. JBF, "Memoirs," Frémont Family Papers, BL, 379; Strother, *A Virginia Yankee in the Civil War*, 65.

68. Charles Francis Adams Jr. to Charles Francis Adams, August 27, 1862, Ford, *A Cycle of Adams Letters*, 176.

69. Strother, *A Virginia Yankee in the Civil War*, 63; JCF to Edwin Stanton, June 27, 1862, *O.R.*, 1:12:437–438.

70. Flower, *Edwin McMasters Stanton*, 362; John Pope to JCF and Nathaniel Banks, June 27, 1862, *O.R.*, 1:12/3:437; Cozzens, *General John Pope*, 80; John Pope to George McClellan, July 4, 1862, *O.R.*, 1:11/3:295; *Washington Evening Star*, February 12, 1863; *Alexandria Gazette*, February 13, 1863.

71. Gordon, *Brook Farm to Cedar Mountain*, 264; Robert Gould Shaw to Josephine "Effie" Shaw, April 16, 1862; Robert Gould Shaw to Sarah Shaw, July 4, 1862, Duncan, *Blue-Eyed Child of Fortune*, 193, 214; JBF to George W. Julian, January 16, 1864, JBF, *Letters of Jessie Benton Frémont*, 362.

72. Strother, *A Virginia Yankee in the Civil War*, 63; *New York Tribune*, August 13, 1862; Robert Gould Shaw to Sarah Shaw, July 28, 1862, Duncan, *Blue-Eyed Child of Fortune*, 222.

73. Blaine, *Twenty Years of Congress*, 1:367; Gallagher, "You Must Either Attack Richmond or Give Up the Job and Come to the Defense of Washington," 3; Cozzens, *Shenandoah 1862*, 3.

74. Schalk, *Campaigns of 1862 and 1863*, 174–181; Cozzens, *Shenandoah 1862*, 3; W. J. Miller, "Such Men as Shields, Banks, and Frémont," 81. Lt. Col. John Pilsen, Frémont's chief of artillery, wrote a pamphlet defending Frémont and pointing out Schalk's many incorrect assumptions; see Pilsen, *Reply of Lieut.-Col. Pilsen to Emil Schalk's Criticisms of the Campaign in the Mountain Department*.

75. JBF to Frederick Billings, January 21, 1862, JBF, *Letters of Jessie Benton Frémont*, 310.

76. U.S. Congress, *Congressional Globe*, 37th Congress, 2nd Session, 18.

77. Baxter, *Orville H. Browning*, 137–139; Blaine, *Twenty Years of Congress*, 1:373. Trumbull's eloquence was borrowed. In a speech in the House of Commons in November 1783, William Pitt the Younger had declared, "Necessity is the plea for every infringement of human freedom: it is the argument of tyrants; it is the creed of slaves." See Trumbull, *Constitutionality and Expediency of Confiscation Vindicated*, 5.

78. U.S. Congress, *Congressional Globe*, 37th Congress, 2nd Session, 3006; Oakes, *Freedom National*, 230–231.

79. Lyman Trumbull to Julia Trumbull, July 13, 1861, Lyman Trumbull Family Papers, ALPL.

80. "To the Senate and House of Representatives," *CW*, 5:328–331, quote on 331.

81. Lyman Trumbull to Julia Trumbull, July 16, 1862, Lyman Trumbull Family Papers, ALPL.

82. U.S. Congress, *Congressional Globe*, 37th Congress, 2nd Session, 3373–3374; *CW*, 5:328–331; Burlingame, *Abraham Lincoln*, 2:359.

83. Lyman Trumbull to Julia Trumbull, July 15, 1862, Lyman Trumbull Family Papers, ALPL; Benjamin Bannan to Lincoln, July 24, 1862, Abraham Lincoln Papers, LOC.

84. Strother, *A Virginia Yankee in the Civil War*, 64; see also McDonald and Gwin, *A Woman's Civil War*, 62–63; Ashby, *The Valley Campaigns*, 134.

85. George B. McClellan to Lincoln, July 7, 1862, Abraham Lincoln Papers, LOC; Stanly, *Letter from the Hon. Edward Stanly*, 9; M. Blair, "The Republican Party as It Was and Is," 426.

86. Welles, *Diary of Gideon Welles*, 1:70; Lincoln to Reverdy Johnson, July 26, 1862, *CW*, 5:343; Lincoln to August Belmont, July 31, 1862, *CW*, 5:350.

Chapter Eight

1. W. C. Harris, *With Charity for All*, 91. The Texas expedition would be led by Frémont's ally, Nathaniel Banks. On Frémont's pay, see JBF to George W. Julian, January 16, 1864, JBF, *Letters of Jessie Benton Frémont*, 362–363; Denton, *Passion and Principle*, 337.

2. JBF to Frederick Billings, August 1, 1862, JBF, *Letters of Jessie Benton Frémont*, 333; *New York Tribune* July 16, 1862.

3. *New York Tribune* July 16, 1862.

4. JBF to Sydney Howard Gay, June 21, 1862, JBF, *Letters of Jessie Benton Frémont*, 329.

5. *New York Herald*, August 29, 1862.

6. *New York Herald*, August 29, 1862; Charles Sumner to Lincoln, August 29, 1862, Abraham Lincoln Papers, LOC.

7. "Appeal to Border State Representatives to Favor a Compensated Emancipation," *CW*, 5:318; Carpenter, *Six Months at the White House with Abraham Lincoln*, 20–22; Oakes, *Freedom National*, 306; Chase, *The Salmon P. Chase Papers*, 1:351; Fehrenbacher and Fehrenbacher, *Recollected Words of Abraham Lincoln*, 38.

8. "Address on Colonization to a Deputation of Negroes," *CW*, 5:370–375; Oakes, *Freedom National*, 310.

9. *New York Tribune*, August 20, 1862. The piece ran in the middle of page 4.

10. Lincoln to Horace Greeley, August 22, 1862, *CW*, 5:388–389.

11. Sydney Howard Gay to Lincoln, August 1862, Abraham Lincoln Papers, LOC.

12. Thurlow Weed to Lincoln, August 24, 1862, Abraham Lincoln Papers, LOC.

13. Douglass, *The Civil War*, 3:266–269.

14. Welles, *Diary of Gideon Welles*, 1:142.

15. "Emancipation Proclamation—First Draft," *CW*, 5:336–337; Oakes, *Freedom National*, 305; Guelzo, *Lincoln's Emancipation Proclamation*, 174; "Preliminary Emancipation Proclamation," *CW*, 5:433–436; Welles, *Diary of Gideon Welles*, 142–144; Chase, *The Salmon P. Chase Papers*, 1:393–396.

16. Finkelman, "Lincoln, Emancipation, and the Limits of Constitutional Change," 350; Fehrenbacher and Fehrenbacher, *Recollected Words of Abraham Lincoln*, 23.

17. William Lloyd Garrison to Fanny Garrison, September 25, 1861, Garrison, *Let the Oppressed Go Free*, 5:114–115; Stewart, *Wendell Phillips*, 240; *The Liberator*, November 28, 1862.

18. Douglass, *The Civil War*, 3:273–274, 280; Theodore Tilton to Lincoln, September 24, 1862, Abraham Lincoln Papers, LOC.

19. William Steel to Frank Ruff, September 26, 1862, and Archbishop Hughes, quoted in Gallman, *Cacophony of Politics*, 78–79, 85; Hannibal Hamlin to Lincoln, September 25, 1862, Abraham Lincoln Papers, LOC; Lincoln to Hannibal Hamlin, September 28, 1862, *CW*, 5:444.

20. B. S. Hedrick to Lincoln, September 23, 1862, Abraham Lincoln Papers, LOC.

21. C. Goodwin, *John Charles Frémont*, 238n.

22. William Lloyd Garrison to Helen Garrison, October 10, 1862, Garrison, *Let the Oppressed Go Free*, 5:123; Wyandot County, Ohio, Citizens to Lincoln, November 1862, and Preble County, Ohio, Citizens to Senate, December 19, 1862, Abraham Lincoln Papers, LOC.

23. *Missouri Democrat*, October 20, 1862.

24. Montgomery Blair to Lincoln, February 19, 1863, Abraham Lincoln Papers, LOC; F. Blair, "Address of F. P. Blair, Jr. to His Constituents," 4.

25. Guelzo, *Lincoln's Emancipation Proclamation*, 187.

26. Cochrane, *American Civil War*, 28; Gallman, *Cacophony of Politics*, 88; Neely, *Lincoln and the Democrats*, 48–59; *The Liberator*, November 21, 1862.

27. JBF to Eliza Benton Jones, early 1863, C. C. Phillips, *Jessie Benton Frémont*, 259; *Missouri Republican*, November 3, 1862; Parrish, *Frank Blair*, 151–154; Lincoln to Frank

Blair, November 14, 1862, *CW*, 5:496; Blair to Lincoln, November 14, 1862, Abraham Lincoln Papers, LOC.

28. Carl Schurz to Lincoln, November 8, 1862; Lincoln to Carl Schurz, November 24, 1862, Abraham Lincoln Papers, LOC; Lincoln to Carl Schurz, November 10, 1862, *CW*, 5:494; Engle, *Gathering to Save a Nation*, 228; Guelzo, *Lincoln's Emancipation Proclamation*, 197.

29. JBF to James T. Fields, May 22, 1862, JBF, *Letters of Jessie Benton Frémont*, 324.

30. JBF to James T. Fields, October 8, 1862, JBF, *Letters of Jessie Benton Frémont*, 334; JBF to James T. Fields, October 22 and 30, quoted in Herr, *Jessie Benton Frémont*, 366.

31. JBF to James T. Fields, October 26, 1862, JBF, *Letters of Jessie Benton Frémont*, 335.

32. *Washington Evening Star*, February 12, 1863; *Atlantic Monthly*, January 1863, 142–143.

33. *New York Tribune*, January 19, 1863; *Missouri Republican*, January 13, 1863.

34. *Daily National Republican*, March 9, 1863.

35. JBF to James T. Fields, January 5, 1863, JBF, *Letters of Jessie Benton Frémont*, 336–337; JBF to Thomas Starr King, early 1863, Jessie Benton Frémont Papers, SCP; *Daily National Republican*, April 27, 1863.

36. Driscoll, *Rogue*, 177.

37. Driscoll, *Rogue*, 178.

38. Driscoll, *Rogue*, 179–180.

39. Driscoll, *Rogue*, 180–181.

40. *Missouri Democrat*, December 30, 1862; *Chicago Tribune*, January 1, 1863.

41. Driscoll, *Rogue*, 181; "Order Approving Sentence of Justus McKinstry," *CW*, 6:82.

42. "Annual Message to Congress," *CW*, 5:529–535.

43. *The Liberator*, January 30 and February 5, 1863; JBF to Eliza Benton Jones, early 1863, C. C. Phillips, *Jessie Benton Frémont*, 259; *Weekly National Intelligencer*, March 26, 1863; *New York Tribune*, February 12 and March 24, 1863; Julian and Child, *Speeches on Political Questions*, 209.

44. J. McPherson, *Struggle for Equality*, 91; *The Liberator*, December 11, 1863.

45. JBF to Eliza Benton Jones, early 1863, C. C. Phillips, *Jessie Benton Frémont*, 259; Bicknell, *Lincoln's Pathfinder*, 264–266; *New York Tribune*, April 1, 1863; *Alexandria Gazette*, April 3, 1863.

46. *New York Tribune*, April 13, 1863.

47. *New York Tribune*, April 13, 1863.

48. *New York Herald*, April 14, 1863.

49. *Weekly National Intelligencer*, April 23, 1863.

50. *Weekly National Intelligencer*, May 21, 1863; Hennessey, "Evangelizing for Union," 536–537.

51. Bates, *Diary of Edward Bates*, 292, 321; W. C. Harris, *With Charity for All*, 56.

52. JBF, "Memoirs," Frémont Family Papers, BL, 379–380; *Alexandria Gazette*, January 31 and February 18, 1863; *New York Tribune*, February 17 and March 27, 1863.

53. Winks, *Frederick Billings*, 182–183; Chaffin, *Pathfinder*, 480–481; *Butte Record* (Oroville, California), July 11, 1863; *Daily National Republican*, April 9, 1863; W. E. Smith, *Francis Preston Blair Family*, 2:89.

54. *New York Tribune*, March 4, 1863; *Daily National Republican*, March 3, 1863; Brooks, *Mr. Lincoln's Washington*, 217; Lincoln to Edwin Stanton, March 7, 1863, *CW*, 6:127.

55. Brown, *Edward Stanly*, 202–203.

56. Brown, *Edward Stanly*, 204; *New York Herald*, May 28, 1862; Edward Stanly to Edwin Stanton, June 12, 1862, *O.R.*, 1:9:400–401; W. C. Harris, *With Charity for All*, 63–65.

57. Brown, *Edward Stanly*, 208–214.

58. Brown, *Edward Stanly*, 238–240, 249–250.

59. Conway, *Autobiography, Memories and Experiences*, 1:377–380; JBF, "Memoirs," Frémont Family Papers, BL, 379.

60. "Proclamation Revoking General Hunter's Order of Military Emancipation of May 9, 1862," *CW*, 5:223.

61. *New York Herald*, January 27, 1863; *New York Tribune*, February 12, 1863.

62. W. C. Harris, *With Charity for All*, 71.

63. Jacob Dodson to Simon Cameron, April 23, 1861, *O.R.*, 3:1:107; Cameron to Dodson, April 29, 1861, *O.R.*, 3:1:133.

64. Kahan, *Amiable Scoundrel*, 200–205; Browning, *Diary of Orville Hickman Browning*, 1:555; Fehrenbacher and Fehrenbacher, *Recollected Words of Abraham Lincoln*, 199; "Memorandum on Recruiting Negroes," July 1862, *CW*, 5:338; *New York Tribune*, March 26, 1863; Eggleston, *President Lincoln's Recruiter*, 134.

65. *The Liberator*, January 30 and June 5, 1863; *Weekly National Intelligencer*, March 19, 1863; *Washington Evening Star*, March 28, 1863.

66. Julian, *Political Recollections*, 229–230; Lincoln to Isaac Arnold, May 26, 1863, *CW*, 6:230; Lincoln to Carl Schurz, March 13, 1864, *CW*, 7:243; Fehrenbacher and Fehrenbacher, *Recollected Words of Abraham Lincoln*, 442.

67. *Daily National Republican*, March 18, 1863.

68. *Washington Evening Star*, April 10, 1863; *Daily National Republican*, April 10, 1863; *Alexandria Gazette*, April 27, 1863.

69. *Alexandria Gazette*, May 7, 1863; Thaddeus Stevens to unknown, June 9, 1863, quoted in Williams, *Lincoln and the Radicals*, 279.

70. *Daily National Republican*, June 2, 1863.

71. New York City Citizens Committee to Lincoln, May 28, 1863, Abraham Lincoln Papers, LOC; "Remarks to New York Committee," May 30, 1863, *CW*, 6:239.

72. *Washington Evening Star*, June 6, 1863.

73. Lincoln to Charles Sumner, June 1, 1863, Abraham Lincoln Papers, LOC.

74. JCF to Charles Sumner, June 9, 1863, Abraham Lincoln Papers, LOC.

75. R. J. Bartlett, *John C. Frémont and the Republican Party*, 95; Wittke, *Against the Current*, 189–191.

76. R. J. Bartlett, *John C. Frémont and the Republican Party*, 89.

77. Elizabeth Blair Lee to Samuel Phillips Lee, March 20, 1863, E. B. Lee, *Wartime Washington*, 254; Elizabeth Blair Lee to Samuel Phillips Lee, October 16, 1861, E. B. Lee, *Wartime Washington*, 86 ("abolition horde"); Elizabeth Blair Lee to Samuel Phillips Lee, December 17, 1861, E. B. Lee, *Wartime Washington*, 93 ("John Brownites"); Elizabeth

Blair Lee to Samuel Phillips Lee, May 26, 1862, E. B. Lee, *Wartime Washington*, 152 ("Frémont proclivities").

78. JBF to John T. Fiala, July 10, 1863, JBF, *Letters of Jessie Benton Frémont*, 354; Julian, *Political Recollections*, 230.

79. JCF to Edwin Stanton, June 6, 1863, in *Daily National Republican*, June 13, 1863.

80. *Washington Evening Star*, July 2, 1863.

81. *Alexandria Gazette*, July 29, 1863; Sigismund Kaufmann, Charles Kessman, and Friedrich Kapp to Lincoln, June 16, 1863; John L. Russell to Lincoln, June 27, 1863; Tewandah to Lincoln, June 29, 1863; Pennsylvania Citizens to Lincoln, June 30, 1863, Abraham Lincoln Papers, LOC.

82. Lincoln to Frederick Kapp and others, June 16, 1863, *CW*, 6:282; JBF to John T. Fiala, July 10, 1863, JBF, *Letters of Jessie Benton Frémont*, 354.

83. *New York Tribune*, July 14, 1863; *New York World*, July 25, 1863; Egan, *Frémont*, 519; Herr, *Jessie Benton Frémont*, 368–369; Strong, *Diary of the Civil War*, 339; Rolle, *John Charles Frémont*, 226.

84. Pickard, *Life and Letters of John Greenleaf Whittier*, 460–463.

85. Pickard, *Life and Letters of John Greenleaf Whittier*, 464–465.

86. JBF to John Greenleaf Whittier, October 17, 1863, JBF, *Letters of Jessie Benton Frémont*, 357–358.

87. Fehrenbacher and Fehrenbacher, *Recollected Words of Abraham Lincoln*, 76; Hay, *Inside Lincoln's White House*, 93; *New York Herald*, August 13, 1863.

88. Lincoln to Montgomery Blair, November 2, 1863, *CW*, 6:554–555; Brooks, *Mr. Lincoln's Washington*, 269.

89. Orville Browning to Thomas Ewing, June 15, 1863, quoted in Baxter, *Orville H. Browning*, 154; Bates, *Diary of Edward Bates*, 301.

CHAPTER NINE

1. Neely, *Lincoln and the Democrats*, 63–65; E. McPherson, *The Political History of the United States of America during the Great Rebellion*, 414.

2. *The Liberator*, February 5, 1864; Thornbrough, *Indiana in the Civil War Era*, 209.

3. William Lloyd Garrison to James Miller McKim, February 27, 1864, quoted in J. McPherson, *Struggle for Equality*, 266; *The Liberator*, February 5 and March 18, 1864; R. J. Bartlett, *John C. Frémont and the Republican Party*, 100; Waugh, *Reelecting Lincoln*, 174.

4. *The Liberator*, March 4, 1864; *New York Herald*, March 2, 1864.

5. *New York Tribune*, March 1, 1864.

6. Rolle, *John Charles Frémont*, 229; Horner, *Lincoln and Greeley*, 342.

7. Zornow, *Lincoln and the Party Divided*, 61–62; Frederick Driscoll to Lincoln, April 12, 1864, Abraham Lincoln Papers, LOC.

8. Bates, *Diary of Edward Bates*, 375.

9. Engle, *Yankee Dutchman*, 167–169; Koerner, *Memoirs of Gustave Koerner*, 2:432.

10. R. J. Bartlett, *John C. Frémont and the Republican Party*, 97; William H. Haase to Lincoln, May 12, 1864, Abraham Lincoln Papers, LOC.

11. *New York World*, January 25 and 28, 1864.

12. W. E. Smith, *Francis Preston Blair Family*, 2:237–240, 248, 251; Hay, *Inside Lincoln's White House*, 124; *New York Herald*, October 8, 1863; Brooks, *Mr. Lincoln's Washington*, 249; James A. Garfield to J. H. Rhodes, April 28, 1864, quoted in Williams, *Lincoln and the Radicals*, 314.

13. Waugh, *Reelecting Lincoln*, 176; Long, *The Jewel of Liberty*, 37, 226; Fehrenbacher and Fehrenbacher, *Recollected Words of Abraham Lincoln*, 148.

14. Cochrane, *American Civil War*, 30; Brooks, *Mr. Lincoln's Washington*, 237; R. J. Bartlett, *John C. Frémont and the Republican Party*, 87; Fehrenbacher and Fehrenbacher, *Recollected Words of Abraham Lincoln*, 375; Burlingame, *Abraham Lincoln*, 2:624; Salmon Chase to Jesse Stubbs, November 1, 1861, Chase, *The Salmon P. Chase Papers*, 3:106.

15. Chase, *The Salmon P. Chase Papers*, 1:432–433.

16. Fehrenbacher and Fehrenbacher, *Recollected Words of Abraham Lincoln*, 505; *New York Herald*, February 23, 1864.

17. *New York Times*, February 24, 1864; *New York Herald*, March 5, 1864; Stahr, *Salmon P. Chase*, 475; Lincoln to Salmon Chase, February 29, 1864, *CW*, 7:213.

18. U.S. Congress, *Congressional Globe*, 38th Congress, 1st Session, 509–514, 1828–1832, and Appendix, 46, 51. For Tyler's abortive 1844 campaign, see Bicknell, *America 1844*, 163–165; Parrish, *Frank Blair*, 195–196.

19. R. J. Bartlett, *John C. Frémont and the Republican Party*, 92–93; Burlingame, *Abraham Lincoln*, 2:620; JBF, "Memoirs," Frémont Family Papers, BL, 380.

20. George McClellan to Samuel S. Cox, June 8, 1863, McClellan, *Civil War Papers of George B. McClellan*, 548–549.

21. George McClellan to Samuel L. M. Barlow, January 20, 1863; George McClellan to Mary Ellen McClellan, February 28, 1863; George McClellan to Lorenzo Thomas, August 4, 1863; George McClellan to Charles J. Biddle, October 12, 1863; George McClellan to Lincoln, November 1863; George McClellan to Elizabeth McClellan, December 6, 1863; all in McClellan, *Civil War Papers of George B. McClellan*, 535, 540, 554, 558–559, 560–562, 563.

22. Sears, *George B. McClellan*, 350–351.

23. George McClellan to Edward H. Wright, March 19, 1864; George McClellan to Samuel L. M. Barlow, June 17, 1864, McClellan, *Civil War Papers of George B. McClellan*, 572, 578; Zornow, *Lincoln and the Party Divided*, 144–145.

24. George McClellan to Francis Preston Blair, July 22, 1864, McClellan, *Civil War Papers of George B. McClellan*, 583–585; *New York Herald*, August 4, 1864.

25. *New York Herald*, February 21, 1861; J. George, "Long-Neglected Lincoln Speech," 27.

26. R. J. Bartlett, *John C. Frémont and the Republican Party*, 106–107.

27. Egan, *Frémont*, 425, 519; C. C. Phillips, *Jessie Benton Frémont*, 262–263; JBF to Thomas Starr King, January 1864, JBF, *Letters of Jessie Benton Frémont*, 360; JBF to John Greenleaf Whittier, March 10, 1864, JBF, *Letters of Jessie Benton Frémont*, 373; JBF to Elizabeth Palmer Peabody, March 20, 1864, JBF, *Letters of Jessie Benton Frémont*, 375, 377n.

28. George Smalley to Wendell Phillips, March 15, 1864, Crawford Blagden Papers, HL; Cirillo, *The Abolitionist Civil War*, 24, 185.

29. W. A. Baldwin to Lyman Trumbull, April 4, 1864, quoted in Williams, *Lincoln and the Radicals*, 313–314.

30. Fehrenbacher and Fehrenbacher, *Recollected Words of Abraham Lincoln*, 125; Lincoln to John H. Bryant, May 30, 1864, *CW*, 7:366.

31. Carpenter, *Six Months at the White House with Abraham Lincoln*, 77.

32. Lester, *Life and Public Services of Charles Sumner*, 360.

33. Francis Lieber to Charles Sumner, February 4, 1864, Donald, *Charles Sumner and the Rights of Man*, 168.

34. Clara Barton to Frances Gage, May 1, 1864, Oates, *A Woman of Valor*, 224.

35. U.S. Congress, *Congressional Globe*, 38th Congress, 1st Session, 1199–1200, 1313.

36. Vorenberg, *Final Freedom*, 112; Lincoln to Albert G. Hodges, April 4, 1864, *CW*, 7:281–282.

37. *New York Herald*, May 3, 1864.

38. R. J. Bartlett, *John C. Frémont and the Republican Party*, 100–101, 105; E. McPherson, *The Political History of the United States of America during the Great Rebellion*, 410.

39. Frederick Douglass to Edward Gilbert, May 23, 1864, Douglass, *The Civil War*, 3:403; J. McPherson, *Negro's Civil War*, 303–304.

40. Wittke, *Against the Current*, 193; *The Liberator*, June 3, 1864.

41. Strong, *Diary of the Civil War*, 453; *New York Herald*, May 30, 1864; Welles, *Diary of Gideon Welles*, 2:43.

42. *New York Tribune*, June 8, 1864; *The Liberator*, June 3, 1864.

43. E. McPherson, *The Political History of the United States of America during the Great Rebellion*, 413; Julian and Child, *Speeches on Political Questions*, 212; Lydia Maria Child to George W. Julian, March 27, 1864, quoted in Cirillo, *The Abolitionist Civil War*, 220.

44. *The Liberator*, June 3, 1864.

45. *The Liberator*, June 3, 1864.

46. Strong, *Diary of the Civil War*, 455; Welles, *Diary of Gideon Welles*, 2:43; Hay, *Inside Lincoln's White House*, 19.

47. E. McPherson, *The Political History of the United States of America during the Great Rebellion*, 413–414; Egan, *Frémont*, 519.

48. E. McPherson, *The Political History of the United States of America during the Great Rebellion*, 413–414; *New York Herald*, June 6, 1864.

49. *New York Dispatch*, June 12, 1864.

50. *New York Herald*, June 2, 1864; Koerner, *Memoirs of Gustave Koerner*, 2:432. For Birney's nonrole in Clay's defeat, see Bicknell, *America 1844*, 229–230; Cheathem, *Who Is James K. Polk?*, 215.

51. Strong, *Diary of the Civil War*, 455.

52. *The Liberator*, June 3, 1864.

53. J. McPherson, *Negro's Civil War*, 304–305.

54. Edwin Cowles to Montgomery Blair, May 31, 1864, Abraham Lincoln Papers, LOC; Solomon Newton Pettis to Abraham Lincoln, May 31, 1864, Abraham Lincoln Papers, LOC.

55. Henry Halleck to Francis Lieber, June 2, 1864; Francis Lieber to Henry Halleck, June 4, 1864, quoted in Rolle, *John Charles Frémont*, 230–231.

56. Wittke, *Against the Current*, 194; *New York Herald*, June 14; *New York Dispatch*, July 3, 1864.

57. Fehrenbacher and Fehrenbacher, *Recollected Words of Abraham Lincoln*, 316.

58. *New York Tribune*, June 6, 1864.

59. Long, *The Jewel of Liberty*, 38; Brooks, *Mr. Lincoln's Washington*, 325; Fehrenbacher and Fehrenbacher, *Recollected Words of Abraham Lincoln*, 448.

60. Korngold, *Two Friends of Man*, 330; Vorenberg, *Final Freedom*, 252.

61. F. Blair, *The Policy of the President for the Restoration of the Union*, 7; W. C. Harris, *With Charity for All*, 4, 8.

62. Brooks, *Mr. Lincoln's Washington*, 358; Cooling, *Jubal Early's Raid on Washington*, 115–117.

63. Lause, *Price's Lost Campaign*, 14.

64. Hay, *Inside Lincoln's White House*, 212; Lincoln to Salmon Chase, June 30, 1864, *CW*, 7:419.

65. Hay, *Inside Lincoln's White House*, 212–216.

66. Hay, *Inside Lincoln's White House*, 124; "First Inaugural Address," *CW*, 4:258; Burlingame, *Abraham Lincoln*, 2:593–594.

67. Burlingame, *Abraham Lincoln*, 2:659.

68. Hay, *Inside Lincoln's White House*, 218–219.

69. "Proclamation Concerning Reconstruction," *CW*, 7:433–434.

70. Julian, *Political Recollections*, 246–247.

71. Brownson, "Approaching Elections," 340–368.

72. White, *When Abe Comes Marching Home Again*, copy in ALPL.

73. Edgar Conkling to Benjamin Butler and Edgar Conkling to JCF, July 18, 1864, Butler, *Private and Official Correspondence*, 4:510–512.

74. JBF to John Greenleaf Whittier, August 22, 1864, JBF, *Letters of Jessie Benton Frémont*, 382.

75. *New York Herald*, August 4, 1864.

76. Schurz, *Reminiscences of Carl Schurz*, 3:103–104.

77. Salmon Chase to George Opdyke, August 19, 1864, Chase, *The Salmon P. Chase Papers*, 1:491n.

78. E. McPherson, *Political History of the United States*, 425–426.

79. Hay, *Inside Lincoln's White House*, 247–248; "Memorandum Concerning His Probable Failure of Re-election," *CW*, 7:514.

80. Long, *The Jewel of Liberty*, 283; Sears, *George B. McClellan*, 371; Grant, *Annotated Memoirs of Ulysses S. Grant*, 755.

81. George McClellan to the Democratic National Committee, September 8, 1864, McClellan, *Civil War Papers of George B. McClellan*, 595–596.

82. Stanly, *Letter from the Hon. Edward Stanly*, 1–3, 7; Fehrenbacher and Fehrenbacher, *Recollected Words of Abraham Lincoln*, 446.

83. Elizabeth Blair Lee to Samuel Phillips Lee, July 2, 1864, E. B. Lee, *Wartime Washington*, 399; Sears, *George B. McClellan*, 382.

84. *New York Herald*, June 7, 1864; Sears, *George B. McClellan*, 382; Bicknell, *Lincoln's Pathfinder*, 29–32.

85. Henry Elliott to Gideon Welles, September 5, 1864, R. J. Bartlett, *John C. Frémont and the Republican Party*, 126.

86. William Lloyd Garrison to Samuel J. May, September 6, 1864, Garrison, *Let the Oppressed Go Free*, 5:235.

87. C. C. Phillips, *Jessie Benton Frémont*, 269–270; JBF to John Greenleaf Whittier, November 19, 1889, JBF, *Letters of Jessie Benton Frémont*, 529–530.

88. JBF to John Greenleaf Whittier, November 19, 1889, JBF, *Letters of Jessie Benton Frémont*, 529–530; JBF to Samuel T. Pickard, May 28, 1893, 548–549; Stewart, *Wendell Phillips*, 254.

89. Bates, *Diary of Edward Bates*, 260; Trefousse, "Zachariah Chandler and the Withdrawal of Frémont," 182; Harbison, "Zachariah Chandler's Part in the Reelection of Abraham Lincoln," 268–269.

90. Trefousse, "Zachariah Chandler and the Withdrawal of Frémont," 183–184; Moore, "Zachariah Chandler in Lincoln's Second Campaign," 476.

91. Trefousse, "Zachariah Chandler and the Withdrawal of Frémont," 184; JBF, "Memoirs," Frémont Family Papers, BL, 390.

92. Trefousse, "Zachariah Chandler and the Withdrawal of Frémont," 185; JBF, "Memoirs," Frémont Family Papers, BL, 390–391; George McClellan to Samuel L. M. Barlow, September 27, 1864, McClellan, *Civil War Papers of George B. McClellan*, 605.

93. E. McPherson, *The Political History of the United States of America during the Great Rebellion*, 426–427.

94. Trefousse, "Zachariah Chandler and the Withdrawal of Frémont," 187.

95. Lincoln to Montgomery Blair and Blair to Lincoln, September 23, 1864, Abraham Lincoln Papers, LOC.

96. Hay, *Inside Lincoln's White House*, 230, 233; Frank Blair to Francis Preston Blair Sr., September 30, 1864, Abraham Lincoln Papers, LOC.

97. Trefousse, "Zachariah Chandler and the Withdrawal of Frémont," 181–182, 186; Elizabeth Blair Lee to Samuel Phillips Lee, September 24, 1864, E. B. Lee, *Wartime Washington*, 433; Welles, *Diary of Gideon Welles*, 2:156.

98. *New York Herald*, September 23, 1864; Wittke, *Against the Current*, 195; J. McPherson, *Negro's Civil War*, 306.

99. Fehrenbacher and Fehrenbacher, *Recollected Words of Abraham Lincoln*, 51; Lincoln to William T. Sherman, September 19, 1864, *CW*, 8:11; Lincoln to Oliver P. Morton, October 13, 1864, and "Estimated Electoral Vote," *CW*, 8:46–47.

100. Schlesinger, *History of American Presidential Elections*, 3:1244; Long, *The Jewel of Liberty*, 224.

101. Cooke diary entry quoted in J. Tracy Power, "In for Four Years More," 93.

102. "Response to a Serenade," *CW*, 8:101.

103. Joseph Medill to Lincoln, January 15, 1865, Abraham Lincoln Papers, LOC.

104. Fehrenbacher and Fehrenbacher, *Recollected Words of Abraham Lincoln*, 2.

EPILOGUE

1. Herr, *Jessie Benton Frémont*, 386; JBF to Alexander McClure, June 25, 1877; JBF to Samuel T. Pickard, May 28, 1893, JBF, *Letters of Jessie Benton Frémont*, 433, 549.

2. Julian, "George W. Julian's Journal," 330.

3. Julian, "George W. Julian's Journal," 335.

4. Webb, *The History of William Webb*, 26, 68.

5. Guelzo, *Lincoln's Emancipation Proclamation*, 275.

6. Gienapp, "Abraham Lincoln and the Border States," 17.

7. "Frémont's Report," *O.R.*, 1:12/3:3–32.

8. Longstreet, "The Seven Days," 2:405; Pryor, "Conflict, Chaos, and Confidence," 60.

9. Parrish, *Frank Blair*, 253. Details of the event and the text of Blair's speech are in the *Missouri Republican*, May 28, 1868; also see *Harper's Weekly*, June 20, 1868.

10. Parrish, *Frank Blair*, 222.

11. JBF to Charles Sumner, January 28, 1868, JBF, *Letters of Jessie Benton Frémont*, 399–400.

12. Herr, *Jessie Benton Frémont*, 387–393; Nevins, *Frémont*, 589–591; Chaffin, *Pathfinder*, 480–484.

13. Chaffin, *Pathfinder*, 485–486; Elizabeth Benton Frémont, *Recollections of Elizabeth Benton Frémont*, 154.

14. Elizabeth Blair Lee to Samuel Phillips Lee, October 14, 1861, E. B. Lee, *Wartime Washington*, 85.

15. Elizabeth Blair Lee to Samuel Phillips Lee, December 18, 1863, and March 27, 1864, E. B. Lee, *Wartime Washington*, 329, 359; Laas, "Elizabeth Blair Lee," 390–391, 396–397.

16. JBF to Samuel Phillips Lee, October 25, 1865, JBF, *Letters of Jessie Benton Frémont*, 394; Herr, *Jessie Benton Frémont*, 380; Herr and Spence, "'I Really Had Something like the Blues,'" 30.

17. Herr, *Jessie Benton Frémont*, 415–417; Herr and Spence, "'I Really Had Something like the Blues,'" 30–31; JBF to Elizabeth Blair Lee, July 29, 1883, JBF, *Letters of Jessie Benton Frémont*, 497–498.

18. Charles S. Homer to Lincoln, September 17, 1861, Abraham Lincoln Papers, LOC.

19. JBF, "Great Events," Frémont Family Papers, BL, unnumbered preface page; C. Goodwin, *John Charles Frémont*, 260.

20. Koerner, *Memoirs of Gustave Koerner*, 2:162.

21. Grierson, *A Just and Righteous Cause*, 60–61.

22. Sinha, *Slave's Cause*, 584; Douglass, *The Civil War*, 4:311.

23. Royce, "Frémont," 548; JCF, *Memoirs of My Life*, BL, 602.

24. Royce, "Frémont," 548.

25. *St. Louis Republic*, January 4, 1903; *Lexington Intelligencer*, January 3, 1903; *New York Sun*, December 29, 1902; *San Francisco Call*, December 28, 1902; *Washington Times*, January 3, 1903.

BIBLIOGRAPHY

BOOKS, ARTICLES, DISSERTATIONS, AND GOVERNMENT DOCUMENTS

Achorn, Edward. *The Lincoln Miracle: Inside the Republican Convention That Changed History*. New York: Atlantic Monthly Press, 2023.

Adams, Charles Francis, Jr. *Charles Francis Adams*. New York: Chelsea House, 1980, reprint of 1900 edition.

Adams, George Rollie. *General William S. Harney: Prince of Dragoons*. Lincoln: University of Nebraska Press, 2001.

Adams, Henry. *Letters of Henry Adams, 1858–1891*. Edited by Worthington Chauncey Ford. Boston: Houghton, Mifflin, and Company, 1930.

Anders, Curt. *Henry Halleck's War: A Fresh Look at Lincoln's Controversial General-in-Chief*. Fort Wayne: Guild Press of Indiana, 1999.

Arenson, Adam. *The Great Heart of the Republic: St. Louis and the Cultural Civil War*. Cambridge, MA: Harvard University Press, 2011.

Armstrong, Richard L. *The Battle of McDowell: March 11–May 18, 1862*. Lynchburg, VA: H. E. Howard, 1990.

Ashby, Thomas. *The Valley Campaigns: Being the Reminiscences of a Non-combatant While between the Lines in the Shenandoah Valley during the War of the States*. New York: Neale Publishing Company, 1914.

Baker, Jean H. *Mary Todd Lincoln: A Biography*. New York: Norton, 1987.

Balsamo, Larry T. "We Cannot Have Free Government without Elections: Abraham Lincoln and the Election of 1864." *Journal of the Illinois State Historical Society* 94, no. 2 (summer 2001): 181–199.

Barnes, Thurlow Weed. *Life of Thurlow Weed, Including His Autobiography and a Memoir*. 2 vols. Boston: Houghton Mifflin and Company, 1884.

Bartels, Carolyn M. *The Civil War in Missouri Day by Day, 1861–1865*. Independence, MO: Two Trails Publishing, 1992.

Bartlett, Irving H. *Wendell and Ann Phillips: The Community of Reform, 1840–1860*. New York: W. W. Norton, 1979.

Bartlett, Ruhl Jacob. *John C. Frémont and the Republican Party*. Columbus: Ohio State University, 1930.

Basler, Roy P., ed. *Collected Works of Abraham Lincoln.* 9 vols. New Brunswick, NJ: Rutgers University Press, 1953–1955.

Bates, Edward. *The Diary of Edward Bates, 1859–1866.* Edited by Howard Beale. Washington, DC: Government Printing Office, 1933.

Baxter, Maurice G. "Orville H. Browning: Lincoln's Colleague and Critic." *Journal of the Illinois State Historical Society* 48, no. 4 (winter 1955): 431–455.

Baxter, Maurice G. *Orville H. Browning: Lincoln's Friend and Critic.* Bloomington: Indiana University Press, 1957.

Bearss, Edwin C. *The Battle of Wilson's Creek.* Springfield, MO: Wilson's Creek National Battlefield Foundation, 1992.

Bell, Virginia. "Trenor Park: A New Englander in California." *California History* 60, no. 2 (summer 1981): 158–171.

Bellows, H. W. "Notes of a Preliminary Sanitary Survey of the Forces of the United States, in the Ohio and Mississippi Valleys, near Midsummer, 1861." In *Documents of the U.S. Sanitary Commission.* Vol. 1. New York: United States Sanitary Commission, 1866.

Bicknell, John. "'A Stream of Clear, Swift-Running Water': Nicollet, Frémont, and the Exploration of the Big Sioux River in 1838." In *Heartland River: A Cultural and Environmental History of the Big Sioux River Valley,* edited by Jon Lauck, 157–170. Sioux Falls, SD: Center for Western Studies, 2022.

Bicknell, John. *America 1844: Religious Fervor, Westward Expansion, and the Presidential Election That Transformed the Nation.* Chicago: Chicago Review Press, 2014.

Bicknell, John. *Lincoln's Pathfinder: John C. Frémont and the Violent Election of 1856.* Chicago: Chicago Review Press, 2017.

Bigelow, John. *Retrospections of an Active Life.* Vol. 1, *1817–1863.* New York: Baker & Taylor Co., 1909.

Blaine, James G. *Twenty Years of Congress.* 2 vols. Norwich, CT: Henry Bill Publishing, 1884.

Blair, Frank, Jr. "Address of F. P. Blair, Jr. to His Constituents, October 8, 1862." *St. Louis: Daily Union,* 1862.

Blair, Frank, Jr. *Frémont's Hundred Days in Missouri.* Washington, DC: Congressional Globe, 1862.

Blair, Frank, Jr. *The Policy of the President for the Restoration of the Union and Establishment of Peace.* Washington, DC: Congressional Globe, 1862.

Blair, Harry C., and Rebecca Tarshis. *Lincoln's Constant Ally: The Life of Colonel Edward D. Baker.* Portland: Oregon Historical Society, 1960.

Blair, Montgomery. "The Republican Party as It Was and Is." *North American Review* 131, no. 288 (November 1880): 422–430.

Blight, David. *Frederick Douglass: Prophet of Freedom.* New York: Simon & Schuster, 2018.

Blum, Virgil C. "The Political and Military Activities of the German Element in St. Louis, 1859–1861." *Missouri Historical Review* 42, no. 2 (January 1948): 103–129.

Bradley, Erwin Stanley. *Simon Cameron, Lincoln's Secretary of War: A Political Biography.* Philadelphia: University of Pennsylvania Press, 1966.

Brooks, Noah. *Mr. Lincoln's Washington: Selections from the Writings of Noah Brooks, Civil War Correspondent*. Edited by P. J. Staudenraus. New York: Smith Brunswick, 1967.

Brooks, Noah. "Two War-Time Conventions." *Century Magazine* (March 1895): 723–736.

Brooksher, William Riley. *Bloody Hill: The Civil War Battle of Wilson's Creek*. Washington, DC: Brassey's, 1995.

Brotherhead, William. *General Frémont, and the Injustice Done Him by Politicians and Envious Military Men*. Philadelphia: W. Brotherhead, 1862.

Brown, Norman D. *Edward Stanly: Whiggery's Tarheel "Conqueror."* Tuscaloosa: University of Alabama Press, 1974.

Browning, Orville Hickman. *The Diary of Orville Hickman Browning*. Edited by Theodore Calvin Pease and James G. Randall. 2 vols. Springfield: Illinois State Historical Society Library, 1925.

Brownson, Orestes. "The Approaching Elections: Lincoln or Frémont? Who Shall Be Our Next President?" *Brownson's Quarterly Review* (July 1864): 339–370.

Bull, William J., and John P. Bull. *Missouri Brothers in Gray: The Reminiscences and Letters of William J. Bull and John P. Bull*. Edited by Michael E. Banasik. Iowa City, IA: Camp Pope Bookshop, 1998.

Bulloch, James D. *The Secret Service of the Confederate States in Europe*. New York: Burt Franklin, 1883.

Bunker, Gary L. "The Campaign Dial: A Premier Lincoln Campaign Paper, 1864." *Journal of the Abraham Lincoln Association* 25, no. 1 (winter 2004): 38–75.

Burlingame, Michael. *Abraham Lincoln: A Life*. 2 vols. Baltimore: Johns Hopkins University Press, 2008.

Burlingame, Michael. *An American Marriage: The Untold Story of Abraham Lincoln and Mary Todd*. New York: Pegasus Books, 2021.

Burlingame, Michael. *Lincoln's Journalist: John Hay's Anonymous Writings for the Press, 1860–1864*. Carbondale: Southern Illinois University Press, 1999.

Butler, Benjamin F. *Butler's Book*. Boston: A. M. Thayer & Co., 1892.

Butler, Benjamin F. *Private and Official Correspondence of Gen. Benjamin F. Butler during the Period of the Civil War*. 5 vols. Norwood, MA: Plimpton Press, 1917.

Carpenter, Francis Bicknell. *Six Months at the White House with Abraham Lincoln: The Story of a Picture*. New York: Hurd and Houghton, 1866.

Castel, Albert. *General Sterling Price and the Civil War in the West*. Baton Rouge: Louisiana State University Press, 1968.

Chaffin, Tom. *Pathfinder: John Charles Frémont and the Course of American Empire*. New York: Hill & Wang, 2002.

Chase, Salmon. *The Salmon P. Chase Papers*. Edited by John Niven. 3 vols. Kent, OH: Kent State University Press, 1993–1996.

Cheatham, Mark. *Who Is James K. Polk: The Presidential Election of 1844*. Lawrence: University Press of Kansas, 2023.

Child, Lydia Maria. *Letters of Lydia Maria Child*. New York: Houghton, Mifflin and Company, 1883.

Cirillo, Frank J. *The Abolitionist Civil War: Immediatists and the Struggle to Transform the Union*. Baton Rouge: Louisiana State University Press, 2023.

Clinton, Catherine. *Mrs. Lincoln: A Life*. New York: HarperCollins, 2009.

Cochrane, John. *American Civil War: Memories of the Rebellion*. New York: Rogers & Sherwood, 1879.

Cochrane, John. *Arming the Slaves in the War for the Union*. New York: Rogers & Sherwood, 1875.

Colfax, Schuyler. *Frémont's Hundred Days in Missouri: Speech of Schuyler Colfax, of Indiana, in Reply to Mr. Blair, of Missouri, Delivered in the House of Representatives, March 7, 1862*. Washington, DC: Scammell, 1862.

Colton, Kenneth E., ed. "The Irrepressible Conflict of 1861: The Letters of Samuel Ryan Curtis." *Annals of Iowa* 24 (1942): 14–59.

Colton, Kenneth E., ed. "With Frémont in Missouri in 1861: The Letters of Samuel Ryan Curtis." *Annals of Iowa* 24 (1941): 105–167.

Conlin, Michael F. "The Smithsonian Abolition Lecture Controversy: The Clash of Antislavery Politics with American Science in Wartime Washington." *Civil War History* 46, no. 4 (December 2000): 300–323.

Conway, Moncure Daniel. *Autobiography, Memories and Experiences*. Boston: Houghton, Mifflin and Company, 1904.

Cooling, Benjamin Franklin. *Jubal Early's Raid on Washington 1864*. Baltimore: Nautical & Aviation Publishing Company of America, 1989.

Covington, James W. "The Camp Jackson Affair." *Missouri Historical Review* 55, no. 3 (April 1961): 197–212.

Cox, Jacob D. "West Virginia Operations under Frémont." In *Battles and Leaders of the Civil War*. Vol. 2: *North to Antietam*, edited by Robert Underwood Johnson and Clarence Clough Buel, 278–281. New York: Castle Books, 1956. First published in 1887 in *Century Magazine*.

Cozzens, Peter. *General John Pope: A Life for the Nation*. Urbana: University of Illinois Press, 2000.

Cozzens, Peter. *Shenandoah 1862: Stonewall Jackson's Valley Campaign*. Chapel Hill: University of North Carolina Press, 2008.

Croffut, William A. *An American Procession: 1855–1914*. Boston: Little, Brown, and Company, 1931.

Croffut, William A. "Lincoln's Washington: Recollections of a Journalist Who Knew Everybody." *Atlantic Monthly* (January 1930): 55–65.

Dahlgren, Madeleine Vinton. *Memoir of John A. Dahlgren*. Boston: James R. Osgood and Company, 1882.

Dallas, George Mifflin. *Diary of George Mifflin Dallas*. Edited by Susan Dallas. Philadelphia: J. B. Lippincott Company, 1892.

Davis, Carl L. *Arming the Union: Small Arms in the Civil War*. Port Washington, NY: Kennikat Press, 1973.

Davis, William C. *Battle at Bull Run: A History of the First Major Campaign of the Civil War*. Baton Rouge: Louisiana State University Press, 1977.

Denslow, Van Buren. *Frémont and McClellan, Their Political and Military Careers Reviewed*. Yonkers, NY: Semi-Weekly Clarion, 1862.

Denton, Sally. *Passion and Principle: John and Jessie Frémont, the Couple Whose Power, Politics, and Love Shaped Nineteenth-Century America*. New York: Bloomsbury, 2007.

Donald, David Herbert. *Charles Sumner and the Rights of Man*. New York: Alfred A. Knopf, 1970.

Dorsheimer, William. "Frémont's Hundred Days in Missouri." *Atlantic Monthly* (February–March 1862): 115–125, 247–258, 372–384.

Douglas, Stephen A. *The Letters of Stephen A. Douglas*. Edited by Robert W. Johannsen. Urbana: University of Illinois Press, 1961.

Douglass, Frederick, *The Life and Writings of Frederick Douglass*. Vols. 3 and 4: *The Civil War*. Edited by Philip S. Foner. New York: International Publishers, 1952.

Driscoll, John K. *Rogue: A Biography of Civil War General Justus McKinstry*. Jefferson, NC: McFarland, 1996.

DuBois, James T., and Gertrude S. Mathews. *Galusha A. Grow: Father of the Homestead Law*. Boston: Houghton Mifflin, 1917.

Duncan, Russell. *Blue-Eyed Child of Fortune: The Civil War Letters of Colonel Robert Gould Shaw*. Athens: University of Georgia Press, 1992.

Eaton, John. *Grant, Lincoln, and the Freedmen: Reminiscences of the Civil War*. Edited by Michael J. Larson and John David Smith. Knoxville: University of Tennessee Press, 2022.

Egan, Ferol. *Frémont: Explorer for a Restless Nation*. New York: Doubleday, 1977.

Eggleston, Michael A. *President Lincoln's Recruiter: General Lorenzo Thomas and the United States Colored Troops in the Civil War*. Jefferson, NC: McFarland, 2013.

Elliott, Charles Winslow. *Winfield Scott: The Soldier and the Man*. New York: Macmillan, 1937.

Emerson, Ralph Waldo. *The Complete Works of Ralph Waldo Emerson*. Vol. 11. Boston: Houghton, Mifflin, and Company, 1904.

Engle, Stephen D. *Gathering to Save a Nation. Lincoln and the Union's War Governors*. Chapel Hill: University of North Carolina Press, 2016.

Engle, Stephen D. *Yankee Dutchman: The Life of Franz Sigel*. Fayetteville: University of Arkansas Press, 1993.

Escott, Paul D. *Lincoln's Dilemma: Blair, Sumner, and the Republican Struggle over Racism and Equality in the Civil War Era*. Charlottesville: University of Virginia Press, 2014.

Etulain, Richard W. "Abraham Lincoln: Political Founding Father of the American West." *Montana: The Magazine of Western History* 59, no. 2 (summer 2009): 3–22, 92–93.

Fehrenbacher, Don E., and Virginia Fehrenbacher, eds. *Recollected Words of Abraham Lincoln*. Stanford, CA: Stanford University Press, 1996.

Fessenden, Francis. *Life and Public Services of William Pitt Fessenden*. 2 vols. Boston: Houghton, Mifflin, and Company, 1907.

Finkelman, Paul. "Lincoln, Emancipation, and the Limits of Constitutional Change." *Supreme Court Review* 2008, no. 1 (2008): 349–387.

Fish, Carl Russell. "Lincoln and the Patronage." *American Historical Review* 8, no. 1 (October 1902): 5–69.

Fleischner, Jennifer. *Mrs. Lincoln and Mrs. Keckly: The Remarkable Story of the Friendship between a First Lady and a Former Slave*. New York: Broadway Books, 2003.

Flower, Frank A. *Edwin McMasters Stanton: The Autocrat of Rebellion, Emancipation, and Reconstruction*. Akron, OH: Saalfield Publishing Company, 1905.

Foner, Eric. *The Fiery Trial: Abraham Lincoln and American Slavery*. New York: W. W. Norton, 2010.

Foote, Shelby. *The Civil War*. 3 vols. New York: Vintage Books, 1986.

Ford, Worthington Chauncey, ed. *A Cycle of Adams Letters*. Boston: Houghton Mifflin, 1920.

Forman, Jacob Gilbert. *The Western Sanitary Commission*. St. Louis, MO: R. P. Studley & Co., 1864.

Freeman, Joanne B. *The Field of Blood: Violence in Congress and the Road to Civil War*. New York: Farrar, Strauss and Giroux, 2018.

Frémont, Elizabeth Benton. *Recollections of Elizabeth Benton Frémont*. New York: Frederick H. Hitchcock, 1912.

Frémont, Jessie Benton. *Far West Sketches*. Boston: D. Lothrop and Company, 1890.

Frémont, Jessie Benton. *The Letters of Jessie Benton Frémont*. Edited by Pamela Her and Mary Lee Spence. Urbana: University of Illinois Press, 1993.

Frémont, Jessie Benton. *Souvenirs of My Time*. Boston: D. Lothrop and Company, 1887.

Frémont, Jessie Benton. *The Story of the Guard: A Chronicle of the War*. Boston: Ticknor & Fields, 1863.

Frémont, John C. "In Command in Missouri." In *Battles and Leaders of the Civil War*. Vol. 1: *From Sumter to Shiloh*, edited by Robert Underwood Johnson and Clarence Clough Buel, 278–288. New York: Castle Books, 1956. First published in 1887 in *Century Magazine*.

Frémont, John C. *Memoirs of My Life*. New York: Cooper Square Press, 2001. Originally published 1887.

French, Benjamin Brown, Donald B. Cole, and John J. McDonough, eds. *Witness to the Young Republic: A Yankee's Journal, 1828–1870*. Hanover: University Press of New England, 1989.

Gallagher, Gary. "You Must Either Attack Richmond or Give Up the Job and Come to the Defense of Washington: Abraham Lincoln and the 1862 Shenandoah Valley Campaign." In *The Shenandoah Valley Campaign of 1862*, edited by Gary W. Gallagher, 3–23. Chapel Hill: University of North Carolina Press, 2003.

Gallman, J. Matthew. *The Cacophony of Politics: Northern Democrats and the American Civil War*. Charlottesville: University of Virginia Press, 2021.

Garrison, William Lloyd. *The Letters of William Lloyd Garrison*. Vol. 5: *Let the Oppressed Go Free, 1861–1867*. Edited by Walter M. Merrill. Cambridge, MA: Harvard University Press, 1979.

George, Joseph, Jr. "Long-Neglected Lincoln Speech: An 1864 Election Preliminary." *Journal of the Abraham Lincoln Association* 16, no. 2 (summer 1995): 23–28.

George, Mary Karl. *Zachariah Chandler: A Political Biography*. East Lansing: Michigan State University Press, 1969.

Gerteis, Louis S. *The Civil War in Missouri: A Military History*. Columbia: University of Missouri Press, 2012.

Gerteis, Louis S. *Civil War St. Louis*. Lawrence: University Press of Kansas, 2001.

Gienapp, William. "Abraham Lincoln and the Border States." *Journal of the Abraham Lincoln Association* 13, no. 1 (1992): 13–46.

Goodwin, Cardinal. *John Charles Frémont: An Explanation of His Career*. Stanford, CA: Stanford University Press, 1930.

Goodwin, Doris Kearns. *Team of Rivals: The Political Genius of Abraham Lincoln*. New York Simon & Schuster, 2005.

Gordon, George H. *Brook Farm to Cedar Mountain: In the War of the Great Rebellion, 1862–62*. Cambridge, MA: Riverdale Press, 1863.

Grant, Ulysses. *The Annotated Memoirs of Ulysses S. Grant*. Edited by Elizabeth D. Samet. New York: Liveright Publishing, 2019.

Greeley, Horace. *An Overland Journey from New York to San Francisco in the Summer of 1859*. New York: Alfred A. Knopf, 1964. First published in 1860 by C. M. Saxton, Barker & Co. (New York).

Grierson, Benjamin H. *A Just and Righteous Cause: Benjamin H. Grierson's Civil War Memoir*. Edited by Bruce J. Dinges and Shirley A. Leckie. Carbondale: Southern Illinois University Press, 2008.

Grimsley, Mark. *The Hard Hand of War: Union Military Policy toward Southern Civilians, 1861–1865*. Cambridge: Cambridge University Press, 1995.

Grinnell, Josiah Bushnell. *Men and Events of Forty Years*. Boston: D. Lothrop Company, 1891.

Guelzo, Allen C. *Lincoln's Emancipation Proclamation: The End of Slavery in America*. New York: Simon & Schuster, 2004.

Hale, Laura Virginia. *Four Valiant Years in Lower Shenandoah Valley, 1861–1865*. Strasburg, VA: Shenandoah Publishing House, 1968.

Hamlin, Charles Eugene. *The Life and Times of Hannibal Hamlin*. Port Washington, NY: Kennikat Press, 1971. First published in 1899 by Riverside Press (Cambridge, MA).

Harbison, Windred A. "Zachariah Chandler's Part in the Reelection of Abraham Lincoln." *Mississippi Valley Historical Review* 22, no. 2 (September 1935): 267–276.

Harris, Nini. *A Most Unsettled State: First-Person Accounts of St. Louis during the Civil War*. St. Louis, MO: Reedy Press, 2013.

Harris, William C. *Lincoln and the Border States: Preserving the Union*. Lawrence: University Press of Kansas, 2011.

Harris, William C. "Lincoln and Wartime Reconstruction in North Carolina, 1861–1863." *North Carolina Historical Review* 63, no. 2 (April 1986): 149–168.

Harris, William C. *With Charity for All: Lincoln and the Restoration of the Union*. Lexington: University Press of Kentucky, 1997.

Hay, John, *Inside Lincoln's White House: The Complete Civil War Diary of John Hay*. Edited by Michael Burlingame and John R. Turner Ettlinger. Carbondale: Southern Illinois University Press, 1997.

Hendrick, Burton J. *Lincoln's War Cabinet*. Boston: Little Brown and Company, 1946.

Hendricks, Gordon. "The First Three Western Journeys of Albert Bierstadt." *Art Bulletin* 46, no. 3 (September 1964): 333–365.

Hennessy, John. "Evangelizing for Union, 1863: The Army of the Potomac, Its Enemies at Home, and a New Solidarity." *Journal of the Civil War Era* 4, no. 4 (December 2014): 533–558.

Herbon, Lorraine D. "Public Wife: The Life of Jessie Benton Frémont." PhD diss., University of Tennessee, 2022. https://trace.tennessee.edu/utk_graddiss/7189.

Herr, Pamela. *Jessie Benton Frémont*. Norman: University of Oklahoma Press, 1988.

Herr, Pamela, and Mary Lee Spence. "'I Really Had Something like the Blues': Letters from Jessie Benton Frémont to Elizabeth Blair Lee, 1847–1883." *Montana: The Magazine of Western History* 41, no. 2 (spring 1991): 16–31.

History of Clay and Platte Counties, Missouri. St. Louis, MO: National Historical Company, 1885.

Hollandsworth, James G., Jr. *Pretense of Glory: The Life of General Nathaniel P. Banks*. Baton Rouge: Louisiana State University Press, 1998.

Hollister, O. J. *Life of Schuyler Colfax*. New York: Funk & Wagnalls, 1886.

Holzer, Harold. *Lincoln President-Elect: Abraham Lincoln and the Great Secession Winter, 1860–1861*. New York: Simon & Schuster, 2008.

Hooper, Candice Shy. *Lincoln's Generals' Wives: Four Women Who Influenced the Civil War—for Better and for Worse*. Kent, OH: Kent State University Press, 2016.

Horner, Harlan Hoyt. *Lincoln and Greeley*. Urbana: University of Illinois Press, 1953.

Howard, Victor B. "Lincoln Slave Policy in Kentucky: A Study of Pragmatic Strategy." *Register of the Kentucky Historical Society* 80, no. 3 (summer 1982): 281–308.

Huse, Caleb. *The Supplies for the Confederate Army*. Boston: T. R. Marvin & Son, 1904.

Imboden, John D. "Stonewall Jackson in the Shenandoah." In *Battles and Leaders of the Civil War*. Vol. 2: *North to Antietam*, edited by Robert Underwood Johnson and Clarence Clough Buel, 282–298. New York: Castle Books, 1956. First published in 1887 in *Century Magazine*.

Johannsen, Robert W. *Stephen A. Douglas*. New York: Oxford University Press, 1973.

Johnson, David. *Decided on the Battlefield: Grant, Sherman, Lincoln, and the Election of 1864*. Amherst, NY: Prometheus Books, 2012.

Joyaux, Georges J. "The Tour of Prince Napoleon." *American Heritage* 8, no. 5 (1957): 65–86.

Julian, George W. "George W. Julian's Journal: The Assassination of Lincoln." *Indiana Magazine of History* 11, no. 4 (December 1915): 324–337.

Julian, George W. *Political Recollections: 1840–1872*. Chicago: Jansen, McClurg & Co., 1884.

Julian, George W., and Lydia Maria Child, eds. *Speeches on Political Questions*. New York: Hurd and Houghton, 1872.

Kahan, Paul. *Amiable Scoundrel: Simon Cameron, Lincoln's Scandalous Secretary of War*. Lincoln, NE: Potomac Books, 2016.

Karcher, Carolyn L. *The First Woman in the Republic: A Cultural Biography of Lydia Maria Child*. Durham, NC: Duke University Press, 1994.

Kelso, John R. *Bloody Engagements: John R. Kelso's Civil War*. Edited by Christopher Russo. New Haven, CT: Yale University Press, 2017.

Kennedy, Elijah R. *The Contest for California in 1861: How Colonel E. D. Baker Saved the Pacific States to the Union*. Boston: Houghton Mifflin, 1912.

Kennedy, Joseph C. G. *Population of the United States in 1860*. Washington, DC: Government Printing Office, 1864.

Keyes, E. D. *Fifty Years' Observation of Men and Events*. New York: Charles Scribner's Sons, 1884.

Kirkpatrick, Arthur Roy. "Missouri in the Early Months of the Civil War." *Missouri Historical Review* 55, no. 3 (April 1961): 235–266.

Kirkpatrick, Arthur Roy. "Missouri on the Eve of the Civil War." *Missouri Historical Review* 55, no. 2 (January 1961): 99–108.

Koerner, Gustave. *Memoirs of Gustave Koerner, 1809–1896*. 2 vols. Cedar Rapids, IA: Torch Press, 1909.

Korngold, Ralph. *Two Friends of Man: The Story of William Lloyd Garrison and Wendell Phillips and Their Relationship with Abraham Lincoln*. Boston: Little, Brown and Company, 1950.

Krick, Robert K. *Conquering the Valley: Stonewall Jackson at Port Republic*. New York: Morrow, 1996.

Laas, Virginia Jeans. "Elizabeth Blair Lee: Union Counterpart of Mary Boykin Chesnut." *Journal of Southern History* 50, no. 3 (August 1984): 385–406.

Larimer, Charles F., ed. *Love and Valor: Intimate Civil War Letters between Captain Jacob and Emeline Ritner*. Western Springs, IL: Sigourney Press, 2000.

Lause, Mark. A. *Price's Lost Campaign: The 1864 Invasion of Missouri*. Columbia: University of Missouri Press, 2011.

Lee, Elizabeth Blair. *Wartime Washington: The Civil War Letters of Elizabeth Blair Lee*. Edited by Virginia Jeans Laas. Urbana: University of Illinois Press, 1991.

Lee, Jacob F. "Unionism, Emancipation, and the Origins of Kentucky's Confederate Identity." *Register of the Kentucky Historical Society* 111, no. 2 (spring 2013): 199–233.

Lester, C. Edwards. *Life and Public Services of Charles Sumner*. New York: United States Publishing Company, 1874.

Letters Sent by Major General John C. Frémont, His Adjutant, and Director of Transportation, 7/1861–11/1861, Record Group 393: Records of U.S. Army Continental Commands, 1817–1947, National Archives.

Lippman, Ellen, and Martin McMahon. "Professionalism and Politics in the Procurement Process: United States Civil War Early Years." *Accounting Historians Journal* 44, no. 1 (June 2017): 63–76.

Long, David. *The Jewel of Liberty: Abraham Lincoln's Re-election and the End of Slavery*. Mechanicsburg, PA: Stackpole Books, 1994.

Longstreet, James. "The Seven Days." In *Battles and Leaders of the Civil War*. Vol. 2: *North to Antietam*, edited by Robert Underwood Johnson and Clarence Clough Buel, 396–405. New York: Castle Books, 1956. First published in 1887 in *Century Magazine*.

Love, James. *My Dear Molly: The Civil War Letters of Captain James Love.* Edited by M. E. Kodner. St. Louis: Missouri Historical Society Press, 2015.

Lovejoy, Owen. *His Brother's Blood: Speeches and Writings, 1838–64.* Edited by William F. Moore and Jane Ann Moore. Urbana: University of Illinois Press, 2004.

Lowe, Robert E. "Lincoln, the Fall of Atlanta, and the 1864 Presidential Election." *Georgia Historical Quarterly* 100, no. 3 (2016): 260–289.

Magdol, Edward. *Owen Lovejoy: Abolitionist in Congress.* New Brunswick, NJ: Rutgers University Press, 1967.

Malanson, Jeffrey J. "The Founding Fathers and the Election of 1864." *Journal of the Abraham Lincoln Association* 36, no. 2 (summer 2015): 1–25.

Manning, Chandra. "The Shifting Terrain of Attitudes toward Abraham Lincoln and Emancipation." *Journal of the Abraham Lincoln Association* 34, no. 1 (winter 2013): 18–39.

Marvel, William. *Lincoln's Autocrat: The Life of Edwin Stanton.* Chapel Hill: University of North Carolina Press, 2015.

Matheny, James H. "A Modern Knight Errant: Edward Dickinson Baker." *Journal of the Illinois State Historical Society* 9, no. 1 (April 1916): 23–42.

Matthews, Glenna. *The Golden State in the Civil War: Thomas Starr King, the Republican Party, and the Birth of Modern California.* New York: Cambridge University Press, 2012.

Mayer, Henry. *All on Fire: William Lloyd Garrison and the Abolition of Slavery.* New York: St. Martin's Press, 1998.

McClellan, George B. *The Civil War Papers of George B. McClellan: Selected Correspondence, 1860–1865.* Edited by Stephen W. Sears. New York: Da Capo Press, 1992.

McClure, A. K. *Abraham Lincoln and Men of War-Times.* Lincoln: University of Nebraska Press, 1996 (originally published 1892).

McDonald, Cornelia Peake, and Minrose C. Gwin, eds. *A Woman's Civil War: A Diary, with Reminiscences of the War, from March 1862.* Madison: University of Wisconsin Press, 1992.

McDonough, James L. *Schofield: Union General in the Civil War and Reconstruction.* Tallahassee: Florida State University Press, 1972.

McKinstry, Justus. *Vindication of Brig. Gen. J. McKinstry, Formerly Quarter-Master, Western Department.* Privately published pamphlet, undated.

McPherson, Edward. *The Political History of the United States of America during the Great Rebellion, from November 6, 1861, to July 4, 1864.* Washington, DC: Philip & Solomons, 1864.

McPherson, James. "Lincoln as Commander in Chief." In *Rediscovering Abraham Lincoln*, edited by John Y. Simon and Harold Holzer, 1–15. New York: Fordham University Press, 2002.

McPherson, James M. *The Negro's Civil War: How American Negroes Felt and Acted during the War for the Union.* New York: Pantheon, 1965.

McPherson, James M. *The Struggle for Equality: Abolitionists and the Negro in the Civil War and Reconstruction.* Princeton, NJ: Princeton University Press, 1964.

Medford, Edna Greene. "Lincoln and the Constitutional Dilemma of Emancipation." *OAH Magazine of History* 21, no. 1 (January 2007): 19–23.

Miers, Earl S. *Lincoln Day by Day: A Chronology, 1809–1865.* Washington, DC: Lincoln Sesquicentennial Commission, 1960.

Miller, Edward E., Jr. *Lincoln's Abolitionist General: The Biography of David Hunter.* Columbia: University of South Carolina Press, 1997.

Miller, Robert E. "Zagonyi." *Missouri Historical Review* 76, no. 2 (January 1982): 174–192.

Miller, William J. "Such Men as Shields, Banks, and Frémont: Federal Command in Western Virginia, March–June 1862." In *The Shenandoah Valley Campaign of 1862,* edited by Gary W. Gallagher, 43–85. Chapel Hill: University of North Carolina Press, 2003.

Moore, Charles. "Zachariah Chandler in Lincoln's Second Campaign." *Century Magazine* 50, no. 3 (July 1895): 476–477.

Moore, William F., and Jane Ann Moore. *Collaborators for Emancipation: Abraham Lincoln and Owen Lovejoy.* Urbana: University of Illinois Press, 2014.

Moran, Benjamin. *The Journal of Benjamin Moran, 1857–1865.* Edited by Sarah Agnes Wallace and Frances Elm Gillespie. 2 vols. Chicago: University of Chicago Press, 1949.

Mulligan, James A. "The Siege of Lexington, Mo." In *Battles and Leaders of the Civil War.* Vol. 1: *From Sumter to Shiloh,* edited by Robert Underwood Johnson and Clarence Clough Buel, 307–313. New York: Castle Books, 1956. First published in 1887 in *Century Magazine.*

Murray, Robert. "The Frémont-Adams Contracts." *Journal of the West* 5 (October 1966): 517–524.

Neely, Mark E., Jr. *Lincoln and the Democrats: The Politics of Opposition in the Civil War.* New York: Cambridge University Press, 2017.

Nevins, Allan. *Frémont: Pathmarker of the West.* Lincoln: University of Nebraska Press, 1992. First published in 1939 by D. Appleton-Century (New York).

Newman, Richard S. "The Age of Emancipating Proclamations: Early Civil War Abolitionism and Its Discontents." *Pennsylvania Magazine of History and Biography* 137, no. 1 (January 2013): 33–55.

Nicklason, Fred. "The Civil War Contracts Committee." *Civil War History* 17, no. 3 (September 1971): 232–244.

Nicolay, Helen. "Lincoln's Cabinet." *Abraham Lincoln Quarterly* 5, no. 5 (March 1949): 255–292.

Nicolay, John, and John Hay. *Abraham Lincoln: A History.* 10 vols. New York: The Century Co., 1904. First published in 1886 by Century Co. (New York).

O'Harrow, Robert. *The Quartermaster: Montgomery C. Meigs, Lincoln's General, Master Builder of the Army.* New York: Simon & Schuster, 2016.

Oakes, James. *Freedom National: The Destruction of Slavery in the United States, 1861–1865.* New York: W. W. Norton, 2013.

Oakes, James. "Reluctant to Emancipate? Another Look at the First Confiscation Act." *Journal of the Civil War Era* 3, no. 4 (December 2013): 458–466.

Oates, Stephen B. *A Woman of Valor: Clara Barton and the Civil War*. New York: Free Press, 1995.

Parker, Wyman W. *Henry Stevens of Vermont: An American Book Dealer in London, 1845–'86*. Amsterdam: N. Israel, 1963.

Parrish, William E. *Frank Blair: Lincoln's Conservative*. Columbia: University of Missouri Press, 1998.

Parrish, William E. "General Nathaniel Lyon: A Portrait." *Missouri Historical Review* 49, no. 1 (October 1954): 1–18.

Parrish, William E. *Turbulent Partnership: Missouri and the Union, 1861–1865*. Columbia: University of Missouri Press, 1963.

Parrish, William E. "The Western Sanitary Commission." *Civil War History* 36, no. 1 (March 1990): 17–35.

Peckham, James. *Gen. Nathaniel Lyon and Missouri in 1861*. New York: American News Company, 1866.

Petersen, Frederick A. *A Military Review of the Campaign in Virginia and Maryland*. New York: S. Tousey, H. Dexter, 1862, 1863.

Phillips, Catherine Coffin. *Jessie Benton Frémont: A Woman Who Made History*. Lincoln: Bison Books, 1995.

Phillips, Christopher. *Damned Yankee: The Life of General Nathaniel Lyon*. Columbia: University of Missouri Press, 1990.

Phillips, Christopher. "Lincoln's Grasp of War: Hard War and the Politics of Neutrality and Slavery in the Western Border States, 1861–1862." *Journal of the Civil War Era* 3, no. 2 (June 2013): 184–210.

Phillips, Christopher. *Missouri's Confederate: Claiborne Fox Jackson and the Creation of Southern Identity in the Border West*. Columbia: University of Missouri Press, 2000.

Phillips, Christopher. *The Rivers Ran Backward: The Civil War and the Remaking of the American Border*. New York: Oxford University Press, 2016.

Phillips, Wendell. *Speeches, Lectures, and Letters, Second Series*. Boston: Lee and Shepard, 1891.

Phisterer, Frederick. *New York in the War of the Rebellion, 1861–1865*. 3 vols. Albany: J. B. Lyon Company, 1912.

Pickard, Samuel T. *Life and Letters of John Greenleaf Whittier*. Cambridge, MA: Riverside Press, 1894.

Pierson, William Whatley, Jr. "The Committee on the Conduct of the Civil War." *American Historical Review* 23, no. 3 (April 1918): 550–576.

Pilsen, John. *Reply of Lieut.-Col. Pilsen to Emil Schalk's Criticisms of the Campaign in the Mountain Department, Under Maj.-Gen. J. C. Frémont*. New York: n.p., 1863.

Piston, William Garrett, and Richard W. Hatcher III. *Wilson's Creek: The Second Battle of the Civil War and the Men Who Fought It*. Chapel Hill: University of North Carolina Press, 2000.

Polk, James K. *The Diary of a President, 1845–1849*. Edited by Allan Nevins. New York: Longman, Green and Co., 1929.

Poore, Benjamin Perley. *Perley's Reminiscences of Sixty Years in the National Metropolis*. 2 vols. Philadelphia: Hubbard Brothers, 1886.

Pope, John. *The Military Memoirs of General John Pope.* Edited by Peter Cozzens and Robert I. Girardi. Chapel Hill: University of North Carolina Press, 1998.

Potter, David M. *Lincoln and His Party in the Secession Crisis.* New Haven, CT: Yale University Press, 1942.

Power, J. Tracy. "In for Four More Years: The Army of Northern Virginia and the United States Presidential Election of 1864." In *Rediscovering Abraham Lincoln,* edited by John Y. Simon and Harold Holzer, 93–111. New York: Fordham University Press, 2002.

Pratt, Harry E. "Simon Cameron's Fight for a Place in Lincoln's Cabinet." *Bulletin of the Abraham Lincoln Association* 49 (September 1937): 3–11.

Procter, Addison G. *Lincoln and the Convention of 1860: An Address before the Chicago Historical Society.* Chicago: Chicago Historical Society, 1918.

Pryor, Elizabeth Brown. "Conflict, Chaos, and Confidence: Abraham Lincoln's Struggle as Commander in Chief." *Virginia Magazine of History and Biography* 129, no. 1 (2021): 2–79.

Rather, Lois. *Jessie Frémont at Black Point.* Oakland, CA: Rather Press, 1974.

Rego, Paul M. *Lyman Trumbull and the Second Founding of the United States.* Lawrence: University Press of Kansas, 2022.

Reynolds, David S. *Abe: Abraham Lincoln in His Times.* New York: Penguin Books, 2020.

Riddle, A. G. *Recollections of War Times: Reminiscences of Men and Events in Washington, 1860–1865.* New York: G. P. Putnam's Sons, 1895.

Roberts, David. *A Newer World: Kit Carson, John C. Frémont, and the Claiming of the American West.* New York: Simon & Schuster, 2000.

Robertson, James I., Jr. *Stonewall Jackson: The Man, the Soldier, the Legend.* New York: Macmillan, 1997.

Rolle, Andrew. *John Charles Frémont: Character as Destiny.* Norman: University of Oklahoma Press, 1991.

Rollins, C. B. "Some Impressions of Frank P. Blair." *Missouri Historical Review* 24, no. 3 (April 1930): 352–358.

Rombauer, Robert J. *The Union Cause in St. Louis in 1861.* St. Louis, MO: Nixon Jones Printing, 1909.

Rorvig, Paul. "The Significant Skirmish: The Battle of Boonville, June 17, 1861." *Missouri Historical Review* 86, no. 2 (January 1992): 127–148.

Rowan, Steven, and James Neal Primm. *Germans for a Free Missouri: Translations from the St. Louis Radical Press, 1857–1862.* Columbia: University of Missouri Press, 1983.

Royce, Josiah. "Frémont." *Atlantic Monthly* (October 1890): 548–557.

Ruess, Claude Moore. *Carl Schurz: Reformer.* New York: Dodd, Mead & Company, 1932.

Salter, William. *The Life of James W. Grimes.* New York: D. Appleton and Company, 1876.

Sandburg, Carl. *Abraham Lincoln, the War Years.* New York: Harcourt, 1939.

Schalk, Emil. *Campaigns of 1862 and 1863.* Philadelphia: J. B. Lippincott, 1863.

Schenck, Robert C. "Notes on the Battle of McDowell." In *Battles and Leaders of the Civil War.* Vol. 2: *North to Antietam,* edited by Robert Underwood Johnson and Clarence Clough Buel, 298. New York: Castle Books, 1956. First published in 1887 in *Century Magazine.*

Schlesinger, Arthur M., Jr. *History of American Presidential Elections, 1789–2001*. 11 vols. Philadelphia: Chelsea House, 2002.

Schofield, John M. *Forty-Six Years in the Army*. New York: Century Co., 1897.

Schurz, Carl. *The Reminiscences of Carl Schurz*. 3 vols. New York: McClure Company, 1907, 1908.

Sears, Stephen W. *George B. McClellan: The Young Napoleon*. New York: Ticknor & Fields, 1988.

Shanks, John P. C. *Vindication of Major General John C. Frémont against the Attacks of the Slave Power and Its Allies*. Washington, DC: Scammell & Co., 1862.

Shannon, Fred Albert. *The Organization and Administration of the Union Army, 1861–1865*. Cleveland, OH: Arthur H. Clark Company, 1928.

Shea, William L. *Union General: Samuel Curtis Ryan and Victory in the West*. Lincoln, NE: Potomac Books, 2023.

Sherman, William T. *Memoirs of General W. T. Sherman*. New York: Library of America, 1990.

Sherman, William T., *Sherman's Civil War: Selected Correspondence of William T. Sherman, 1860–1865*. Edited by Brooks D. Simpson and Jean V. Berlin. Chapel Hill: University of North Carolina Press, 1999.

Simon, John Y., ed. *The Papers of Ulysses S. Grant*. Vols. 2–5. Carbondale: Southern Illinois University Press, 1969–1973.

Simon, John Y., and Harold Holzer, eds. *Rediscovering Abraham Lincoln*. New York: Fordham University Press, 2002.

Simpson, Brooks D. "Lincoln and His Political Generals." *Journal of the Abraham Lincoln Association* 19, no. 1 (winter 2000): 63–77.

Sinha, Manisha. *The Slave's Cause: A History of Abolition*. New Haven, CT: Yale University Press, 2016.

Smallwood, Osborn T. "The Historical Significance of Whittier's Anti-slavery Poems as Reflected by Their Political and Social Background." *Journal of Negro History* 35, no. 2 (April 1950): 150–173.

Smith, Elbert E. *Francis Preston Blair*. New York: Free Press, 1980.

Smith, Willard H. *Schuyler Colfax: The Changing Fortunes of a Political Idol*. Indianapolis: Indiana Historical Society, 1952.

Smith, William E. "The Blairs and Frémont." *Missouri Historical Review* 23, no. 2 (January 1929): 214–260.

Smith, William E. *The Francis Preston Blair Family in Politics*. 2 vols. New York: Macmillan Company, 1933.

Snead, Thomas L. *The Fight for Missouri*. New York: Charles Scribner's Sons, 1886.

Snead, Thomas L. "The First Year of the War in Missouri." In *Battles and Leaders of the Civil War*. Vol. 1: *From Sumter to Shiloh*, edited by Robert Underwood Johnson and Clarence Clough Buel, 262–277. New York: Castle Books, 1956. First published in 1887 in *Century Magazine*.

Stahr, Walter. *Salmon P. Chase: Lincoln's Vital Rival*. New York: Simon & Schuster, 2021.

Stanly, Edward. *Letter from the Hon. Edward Stanly: His Reasons for Supporting Gen. Geo. B. McClellan*. San Francisco: McClellan Central Club, 1864.

Starr, Kevin. *Americans and the California Dream, 1850–1915*. New York: Oxford University Press, 1973.

Statutes at Large. Vol. 12. Boston: Little, Brown and Company, 1863.

Stevens, Walter B. "Lincoln and Missouri." *Missouri Historical Review* 10, no. 2 (January 1916): 63–119.

Stewart, James Brewer. *Wendell Phillips: Liberty's Hero*. Baton Rouge: Louisiana State University Press, 1986.

Strong, George Templeton. *Diary of the Civil War, 1860–1865*. Edited by Allan Nevins. New York: Macmillan Co., 1962.

Strother, David Hunter. *A Virginia Yankee in the Civil War: The Diaries of David Hunter Strother*. Edited by Cecil D. Eby Jr. Chapel Hill: University of North Carolina Press, 1961.

Tanner, Robert G. *Stonewall in the Valley: Thomas J. "Stonewall" Jackson's Shenandoah Valley Campaign, Spring 1862*. Mechanicsville, PA: Stackpole Books, 1996.

Tap, Bruce. "Amateurs at War: Abraham Lincoln and the Committee on the Conduct of the War." *Journal of the Abraham Lincoln Association* 23, no. 2 (summer 2002): 1–18.

Tap, Bruce. "Reconstructing Emancipation's Martyr: John C. Frémont and the Joint Committee on the Conduct of the War." *Gateway Heritage* 14 (spring 1994): 36–53.

Tap, Bruce. *Over Lincoln's Shoulder: The Committee on the Conduct of the War*. Lawrence: University Press of Kansas, 1998.

Tasher, Lucy Lucile. "The Missouri Democrat and the Civil War." *Missouri Historical Review* 31, no. 4 (July 1937): 402–419.

Taylor, Grace N. "The Blair Family in the Civil War." *Register of the Kentucky Historical Society* 39, no. 126 (January 1941): 47–57.

Teters, Kristopher A. *Practical Liberators: Union Officers in the Western Theater during the Civil War*. Chapel Hill: University of North Carolina Press, 2018.

Thornbrough, Emma Lou. *Indiana in the Civil War Era, 1850–1880*. Indianapolis: Indiana Historical Society, 1995.

Townsend, George Alfred. *Rustics in Rebellion: A Yankee Reporter on the Road to Richmond*. Chapel Hill: University of North Carolina Press, 1950.

Tracy, Albert. "Frémont's Pursuit of Jackson in the Shenandoah Valley: The Journal of Colonel Albert Tracy, March–July 1862," edited by Francis F. Wayland. *Virginia Magazine of History and Biography* 70, no. 2 (April 1962): 165–193, and 70, no. 3 (July 1962): 332–354.

Trefousse, Hans L. *Benjamin Franklin Wade, Radical Republican from Ohio*. New York: Twayne, 1963.

Trefousse, Hans L. "The Joint Committee on the Conduct of the War: A Reassessment." *Civil War History* 10, no. 1 (March 1964): 5–19.

Trefousse, Hans L. "Owen Lovejoy and Abraham Lincoln during the Civil War." *Journal of the Abraham Lincoln Association* 22, no. 1 (winter 2001): 14–32.

Trefousse, Hans L. *The Radical Republicans: Lincoln's Vanguard for Racial Justice*. New York: Knopf, 1969.

Trefousse, Hans L. "Zachariah Chandler and the Withdrawal of Frémont in 1864: New Answers to an Old Riddle." *Lincoln Herald* 70, no. 4 (winter 1968): 181–188.

Trumbull, Lyman. *The Constitutionality and Expediency of Confiscation Vindicated: Speech of Hon. Lyman Trumbull, of Illinois, on the Bill to Confiscate the Property and Free the Slaves of Rebels.* Washington, DC: Congressional Globe, 1862.

Trumbull, Lyman. "A Statesman's Letters of the Civil War Period," edited by Duane Mowry. *Journal of the Illinois State Historical Society* 2, no. 2 (July 1909): 43–50.

Tuffnell, Stephen. "Expatriate Foreign Relations: Britain's American Community and Transnational Approaches to the U.S. Civil War." *Diplomatic History* 40, vol. 4 (September 2016): 635–663.

Turkoly-Joczik, Robert L. "Frémont and the Western Department." *Missouri Historical Review* 82, no. 4 (July 1988): 363–385.

Turner, Justin G., and Linda Levitt Turner, eds. *Mary Todd Lincoln: Her Life and Letters.* New York: Fromm International, 1987.

U.S. Congress. *Congressional Globe.* 37th and 38th Congresses, 1st and 2nd Sessions. Washington, DC: Congressional Globe Office, 1861–1864.

U.S. Congress. *Report of the Joint Committee on the Conduct of the War.* Vol. 3: *Western Department, or Missouri, Miscellaneous.* Washington, DC: Government Printing Office, 1863.

U.S. Congress. *U.S. House Journal.* 37th Congress, 2nd session. Washington, DC: Government Printing Office, 1862.

U.S. Congress. *War Claims at St. Louis.* 37th Congress, House of Representatives, Ex. Doc. No 94, 1862.

U.S. Department of War. *The War of the Rebellion: A Compilation of the Official Records of the Union and Confederate Armies.* 128 vols. Washington, DC, 1880–1901.

Van Deusen, Glyndon G. "Thurlow Weed's Analysis of William H. Seward's Defeat in the Republican Convention of 1860." *Mississippi Valley Historical Review* 34, no. 1 (June 1947): 101–104.

Varon, Elizabeth R. *Armies of Deliverance: A New History of the Civil War.* New York: Oxford University Press, 2019.

Vasvary, Edmund. *Lincoln's Hungarian Heroes: The Participation of Hungarians in the Civil War.* Washington, DC: Hungarian Reformed Federation of America, 1939.

Villard, Henry. *Lincoln on the Eve of '61.* New York: Alfred A. Knopf, 1941.

Volpe, Vernon L. "The Frémonts and Emancipation in Missouri." *The Historian* 56, no. 2 (winter 1994): 339–354.

Vorenberg, Michael. *Final Freedom: The Civil War, the Abolition of Slavery, and the Thirteenth Amendment.* New York: Cambridge University Press, 2001.

Walpole, Frederick. *Four Years in the Pacific.* London: Richard Bentley, 1850.

Wasson, R. Gordon. *The Hall Carbine Affair: A Study in Contemporary Folklore.* New York: Pandick Press, 1948.

Waugh, John C. *Reelecting Lincoln: The Battle for the 1864 Presidency.* New York: Crown, 1998.

Webb, William. *The History of William Webb, Composed by Himself.* Detroit, MI: Egbert Hoekstra, 1873.

Weigley, Russell F. *Quartermaster General of the Union Army: A Biography of M. C. Meigs.* New York, Columbia University Press, 1959.

Welles, Gideon. *Diary of Gideon Welles*. Edited by Howard Beale. 3 vols. New York: W. W. Norton, 1960.

Wendte, Charles W. *Thomas Starr King: Patriot and Preacher*. Boston: Beacon Press, 1921.

Wherry, William M. "Wilson's Creek, and the Death of Lyon." In *Battles and Leaders of the Civil War*. Vol. 1: *From Sumter to Shiloh*, edited by Robert Underwood Johnson and Clarence Clough Buel, 289–297. New York: Castle Books, 1956. First published in 1887 in *Century Magazine*.

White, Andrew Dickson. *When Abe Comes Marching Home Again*. Philadelphia: Mason & Co., 1864.

Whittier, John Greenleaf. *In War Time and Other Poems*. Boston: Ticknor and Fields, 1864.

Whittier, John Greenleaf. *The Prose Works of John Greenleaf Whittier*. Boston: Houghton Mifflin, 1892.

Widmer, Ted. *Lincoln on the Verge: Thirteen Days to Washington*. New York: Simon and Schuster, 2020.

Wilkie, Franc B. *Missouri in 1861: The Civil War Letters of Franc B. Wilkie, Newspaper Correspondent*. Edited by Michael E Banasik. Iowa City, IA: Camp Pope Bookshop, 2001.

Williams, T. Harry. *Lincoln and His Generals*. New York: Dorset, 1952.

Williams, T. Harry. *Lincoln and the Radicals*. Madison: University of Wisconsin Press, 1969.

Winks, Robin W. *Frederick Billings: A Life*. New York: Oxford University Press, 1991.

Winter, William C. *The Civil War in St. Louis: A Guided Tour*. St. Louis: Missouri Historical Society Press, 1994.

Wittke, Carl. *Against the Current: The Life of Karl Heinzen (1809–80)*. Chicago: University of Chicago Press, 1945.

Work, David. *Lincoln's Political Generals*. Urbana: University of Illinois Press, 2009.

Wurthman, Leonard B., Jr. "Frank Blair: Lincoln's Congressional Spokesman." *Missouri Historical Review* 64, no. 3 (April 1970): 263–288.

Zornow, William Frank. *Lincoln and the Party Divided*. Norman: University of Oklahoma Press, 1954.

MANUSCRIPTS AND ONLINE RESOURCES
Abraham Lincoln Presidential Library
E. H. Owen Papers
Edward Bates Papers
James Shields Papers
John C. Frémont Papers
Lyman Trumbull Family Papers
Orville Hickman Browning Papers
Ransom Bedell Letters
Wendell Phillips Papers

Bancroft Library, University of California
Frémont Family Papers (typescript "Great Events" and "Memoirs")
Thomas Starr King Papers

William L. Clements Library, University of Michigan
Henry W. Stevens Papers
Owen Lovejoy Papers

Houghton Library
Crawford Blagden Papers

Library of Congress
Abraham Lincoln Papers
Blair Family Papers

Lincoln Archives
Lincoln Archives Digital Project (http://www.lincolnarchives.us)

Massachusetts Historical Society
Charles Francis Adams Civil War Diary (https://masshist.org/publications/cfa-civil-war)

Missouri Historical Society
Frank and Montgomery Blair Papers
Hamilton Gamble Papers
James O. Broadhead Papers
John C. Frémont Collection
John T. Fiala Papers
Robert Julius Rombauer Papers
Robert White Papers
Thomas Hart Benton Papers
William Greenleaf Eliot Papers

National Archives
National Archives Record Group 393 (Records of U.S. Army Continental Commands, 1821–1920), Letters Sent by Maj. Gen. Frémont, July to November 1861

Office of the Historian, U.S. Department of State
Message of the President of the United States to the Two Houses of Congress, at the Commencement of the Second Session of the Thirty-Seventh Congress (https://history.state.gov/historicaldocuments/frus1861/d123)

Society of California Pioneers
Jessie Benton Frémont Papers

State Historical Society of Missouri
Charles M. Chase Papers

NEWSPAPERS AND MAGAZINES
Alexandria Gazette
Atlantic Monthly
Butte Record (Oroville, California)
Chicago Daily Democrat
Chicago Tribune
Christian Recorder
Daily Alta California
Daily National Democrat
Frank Leslie's Weekly
Illinois State Journal
The Liberator
Missouri Democrat
Missouri Republican
National Anti-Slavery Standard
National Era
National Intelligencer
National Republican
Nevada Democrat
New York Herald
New York Sun
New York Times
New York Tribune
San Francisco Bulletin
San Francisco Call
St. Louis Republic
Washington Evening Star
Washington Times

ABBREVIATIONS
ALPL—Abraham Lincoln Presidential Library
BL—Bancroft Library
CW—Collected Works of Abraham Lincoln (see Basler)
JBF—Jessie Benton Frémont (see Frémont)
JCF—John Charles Frémont
JCCW: Missouri—Report of the Joint Committee on the Conduct of the War (see
  U.S. Congress)

LADP—Lincoln Archives Digital Project
LOC—Library of Congress
HL—Huntington Library
MassHS—Massachusetts Historical Society
MHS—Missouri Historical Society
O.R.—*The War of the Rebellion: A Compilation of the Official Records of the Union and Confederate Armies* (see U.S. Department of War)
SCP—Society of California Pioneers
SHSM—State Historical Society of Missouri
WLC—William L. Clements Library, University of Michigan

INDEX

54th Massachusetts Regiment, 206, 234, 289

abolition: Cameron and, 159; Douglass and, 260; and election of 1864, 266; Frémont and, 11, 214, 246, 273; military attitudes toward, 75–76; political effects of, 175
abolitionists: and affection for Frémont, 214; and cause of war, 86; and defense of Frémont, 148; and election of 1864, 245–246, 256–259, 265, 271, 276; and Emancipation Proclamation, 218, 227; and Frémont's proclamation, 95, 112; and growth of emancipation sentiment, 177; and Lincoln's reversal, 104–105; and Second Confiscation Act, 209; and Smithsonian lecture series, 161–163
access issues, Frémont and, 121–124; investigation and, 168
Adams, Charles Francis, 18–19, 30–34, 66
Adams, Charles Francis, Jr., 110, 205–206
Adams, Henry, 19
Adams, Theodore, 153–154
African Americans: and election of 1864, 260–261, 265, 279; and Frémont, 40–41, 104, 233, 283–284; and Lincoln, 105, 215; and Smithsonian lectures, 178. *See also* black troops; Douglass, Frederick
Allegheny Mountains. *See* Mountain Department
Allen, Robert, 116

ambition, Frémont and, 2, 117
Ames, Oakes, 232
Anaconda Plan, 55–56
Anderson, Galusha, 162
Anderson, Robert, 94
Andrew, John, 213, 222
Antietam, Battle of, 217
Anzelm, Albert, 63
Arion Singing Society, 148
Arizona, 287
arming slaves. *See* black troops
arms acquisitions, 29–36, 55, 66, 119, 157
Army Corps of Topographical Engineers, 7–8
Arnold, Isaac, 235
Asboth, Alexander, 57, 63, 132
Ashby, Turner, 199
Astor House, 28, 57, 148
Atlanta, Georgia, 266, 267, 275
authority: Frémont and, 51–54, 64–65, 85–113, 165–166; Hunter and, 192; investigation and, 167; Lincoln and, 194, 210, 212, 217–218

Baker, Edward D., 3–6, 22, 139, 228
Baltimore, Maryland, 55
Baltimore & Ohio Railroad, 184, 185
Bancroft, George, 159
Banks, Nathaniel, 41, 53–54, 187, 240; and Army of Virginia, 205, 206; and cabinet, 18; and election of 1864, 249; and Frémont, 55, 207; and Front Royal, 195; and Mountain Department, 186–187

351

About the Author

John Bicknell was a journalist for more than thirty years, more than half of that in Washington, where he was an editor at *Congressional Quarterly* and *Roll Call* and served as senior editor of four editions of *The Almanac of American Politics*. He is author of *America 1844: Religious Fervor, Westward Expansion, and the Presidential Election That Transformed the Nation* and *Lincoln's Pathfinder: John C. Frémont and the Violent Election of 1856*.